THE PSYCHOPATH

A Comprehensive Study of
Antisocial Disorders and Behaviors

The Psychopath

A Comprehensive Study of
Antisocial Disorders and Behaviors

Edited by

WILLIAM H. REID, M.D., M.P.H.

Nebraska Psychiatric Institute
and
Department of Psychiatry
University of Nebraska College of Medicine (Omaha)

BRUNNER/MAZEL, *Publishers* • New York

Library of Congress Cataloging in Publication Data

Main entry under title:
The Psychopath: a comprehensive study of antisocial disorders and behaviors.
    Includes bibliographies and index.
    1. Sociopathic personality—Addresses, essays, lectures. I. Reid, William H., 1945-

[DNLM: 1. Antisocial personality. 2. Social behavior disorders. WM190 P974]
RC555.P77   616.8'582   78-8629
ISBN 0-87630-172-3

Published by
BRUNNER/MAZEL, INC.
19 Union Square, New York, New York 10003

MANUFACTURED IN THE UNITED STATES OF AMERICA

To Our Teachers

and

Our Students

Acknowledgments

Over the two years it has taken to write, compile and edit this volume, a large number of people have contributed to its completion. At the outset, valuable advice was offered by Richard Rada and Edward T. Hall. As the project progressed, each of the authors proved not only expert in his or her field but wholly professional in our dealings and prompt with data and mansucripts. Finally, for considerable administrative assistance and typing of the final manuscript, many thanks to Claire G. Reich and Marilyn Heitman.

Foreword

During the past few years notable changes of outlook in psychiatry have been reported in the United States. Some psychiatrists have been significantly influenced by political events and activist groups have sometimes utilized them in seeking to advance legalistic and bureaucratic control over decisions heretofore agreed upon between physician and patient. An observer, perhaps a more compassionate representative of our field, might call to mind the old limerick:

> There was a faith healer of Deal
> Who said, "Although pain isn't real,
>   If I sit on this pin
>   And it punctures my skin
> I dislike what I fancy I feel.

Recently I have, on a few occasions, encountered opinions suggesting that the psychopath should not be considered a person with psychiatric illness and that his behavior is perhaps not an appropriate subject for psychiatric study. It has, indeed, seemed to me that the words "sick" and "illness" have often been used very loosely and euphemistically, and sometimes unfortunately, in connection with criminal behavior. Often this use implies that psychiatry has powers that I believe are imaginary. I recall incidents published in the lay press referring to brutal murderers and to persons who repeat brutal crimes as being "sick." In such reference emphasis is often sought by repetition: "He is *sick, sick, sick!*"

The word "sick" has become quite popular during recent years to indicate atrocious, and, sometimes, disgusting acts of criminal violence. I have been impressed by letters in news magazines from laymen protesting the punishment of brutal murderers and insisting that they be turned over to psychiatrists for cure. If we possessed a truly effective cure for criminals, I would be less inclined to doubt that the term "sick" or "ill" is appropriate or accurate, and that these people should be regularly referred to us for transformation. Our record, however, does not indicate that we have been even modestly successful in our efforts to cure ordinary criminals. It is even less impressive in our efforts with the typical psychopath.

Although it has become popular to call the vicious murderer sick, and to hail psychiatry as an appropriate (and, presumably, effective) cure for him, I have not encountered vehemently expressed opinions that Hitler, however many features of psychiatric illness he may have shown, should be exonerated of blame and responsibility for the tragic disasters he brought upon the world.

If the psychopath's disorder is officially classed as a *mental disease* it would seem that he must, if the Durham Rule is applied in Court, be pronounced not legally responsible for his antisocial acts. This rule was extravagantly praised approximately two decades ago and hailed as a means of bringing, at last, through psychiatry, scientific knowledge to bear on serious and complex questions of law. What was assumed by many to be the scientific enlightenment that psychiatry could shed on these questions has apparently proved less than adequate, or perhaps less than scientific. The Durham Rule has been substantially altered and even, in some jurisdictions, supplanted by the *New Penal Code*.

When I first became interested in the psychopath many years ago, it was difficult to find much about him in psychiatric textbooks. In a big volume, some obscure paragraph or, occasionally, a few pages were set aside to deal with this condition. It was usually found under a heading that also embraced a number of other conditions, perhaps as many as a dozen or more, each briefly mentioned under a single identifying term having little to do with the psychopath as I believe him to be. The present volume, in my opinion, reflects the real and promising efforts that have been made in recent years to gain additional knowledge of the psychopath and other types of antisocial disorders. I still feel that less is truly known about psychopathy than about any other personality disorder or deviation from normal behavior.

I have been impressed and encouraged especially by the excellent experimental work done by Dr. Robert Hare and his colleagues in attempts to test objectively concepts of the psychopath that have been tentatively and speculatively advanced to account for his specific and persistent patterns of failure despite his many assets and his often brilliant abilities. It seems to me that the typical psychopath is less capable of leading an adequate life in the community, or of behaving in an acceptable manner, than most patients with schizophrenic illness. Nevertheless, there have been almost no well focused efforts toward developing specific methods to understand, control or restrain his antisocial or his self-destructive activity.

I feel that this volume will contribute substantially to placing the psychopath in focus. We still lack adequate means, social and medical, of curing him, of controlling him, or of significantly altering his self-destructive and socially destructive ways. Because of this, better realization of the nature of his problem, and how it differs from other problems, must be sought. Even if effective therapy for some sociopathic syndromes is never achieved, such knowledge would help those working in the fields of medicine, psychology, law, and education eventually to develop more appropriate and effective methods of coping with the bewildering and tragic consequences of the primary disorder.

In pursuing efforts to gain understanding of the psychopath's paradoxical manifestations of brilliance and folly, of charm and irresponsibility, of how those possessing virtually all gifts can so sharply lack the ability to use them in any sustained purpose, good or evil; in this quest, perhaps we may be led to ponder again, and perhaps with feelings that surprise and freshly stir us, on the Psalmist's memorable question: *What is man that thou art mindful of him?*

HERVEY M. CLECKLEY, M.D.

Augusta, Georgia
April, 1978

Contents

III. TREATMENT ... 259

Contributors

James B. Bakalar, Lecturer in Law in the Department of Psychiatry, Harvard Medical School and Massachusetts Mental Health Center, Boston, Massachusetts.

Francis L. Carney, Ph.D., Supervising Psychologist, Patuxent Institution, Jessup, Maryland.

David N. Cox, Ph.D., Instructor, Department of Psychology, University of British Columbia, Vancouver, British Columbia.

Frank A. Elliott, M.D., Professor of Neurology, Department of Neurology, University of Pennsylvania Medical School, and Director, The Elliott Neurological Center, Pennsylvania Hospital, Philadelphia, Pennsylvania.

Lester Grinspoon, M.D., Associate Professor of Psychiatry, Department of Psychiatry, Harvard Medical School and Massachusetts Mental Health Center, Boston, Massachusetts.

Robert D. Hare, Ph.D., Professor, Department of Psychology, University of British Columbia, Vancouver, British Columbia.

Robert Kellner, M.D., Ph.D., Professor of Psychiatry and Director of Research, Department of Psychiatry, University of New Mexico School of Medicine, and Chief, Psychiatry Service, Veterans Administration Hospital, Albuquerque, New Mexico.

Louis A. Leaff, M.D., Associate Professor of Psychiatry and Director of Residency Training, Department of Psychiatry, Medical College of Pennsylvania, Philadelphia, Pennsylvania.

John R. Lion, M.D., Professor of Psychiatry, Department of Psychiatry and Institute of Psychiatry and Human Behavior, University of Maryland School of Medicine, Baltimore, Maryland.

Russell R. Monroe, M.D., Professor and Chairman, Department of Psychiatry, and Director, Institute of Psychiatry and Human Behavior, University of Maryland School of Medicine, Baltimore, Maryland.

Helen L. Morrison, M.D., Madison, Wisconsin.

Richard T Rada, M.D., Associate Professor and Assistant Chairman, Department of Psychiatry, University of New Mexico School of Medicine, Albuquerque, New Mexico.

Howard C. Reid, M.D., Medical Director, Upper Mississippi Mental Health Center, and Director, Upper Mississippi Research Project, Bemidji, Minnesota.

William H. Reid, M.D., M.P.H., Assistant Professor of Psychiatry, Department of Psychiatry and Nebraska Psychiatric Institute, University of Nebraska College of Medicine, Omaha, Nebraska.

Don A. Rockwell, M.D., Associate Professor of Psychiatry, Department of Psychiatry, University of California, Davis, School of Medicine, Davis, California.

John Edward Talley, M.D., Training Analyst, Institute of the Inter-Regional Society of Jungian Analysts, Santa Fe, New Mexico.

THE PSYCHOPATH
A Comprehensive Study of
Antisocial Disorders and Behaviors

I

PERSPECTIVES ON PSYCHOPATHY

The following section, more than the remainder of this volume, addresses the philosophy and sociology which surround antisocial disorders in our society. The need for adequate and consistent diagnosis is central to any theme of research or treatment, as well as the establishment of coherent discourse. Some aspects of the editor's personal views are outlined in Chapter 2, "The Sadness of the Psychopath." Chapter 3 on "The Asocial Child" addresses the foundations of character development which contribute to later sociopathy. Finally, some descriptions of antisocial or psychopathic behavior which may be less commonly seen by many readers are presented in Chapter 4, "The Psychopath in Rural Areas."

1

Diagnosis of Antisocial Syndromes

WILLIAM H. REID, M.D., M.P.H.

At the 1977 VI World Congress of Psychiatry, a symposium was offered on the "diagnostic dilemma" of sociopathy. We did not solve the dilemma. What did occur was a highlighting of some of the diagnostic problems, professional stereotypes, and clinical variants that come to mind when the issue of antisocial behavior is discussed. It is frequently the case that one's personal point of view regarding the sociopath (psychopath, antisocial character) seems totally clear and unassailable. As one reads the following chapters, however, there ensues a growing feeling of confusion about the diagnosis of sociopathic disorders.

The author proposes a diagnostic structure which allows for the differentiation of symptomatic behavior, characterologic disorder, and core personality deficit. This format is not incompatible with either the old or the new diagnostic and statistical manuals of the American Psychiatric Association (1, 2).

An early 1978 draft of *DSM III* lists the proposed operational criteria for diagnosis of "antisocial personality" (2). Since these seem useful and since they are likely to become part of the standard nomenclature in the United States and other parts of the world without a great deal of alteration, these criteria will be listed at this point in the text. The criteria attempt in a number of ways to limit the diagnosis to that of a true personality disorder, differentiating it from specific problems of conduct or behavior, as well as from symptoms which stem from other underlying cardinal disease. At this writing, the proposed *DSM III* criteria are:

A. Current age at least 18 and a history of continuous and chronic antisocial behavior in which the rights of others are violated.

and

B. onset before age 15, as indicated by a history of two or more of the following:
   1. Truancy (positive if at least five days per year for at least two years, not including the last year of school).
   2. Expulsion from school.
   3. Delinquency (arrested or referred to juvenile court because of behavior).
   4. Running away from home overnight at least twice while living in a parental or parental surrogate home.
   5. Persistent lying.
   6. Unusually early or aggressive sexual behavior.
   7. Unusually early drinking to excess.
   8. Thefts.
   9. Vandalism.
   10. Required to repeat school grades, or grades markedly below those expected on the basis of estimated or known "IQ."
   11. Chronic violations of rules at home and/or at school (other than truancy).

and

C. at least three of the following since age 15:
   1. Poor occupational performance over several years, as shown by either (a) frequent job changes (three or more jobs in five years not accounted for by nature of job or economic or seasonal fluctuation), (b) significant unemployment (six months or more in ten years when expected to work), or (c) serious absenteeism (average three or more days late or absent per month). *N.B.*: Poor academic performance for the last few years of school may substitute for this criterion in individuals who, by reason of their age or circumstance, have not had an opportunity to demonstrate occupational adjustment.
   2. Three or more non-traffic arrests, or one felony conviction.
   3. Two or more divorces or separations (whether married or not).
   4. Repeated physical fights or assaults (not required by job or to defend someone).
   5. Repeated thefts, whether caught or not.
   6. Illegal occupation (e.g., prostitution, pimping, drug sales).
   7. Repeated defaulting on debts or other major financial responsibilities (e.g., child support).
   8. Traveling from place to place without a prearranged job or clear goal, or without a clear idea of when the travel will terminate.

and

D. no period of five years or more during which the individual behaved in a conforming manner, with the exception of time spent bedridden, confined to a hospital or penal institution, or under treatment.

and

E. does not meet established criteria for a diagnosis of Schizophrenia or severe Mental Retardation.

In addition, the following "essential features" of the antisocial personality disorder are described by the *DSM III* draft:

> . . . antisocial behavior in many areas beginning before the age of 15 and typically from earliest school years or before, and persisting into adulthood. As an adult there is invariably a markedly impaired capacity to sustain lasting, close, warm and responsible relationships with family, friends, or sexual partners, and a failure to sustain good job performance over a period of several years (2).

Later chapters will address some of these criteria. One which deserves some discussion here is the "relationship" feature quoted above. That description contains a number of adjectives which leave considerable room for clinical interpretation ("lasting," "close," "responsible," etc.).

The matter of the sociopath's capacity for relationships is of such importance, either in terms of its intrinsic value as a characteristic or in terms of its position as a symptom of core deficits involving basic trust, for example, or one's ability to internalize important parts of his infant environment, that the issue should be clear in the mind of the clinician or researcher before the diagnosis of antisocial personality is made. Indeed, one might make a case for presence of stable—if aberrant—object relations which might avoid humans altogether, in favor of some emotionally safer and more concretely predictable inanimate object.

The ability of the clinician or researcher to separate persons exhibiting antisocial *behaviors* from those involved in character pathology is crucial. Persistence of stereotypes regarding diagnosis serves to confuse our efforts at research into these conditions and to decrease our chances for the specificity of diagnosis which is vital to good treatment. It is our contention that much of the pessimism with regard to treatment of antisocial disorders is related to an inability to separate, both clinically and in our minds, patients with core sociopathic disorders from those whose behavior is a manifestation of something else. Although many or all of these conditions, including antisocial personality, may be treatable via one modality or another, applying any one treatment method to the entire range of people with antisocial symptoms is virtually fruitless. Much of what follows is concerned with correlates of antisocial behavior which may be of assistance in teasing out the differing underlying characteristics of overtly similar syndromes, so that they may be addressed and treated separately from each other. The chapters on treatment tend to address the antisocial personality disorder itself, although Dr. Kellner's review of psychopharmacology stresses the importance of treatment of underlying cardinal disorders and of a symptomatic approach with these agents.

Finally, I should like to propose a description of a disorder at the end of the "antisocial" continuum. Although the proposed *DSM III* criteria limit themselves to what seems to be a specific and chronic condition, there exists a rarer person whom I should like to call a "core psychopath." This concept seems related to that of the "anethopath" described by Ben Karpman many years ago (3) and it is essentially this person who is addressed in Chapter 2 entitled "The Sadness of the Psychopath." The diagnosis of this disorder would be at once difficult and very serious, since we are speaking of a preconflictual, developmental etiology and a chronic, markedly refractory condition. Karpman's original diagnoses were made using psychoanalytic criteria and sufficient time to determine, to the examiner's satisfaction, that no underlying cardinal psychosis or neurosis existed. This method would befit both the complexity and the severity of such a condition. It seems comparable to some of the principles of diagnosis of the narcissistic personality as described by Kohut (4) and Offenkrantz and Tobin (5).

REFERENCES

1. *Diagnostic and Statistical Manual of Mental Disorders*, 2nd ed. American Psychiatric Association, Washington, D.C., 1968.
2. SPITZER, R. L. Personal Communication.
3. KARPMAN, B. On the Need for Separating Psychopathy into Two Distinct Types: The Symptomatic and the Idiopathic. *J. Crim. Psychopathol.* 3:112, 1941.
4. KOHUT, H. The Psychoanalytic Treatment of Narcissistic Personality Disorders. In: *Psychoanalytic Study of the Child*, Vol. 23. New York: International Universities Press, 1968.
5. OFFENKRANTZ, W. and TOBIN, A. Psychoanalytic Psychotherapy. *Arch. Gen. Psychiatry* 30 (5):593-606, May, 1974.

2

The Sadness of the Psychopath

WILLIAM H. REID, M.D., M.P.H.

". . . Evening comes again before too long.
And knowing that's the hardest time, I look for lights
   and any voices.
But when they come I know it's not the same;
The night is just outside the door,
And with it all the memories of the past I want to see:
The people and the places I'm looking for
And can never find again."*

The phrase "sadness of the psychopath" seems to summarize the tremendous variety and depth of pain and difficulty that are intertwined among all of the following chapters, a prophecy of pain for the patient and a legacy of cost and sorrow for those around him, losses that can be seen in the microcosm of the individual and his family, in his community, and in society itself.

In this chapter it seems useful to speak less specifically of the many differences among psychopathic behaviors, psychopathic symptoms and the full-blown "anethopath" (1, 2). A more philosophical approach is necessary in order to consider these pains and sadnesses. Where relevant, proper separation is made; elsewhere the reader's own experience should be sufficient to help make our point and crystallize the concepts that are, in the last analysis, the basis for our seeing the understanding of these syndromes as an extremely important goal of this book.

---

* From *Merryville Highway Song*, copyright 1972 by Fewer Sorrows Music. Used by permission.

7

THE INDIVIDUAL

We will see in the later chapters on presentation and dynamics that
the psychopath does indeed feel pain. Although the instruments of discomfort and the sites of vulnerability may often be different from those
of other people, he is not the impenetrable shield that he continuously
presents to the public. In many instances he responds to the same stresses
as do the rest of us, although he may respond differently and one may
have to search harder to find the wound or the defense against it.

With respect to pain and anxiety, the true psychopath, who may or
may not be limited to the "anethopath" discussed later, seems different
from the neurotic or psychotic person who manifests sociopathic behavior
in addition to, or as part of, his disease. The person whose antisocial
behavior defends against neurotic conflict is well equipped to feel anxiety
and depression and thereby to suffer from the onslaught of both internal
and external attack. Dynamic theorists, therapists, phenomenologists and
casual observers all agree that to consider this individual as free of
anxiety/guilt/pain is erroneous, no matter what his sociopathic symptomatology.

The borderline psychotic with sociopathic symptoms is, in many ways,
protected from real pain. His emotional structure has developed in such
a way as to permit access to the "last ditch" defenses of primitive neurosis
and psychosis. Although there is much evidence to indicate anxiety and
discomfort within many psychotic processes (3, 4), withdrawal and isolation can be impenetrable walls against the demons of the unconscious.
Dissociation and fugue may unassailably separate responsibility from the
self; uncomfortable paranoia may prohibit even greater pain from
reaching consciousness; and in florid psychosis the imperative need to
deal with a continuous bombardment of sensation and primary process
may serve well to keep terrifying images of disintegration at bay.

The true psychopath certainly feels "objective" anxiety. That is, certain
environmental stresses such as acute object loss, awaiting trial or facing
drug withdrawal—concerns *of the moment*—worry him as much as they
do anyone. Indeed, the guilt-ridden neurotic may be more comfortable
here than the psychopath, feeling in some instances that he awaits his
"just reward." This objective anxiety can perhaps be measured in terms
of how strongly the individual strives to escape the uncomfortable
situation.

Signs of deeper anxiety are there as well. The intolerance of boredom
and search for stimulation seen in these individuals are in all likelihood
felt, viscerally if you will, as an anxiety (5, 6, 7). Psychopaths trained in

long-term studies to locate and recognize their own affects often describe a free-floating, don't-know-why-it's-there discomfort that must be quelled. Their descriptions remind one of a neurotic's "anxiety attack," the symptoms of which may be vague but are still intolerable.

Some reflection on the following chapters makes me feel that we *do* know "why-it's-there." The psychopath must protect himself from the fearsome contents of his unconscious, as we all must protect ourselves. There is, however, a large volume of dynamic and analytic evidence that indicates in the psychopath different contents at the core of his emotional makeup. Where the rest of us have the awesome power of primitive drives and introjects and the frightening images of archetypal forms, he has, to many observers, nothing.

He has nothing. This is not really a correct statement but it conveys more than any I can think of the very real void that exists at the core of the psychopath (especially the anethopath). Karpman (2) and others have elegantly described their long work unraveling the situational dynamics and objective defense structures of sociopaths to find below, over and over again—nothing.

There are perhaps two forms of nothing in psychiatry. One is the familiar and terrifying destruction of the ego alluded to earlier, an obliteration and a "floating into the void" (universe) (8) so feared by schizophrenics.

The other—the nothing which, I feel, lies at the center of the psychopath—is a lack of energy, of living force, a compendium of the *parts* of an emotional self without the spark of life. This is a concept reminiscent of Cleckley's "Mask" (9), with all its features present but lacking true life (although I do not imply that this is Cleckley's basic assertion). All the molecules are apparently there but unable to interact, unable to generate heat and light, in some absolute zero state.

One might think of a person outside on a cold, snowy night looking through a window into a warm room, seeing a family, sensing happiness, almost able to feel the warmth but realizing he can never be inside. This description is close to that one affect, mentioned in Chapter 15, that does seem deep and real for the psychopath: the hopelessness of endogenous depression (10).

The psychopath is not, cannot allow himself to be, truly aware of his depression. Indeed, avoidance of it plays a major role in his symptomatology. When forced into depression (a rare event) he still remains far from a conscious viewing of his emptiness. Consistent with the many accounts of his emotional resilience, he does not feel this *ennui* as such any more than the schizophrenic in remission continued to look over the brink of oblivion. Neither could survive such loss. Nevertheless, it is there, with bits showing through as holes in the sociopathic armor, as brief and vague anxieties, as reactions to situations of vulnerability, as an unquenchable drive for stimulation and escape.

The psychopath often is aware intellectually of that which he lacks. In a pensive (or manipulating) moment he may discuss with a therapist, interviewer or friend this basic difference between others and himself. He may betray it in his descriptions of pseudo-feelings about his behaviors. His (our) literature and songs are often replete with gaiety and bravado but also with an underlying sadness that seems omnipresent.

It should be of concern to therapists and social scientists that as the psychopath grows older he may "meet himself coming back." He will have had failure after failure in life; he will have seen in others hundreds of times the warmth that for him is unattainable. He will have expended tremendous psychic energy fighting off emptiness. If these energies are exhausted or if he has indeed "learned" from the continuous battering of his armor,* then he must eventually decompensate.

The most visible form of decompensation of the psychopath is deterioration into inadequacy. No longer carrying an active, resilient shell of narcissism, his protection becomes one of passivity and resignation, still giving up his destiny to "fate" but now appearing defeated and small. He may become a skid-row alcoholic. He may become "disabled" by one of the variety of chronic afflictions that hover between the "medical" and the psychosomatic (e.g., back injury). He will continue to be a "taker" from society via welfare rolls, public hospitals, family support and the like. He is depressed but the depression is reactive, part of his passivity and defeat and of his loss of a major outlet for his projective anger.

Another form of decompensation, often overlooked in the "true" psychopath, is primary depression. I think that being finally and internally convinced of the terrible "nothing" at one's core must lead in a significant number of (especially older) sociopaths to devastating depression, either as a last-resort dissociative defense or as a concomitant to finally having to live with one's personal and very permanent emptiness. This concept seems similar to Bibring's thoughts of depressive reaction to helplessness in the face of loss (10).

The therapeutic usefulness (and even inevitability) of this or a related depression will be discussed in Chapter 15. Here I should like to consider

---

* C.f., an analyst's patiently repetitious observations that eventually "saturate" the neurotic patient's defensive structure and lead to true insight.

it in its "natural" state, that is, encountered outside the controls and supports of careful psychotherapeutic treatment.

By his very nature, at the time the psychopath discovers his own depression, his "core" in a sense, he is likely to be at his most vulnerable. He is probably older and has lost much of his reserve of psychic energy. He may be ill. He may be facing other loss, either within his tenuous object relations or, more likely, within his narcissistic character. He may be in prison. He is likely to be away from most of his usual supporting structure and he may know that he has himself caused its removal.

Such a position is no less serious for the psychopath than for anyone else. He is now in pain; it is seemingly inescapable. He is helpless against it and ill-equipped to live with it. His depression is quite serious; it is largely from within and will not pass of its own accord. Indeed, *he has now lost many of the trappings of sociopathy.* He may, in the face of much scholarly thought to the contrary, commit suicide.

THE FAMILY AND SIGNIFICANT OTHERS

The sadness of sociopathy extends well beyond the individual. Some of the greatest pain and most significant loss, by personal or social measures, occurs among those whose lives he has touched. Most closely touched, and therefore most directly influenced, is the family.

The family from which he comes. Cleckley (9) presents one of the most insightful and complete treatments of family disruption and pain resulting from the psychopath. Without discussing (to any large extent) dynamic causation or chastising already unhealthy families, he sympathizes with the family and speaks of their feelings of despair and dashed hopes as well as of failure after failure of their efforts to help their offspring. He does not condemn the family for scapegoating or vicarious acting out but instead focuses upon the difficulties that exist once the psychopath has emerged.

Some families of sociopathic offspring may already be "borderline" in terms of emotional, marital, or financial difficulty. The emergence of a chronically antisocial child or adult is often related to the prior and continuing presence of disruptive influences in the family, influences which are already having their effect on all of the members. Low socioeconomic status, although not causative (11), often coexists with sociopathy and places extra burdens on the limited coping energies within the group. Similarly, concomitant occurrence of other family pathology not confined to the "lower classes" may make the home particularly vulnerable to additional drains on its resources. The presence of psychopathic offspring then becomes not an isolated problem but one added to a constellation of interrelated difficulties.

Most important of the internal family pains may be deep feelings of personal failure. "As the twig is bent . . .", and so the parents feel they have not accomplished what may be their primary mandate in life: to be good parents. On the surface lie embarrassment and shame for the acts of their offspring, held up to them by the community and reflected in the apparent successes of others' children. Deeper, serious feelings of "What's wrong with me?" compound depression and guilt for personal and vicarious acting out within the family. Often the parent's superego may be overly harsh and restrict other more productive activity.

As with other social and emotional problems, such as divorce or schizophrenia, siblings often wonder, "Am I next?" They feel a genetic and environmental bond to the psychopathic kin and his background. Phrases such as "You're just like your sister" may carry strong prophetic influence when the sibling realizes, at a variety of levels, that she *is* similar in appearance, behavior, and genetic constitution. Given consistent reinforcement and/or a vulnerable stage of development, a small kernel of similarity may be extrapolated by the child to become a significant issue for emotional defenses and a driving force for external behavior. These may be manifested in the development of similar (sociopathic) behavior which fulfills a variety of subtle expectations from family and self. On the other hand, some sort of overcompensation may occur to produce a rigid, obsessive symptomatology felt to be the opposite of the pathology of the psychopathic sibling.

The nuclear family is usually the easiest group for the adolescent or adult sociopath to manipulate. Motivated by a variety of concerns from guilt to protectiveness to a powerful variable-ratio schedule of reinforcement, the family repeatedly becomes involved in the sociopath's difficulties. Each involvement is likely to be costly. Repairs to the family car after an adolescent spree, restitution to a neighboring businessman for a minor burglary, bail for misdemeanors, and finally bond for felonies or perhaps bailing the offspring out of business problems may be part of an escalating series of financial drains. Of course, the family need not (and should not) maintain its psychopathic offspring's fiscal support but it is the rare family that has not spent outside of its budget in an effort to "help" such a family member.

Cost to the family is present in other forms as well. In addition, to the social and personal embarrassment mentioned above and the energy and resources spent as a result of the destruction the psychopath often leaves in his wake, as well as making good his promises and apologizing for his irresponsibilities, there is the pain of wondering where he is. Is he all right? Is he in jail? Comfort rarely comes from a letter or telephone call. Although communication may in some cases be frequent, the brief amenities and statements of his love are always followed by an account of his latest problems, along with his latest request for help. In this regard it is not unusual to hear families of those who have been incarcerated express relief at having a bit of peace of mind, knowing where the individual is for some length of time.

One of the most difficult to bear of those costs to the family is the lack of reward for their efforts. Again and again the psychopath returns to the family to bail him out of trouble. The story is always the same: He sees the error of his ways (and may even call himself "sick") and needs money just one more time in order to start again. This time he will stay on the "right track," the path to solvency and honor. Most of all, he will this time "succeed" and thereby reaffirm his love for the family and his deservedness of their respect. He may plead for money or he may bargain for someone to intervene in his legal problems. He may beg them not to commit him to a drug treatment program or ask that they cosign his latest loan. Always there is the promise that things are now "different." He knows how to hold reward within view but just out of reach, since he will never willingly give control of himself to someone else.

Parents, especially, want desperately to believe him. In each loan or gift there is the hope that something good and lasting will happen. Unfortunately, they are always disappointed and left a little poorer, a little more hopeless.

Why, then, does the family continue to be a ready source of support for the psychopath? The family would (and does, if we ask) say, "He's our son, our flesh and blood . . . We can't turn our backs on him . . . If he didn't have us there would be no one to help him."

In this regard I would allude to the guilt mentioned earlier. By continuing to be available the family is trying to undo its wrongs. By continuing to suffer, it atones. More deeply, the family may be atoning for the offspring's behavior *as if it were the family's own,* acting within some unilateral failure of early symbiotic resolution, in this case on the part of the family, or one of its members, rather than on the part of the child.

Continuing reward for the offspring's acting out the fantasies of the family may be another relevant dynamic. In addition, the author feels that such living through the other person is related to unconscious guilt for previously exploiting the psychopath, as well as to a primitive vision of him as an extension of the parental (or sibling, especially in the case of a twin) self.

An interesting and easily supported hypothesis comes to us from the field of experimental psychology. Operant conditioning principles predict that the most consistent and difficult to extinguish sets of behaviors will be those that are reinforced *variably*. That is, if one is rewarded at unpredictable intervals for a behavior and is given varying amounts of reinforcement, sometimes very little, the probability of that behavior's continuing for long periods of time, unabated and without further reinforcement, becomes very high.

Certainly there are few visible rewards for families' supportive behavior. Childhood smiles and later hopes that everything will turn out for the best become reinforcers (hope in this case has become a "secondary reinforcer"), perhaps providing brief respite from pain and apprehension while the offspring spends the family's money or moves to another town. The reinforcement is varied both in time and amount. The chance for the family's reward is present, though minute, and secondary reinforcers may be enough to sustain the supportive behavior for years.*

The family to which he comes. Problems associated with families in which a spouse has a severely antisocial character are discussed in detail in Chapters 3 and 7. Many of the difficulties are similar to those seen in his earlier family and some of the same dynamics may be in process. In addition, however, there appear some new problems associated with marital relationships, adult responsibility, and parenthood.

The wife of a sociopath may feel a strong obligation from personal and cultural mores to "stand by her man"; the husband of a sociopathic woman may for a variety of reasons need to support or hide his wife's inappropriately antisocial behavior. Spouses of either sex may have a variety of internalized feelings dating from childhood concerning conjugal relationships or what a marriage or family "should be." Problems in a parent's own early family may have instilled a need to give the new children a "better" home than the one that he or she experienced, a need expressed in inappropriate support for the psychopathic spouse in an effort to save the marriage.

There may also be a neurotic searching by the non-sociopathic spouse for a supportive, nurturing family perceived as missing in early childhood. The dream of a warm, stable home life never before experienced can give rise to a tenacious clinging to a pathologic spouse in order to

---

* One interesting study of "hope," which actually seems to be a study of a very powerful reinforcer in a variable-ratio situation with only one instance of reward, was done with mice in rapidly churning water. Placed in the water, each control mouse swam for a few seconds, sank and drowned. Other mice were placed in the water and then removed ("rescued") quickly. When these latter mice were again placed in the water, they all swam for extended periods, some for hours, before drowning.

build, in fantasy at least, a family which will at last fill the unmet needs of the past.

Feelings of failure and inadequacy are also well-known concomitants of family disruption. Although these are adequately discussed in later chapters and elsewhere in the literature, it is appropriate to point out that the psychopathic partner, with his continuous disruption and resistance to change, is likely to supplement these painful affects in spouse and children on a regular basis. At the same time, he may often use his exploitative abilities to fill his needs and to provide himself with external supports which paradoxically may prevent actual divorce for months or years, thereby prolonging the family's discomfort. Even after divorce, a surprising number of spouses and families keep supportive contact with, or even accept the return of, the aberrant member.

It should be pointed out that I do not mean to discount the large number of other factors that add to family problems and to chronic pathologic patterns of interaction. The presence of other predisposing characteristics in spouses is, of course, a heavily contributing factor to the outwardly visible pain within the family. These neurotic and characterologic precursors often are coupled with damaging socioeconomic conditions, leading to a family which is already burdened by the odds against it. Adding an acting-out sociopath to the matrix may be like pouring gasoline onto smoldering coals.

Children

Spouses are able to choose each other. Their reasons may be good or bad, destructive or growth producing, neurotic or not. They can generally pick the life they shall lead and they can escape from it in a variety of ways.

These statements are not true for the child. A child does not choose his parents. He or she must cling to the family structure that is offered from birth and go about the full-time business of growing within it. He knows no other life; nor does any other life (usually) present itself to him. Prior to latency he lives with no knowledge or chance of choice; further, such choice should not be his anyway, since play is the work of childhood and the frightening responsibilities of adult decisions should not be his with which to wrestle.

Even the so-called "family romance" (12) of the latency-age child, in which he may fantasize a different or "better" home environment, is only temporary and incomplete relief from home problems. Perhaps part of a normally maturing ego defense system or perhaps a way of holding discomfort at bay while the child strengthens other coping mechanisms, such imaginative flights nevertheless cannot, without entering psychotic proportions, compete with the adult-controlled world around him.

The child, then, is trapped. He may be loved or insignificant, nourished or exploited; and he cannot escape that which may hurt him terribly without suffering severe and perhaps even more damaging consequences.

Again, it is not my purpose to discuss at length the pathology to which children are subjected and prone. The specific issue of family genesis of psychopathic disorders is reviewed elsewhere in this book. It must be obvious, however, that the inconsistency of the sociopathic parent is a significant detriment to family structure. The lack of appropriate role model in the affected parent may be devastating. The *absences* of person, of affect, of appropriate milieu for testing and ego development seem conspicuous.

The child, even more than the psychopath's siblings (with the exception of a twin), is susceptible to strong influence from family prophecy. He knows whose child he is, even if the aberrant parent has left the family very early. He is open to the prophecies and internalized models of his childhood.

In addition he has the genes of his parents. Those therapists who have observed the fear felt by a patient who wonders whether he will become schizophrenic as his parent did, or by one whose relatives died of heart disease at an early age, are aware that familial transmission of pathology can produce as much discomfort from anticipation as from biological occurrence.

There are other people whose lives may be closely mingled with that of the sociopath. Friends may be more or less invested in relationships with a sociopath and, although they often choose to leave and avoid the problems of such an association, they are subject to some of the same emotional loss as that seen in relatives. Financial loss may be greater, since they may have invested in his schemes or given him "loans." Social loss may be significant. The psychopath may endanger his friend's job, encourage him to act out in socially destructive ways or sleep with his/her wife or husband.

As we have seen, disruption often accompanies the psychopath. Those injured may be his followers or companions rather than himself (13). The sociopath is not concerned with the consequences or "spin-offs" of his activities. Even during dangerous behaviors such as fast driving, borderline business activity, drug abuse or criminal acts, *his* own goals, *his* stimulation, are paramount. That *people* are involved is not relevant.

Those who are along for the ride have no more meaning for him than do the other "things" which he uses for his purpose—the automobile, the sales merchandise, the pill bottle, or the pen with which he forges a check.

The psychotherapist, who in some ways may have a unique relationship with the psychopath, can in other ways be an example of much of the sadness and loss cited above. He allows himself to become a "significant other" in his patient's life. If the patient accepts this relationship the therapist then becomes vulnerable, although he tries not to be, to the same problems that befall the family and friends.

The therapist invests in his patient. He invests his time, which could be used for other patients or pursuits; he invests his efforts and expertise, often his money (e.g., via non-paying patients), and some aspects of his emotional self. Much of Dr. Lion's chapter in Part III has been devoted to countertransference issues in the analytic and nonanalytic therapist or counselor. The frustration of such a relationship, the feeling of professional and personal failure which may ensue, and the personal and societal loss through depression and wasted therapy time are certainly valid examples of the costs that can derive from relationships with the psychopath.

COMMUNITY AND SOCIETY

The most visible loss to the community from psychopathic behavior is that related to crime. Although we stress that not all psychopaths are criminals and vice versa, criminal activity is easily seen by the public as a community liability and is often traced to persons exhibiting sociopathic behavior.

Property loss related to crime continues to rise both in absolute terms and in terms of public concern. At the community level dollar-equivalents of loss through robbery, burglary and the like cause a great deal of individual hardship to the businessman or resident. In the case of significant losses to large employers there may also be a burden on an entire town through eradication of jobs, lowering of tax revenues and decreased economic stimulation.

Personal losses via crimes of assault, rape, and murder are even greater, involving loss of productive citizens and costs of their treatment and compensation. Fear among the citizenry has become a major issue, especially in population centers. Even parks and areas of urban redevelopment have, in large measure, been kept from productive use and subverted to the purposes of aberrant* segments of the population. When the aberrant group is in conflict with the "normal" population, the park (or downtown area or ghetto) becomes a jungle wherein the psychopath has all the advantages and usually makes use of them. A variety of sacrifices then ensue: loss of productive use of the environment, loss of the resources used to provide that environment, and material and personal loss of quality of life and the "pursuit of happiness" to those persons who may need them most (e.g., the poor, elderly, or ethnic minorities).

Other expenses due to criminal activity are well known and can be easily documented. Costs of law enforcement are extremely high both in terms of preventing crime and of apprehending and prosecuting the perpetrators.

Crime prevention is a popular goal, actively pursued and publicized throughout the country. In the long run it should be less expensive than after-the-fact measures but vital knowledge is lacking, perhaps because there may be no viable answers to the complex questions raised. Monetary outlay is high, especially for pilot studies, experimental programs and initial "tooling up." Moreover, prevention and enforcement methods ask us more and more to choose between our own freedoms and protection from crime. Shall we, for example, give up some of our rights of privacy to the laudable end of preventing "worse" crimes, as is often suggested? Or should we tenaciously guard our individual freedoms, lest in apprehending criminals we mortally wound our democracy? Do virtuous ends justify questionable means? Should virtuous means be upheld even in the face of seemingly dangerous consequences?

The sociopath, of course, has no such conflict. He chooses his own personal ends and the most efficient means to them. He may chuckle a bit as we wrestle with philosophical questions while he uses our cumbersome system, our guilts and fairmindedness, to his own advantage. He contributes to an erosion of our societal philosophy by his misuse of it. He has thus *taken from us* very deeply and in the process takes from himself.

Other losses to the community and society may be seen wherever resources are expended for the sociopath's needs. When he is injured, perhaps through his own negligence, society often compensates him for his damages. When he spends non-productive time in mental institutions, society pays in a variety of ways. When he is out of work or otherwise

---

* I am aware of the value judgments voiced in this section. They are used because they reflect current popular thought and are, in that light, appropriate communicative tools.

cannot support himself and his family, someone else assumes the responsibilities that should be his.

With some notable exceptions, society usually loses the true psychopath as a productive person. He may be bright and healthy, with many useful qualities and abilities, but these are not often destined for the common good. Often an entire family is lost, thrown out of its precarious balance and into a downward spiral of economic and social failure. As we have seen, such a spiral often, if not usually, leads to family inadequacy, social dependence, and pessimism concerning the success of the following generation.*

The sociopath, then, carries an habitually negative balance in his accounts with society. He or she is supported, cared for, handled, or kept by the State without compensatory contribution to it. Although the same can be said of many persons with severe physical illness, congenital deficits, and so on, the sociopath's condition is somehow different from these. I agree with Cleckley's findings of serious emotional deficit in the psychopath, almost to the point of accepting his "semantic aphasia" (9); however, I am reluctant to exempt the psychopath from basic social responsibility. I will join in the search for effective and appropriate treatment or control of these various disorders and behaviors, but I have difficulty justifying removal of psychopaths entirely from social/forensic responsibility to an arena which is wholly medical. Although most of the primary problems for these people lie in difficulties with the "psycho-" portion of the self rather than with the "socio-" (hence the lack of prejudice against the use of the term "psychopath" in the text), I must agree with the volume of statute and public feeling which, except in unusual circumstances, holds the individual to task when the community is threatened. This position also seems defensible from the point of view of civil liberties and, paradoxically, with respect to protection of the accused under the law. Consider, for example, the morass of problems which can result when an individual escapes prosecution for a minor crime through the efforts of a defense attorney who has him declared schizophrenic. He is now "insane" rather than antisocial.

This "negative balance" may additionally be seen in the members of society who surround the psychopath. Harrington (13) has noted a number of ways in which the psychopath may be a leader, a "pied piper" encouraging others to follow. In most instances, although not all, one's following would seem to be at his (or others') peril. Examples such as

---

* It will be recalled that we are speaking primarily of the accumulated effects of family influences and not of external socioeconomic correlates; c.f., Chapter 7.

the injury caused by followers of drug "prophets" and violent cultists come to mind, as do a number of lesser "I dare you" situations of vicarious stimulation and acting out (c.f., the subtle encouragements found within the families cited earlier in this chapter).

Occasionally, of course, sociopathic charisma may aid in encouragement of others to more constructive ends. Consider the teacher who is able to inspire interest among his students or the politician who, while serving his own needs, may generate revenue and support for a number of worthwhile public causes. A few people even envision the psychopath as a person "whose time has come," some going so far as to call him a Messiah (13) who can, by sharing with us his ability to stimulate himself, help us repress fears of death and stem the currently rising tide of personal and societal *ennui*.

It seems clear that such a position regarding sociopathy is not easily tenable. *Ennui*, although uncomfortable, is not new, nor has it historically been limited to societies such as ours. To regard the psychopath as having the answers to some universal questions and ills seems unwise. Even as the schizophrenic who has been seen by some ages as an oracle (or witch), *the psychopath's condition is, at its core, one of personal deficit*, though it may at times seem of social advantage.

There are many people who would like to see changes in mental health fields and in society as a whole. Their well-meaning but varied positions include those advocating less (or different) labeling of aberrant behaviors, new points of view, and sometimes changes in entire bodies of social and psychiatric thought (14-17). Dialogue, questioning and re-examination must continue if we are to survive together; however, there seems much lack of organization in this sort of attack upon the unanswered.

Confusion—especially in the light of our many never-before-faced problems of population, energy, environment, even of species survival—makes a place for any organizing force, for man hates entropy. It is not surprising that answers are sought outside the disappointing realm of conventional sources. Stories of unidentified flying objects are reminiscent of descriptions of gods of past fearful eras. Insulating isolation has become a "normal" coping mechanism for the urban dweller (18). Religions and other movements which offer protection and answers (logical or not) are rapidly growing.

It is no wonder that the psychopath, who seems so comfortable and unconcerned, should be looked to as a possible route of escape. His ideas are attractive; he may be a leader within some of these often maladaptive areas. In reality, however, although he may offer some entertaining compromise to a humdrum life or to compulsive "straightness," to project upon the psychopath's mask (9) the raiment of true depth of meaning would be a serious error in judgment.

REFERENCES

1. KARPMAN, B. On the Need for Separating Psychopathy into Two Distinct Types: the Symptomatic and the Idiopathic. *J. Crim. Psychopathol.* 3:112, 1941.
2. KARPMAN, B. The Myth of the Psychopathic Personality. *Am. J. Psychiat.* 104:523, March, 1948.
3. MEADOW, A., DONLON, P. T., BLACKER, K. H. Effects of Phenothiazines on Anxiety and Cognition in Schizophrenia. *Dis. Nerv. Syst.* 36 (4):203-208, April, 1975.
4. DONLON, P. T. Personal Communication.
5. HARE, R. D. *Psychopathy: Theory and Research.* New York: Wiley, 1970.
6. HARE, R. D. Psychopathy and Physiological Responses to Adrenalin. *J. Abnormal Psychol.* 79:138-147, 1972.
7. HARE, R. D. and QUINN, M. J. Psychopathy and Autonomic Conditioning. *J. Abnormal Psychol.* 77 (3):223-235, 1971.
8. BURESCH, J. Personal Communication.
9. CLECKLEY, H. M. *The Mask of Sanity* (5th Ed.). St. Louis: Mosby, 1976.
10. BIBRING, E. The Mechanism of Depression (1953). In: W. Gaylin (Ed.), *The Meaning of Despair.* New York: Science House, 1968.
11. ROBINS, L. N. *Deviant Children Grown Up.* Baltimore: Williams and Wilkins, 1966.
12. FREUD, S. Family Romances. In: J. Stracey (Ed.), *Standard Edition of the Complete Psychological Works of Sigmund Freud.* London: Hogarth Press, 1964.
13. HARRINGTON, A. The Coming of the Psychopath. *Playboy.* 18 (12):203, December, 1971.
14. SZASZ, T. S. *The Myth of Mental Illness: Foundations of a Theory of Personal Conduct.* New York: Hoeber Medical Division, Harper and Row, 1961.
15. HALL, E. T. *The Silent Language.* Garden City, New York: Doubleday, 1959.
16. HALL, E. T. *The Hidden Dimension.* Garden City, New York: Anchor Books, Doubleday, 1969.
17. LAING, R. D. *The Divided Self: An Existential Study in Sanity and Madness.* Baltimore: Penguin, 1971. Orig. Tavistock Publications, 1960.
18. REID, W. H. Survivor's Guilt in the New City. Paper: Annual Meeting, Univ. California, Berkeley, School of Public Health, 1975.

3

The Asocial Child: A Destiny of Sociopathy?

HELEN L. MORRISON, M.D.

The acceptance of the existence of sociopathy in children has not been without controversy (1-4). One of the basic confusions attendant to this controversy seems to be the equation of "concept" with "diagnosis." Briefly, a concept is a device involving basic, descriptive categories which are used not only in a theoretical sense but also in an observational sense. Observation as used here implies an experience which rests on theoretical assumptions. Concepts are measured by their conversion into variables. Once this is done, attempts are made to relate these variables, to find their connections. Health and illness are concepts which imply consensus of identification or understanding of the condition. They can also imply treatment. These concepts can be subsequently subdivided into various levels of the understanding of the conditions.

In attempts to define sociopathy, distinction must be made as to the level at which we are using the concept, as well as the context in which it is observed. Attention must be paid to an important variable existent to a greater degree in the diagnostic process in children than in adults: A child exists in a developmental context, fluid and sometimes felt to be without boundaries. Thus, a deficit in functioning at one age may not necessarily be a deficit at a later age. A child cannot be viewed in isolation from his environment, physical or psychological, considering especially his parents, siblings, and peers. An understanding of relationships of the child's developmental status in the areas of ego libidinal advances, motor skills, language and social interaction (to name a few)

22

to the presenting behavior—as well as to the effect of this behavior on the process of continuing and continuous development—is essential not only in diagnosis but in planning for treatment.

As a specific abnormality or behavior, sociopathy can be a symptom of many psychiatric disorders in children. As a syndrome, however, the concept of sociopathy in childhood does not find support. For example, problems in adult socialization are commonly related to character deficits in the area of empathy. However, one will not find this source of aberrant socialization included in the cluster of symptoms which define behavior disorders of childhood. Thus, theoretical concepts derived observationally from symptom clusters seen in children have not lead to the inclusion of these disorders in the childhood nomenclature, i.e., the distinct diagnosis of sociopathy in childhood does not exist.

The description of presenting clinical material, then, is not limited to a single prominent symptom or one symptom cluster. It does not include only one precipitating factor, social characteristic or age of onset. In addition, other behavioral characteristics do not provide clear definition of a core group membership. Response to treatment and follow-up data do not define a homogeneous entity in childhood in most cases. Perhaps the only agreement that can be reached is that the adult syndrome of antisocial personality does somehow manifest its presence in childhood and that treatment is difficult and complex.

With this introduction, the remainder of this chapter will focus on the concept of antisocial disorders in childhood, not as one diagnosis but as a range of diagnoses. Proposed etiologies with physical and familial background, developmental characteristics, childhood predictors of later adult antisocial behavior, and physical and psychological correlates of sociopathic behavior, as well as a review of treatment, will complete the chapter.

HISTORY OF THE SOCIOPATHIC CONCEPT IN CHILDHOOD

Although his classification "moral insanity" has been criticized for being too broad and probably due to the presence of borderline or latent psychosis in his patients, Prichard is credited with the introduction of the concept of psychopathy (5). The classification "born criminal" was described by Lombroso (6) and refined by Gouster (7). Indeed, these terms were used synonymously with psychopathy until Koch coined the term psychopath (8). Again, criticism was made that the term was overly inclusive, with organic brain syndrome and neuroses among many conditions possibly present in his cases. Koch described these persons as being nonpsychotic and having the appearance of complete mental normality

(8). Subclassification of psychopathic conditions, along with prevalence and distribution according to sex, was done by Kraepelin, who ascribed the condition to developmental inhibitions or infantilism, albeit circumscribed (9).

The concern over the problems of children who showed signs of delinquent behavior led to the formation in 1909 of the Juvenile Psychopathic Institute, directed by Dr. William Healy. Healy had been commissioned to study causes and prevention of delinquency and discovered only two American clinics which concerned themselves with psychological evaluation of these children. His book (10) was important to the definition of socioeconomic factors felt to contribute to the development of delinquency as well as to putting an end, at that time, to speculations that genetic or intellectual defects caused the condition.

Glueck, a psychoanalyst, studied early development and its relationship to later criminal behavior of Sing Sing prison inmates. Although his study included broad categories of other disorders, it aided understanding of some of the early roots of delinquent behavior (11). The publishing of *Crime, Its Causes and Treatment* by Darrow in 1922 pointed out that prevention needed to be based on an understanding of the causes of the disorder (12). That same year, a description of the character traits of the psychopath was presented by Vishner. They included a central deficit of "uninhibited social nihilism and guiltlessness," as well as "marked egotism, extreme impulsivity, lack of concentration and abnormal projection" (13). The founding of the American Orthopsychiatric Association in 1924 is described by Alexander and Selesnick as being primarily by professionals interested in further delineation of the multiple facets of delinquency (14). Partridge further defined the term "psychopathic personality" in 1930 (15).

By this time, the psychoanalytic movement had begun to describe the relationship of an incomplete or pathological superego to the behavior of these patients (16-18). More detailed description of the psychoanalytic view is discussed in Chapters 5 and 6 of this volume.

Following Freud's identification of the character type "criminals from a sense of guilt" (19), Alexander described the neurotic character and attempted to classify those patients who exhibited throughout their lives behavior which was aimed at relieving unconscious tension (20). These behaviors were not *adapted* to reality but were present *in spite of* the presence of reality. The patients had the same oral dynamic structure as impulse neurotics. Further attempts at classification and correlation of aspects of psychopathy were made by Kahn in 1931 and Kretchmer in 1934. Kahn assigned 16 types of personality to either a character aspect of the personality, a temperament or a drive (21). Kretchmer defined four psychological states with three reactions possible. The four states (uptake, retention, working through and release), in different constellations, characterized the three reactions of "primitive," "expansive," or "sensitive" (22).

The emergence of a discrete syndrome was slowed due to initial concepts, especially in the British literature, which viewed sociopathy as consisting mainly of a moral defect. The first purely descriptive classifications were made by Henderson in 1939 (23), followed by Curran and Mallinson (24). The unification of psychoanalytic and descriptive principles relative to psychopathy (25), as well as its subclassification into neurotic or constitutional (26, 27), continued through the next decade.

Aichhorn, an analyst, initiated many investigations into delinquency, including some concerned with cause and treatment (28). His initial cases often fit the category of a neurotic delinquent, similar to Alexander's neurotic character whose motive for antisocial behavior was proposed to be that of self-punishment. Later, Eissler wrote that the criteria for delinquent behavior should be based on underlying motivation and not legal codes (29), but theoretical description was needed. Johnson considered the term "superego lacunae" to define the choice of behavior rather than motives underlying that behavior (30).

CURRENT CHILDHOOD DISORDERS

In 1952, "sociopathic personality disturbance," which included dyssocial reaction, antisocial reaction, sexual deviation and addiction, was included in the *Diagnostic and Statistical Manual* of the American Psychiatric Association *(DSM I)* (31). No provision for most childhood disorders was made. In 1968, *DSM II* (32) was felt to advance a more common frame of reference for the diagnostic classification of behavioral disorders of childhood. Taken from the GAP report of 1966 (33) and the Eighth International Classification of Diseases, seven categories were included to bridge the gap between more fixed disorders such as neurosis and more transient behavioral reactions (34-35). For the purposes of this chapter, three will be mentioned here, along with discussion related to the inconsistencies and inappropriateness inherent in these classifications.

The "runaway reaction" is a symptom cluster characterized by overnight running away from home, seclusion, apathy, immaturity, timidity, lack of socialization or loyalty to peers (save for a need for protection from them), and gross distortions in self-concept with lack of confidence (36). There is difficulty accepting this category because it is arranged not in terms of characterizing personality but in terms of partial responses to other possible, but not named, primary psychiatric disturbance.

A socialized reaction, with basic capacity for social relations, is shown in the "group delinquent reaction." Behavior here is felt to be learned and is expressed as group rather than individual dysfunction. It has also been described as rebellion with the presence of functional adaptive behavior. The capacity for loyalty is much greater than with the runaway reaction, although there is limitation of this loyalty to the group only, not to society as a whole. Behaviors, though, are similar, especially that of stealing (37).

Another reaction, also considered secondary to a basic defect in socialization, is the unsocialized aggressive reaction. The appearance of aggressive behavior is felt to be in response to frustration. In this category of reaction, the child often shows this frustration in a repetitive and maladaptive fashion. Other behaviors felt to be characteristic of this group include lying, teasing others in a hostile fashion, temper tantrums and stealing. Enuresis is described as being particularly persistent (38). It has been suggested that the antisocial or sociopathic personality of adulthood develops from extreme cases of unsocialized aggressive reaction of childhood (39).

ANTECEDENTS OF ANTISOCIAL DISORDERS

The attribution of major sociopathic behaviors in children and adolescents only to maternal deprivation as a primary etiology is reminiscent of the singular "trauma" origin of psychoses and neuroses. A single event, however serious, cannot be viewed in isolation. Consideration of genetic or constitutional determinants, as well as physiologic and environmental factors attendant to deprivation, is more helpful than any singular viewpoint. Clearly, conclusions as to the importance of the event of deprivation indicate that loss of one or both parents in childhood is more frequent in those persons diagnosed as having mental illness than in non-affected populations. The question most relevant for our purposes is that of incidence of parental deprivation in various forms of mental illness (40), with special regard to the child who in adulthood will be diagnosed sociopathic.

The evaluation of environment relative to risk of developing sociopathic personality was initially studied by several authors (41, 42). These and all subsequent studies need to be reviewed in the context of the following information. The investigation of statistical and temporal relationships of one "risk" factor to another factor felt to be predictive of the diagnosis of sociopathic personality must be a simultaneous one.

For an environmental variable such as deprivation to be an antecedent of a chief predictive variable, such as antisocial behavior in the child, the environmental variable must be shown to contribute to the expression of antisocial behavior in the child and subsequent adult sociopathic personality. Thus, antecedents of child antisocial behavior, with regard to environmental variables, must meet the conditions described by Robins (43). The environmental variable must be present before the onset of antisocial behavior and it must be related statistically to antisocial behavior of the child as well as to the adult sociopathic diagnosis. If a constant degree of childhood antisocial behavior is present, there is no statistical association found between sociopathic personality and the variable; when the variable is held constant, there is no diminishing of the relationship between childhood antisocial behavior and adult sociopathic personality.

If an environmental variable appears after the occurrence of childhood antisocial behavior, or is not present in every case, then it cannot be said with assurance that the variable contributes to the illness. The presence of an associated environmental variable does not necessarily imply an increased probability of the antisocial child being diagnosed adult sociopath; in order to infer cause, one needs to know the chronology of the relationship of the variable to the exhibited disease. To define diagnostic determinants based upon antecedents of childhood antisocial behavior requires investigation of a third variable known to occur prior to that behavior.

Deprivation

The concept of deprivation has been examined until at present it is almost worthless. It has been described in various conditions ranging from insufficient interaction with parental figures to undesirable interaction, primarily with the mother, in early childhood. Examples of deprivation and/or the mechanisms by which deprivation exerts its effects can be summarized in the following ways. Economic deprivation describes an inability to have financial resources, ignoring the mechanisms of interchange between individual behavior and environment. Little is considered about the effect which increased resources might have on emotional or social development. Lack of stimulation is another proposed cause of deprivation, one in which the child has inadequate opportunity for acquisition of experiences for effective social and cognitive growth. Closely related to lack of stimuli is the child's inability to be exposed to cause and effect, the absence of patterns, sequence and association in the stimuli. The environment of the deprived child is also felt to be related to the lack of appropriate reinforcement schedules which promote fitting or desired behavior. Stimulation from environmental sources has been known to foster neural structural growth. Thus, psychosocial deprivation contributes to deficiencies in cognitive development in the human.

Sociologic and anthropologic writers have attempted to delineate cultural antecedents of psychosocial deprivation. Cultural differences are felt to restrict educational and occupational opportunities. Self-imposed or involuntary segregation from the rest of society induces a number of disadvantages. The learning of behavior appropriate to the home environment but disruptive or not useful outside the home is often characteristic of childhood in a disadvantaged area, and may portend later social adaptive difficulty.

Delinquency and Deprivation

Early maternal deprivation is especially questionable as a basis for delinquency. The implication often seen is that maternal deprivation is pathogenic for and causes delinquency. Although this remains a somewhat widely held belief, delinquency has not been reported to be singularly or commonly associated with maternal deprivation. It is also not frequently reported that early mother-child attachment disruption consistently precedes delinquency. The following review will focus on the contributions of deprivation to subsequent sociopathic behavior. It does not, however, imply a causal relationship.

RETROSPECTIVE STUDIES

Grossly disturbed relationships with a mothering figure and the contribution of this factor to the development of repeated delinquency were reported in 1937 by Levy (44). He described the case of a child in whom multiple early placements followed illegitimate birth. General inattention, deceitfulness and evasiveness, combined with good intelligence, seemed to lead to what still can be considered typical features of the sociopathic individual: no capacity to make true friends, with characteristically superficial relationships; lack of concern or emotional response; stealing; and deceit and evasion with, more regularly than in the case reported above, impaired school performance.

Powdermaker et al. (45), in defining three groups of delinquent girls, recognized one group that was nonresponsive to treatment, with a central difficulty of an incapacity to enter into an emotional relationship with others. They described the inability to relate as a core feature of the disturbance in the delinquent. Its cause was felt to be a history of multiple or institutional placements and concomitant lack of affective relationships in infancy.

This theme was consistently repeated by many authors, including Bender (46,47), Lowrey (48), Goldfarb (49-53), and Bowlby (54, 55), and led to more scientifically oriented and prospective studies. Bender's studies were essentially retrospective. For a nine-year period, she observed that 5-10% of children hospitalized for behavior disturbances could be classified as "psychopathic behavior disorder of childhood." Her follow-up study of 10 children from the initial sample revealed that reevaluation five years later showed no improvement of social or affectual functioning.

Bowlby described a syndrome of "affectionless character," closely resembling Bender's description, in a sample of 88 children. Half of these children, the control group, were emotionally disturbed but did not exhibit stealing. The other group of 44 children ("thieves") had been reported as showing stealing behavior. Among the 88 children, the thieves group included 17 who had experienced separations of greater than 6 months duration prior to age 6. Fourteen of the "thieves" group fit the criteria of the "affectionless character." A significant overlap was described between character type ("affectionless") and rearing experience (prolonged separation) and the idea of an early connection between separation and delinquency was formulated. Although Bowlby's studies are considered classic ones, several difficulties must be considered in the interpretation of the results. Bowlby did not specify that separation, in and of itself, was the primary antecedent for the affectionless character. It is apparent that a combination of factors were contributory. These were, most frequently, a combination of deprivation of maternal care, separation, multiple parenting and multiple placements, which led to further deprivation.

Edelston hypothesized that the experience of separation would result in extreme sensitivity of the child to the further *possibility* of separation. The examination of the records of 200 children seen in a child guidance clinic during the years 1942-1946 in wartime London defined the cause of disturbance in 33% of those children as separation and not the bombing experience (56).

In 1949, a retrospective study was done of 199 children aged 13 to 17. Considering all diagnostic categories (psychopathic personality, 10%; primary behavior disorder, 13%; character neurosis, 19%; schizophrenia, 21%; and psychoneurosis, 28%), only 25% of the children were reared by both parents (57). Clarke and Clarke studied a series of mentally retarded children who experienced both separation and preseparation deprivation. They reported that greater gains in measurable intelligence occurred in "less adverse" preseparation experiences (58). Pathogenic preseparation experiences were also noted in the Mershal experiment, conducted by Lewis. In the study of 500 children, prolonged separation before 24 months of age was positively correlated with degree of behavioral disturbance (59). Wooton further emphasized that temporary separations (greater than three months) or separations after age two were not related to the specific personality patterns in later life (60). However, the questions of substitution of parenting and degree of preseparation disturbance seem to preclude the unconditional acceptance of the conclusions of his study.

Subsequent work by several authors, including Miller and Dollard (61), Mowrer (62) and Shoben (63), focused on behavior as a result of interaction of variables. Wilkin's findings, that traumatic experiences at age five could contribute to delinquency, added to the modern turning away from the singular cause-and-effect paradigms of early investigators (64). Earle and Earle found that 14% of a group of 1,423 psychiatric patients had experienced separation. Of the separated group, sociopathic personality was diagnosed in 25% of the cases while the prevalence of sociopathic personality was only 3% in the control or nonseparated group. In the separated group, the incidence of depression was higher in those who had lost a parent through death than through other causes (65).

The link between sociopathic disorders and separation remains controversial. Glueck and Glueck reported that delinquents had twice the frequency of early separation experience (prolonged absence, divorce, marital separation, death) as did nondelinquents (66). Wardle studied conduct disorders in children and concluded that these children suffered from greater than average incidence of separation (67). Andry did not support Bowlby's early findings, although many criticisms are directed toward his method of history-collection (questionnaire) and his view that the maternal deprivation syndrome cannot be empirically tested (68). Naess also concluded that deprivation was not causal as an antecedent of delinquency (69).

More recently Bowlby discussed antecedent conditions correlated with environmental and genetic factors. This retrospective study defined persistent delinquency, suicide, psychopathic personality and depression relative to disrupted childhood bonds (70). Humphrey reported on an adult inpatient population in which childhood institutionalization was significantly higher among patients given sociopathic personality diagnoses than those given other psychiatric diagnoses (71), a finding also noted by Tringer (72).

The use of retrospective studies has been criticized from many viewpoints. Cases are generally limited to those who are referred for treatment while other persons who may have been subjected to similar experiences are not generally found. The inability to remember details of child-rearing, as well as selective reporting of information, often does not allow accurate collection of data. Time sequences, such as which occurrences came first or which behaviors followed, are easily forgotten. Also, the unavailability of control groups and lack of consistency among variables make these studies more difficult to evaluate and often less than fruitful. Nevertheless, the weight of the studies reported above tends to press for an association between early, severe maternal deprivation and an inability to form affectional bonds—the core characteristic of the child who is classified as delinquent.

LONGITUDINAL STUDIES

The selection for study of subjects who have known some environmental experience, such as deprivation, and subsequent questioning with regard to outcome are attempts to answer some of the criticisms inherent in the retrospective technique. Longitudinal studies also have many methodologic difficulties, however. Anthony (73) describes the "built-in obsolescence" principle whereby concepts and procedures chosen to study an initial hypothesis are often outmoded during the course of the study. Problems in later continuity or availability of cases and the definition of valid groups of control patients are also of concern with this type of study.

The patient populations in most early longitudinal projects included children referred for clinic evaluation, names from birth registries, school children, orphanage inhabitants and foster home children. Most of the theoretical hypotheses of these studies can be stated—admittedly simply—as "a problem child grows to become a problem adult." Many of the reports cited below have added dimension to this hypothesis.

One of the first studies concerned with adult outcome was reported by Thies in 1924 (74). Foster home placement occurred during childhood in 910 persons. Of this sample, two matched groups (same age at foster home placement, similar heredity, equivalent foster home environment) were studied relative to social competence and capability. The first group consisted of 95 children who had been in institutions for at least five years of childhood. The second group was 84 children who lived at home, 80% in an environment described by the author as "bad homes." Percentages of "successful" offspring raised at home, whether by good or psychopathic parents, did not differ significantly. Children who had lived in institutions had poor adjustment compared to the above group and at least 35% of the institutionalized children were judged socially incompetent. Of these 35% at adulthood, 16% were either involved in court proceedings or were institutionalized. None of the patients was evaluated psychiatrically. Overt social incompetence thus may not speak to the presence or absence of psychiatric disturbance, although evaluation of these patients might reveal a higher incidence of mental disorder.

A later study, by Beres and Obers, concerned follow-up of 38 subjects who had been placed in institutions for the first three to four years of life (75). Severe character disorders were seen in 22 of the patients and seven of these were diagnosed "affectionless" psychopath. Four patients were diagnosed schizophrenic. Seven were considered to have made a relatively successful adjustment although none of these cases had developed close affectional ties with marriage partners or their children. This study has been criticized for biased selection of subjects (choice of severely disturbed patients, not a randomized sample). In Europe, Arctander studied boys referred to the Child Welfare Board in Oslo (76). Delinquent boys, when compared to a control group, had less frequent employment as skilled workers (clerical jobs) than as unskilled (laborers). Ahnsjo's investigation, which covered a 38-year period of admission to detention homes, revealed greater recidivism in males than females (77).

A report by Otterstrom compared occupational status, court record, use of alcohol and marital status among four groups of children and the general population (78). The children had been in inadequate homes and either had or had not committed overt delinquent acts. The delinquents either had or had not been through the court system. Outcome was also correlated with histories of parental disturbance. Criminal parents, "drunkard" fathers and "bad homes" were associated with later criminality. Illegitimacy and low intelligence were not significantly related to adult social problems. In criminals, age of first contact with social authority and length of detention were not predicted by early developmental factors.

Questionable results with regard to effects of early experience of rearing in family versus institution are reported by a number of authors. Brown and Tyler (79) concluded that familial disturbances or non-intact homes did not differ from early institutionalization in preceding pathological outcome; however, his study has two main drawbacks. The first is a lack of data regarding age of institutionalization. Secondly, diagnosis of psychological dysfunction was made only on the basis of personality inventory. A study by Bodman reported outcome for 103 children, age 15, with one group of 52 who lived at home and another of 51 who had lived in institutions (80). Both groups had been in their respective environments for at least three years prior to the studies. The Vineland Social Maturity Scale revealed that the "institutionalized" children received lower scores than "home" children; however, no statistical tests of significance were performed. Bowlby discusses this study and notes that when the data are viewed in the light of the presence or absence of adverse or non-adverse hereditary factors, the groups do not differ (81). He also makes note of the early childhood history of these children, citing varied separation experiences among even the "home" children.

Other studies related to long-term follow-up with regard to both early experience and outcome led in large part to the conclusions described in the early part of this section. Ability to predict adult psychiatric status by means of correlation with behavioral symptoms in childhood, and the strength of a single criterion such as IQ in the child to foretell adult behavior were basic views (82-88). A discussion of these two areas will allow the reader to relate our review of the "deprivation" literature to the following clinical and experimental material.

SOCIOPATHIC OUTCOME—EARLY CHILDHOOD DISORDERS

A survey of children's psychiatric clinics throughout the country has revealed that the most common problem of referred children is that of antisocial behavior, particularly among boys (89). Many studies have discussed the relationship of these behavioral problems of childhood to adult outcome. This section will focus on the predictive value of these studies.

Morris et al. and O'Neal and Robins used old clinic records in a sophisticated and scientifically designed follow-up of over 500 adults who were referred as children to a child guidance center for evaluation (90, 91). Control subjects were matched with the study sample for year of birth, place of residence, race, sex and IQ. None of the control subjects was reported—on the basis of educational records—to have had behavioral difficulties. The natural history of the study children, diagnosed as antisocial reaction or delinquent, revealed 35% eventually diagnosed as sociopathic personality disorder as adults (92). Nineteen percent of the adult study sample were diagnosed neurotic and 23% were judged psychotic. The authors concluded that irritability, tantrums, sleep disturbance (insomnia), tics, shyness and nervousness were unrelated to later psychiatric diagnosis.

Plude reported a study which evaluated adjustment among adults who had a childhood history of withdrawal behavior or shyness. Little adult pathology was found (93). Comparisons of a total of 226 children and adolescents up to age 16 showed similar results. With regard to diagnosis and progress of disease, however, 76 of 102 cases of children with schizoid features had outcomes of gradual onset and continuous course schizophrenia. In 47 children with psychopathic personality a continuous course schizophrenia was encountered.

Bender discusses a clinic population of 12 schizophrenic boys who had presented psychopathic personalities during adolescence (94). These cases were part of the 1935-52 Bellevue group. The control group was 12 schizophrenic boys who did not show psychopathic disturbance. Adult life for the "psychopathic" schizophrenic was marked by legal entanglements, sexual identity problems, and community difficulties. The comparison group had no legal difficulties and a generally more stable life situation.

At the Maudsley, Prichard and Graham studied a group of patients seen continuously in the psychiatric clinic, where they had been followed from childhood (95). Neurotic symptoms in childhood were consistently associated with affective disorders (anxiety and depression) in adulthood. Childhood phobias (anxiety) were clearly related to anxiety states in the adult. Children diagnosed as antisocial reaction (delinquency and theft) were later significantly associated with diagnoses of adult sociopathic disorder. Children diagnosed as being neurotic had no history of diagnosis of adult antisocial personality disorder.

Douglas studied school performance in 1,230 children, 942 nondelinquents and 288 delinquents (96). Teachers' ratings of the delinquent children noted both aggressiveness and nervousness accompanied by little concern with discipline, work or following rules. Swap studied disruptive interaction patterns between two groups of children (97). Unsocialized/psychopathic children and inadequate/immature children were compared in teacher interaction. Active rule-breaking in the form of verbal and physical aggresssion, threatening and resistance to discipline were characteristic of the unsocialized/psychopathic child. The inadequate/immature child was more frequently engaged in withdrawal activities and his behavior was more variable across all environmental settings. Unsocialized/psychopathic children were more disruptive (showed more problem behaviors) in nonacademic environments.

In the preschool child, symptoms correlating with the occurrence of antisocial behavior of adolescence were studied in 25 children 10 years after the first appearance of delinquency. Criteria for inclusion in the study included general patterns of overactivity and defiance, nursery school or neighbors' complaints and behaviors frequently associated with older delinquents, i.e., lying, frequent aggression towards others, hurting animals and setting fires. Rosenberg and Mueller's summary speaks of primary defects in the egos of these children, including poor object relationships, defects in the stimulus barrier and in reality testing, difficulty controlling anxiety and instinctual tension, and low self-esteem (98). This notation of "hyperactivity" is reminiscent of Weiss et al.'s study in which a six-year follow-up of children originally diagnosed "hyperactive" revealed rather high percentages of delinquency (99). The difficulty of separating and making a differential diagnosis between antisocial behaviors and hyperkinesis is well described by Werry (100).

Robins (43) noted that, in the study reported here, boys were more frequently held back one year in school than were girls, and many had not completed elementary school. Discipline problems were also apparent in the educational setting, with truancy a frequent occurrence.

In another study the social outcome of childhood neurotics was compared to that of sociopathic children. In neurosis, remissions and exacerbations were inconstant and did not change with adolescence. The sociopathic children, in contrast, had a more constant course with a poor prognosis (101).

Twenty-year follow-up of all children hospitalized for "neurotic development" in Moscow during the years 1944-1948 studied adult outcome in 63 patients (102). The group included 10 diagnosed hypochondriac, two called hysteric and 51 who were classified as "asthenic personality development." The asthenic group had 11 who were later considered normal, 15 who developed isolated pathological difficulties, seven later schizophrenics and 18 who became psychopathic personalities.

Five hundred fifteen Austrian adults who had been referred either to health or legal authorities, and 319 Austrian school children were part of a study reported by Strotzka et al. (103). The children were divided into three groups: 123 were "special," slow learning students; 98 were school failures, and 98 were "normal" classmates. In the adult population, 172 adults were classified "criminals," 42 were described as having "sociopathic" behavior on record and the remainder were diagnosed as neurotic or mentally ill. "Criminals" and "sociopaths" were similar to each other in terms of socioeconomic class and other ecological variables and were markedly different from the general population. Many children in both the "slow" and the "school failure" groups were found to be related to the adults in the "criminal" and "sociopathic" groups.

OBJECTIVE EVALUATION

There are a number of concerns of the clinician who attempts diagnosis of antisocial personality, especially in the child. While many authors have noted that the core or central tool for diagnosis in adults is the clinical interview (104), the establishment of diagnosis in the child before adolescence is fraught with difficulties. The general adult criteria include the condition that symptoms of the disorder be documented prior to age 15. This is feasible when the adolescent has shown manifestations of overt social/delinquent dysfunction. For the younger children or the child who may have engaged in sociopathic behavior without becoming involved with the legal establishment, more objective criteria and valid, reliable evaluations are needed. Several methods of evaluation will be discussed here although space limitations do not permit elaborate presentation of all of these. The reader who desires further information is referred to several papers listed at the end of the chapter (105-110).

Hathaway and Monachesi, utilizing the Minnesota Multiphasic Personality Inventory (MMPI), began a study of rate of delinquency development among 4,000 ninth grade students in Minneapolis in 1948 (111). In 1950 and 1952, by which time the subjects' ages averaged 17, ratings of delinquency, on a scale from 1 (minor difficulty with official legal records) to 4 (repeated serious offenses), were made of all students. General life adjustment was also assessed in the 1952 series. The results of that study revealed several major relationships of delinquency to MMPI code. Decreased delinquency rates were associated with the scales of Depression (D), Social Introversion (Si) and Masculinity-Feminity (Mf)—the "suppressor" category. The scales of Psychopathic Deviate (Pd), Schizophrenia (Sc) and Hypomania (Ma) were associated with high rates of delinquency—the "excitor" category (111). Group generalizations with regard to the diagnostic aspects of the MMPI could not be made with reliability; 17% of those classified as "suppressors" showed delinquency during the four years of follow-up and 67% of those classified as "excitors" showed no delinquent behavior.

The design of a subsequent study utilizing the Hathaway and Monachesi data focused on individual differences and environmental/experiential factors active in the various MMPI groupings (112). Four groups were defined. The "suppressor" and "excitor" groups were further divided into delinquent or nondelinquent categories, with 75 cases assigned to each group. Historical and attitudinal material and clinical interviews were used to collect information. Differential history of early experiences was obtained. Common events most prominent prior to age 13 in the delinquent boys were chronic illness of a sibling or parent, death of a sibling, chronic social agency assistance, removal of the child from the home and history of crime in other family members. Incidents occurring after age 13 and positively related to delinquency were social agency counseling, crime in a family member, chronic illness of a sibling and death of mother. Family histories of the delinquent boys were most often suggestive of dyssocial behavior, psychological problems and family disruption, with effects most differential prior to birth. The degree of seriousness of delinquent behavior was also correlated with family disturbance such as dyssocial behavior, marital disruption and economic need. Family relationship data analysis revealed that boys classified as "suppressors" came from homes described as "permissive," with little punishment from the parents and greater freedom to experiment with alcohol in the home as a child. Personal characteristics of delinquents were described as critical, sensitive to demands, having a low frustration tolerance, envious, deceitful, nonconforming, overly punitive and "acting-out." That these behaviors were seen prior to exhibition of the delinquent behavior led to more consideration and an attempt to develop methods to further define this population.

The Weschler Intelligence Scale for Children (WISC) has been used as an instrument of diagnosis through analysis of subtest scatter, subtest patterning and discrepancy between Verbal and Performance scores. Conflicting results have been reported with respect to the usefulness of the WISC in diagnosis. This is exemplified in a report in which 351 outpatient children who presented with a wide range of diagnoses were given the WISC in an attempt to clarify its distinguishing abilities (113). Comparisons of subtest scatter and patterning, subtest scores, Verbal IQ, and Performance IQ revealed no useful differentiation among nine diagnostic categories. It has been noted that subtest picture arrangement scores can differentiate between impulsive and sociopathic disorders (114); "cause and effect" relationships are recognized by the sociopathic child but are not as evident to the impulse-disordered child.

The use and interpretation of projective tests, as with all other diagnostic procedures, must be viewed in the context of the individual child. Childrens' drawings are developmental and reflect the ongoing maturational process, both somatic and psychic. Konecky's evaluation of drawings led to the conclusion that, if generalizations were to be made regarding diagnostic categories, neurotic children more frequently drew darkened human figures and psychopathic children drew figures in oblique line (115). Another projective measurement used to ascertain personality characterization is the House-Tree-Person technique (H-T-P). This technique has been described, especially with respect to the 'neutral" tree figure, as allowing less defensive access to the unconscious (116). It has been suggested that the addition of detail to the tree (height, presence of defects such as broken limb or knothole) correlates with severity of pathology and age at which trauma has occurred (117).

However, Navar, comparing H-T-P drawings scored for impulsiveness, hostility, and suspiciousness, found no differences between delinquents and nondelinquents on any of these measures (118).

A recent study evaluated 1,844 detailed and complete case reports of delinquents over a two-year period (119). Of these cases, only 12% of the tree drawings revealed a "scar" on the tree. Correlation of data from MMPI profiles and IQ tests with those children who drew a defect on the tree revealed a higher IQ and lower Mania scale on the MMPI. The interpretation of this finding by the author was that these children were less prone to physical acting out and expressed inner tension subtly. The assumption is that the H-T-P technique, if limited to presence or absence of tree defect, is not a valid indicator of childhood sociopathy.

The development and expression of moral values are again apparent during adolescence. The early measurement of a value system has been suggested to be of predictive value for later sociopathic development. The Values Inventory for Children (VIC) is composed of pictorial representations and objects. The child is asked to relate to the examiner a judgment as to whether he "likes" what is shown (120, 121). This instrument was used to sample 107 delinquent junior high school age children and 180 matched nondelinquents (122). Delinquents scored significantly higher than nondelinquents on Sociopathic, Alienated and Delinquent factors, while a higher Masculine factor was seen in nondelinquents. The authors note that this test is less susceptible to and less biased toward expectations of the examiner and expected desirability of response.

Another attempt to measure values and moral judgment in young adolescents classified as normal or antisocial personality was reported recently (123). IQ and mental age matched 10-13 year olds were given the WISC and the Kohlberg Moral Development Interview. Sociopathic subjects had lower levels of "moral reasoning." Higher moral judgment scores were obtained from high mental age subjects than from low mental age subjects. These results tend to suggest that a cognitive factor may be necessary for moral development.

BIOLOGICAL FACTORS

Genetic Dysfunction: Introduction

Suggestions that sociopathy could have a genetic background are related to observations that families of index patients diagnosed sociopathic have a higher incidence of similar disorders. This factor is frequently coupled with the observation of an apparent predominance of males versus females in psychopathic disorder, suggesting that it may be related to some role of the Y chromosome.

That individual responses to similar events, such as separation or deprivation, are not equivalent leads to consideration that these differences may be related to genetic isues—the "nature" question. One can find himself reflexively setting up the age-old dichotomy of "nature versus nurture." Any attempt to speak to this issue is as hopeless a task as sorting out the intertwined possible genetic factors and documented environmental disturbances proposed as causal in the development of the syndrome. With this in mind, this section considers genetic influences in the development of the behaviorally disturbed child and the association of genetic factors with the behavioral disorders.

Family Studies

Familial morbidity risk studies are not of primary assistance in unraveling genetic factors. In an earlier section of this chapter, the significant effect of chronic physical illness of a parent on the development of behavioral disorders in their children was discussed. The psychiatric literature also notes that severely disturbed parents have children who show increased psychiatric disturbance and antisocial behavior (124-128). One of the earliest of these studies found that in a clinic population of children referred for behavior disorder, 46% of the mothers were reported to show difficulties such as depression and neurotic symptoms (129). Neurotic difficulties in the child were also reported to be statistically significantly associated with symptoms of psychopathy or neurosis in the parent (130). Neurotic mothers were reported to be present in the histories of 26% of juvenile delinquents in a study by Litauer (131). Looking at presenting complaints and diagnostic processes in another clinic, Shepherd et al. felt that several factors contributed to the high referral rate. One major factor contributing to differences in the children was whether the mother was described as "complaining" or "non-complaining" (132).

The finding that mothers show psychiatric disturbance more frequently than do fathers has been reported in many studies (133-135). Rutter's work does not support the contention that fathers are less disturbed, especially when disturbance is viewed in a context of work disruption due to both personality and physical factors (136). Fathers of another clinic population (137) were reported to be more sociopathic or psychiatrically disturbed than non-clinic fathers. The authors explained the difference between their conclusions and those of Rutter as differences in index of illness, the latter index being admission to hospital. Neither parent of disturbed children has been reported to have experienced excessive family disruption or separation when compared as a group to non-clinic populations.

Another study at variance with the report that the father is less important in the development of psychopathic characteristics in the child is one by Fodor (138). A comparison between the parents of psychopathic and nonpsychopathic hospitalized delinquents was done by means of the Cornell Parent Rating Scale. Psychopathic subjects rated their mothers as being less demanding with regard to achievement than did non-psychopaths. Fathers of psychopathic children were described as being more rejecting, less involved in their child's education, less nurturing and less giving of praise for their sons.

Of course, the question of whether parental disturbance leads to an inappropriate or inadequate socialization of the child must be entertained in view of its genetic overtones.

The incidence of psychopathic symptoms in families of schizophrenics was described by Kallman as occurring in 10.7% of siblings, 17.0% of their children and 12.8% of the parents (139). The figures for the general population ranged from 3.5% to 10%, an estimate not found by Hallgren and Sjögren, who reported a range of 0.10% to 0.35% general population incidence (140). They also showed lower incidence figures for parents (1.7-2.5%) and siblings (1.1-1.3%). Rosenthal has suggested that these discrepancies are related to differences in upper limits of age for risk and differences between the two countries (141).

Twin Studies

The effects of environment and the question of individual responses to those environments versus genetic influences are the subject of twin studies of sociopathic behavior. The first reported concordance rates for criminality in monozygotic (MZ) versus dizygotic (DZ) twins were reported as 77% and 12% respectively (142). Concordance of 100% for MZ pairs and 20% for DZ pairs was reported in 1932 by Legras (143). Female concordance in three MZ pairs was reported at 75% and in 22 male MZ pairs at 66.7%, although this study had no control subjects reported (143). None of these results can be totally accepted due to questions regarding problems in sampling, lack of clarity in determination of zygosity and sample bias. Marked differences also occur in concordance between opposite- and same-sex dizygous pairs.

Christiansen, in retrospective reviews of criminal records of Danish twins born between 1870 and 1920 (144, 145), described concordance of 52.1% in MZ males and 35.3% in MZ females. Dizygotic concordance was reported at 22% for males and 13.8% for females. Prevalence ratios would be expected to be 14.8 and in DZ males the expected rate is 11%. For females, a greater difference is seen in prevalance ratios: 13.6 times the expected rate for MZ pairs. Potential explanations for this difference in rate of female criminality have ranged from biological factors being more important in female crimes, to a history of more severe environmental deprivation than is found in male offenders (146). The above reported studies suggest that genetic factors play *some* part in criminality.

Adoption Studies

Separation of the confounding variables of "nature" and "nurture" is most directly accomplished by adoption studies. In these, the frequency of psychiatric disorder is studied in adoptive and biological parents of both index and control cases.

Controlled adoption studies of the occurrence of sociopathic personality in children of schizophrenic mothers, in which the children were separated from their mothers at birth, found nine cases of sociopathy in the children of mothers diagnosed schizophrenic and two cases in those of mothers diagnosed "normal" (147). Difficulty in interpretation of this data comes from the fact that after separation at birth, the children were placed either in the care of a family member of the father or in a foundling home. The functioning of the mother during pregnancy is also a question to consider, especially if covert organic damage could have occurred secondary to malnutrition or other factors.

Kety et al. reported a higher prevalence of psychopathic disorder in biological relatives of adopted schizophrenics than in adopted controls (148). However, this finding was not replicated by Rosenthal et al. (149).

A recent adoption study tends to support the importance of heredity and its role in the etiology of psychopathic disorders (150). Eight hundred fifty-four adoptive and biological relatives of 57 adopted psychopaths and 57 matched controls were evaluated. Rates of psychiatric illness were about the same in both groups of biological and adoptive relatives. The overall rate of illness for the biological relatives of the index cases (19.0%) was higher than that of the other three subgroups of relatives (range 12.0-13.7%). More than 14% of the biological relatives of index cases had psychopathic disorders, compared to 5.3% to 7.6% of the other groups. Prevalence of psychopathy in index biological relatives was 3.9% with the other group rates ranging from 0.8-1.5%. Psychopathy was also five times more frequent in the index proband biological fathers. No mothers were diagnosed psychopathic. In contrast to the Heston study, environmental deprivation, brain damage, and pregnancy or birth complications were not found to be etiologically significant.

Similar results were obtained in other Danish studies (151, 152). Male adoptees, 1,145 in all, were studied from registers of police records, and adoption records from the years 1927-1941. If both the adoptive and biologic fathers had police records or legal entanglements, 35% of the adoptees had criminal records. If neither father had a criminal record, that of the adoptees was about 10%.

Correlative Diagnoses

Besides attempts to correlate psychopathy and schizophrenia one finds reports of psychopathic disorders, especially in males, related to diagnoses of alcoholism and depression (153). Unipolar depressed parents of depressed children were reported to have depressed daughters and sons who were either alcoholic or sociopathic. This group of patients, typified by the early onset female depressive, were classified as having depressive spectrum disease. In 1938 Slater questioned the sex-linkage of affective disorder and found no evidence for the linkage hypothesis in the bipolar or unipolar groups (154). Shields discusses these two studies in the context of ruling out sex-linked inheritance in both unipolar and bipolar groups (155).

Other Behavioral Disorders

The influence of genetics in other areas, especially behavior disorders, is not well known. Polygenic inheritance implies a relationship to disorders in which sex ratios deviate, sometimes quite markedly. The more frequently affected sex will be less deviant than the less frequently affected sex. This principle holds for the disorder of stuttering, in which boys are affected at more than twice the rate of girls. Parents and siblings of female stutterers are more often affected than are the parents and siblings of males (156). Kay theorized that girls required a greater number of the genes which predisposed them to stuttering in order to develop the disorder. Therefore, more stutterers would be found in girls' families because they would carry more of the genes. More severe cases were also found to lead to higher risk in the families. Carter states that this relationship between risk and severity is another criterion of polygenic inheritance (157). We have seen that this holds true for the sociopathic disorders, especially in the Danish reports noted above.

In twins, the prevalence of behavior disorders was found to be similar in both MZ and DZ pairs studied by Bakwin (158-162). Reading disability was present in 14.9% of DZ pairs and 14% of MZ pairs. However, concordance rates were 91% for MZ pairs and 45% for DZ. In calculating prevalence, the DZ rate was 3.1 times the expected rate while MZ pairs had 6.5 times the total sample prevalence. The same significance levels of MZ:DZ difference were seen in carsickness, nailbiting, enuresis and sleepwalking. Risk was not felt to be higher for families of female enuretics or females with reading disability, both disorders which occur more frequently in males. Hallgren states that this lack of increase in risk is related to a dominant gene present in some cases of dyslexia (163). Shields has noted that various disorders in Bakwin's studies were not related and feels that a disorder's "nature" is more influenced by genetic factors than is its presence or severity (164).

ORGANIC DYSFUNCTION: HYPERACTIVITY AND SOCIOPATHY

Learning and behavior problems, in every age child, require specific, appropriate and adequate treatment. The effectiveness of treatment depends on the recognition of the underlying dysfunction. Once again we find ourselves in an area of controversy, that of "minimal brain damage." As a concept, this term is used as it was in the introduction, as a pattern set of disturbed behavior, and the definition of its role in the etiology of childhood behavior disorders is fraught with confusion. The clinician is obligated to demonstrate, validly and reliably, that damage to the brain has resulted in the patient's disruptive, antisocial or sociopathic behavior. Extent, rate, location, and cause of damage, susceptibility of the organism, and relationship to developmental stage correlate with a variety of behaviors of the child with CNS damage (165-168). One cannot assume, however, that a child with brain injury will show characteristic behavior disturbances, just as behavior disturbances do not always present against a background of predisposing intracranial damage.

Delinquency has been related to toxoplasmosis, cerebral trauma, diffuse cortical atrophy, and epilepsy (169-172), but simplistic views that similarity of behaviors can be associated with dissimilar brain damage should be considered erroneous (173-177). These too frequently held attitudes are often based on data other than that obtained in rigid experimental paradigms.

The most frequent complaints of parents and teachers concerning a young child brought for evaluation are related to restlessness and overactivity. In older children, this overactivity may be characterized by lack of object, focus or direction. Inconsistent attention, unpredictable mood or expression, poor peer relationships, school failure and truancy, little or no control over impulses, and inappropriate aggression toward persons or the environment are frequent complaints regarding the school-age child.

The child with a history of perinatal anoxia (implying brain damage) has been described as having a deficit in the ability to abstract, lower perceptual-motor functioning, decreased reading ability and decreased social competence (178-182).

Children have also been found to be influenced in cognitive development by many environmental variables (183-185). On WISC measures, Yarrow et al. noted that total IQ in boys was correlated with the degree of positive emotional expression, acceptance and physical contact with the mother (186). On the Cattell test, developmental level was related to these same maternal care characteristics for both sexes (187). Equally sound is the observation that organic factors can contribute to ego regression. Examples often given include explosive acting out under toxic effects of medication or drugs (188). Rates of cerebral trauma as high as 54% have also been described in this syndrome (189). It seems, therefore, that nature and nurture are not mutually exclusive in the development of the organism.

Electroencephalographic Correlates

Significantly increased tendencies for EEG abnormalities have been described for many aspects of abnormal behavior (190), with sites of damage most often ascribed to the limbic system, including the medial frontal cortex, temporal lobes and hypothalamic nuclei (191, 192). The specific abnormality of the EEG has been noted to be bilateral rhythmic slow wave activity (193-195) which, when present in childhood antisocial disorders, has been related to delayed cortical maturation (195). A higher frequency of abnormal EEG with similar slow wave patterns has been seen in biological parents of these children (196).

Retrospective studies of 285 children referred over a two-year period to a juvenile court described the presence of psychomotor symptoms and paranoid ideation (delusions) in 6% of the cases (197). However, this population had a history of cerebral trauma (head injury—85%, perinatal trauma—33%) and no history was given with respect to early family conditions. Thus, no generalization can be made to any wider group of children other than the inclusion of the possibility of this triad (delinquency, psychomotor epilepsy and paranoid ideation) in differential diagnosis.

Drug Response

Increased sensitivity of late adolescent personality disordered patients to alcohol (198), greater tolerance to amphetamines, and decreased tolerance to depressant drugs has been reported (199).

Asthma

An interesting correlation has been found regarding the clinical and therapeutic response of asthma to sociopathic disorder (200). Two hundred sixteen subjects were studied, 161 who had been referred to a children's hospital and 55 who were in a residential school. Increased "sociopathic stress," i.e., stress of association with sociopathic situations, was found to contribute to relapse of the disorder as defined by decreased ventilatory function.

Neurochemical Correlates

Cerebrospinal fluid and serum evaluations of sialic acid levels were performed on 105 children ages 3-16 who had been diagnosed as schizophrenic and on three control groups from 44 children diagnosed with rheumatic psychosis (n = 12), organic pathology (n = 10) and psychopathic character traits (n = 22) (201). Aside from the changes noted in the children diagnosed schizophrenic, the lowest mean concentration occurred in organic lesions of the CNS, 142.5 Molar (range 120-165), and highest concentrations were in the rheumatic psychoses, 354.5 M mean (range 290-445 M). The mean molarity in the children categorized psychopathic was 194.3 (range 180-230 M). This was higher than the mean in schizophrenics with catatonic course (171.7 M, range 140-210), but lower than in the acute onset schizophrenics (260.5 M, range 230-300).

Serotonin, a biogenic amine also called 5-hydroxytryptamine (5-HT), has been reported to be abnormal in several syndromes of childhood (202). Whole blood levels of 5-HT have been reported to be low in mentally retarded patients who exhibit hyperactive behavior (203) as well as in hyperactive children with normal intelligence (204).

Attentional Correlates

Whitehill et al. found that objective measurement of attention in children described as emotionally labile, lacking in impulse control, inattentive and aggressive was associated with decreased visual reaction time and decreased overall response speed (205). However, that the two populations compared cannot be considered to demonstrate the relationship of this finding to sociopathic disorders is evident from statements that 25% of the children in the deviant group had to be dropped from the study due to "uncooperative" behavior.

Response characteristics of adult and adolescent sociopathic subjects to situations requiring attention have generally been lower than those of neurotic or normal subjects (206, 207). Since this seems to imply a constitutional factor, a study was designed to look at this lowered reactivity in younger populations of antisocial children exposed to a "boring" situation (photographic slide sequence) and compare their responses to those of normal or neurotic children. Antisocial children showed an earlier decrease in time spent viewing slides than did the normal children although both groups showed decreases in viewing time across trials. Neurotic children did not show the decrease across time. Sharp differentiation occurs between antisocial and neurotic subtypes in this stimulus-seeking dimension *if* one can view the child's changing slides frequently as a measure of this dimension. Infants age 11 weeks exhibit a variety of "habituation" patterns (208). One is also reminded of the studies by Thomas, Chess and Birch (209), with their findings of early and innate temperamental differences seen in the first few days of life. If certain of these findings represent a predisposition to the antisocial character, earlier identification could possibly be made by the clinician.

Biological investigation into this syndrome in the child is obviously incomplete. Barriers to progress are not only related to difficulties in developing techniques, measurements or methodology, but, also, many investigators are unable to perform "research" on the child patient because of legislative or political restrictions.

FAMILIES—ATTITUDES AND INTERACTIONS

Simplistic comparisons, such as those involving the presence or absence of a particular problem, assume homogeneity of population. No aspect of this chapter can accept this assumption and, although divisions and sub-headings have been made, they are clearly arbitrary. Such is the case for the family. Relationship of family factors to the development and maintenance of sociopathic behaviors has great value for the understanding of the disorders. Assessment of these family factors is less than ideal, but has been most successful when a multifaceted approach has been utilized.

The emphasis on relationships, as shown in the genetics section, has most frequently been between son and mother, although the role of the father is now more often being included for study. Early researchers reported higher incidences of delinquency in homes marked by submissive, inadequate fathers and domineering, aggressive mothers (210-212).

More objective study of the multiple dimensions in the family of the delinquent has led to two studies reported here. In an evaluation of two groups of delinquent adolescent girls and a control group, results indicated that differentiation could be made between mothers and fathers and among the groups (213). Delinquents classified as socialized had parents who were often more restrictive in the area of control and who had higher activity levels than did parents of nonsocialized delinquents. Parents of nondelinquents, when compared to parents of delinquents, showed better parental adjustment, higher levels of activity, lower consistency of controls and higher consistency of feelings. In general, fathers of nondelinquents were felt to be more authoritarian, more demanding with regard to conformity, less demonstrative affectionally to the child but more able to allow environmental exploration by the child.

Quay defined three factors felt to be consistent in delinquency (214). A *neurotic-delinquent* dimension was described as being associated with guilt, anxiety, depression and withdrawal from social contact. Identification with the social norms of the delinquent subgroup was seen as characteristic of a *socialized subculture. Unsocialized-psychopathic* persons were felt to manifest impulsiveness, assaultiveness, lack of socialization, and an anti-authority, amoral attitude with a lack of concern for others.

Groups of both male and female subjects were selected for a later study in which family interaction patterns were studied relative to the above factors (215). The unsocialized-psychopathic person's family was reported to be dominated by the father, with the mother being overtly passive and non-dominant, shifting her position with little obvious resistance. These "passive" mothers also apparently have trouble reaching "final agreement" with their husbands. In contrast, the neurotic-delinquent's family is dominated by the mother, who controls the decision-making process and the interactions with her husband. The father resists, often leading to arguing and conflict in the family situation.

Relationships with mother are reported to vary with the above classifications. There is no evidenced conflict between mother and son in the neurotic-delinquent's family, but in either the psychopathic delinquent's or the non-delinquent's family one finds greater disagreement and aggression between mother and son. This difference has been explained in part by the choice on the part of the neurotic delinquent toward assertion in delinquent acts. Conflict with father is chosen instead of conflict—that is not rewarding—with a controlling mother. Social delinquent sons are characterized by an unwillingness to compromise with the opinions of the father and by passive resistance on the part of the mother. The family of the non-delinquent shows no stable pattern of differential parental dominance; parents will disagree openly in the process of decision-making. Considerable assertiveness is evident among family members.

With regard to restrictions and limitations, rigid activity restrictions are apparent in both parents of psychopathic delinquents and aggression is not encouraged in the home (216). Neurotic delinquents' parents, on the other hand, find aggression to be anxiety provoking, rate high in frequency of physical punishment and denial of privileges to their delinquent children, and have little confidence in the self-control or value development of the child. They also are reported to more significantly reject their children. The families of socialized delinquents use wide ranges of discipline, less severe physical punishment than psychopathic delinquents' families and greater permissiveness than families of neurotic delinquents.

Delinquent daughters and their families show less apparent or consistent differences. Active dissension is apparent in both socialized delinquent and psychopathic delinquent daughters and their parents. The non-delinquent daughter seems less assertive, particularly with the father. Mother is seen as being less powerful in families with neurotic delinquent daughters but the father in these same families is not clearly dominant. Parents of non-delinquent daughters were found to have fewer negative expectations for their daughters when compared to parents in delinquent groups. These parents also had confidence in the ability of their daughter to show self-control, as well as guilt and anxiety, when appropriate, with respect to acts of wrong doing.

Aggression anxiety was not different across parent groups, unlike findings with parents of male delinquents. Reinforcement and encouragement of aggression were apparent in the mothers of delinquent girls. Deprivation of privileges, including physical punishment by the mother was seen in families of neurotic delinquents. Fathers of sociopathic delinquent girls had the lowest expectation of any father group that the daughter would be either morally remorseful, responsible or inhibited in expression of antisocial impulses. These fathers were also the most permissive with their daughters.

No consistent differences in patterns of interaction were seen among delinquent versus non-delinquent groups of families in any of these studies. Few differences were seen among families of male versus female delinquents. In fact, maternal dominance was more frequently seen with neurotic delinquents of both sexes than was paternal dominance.

Family correlates of delinquency are clearly in need of more study (see Chapter 7), especially in view of the above reports. More investigation of varied population types is required, as well as expansion of the methodologies of family interaction studies in delinquency.

Introduction

Perceptions of some educators, regardless of experience, are affected by labels applied to exceptional children. These effects may not be consistent in our view of children called "mentally deficient," but in at least one study negative percepts accompanied labels of "psychopath," "schizophrenic" and "cerebral palsy" (217).

Many retrospective follow-up studies examining the question of permanence or reversibility of the effects of deprivation, either in terms of improved intellectual function or of maturation in adolescence, reach conclusions that are less than optimistic (218). Other researchers feel that the intellectual deficits, if not reversible, are at least arrested by placement in another environment (219).

In viewing sociopathic behavior in the child not as a socially defined disease but as psychopathology, the question of effective treatment turns to two major viewpoints, one pessimistic and one optimistic. In spite of Tunley's view that science is incapable of solving the problem (220), advances have been made in the management of the antisocial child. To benefit from these, distinctions must be made between group and individual reaction, between the social and the asocial, and between the neurotic and the character disordered.

Background

August Aichhorn began as a teacher and became known for his ability to work with aggressive children. Following his establishment of two residential centers in the years prior to 1920, he received psychoanalytic training and in 1935 published *Wayward Youth* (28). Aichhorn viewed these delinquent youngsters as having difficulty in establishing relationships. Although most of his patients could be classified as neurotic delinquents, who have defects of more advanced and more integrated egos than the antisocial child, demonstration of the effectiveness of his methods led to further investigation.

Prevention

Three major types of prevention programs were described by Witmer and Tufts (221). Programs designed to reduce the probability of recidivism are one type. These generally include multidisciplinary involvement in rehabilitation. Second are projects which attempt to intervene in the development of the child who has a potential for delinquency.

Third are those which attempt to change the social environment of the child, best exemplified by the Chicago Area Project (222). This project was based upon the theory that a sense of community identification and responsibility would decrease delinquency. Some positive results were obtained, shown as a decrease of delinquency in three of four communities included in the project.

Robins makes an important point when defining treatment versus prevention: The selection of a child by a researcher for study on the basis of teacher reports of behavior difficulties is usually called prevention; selection on the basis of a referral for help is often called treatment (223). One example of primary prevention might be working with children chosen solely on the basis of their high-risk family backgrounds, without regard for behavioral symptoms.

Psychotherapy

There have been few reported controlled studies of psychotherapeutic treatment of the antisocial child. One study described individual intervention in three groups of children (224). When compared with the neurotic or prepsychotic child, the psychopathic child was reported not to accept the social integration attendant in therapy.

A series of studies reviewed by Levine and Bronstein involved follow-up data obtained up to five years following treatment of juvenile offenders (225). Group as well as individual psychotherapy, therapy oriented toward vocational needs, and therapeutic communities, either in an institution or on an outpatient basis, led to improvement in seven of eight studies. The one exception, the Cambridge-Sommerville Youth Study, matched 325 potential delinquents with 325 control cases. The research group received either outpatient psychoanalytically-oriented psychotherapy or client-centered therapy. The control group received no therapy. At 10 year follow-up, no difference was seen in terms of involvement with crime in either group (226).

Levy describes the therapy of the antisocial child as having a very poor prognosis (227). This is aptly expressed in the study by Powdermaker et al. (45), who had a 50% success rate for delinquent girls ages 12-16. Factors which seemed to determine failure in therapy included rejection of the child or lack of libidinal tie (50%) and neurotic or ambivalent relationship (30%).

Psychoanalysis

Eissler describes the psychoanalytic treatment of delinquents in the context of phases in the treatment situation (228). Creation of positive transferences of the patient is needed because of the primary narcissistic aspect of his personality. Subsequent to this the psychoanalysis begins. Rosenberg extends this phase approach to treatment of the antisocial patient (98).

Establishment of the relationship between therapist and patient usually begins on the oral, narcissistic level, proceeds to formation of the therapeutic alliance in which the therapist often needs to teach the use of fantasy play, and then leads to the therapeutic correction of patterns, much as with the neurotic child. Zavitzianos expands upon the difficulties of technique in the analysis of a juvenile delinquent who is characterized by disturbances in transition from primary narcissism to object love (229). Depersonalization is frequent in these patients and it is often difficult for them to internalize objects.

Behavior Modification

The last non-organic mode of treatment to be considered is that of behavior modification. Interventions in delinquent behaviors have been concerned with control of aggression through, for example, token economy and "time-out" procedures (230), or contingency programs in which cessation of the behavior of stealing led to home visits (231). "Isolation" of brief duration was reported to lead to decreased aggressive behavior in a 16-year-old institutionalized delinquent (79).

Parent training in behavior management of their delinquent children in the home situation revealed a success rate—based on parent report—of 75% (232). Decreased runaway behavior followed negative verbal feedback from staff when girls threatened to run away (233).

Community-based studies in areas of intervention are reported by one group of researchers (234-236). Forty subjects, all delinquents, divided into two groups each of 20 experimentals and 20 controls, were used in the study. The experimental group members were "shaped" for attendance and content in interview situations by means of reinforcements of money, food or other items. A three-year follow-up showed less time in correctional institutions, decreased hostile comments and increased positive view toward self for the experimental group. Alexander and Parsons reported a comparative study among client-centered groups, psychodynamic groups, short-term behavioral intervention and no intervention in delinquent families (237). Less recidivism was seen in the behavioral intervention families within 6-18 months.

Theoretical interpretation of these data is extremely difficult because of problems found in all of the therapeutic approaches outlined. Consideration of Chapters 14 and 15 in this volume will be of interest for a more in-depth discussion of this aspect of treatment.

Pharmacotherapy

Pharmacologic treatment is a relatively uncharted area in childhood, especially with regard to antisocial behavior disorders. Not only would advances in this area aid definition of better management but they would also assist our understanding of etiology. Difficulties in the use of medications in the child are different in many respects from those in adults. One major distinction is that the younger child must depend on his parents for correct timing and dosage. The child's view of the meaning of taking medication, as well as that of the parents, must be understood by the clinician in order to ensure compliance and acceptance of the medication.

Pharmacokinetic studies in children are extremely rare, so differences in drug response, metabolism and side effects must be considered. Appropriate dosage is expected by many clinicians to be less than that for adults; the opposite is often the case. Nonspecific responses to side effects should also be considered in young patients, as should interference with any aspect of the growth or development of the child. With these precautions in mind, the following review addresses the use of pharmacologic agents in treatment of the antisocial child.

Neuleptil, a European preparation not licensed in the United States but reported to be similar to chlorpromazine, has been used for its ability to decrease impulsive behavior and excitability in child and adolescent psychopaths (238).

Diphenylhydantoin (DPH) has been reported to be beneficial in improving mood and affect in adolescents at doses of 150-200 mg/day (239). This finding is disputed by another study which showed equal effects of placebo and DPH at 200 mg/day. The subjects were juvenile delinquents who were court committed; target symptoms were disruptive and disturbed behavior (240). In another study, children between the ages of five and 14 with suspected minimal brain dysfunction and severe tantrums showed no response to DPH (241).

The use of stimulant drugs such as dextroamphetamine and methylphenidate has been effective in the treatment of hyperactive children. Extension of this use to children with antisocial behavior, aggressive behavior and overactivity has been noted to improve overactivity (242). Improvement in delinquent behavior was also noted to occur with dextroamphetamine in comparison to placebo (243). Satterfield and Cantwell

(244) propose that the use of stimulants may be related to remission of symptoms because of increased inhibitory cortical control. This may be related to the findings reported in the low response rate studies reviewed in the previous section on physiology.

Long-term studies are lacking in this area. The impetus for further research will come from successful treatment of the child as well as from positive results in decreasing the number of antisocial adults because of early treatment. For further discussion of the use of psychotropic medication in sociopathic syndromes, see Chapter 16.

AFFECTUAL "DEVIANCE"

Affective functioning is clearly impaired in the sociopathic disorders. Without attempting a detailed exposition of current theoretical views concerning the development and expression of affect, a basic premise of many writers is the general importance of affect in the continuing development of the organism. The author believes that competence, or the syndrome of competence in the normal child, depends upon early attachment and affectual experiences (245).

The child has the ability to form attachments in the first year of life (246). Although there are individual differences in exact timing and appearance, the basic process is similar. One of the necessary concomitants to this development is the presence of environmental stimulation. Early asocial phases are characterized by equal responsiveness to all parts of the infant's environment. As development progresses, attachment occurs with many objects in the environment until attachment to a specific object develops.

THE PSYCHOANALYTIC PERSPECTIVE

The assumption that impulsive characters have no superego, a state which was believed to allow for gratification of demands without consideration for others, has not been confirmed. The recognition that a key variable—among many physiological and psychological variables—in the development of psychopathology is related to the nature of the parent-child bond enables further theorizing about the impulse-ridden character. A lack of lasting object relationships in early development was understood by Fenichel (247) to be the result of inconsistent environmental influence, frequent environmental change, and lack of love in the infant's surroundings. Correlated with this history was a weak, inconsistent and disorganized superego.

Thus, object constancy which is needed for object-related experience is missing in the antisocial child with lack of opportunity for attachment. This need for object constancy is a core aspect of the development of the ability to internalize and of the subsequent appearance of structures which are crucial in order that the child may be able to tolerate frustration and delay and control his impulses (248, 249).

This disruption of early opportunity for development of attachment is seen also in depression. Depression is used here in the context of a "general system dysfunction" as described by Basch (250). In both depression and sociopathy, low arousal rates are postulated, with responses to these low arousal rates seen by many as being related to the exhibition of withdrawal (in depression) and overactivity (in the sociopathic child). These major diagnostic categories can be significantly differentiated by psychomotor research (251) and the two conditions occasionally have been found to be associated. Psychopathic depression, more frequently described in the French literature (252) than in the English, implies a history of overlapping forms of basic interruptions in attachment. It has been postulated that the depressed patient generally has lost hope of reaching his goals but has not "given up" on his future. The sociopathic patient also exhibits hopelessness, but without orientation to the future (253). The depressed patient cannot satisfy his ego-ideal and superego. Depression can therefore exist in the sociopathic child, although it is based on a different developmental stage, object relationships and psychological structure. Awareness of this possible correlation must demand from the clinician *consideration of the position of affect in the sociopath.* Viewing an absence of affect from the position of deviance in *development* rather than from the position of the deviant *person* may permit less negative approaches to management of the child.

SUMMARY

To attempt any brief summary of the concept of the sociopathic child would deny the overwhelming number of multifaceted factors which are thought to contribute to its predisposition, maintenance, biologic concomitants and outcome. What may be more valuable for the reader is clarification of the fact that the consideration of antisocial or sociopathic behavior in the child does not attempt an equation of behavior or social attitude with psychopathology. That an event such as deprivation, genetic predisposition or organic damage can be found to contribute to behavior does not imply etiology nor does it excuse outcome. The same can be said for family and peer interactions, biologic concomitants and educational environments. Treatment demands an interactional approach.

Consideration of the individual situation and child is more important than limitation of behavior because of societal demands. A child does not "grow out of" this position. More frequently, sociopathy in adulthood can be related to childhood, as is abundantly evident from the material cited in this chapter. Early intervention and continued research may help prevent this continuity of outcome.

Advocacy of any simplistic view of this syndrome, or denial of its existence, does not lend itself to the goal of every clinician and researcher. In the context of the child "destined" to become sociopathic, this goal is the delineation of etiologic factors, alteration of psychopathology by appropriate treatment and alleviation of the distress of the child in his family and society.

REFERENCES

1. JENKINS, P. L. Was "sociopathy" ever a diagnosis? Letter to Editor, *Am. J. Psychiatry* 133:4, 456-457, 1976.
2. LEWIS, D. L. and BALLA, D. Sociopathy and its Synonyms: Inappropriate Diagnoses in Child Psychiatry. *Am. J. Psychiatry* 132:7, 720-722, 1975.
3. MATOUSEK, O. and NESNIDALOVA, R. Research in Pedopsychopathy. *Ceskoslovenska Psychiatric* 70:257-262, 1974.
4. VAN KREVELEN, D. A. The Concept of Psychopathy in Child Psychiatry. *Acta. Paedopsychiatr.* 37:67-84, 1970.
5. PRICHARD, J. C. *A Treatise on Insanity and Other Disorders Affecting the Mind.* Philadelphia: Haswell, Barington and Haswell, 1837.
6. LOMBROSO, C. *Crime, Its Causes and Remedies.* Horton, H. P. (transl.). Boston: Little Brown, 1911.
7. GOUSTER, M. Moral Insanity, Revue des Sciences *Médecaus* (abstract: *J. Nerv. Ment. Dis.* 5:181-182, 1878).
8. KOCH, J. L. A. *Die Psychopathie Minderwertigkieten (The Psychopathic Inferiorities).* Ravensberg, Maier, 1891.
9. KRAEPELIN, E. *Psychiatrie.* Eighth Edition, Volume 4. Leipzig: Barth, 1915.
10. HEALY, W. *The Individual Delinquent: A Textbook of Diagnosis and Prognosis.* Boston: Little Brown, 1915.
11. GLUECK, B. A Study of 608 Admissions to Sing Sing Prison. *Ment. Hyg.* II:85-151, 1918.
12. DARROW, C. *Crime, Its Causes and Treatment.* 1922.
13. McCORD, W. and McCORD, J. *Psychopathy and Delinquency.* New York: Grune and Stratton, 1956.
14. ALEXANDER, F. G. and SELESNICK, S. T. *The History of Psychiatry: An Evaluation of Psychiatric Thought and Practice From Prehistoric Times to the Present.* New York: Harper and Row, 1966.
15. PARTRIDGE, G. E. Current Conceptions of Psychopathic Personality. *Am. J. Psychiatry* 10:53, 1930.
16. BALLY, G. Ueber Hochstapler und Verwahrloste. *Zeitschrift für Psychoanalytische Paedogogik,* IX, 1935.
17. MENG, H. Zur Psychologie des Triebhaften Narzissten. *Zeitschrift für Psychoanalytische Paedogogik,* IX, 1935.
18. REICH, W. Der Triebhafte Charakter. *Inter Psa Verlag,* Wien, 1935.
19. FREUD, S. (1916) Some Character Types Met Within Psychoanalytic Work. *Standard Edition* 14:309-333. London: Hogarth Press, 1957.

20. ALEXANDER, F. The Neurotic Character. *Int. J. Psychoanal.* 11:292-311, 1930.
21. KAHN, E. *Psychopathic Personalities.* New Haven: Yale University Press, 1931.
22. KRETCHMER, E. Cited in Schneider, K., *Die Psychopathischen Personlichkeiten.* Leipzig: Thieme, 1934.
23. HENDERSON, D. K. *Psychopathic States.* New York: W. W. Norton & Co., 1939.
24. CURRAN, D. and MALLINSON, P. Psychopathic Personality. *J. Ment. Sci.* 90:266, 1944.
25. GREENACRE, P. Conscience in the Psychopath. *Am. J. Orthopsychiatry* 15:495, 1945.
26. KARPMAN, B. On the Need for Separating Psychopathy Into Two Distinct Clinical Types: Symptomatic and Idiopathic. *J. Clin. Psychopathology* 3:112-137, 1941.
27. LINDNER R. M. Experimental Studies in Constitutional Psychopathic Inferiory. *J. Crim. Psychopathology* 4:252-484, 1942-43.
28. AICHHORN, A. *Wayward Youth.* New Yorks Viking Press, 1935.
29. EISSLER, K. R. *Searchlights on Delinquency.* New York: International Universities Press, 1949.
30. JOHNSON, A. M. Sanctions for Superego Lacunae of Adolescents. In: K. R. Eissler (Ed.), *Searchlights on Delinquency.* New York: International Universities Press, 1949, 225-234.
31. *Diagnostic and Statistical Manual, Mental Disorders (DSM I).* American Psychiatric Association, Mental Hospital Service, Washington, 1952.
32. *Diagnostic and Statistical Manual, Mental Disorders (DSM II).* American Psychiatric Association, Washington, 1968.
33. Group for the Advancement of Psychiatry, Report #62, *Psychopathological Disorders in Childhood: Theoretical Considerations and a Proposed Classification.* New York: Group for the Advancement of Psychiatry, 1966.
34. JENKINS, R. L. Classification of Behavior Problems of Children. *Am. J. Psychiatry* 125:68, 1969.
35. FISH, B. Problems of Diagnosis and the Definition of Comparable Groups: A Neglected Issue in Drug Research With Children. *Am. J. Psychiatry* 125:900, 1969.
36. JENKINS, R. L. and BOYER, A. Types of Delinquent Behavior and Background Factors. *Int. J. Soc. Psychiatry* 14:65-76, 1967.
37. JENKINS, R. L. Diagnoses, Dynamics and Treatment in Child Psychiatry. *Psychiatr. Res. Rep. Am. Psychiatry Assoc.* 18:91-120, 1964.
38. JENKINS, R. L., NUR EDDIN, E. and SHAPIRO, I. Children's Behavior Syndromes and Parental Responses. *Genet. Psychol. Monogr.* 74:261-329, 1966.
39. JENKINS, R. L. The Psychopathic or Antisocial Personality. *J. Nerv. Ment. Dis.* 131:318-334, 1960.
40. BRATFOS, O. Parental Deprivation in Childhood and Type of Future Mental Disease. *Acta Psychiatr. Scand.* 43:453-461, 1967.
41. KENDALL, P. and LAZARSFELD, P. F. Problems of Survey Analysis. In: R. K. Merton and P. F. Lazarsfeld (Eds.), *Continuities in Social Research.* Glencoe: The Free Press, 1950, 113-196.
42. GOLD, D. *Spuriousness, Developmental Sequences, and Independent Causation in Non-Experimental Social Research.* New York: American Sociological Association, 1960.
43. ROBINS, L. *Deviant Children Grown Up.* Baltimore: Williams and Wilkins, 1966.
44. LEVY, D. M. Primary Affect Hunger. *Am. J. Psychiatry* 94:643, 1937.
45. POWDERMAKER, F., LEVES, H. T. and LOURAINE, S. Psychopathology and Treatment of Delinquent Girls. *Am. J. Orthopsychiatry* 7:58, 1937.
46. BENDER, L. and YARNEE, H. An Observation Nursery: A Study of 250 Children in the Psychiatric Division of Bellevue Hospital. *Am. J. Psychiatry* 97:1158, 1941.
47. BENDER, L. Psychopathic Behavior Disorders in Children. In: A. M. Linder and

R. V. Seliger (Eds.), *Handbook of Correctional Psychology*. New York: Philosophical Library, 1947.

48. LOWREY, L. G. Personality Distortion and Early Infant Care. *Am. J. Orthopsychiatry* 10:576, 1949.
49. GOLDFARB, W. Effects of Psychological Deprivation in Infancy and Subsequent Stimulation. *Am. J. Psychiatry* 102:18, 1945.
50. GOLDFARB, W. Psychological Deprivation in Infancy and Subsequent Adjustment. *Am. J. Orthopsychiatry* 15:247, 1945.
51. GOLDFARB, W. Infant Rearing as a Factor in Foster Home Placement. *Am. J. Orthopsychiatry* 14:441, 1944.
52. GOLDFARB, W. Effects of Early Institutional Care on Adolescent Personality. *Child Dev.* 14:213, 1943.
53. GOLDFARB, W. Infant Rearing and Problem Behavior. *Am. J. Orthopsychiatry* 13:249, 1943.
54. BOWLBY, J. *Forty-four Juvenile Thieves, Their Characters and Home Life.* London: Baillière, Tyndall and Cox, 1946.
55. BOWLBY, J. The Influence of Early Environment in the Development of Neurosis and Neurotic Character. *Int. J. Psychoanal.* 21:154, 1940.
56. EDELSTON, H. Separation Anxiety in Young Children: A Study of Hospital Cases. *Genet. Psychol. Monogr.* 28:3-95, 1943.
57. CAREY-TREFZER, C. The Results of a Clinical Study of War-Damaged Children Who Attended the Child Guidance Clinic, the Hospital for Sick Children, Great Ormond Street, London. *J. Ment. Sci.* 95:535-559, 1949.
58. CLARKE, A. D. B. and CLARKE, A. M. Cognitive Changes in the Feebleminded. *Br. J. Psychology* 45:173, 1957.
59. LEWIS, H. *Deprived Children (The Mershal Experiment). A Social and Clinical Study.* London: Oxford University Press, 1954.
60. WOOTON, B. *Social Science and Social Pathology.* London: Allen and Unwin, 1959.
61. MILLER, J. and DOLLARD, J. *Personality and Psychotherapy.* New York: McGraw Hill, 1950.
62. MOWRER, O. H. *Learning Theory and Behavior.* New York: Wiley, 1960.
63. SHOBEN, E. J., JR., Psychotherapy as a Problem in Learning Theory. *Psychol. Bull.* 46:173, 1949.
64. WILKINS, L. T. *Delinquent Generations.* London: H. M. Stationary Office, 1960.
65. EARLE, A. M. and EARLE, B. V. Early Maternal Deprivation and Later Psychiatric Illness. *Am. J. Orthopsychiatry* 31:81, 1961.
66. GLUECK, S. and GLUECK, E. *Unraveling Juvenile Delinquency.* Boston: Harvard University Press, 1950.
67. WARDLE, C. J. Two Generations of Broken Homes in the Genesis of Conduct and Behavior Disorders in Childhood. *Br. Med. J.* 2:349, 1961.
68. ANDRY, R. G. *Delinquency and Parental Pathology.* London: Methuen, 1960.
69. NAESS, S. Mother-child Separation and Delinquency. *Br. J. Delinquency* 10:22, 1959.
70. BOWLBY, J. Description of Affectional Bonds and its Effects on Behavior. *J. Contemp. Psychotherapy* 2:75-86, 1971.
71. HUMPHREY, J. A Study of the Etiology of Sociopathic Behavior. *Dis. Nerv. Syst.* 35:432-435, 1974.
72. TRINGER, L. Mental Disorder from the Standpoint of Socialization. *Ann. Med. Psychol.* 2:141-152, 1975.
73. ANTHONY, E. J. The Behavior Disorders of Childhood. In: P. H. Mussen (Ed.), *Carmichael's Manual of Child Psychology.* New York: Wiley and Sons, 1970.
74. THIES, S. *How Foster Children Turn Out.* New York: State Charities Aid Association, 1924.
75. BERES, D. and OBERS, S. J. The Effects of Extreme Deprivation in Infancy on

Psychic Structure in Adolescence: A Study of Ego Development. *Psychoanal. Study Child* 5:212, 1950.

76. ARCTANDER, S. Cited in Otterstrom, E., Delinquency and Children from Bad Homes. *Acta Paediatr.* 33:5, 1936.

77. AHNSJO, S. Delinquency in Girls and its Prognosis. *Acta Paediatr.* (Supplement III) 28:1-335, 1941.

78. OTTERSTROM, E. Delinquency and Children from Bad Homes. *Acta Paediatr.* (Supplement V) 33:1-326, 1946.

79. BROWN, G. and TYLER, V. Time Out from Reinforcement: A Technique for Dethroning the "Duke" of an Institutionalized Delinquent Group. *Child Psychol. Psychiatry* 9:203-211, 1968.

80. BODMAN, F. The Social Adaptation of Institution Children. *Ment. Health.* London 9:68-69, 1950.

81. BOWLBY, J. *Maternal Care and Mental Health.* Geneva: World Health Organization, 1951.

82. ROHRER, J. H. and EDMONSON, M. S. *The Eighth Generation.* New York: Harper and Brothers, 1960.

83. STEWART, L. H. Social and Emotional Adjustment During Adolescence as Related to the Development of Psychosomatic Illness in Adulthood. *Genet. Psychol. Monogr.* 65:175-215, 1962.

84. SMELSER, W. T. Adolescent and Adult Occupational Choice as a Function of Family Socioeconomic History. *Sociometry* 26:393-409, 1963.

85. MACFARLANE, J. W. From Infancy to Adulthood. *Childhood Education,* Vol. 3, 1963.

86. ANDERSON, J. E. Experience and Behavior in Early Childhood and the Adjustment of the Same Persons as Adults. Minnesota: Institute of Child Development, 1963.

87. KAGAN, J. and MOSS, H. A. *Birth to Maturity.* New York: John Wiley and Sons, 1962.

88. SKEELS, H. M. and SKODAK, M. Techniques for a High-yield Follow-up Study in the Field. *Public Health Reports* 80:249-257, 1965.

89. ROSEN, B. M., BAHN, A. K. and KRAMER, M. Demographic and Diagnostic Characteristics of Psychiatric Clinic Outpatients in the U.S.A., 1961. *Am. J. Orthopsychiatry* 34:455-468, 1964.

90. MORRIS, D. P., SOROKER, E. and BURRUSS, G. Follow-up Studies of Shy, Withdrawn Children I. Evaluation of Later Adjustment. *Am. J. Orthopsychiatry* 24:743-754, 1954.

91. O'NEAL, P. and ROBINS, L. N. The Relation of Childhood Behavior Problems to Adult Psychiatric Status: A Thirty Year Follow-up Study. *Am. J. Psychiatry* 114:961, 1958.

92. O'NEAL, P. and ROBINS, L. N. Childhood Patterns Predictive of Adult Schizophrenia: A Thirty Year Follow-up Study. *Am. J. Psychiatry* 115:385, 1959.

93. PLUDE, V. Y. Premorbid Features of Schizophrenic Children. *J. Neuropathologic in Psychiatry* 68:1544, 1968.

94. BENDER, L. Psychopathic Personality or Schizophrenia in Adolescence. *Biol. Psychiatry* 3:197-204, 1971.

95. PRICHARD, M. and GRAHAM, P. An Investigation of a Group of Patients Who Have Attended Both the Child and Adult Department of the Same Psychiatric Hospital. *Br. J. Psychiatry* 112:487-603, 1966.

96. DOUGLAS, J. W. The School Progress of Nervous and Troublesome Children. *Br. J. Psychiatry* 112:115-116, 1966.

97. SWAP, S. An Ecological Study of Encounters Between Pupils and Teachers. Proceedings, 81st American Psychological Association, 1973.

98. ROSENBERG, R. and MUELLER, B. Preschool Antisocial Children: Psychodynamic

Considerations and Implications for Treatment. *J. Amer. Acad. Child Psychiat.* 7:421-441, 1968.

99. WEISS, G., MINDE, K., WERRY, J. S., DOUGLAS, V. and NEMETH, E. Studies on the Hyperactive Child VIII. Five Year Follow-up. *Arch. Gen. Psychiatry* 24:409-414, 1971.

100. WERRY, J. S. Organic Factors in Childhood Psychopathology. In: H. C. Quay and J. S. Werry (Eds.), *Psychopathological Disorders in Childhood.* New York: Wiley, 1972.

101. ERNST, K. and ERNST, C. Follow-up Studies of Childhood Neuroses. *Acta Paediatr.* 38:316-324, 1972.

102. BUYANOV, M. I. Catamnesis of Asthenic Developments in Children. *J. Neuropatologii i Psikhiatrii* 68:1562-1566, 1968.

103. STROTZKA, H., SIMOR, M. D., SIEVY, P., KUNZE, E. and STADLER, H. Interdependenzen Sozialer Desintegration. *Soc. Psychiatry* 6:158-166, 1971.

104. WINOKUR, G. and CROWE, R. Personality Disorders. In: A. Freedman, H. Kaplan and B. Sadock (Eds.), *Comprehensive Textbook of Psychiatry*, Vol. 11, 1975, 1279-1297.

105. SZUREK, S. A. Childhood Orgins of Psychopathic Personality Trends. In: S. A. Szurek and I. N. Berlin (Eds.), *The Antisocial Child: His Family and His Community.* San Francisco: Langley Porter, 1969.

106. KVARCEUS, W. C. *KD Proneness Scale and Check List.* Yonkers: World Book, 1953.

107. GUNDERSON, E., BALLARD, K. and HUGE, P. The Relationship of Delinquency Potential Scale Scores of Naval Recruits to Later Military Performance. California: United States Naval Retraining Command, 1958.

108. JESNESS, C. Redevelopment and Revalidation of the Jesness Inventory. California: California Youth Authority, 1963.

109. MELGAR, M. Influence of the Social Milieu on Personality Development Judged from Responses to the Rorschach. *Acta Psiquiatrica y Psicoloigica de America Latina* 13:229-234, 1967.

110. BERGMAN, R. E. (Ed.). The Sociopath: *Selections in Antisocial Behavior.* New York: Exposition Press, 1968.

111. HATHAWAY, J. and MONACHESI, E. (Eds.). *Analyzing and Predicting Juvenile Delinquency With the MMPI.* University of Minnesota Press, 1953.

112. WIRT, R. and BRIGGS, P. Personality and Environmental Factors in the Development of Delinquency. *Psychol. Monogr.* 73:1, 1959.

113. SCHOONOVER, S. and HERTEL, R. Diagnostic Implications of WISC Scores. *Psychol. Reports* 26:967, 1970.

114. CLUNE, C. Personal Communication.

115. KONECNY, R. Clinical Applications of the Projective Drawings of Children. *Psycholόgia a Patopsychológia Dietata* 2:79-84, 1967.

116. BUCK, J. The H-T-P Techniques: A Qualitative and Quantitative Scoring Manual. *J. Clin. Psychol. Monogr.* Supp 5, 1948.

117. HAMMER, E. F. *The House-Tree-Person (H-T-P) Clinical Research Manual.* Los Angeles: Western Psychological Services, 1955.

118. NAVAR, R. An Attempt to Differentiate Delinquents From Non-delinquents on the Basis of Projective Drawings. *J. Crim. Law, Criminol. Police Sci.* 55:107-110, 1964.

119. DEVORE, J. and FRYREAT, J. L. Analysis of Juvenile Delinquent's Role Drawing Responses on the Tree Figure of the House-Tree-Person Technique. *J. Clin. Psychol.* 32:731, 1976.

120. GUILFORD, J. and GUPTA, W. Development of the Values Inventory for Children. Proceedings, 79th Annual Convention, American Psychiatric Association, 1971.

121. GUILFORD, J., GUPTA, W. and GOLDBERG, L. Development of a Values Inventory for

Grades 1 to 3 in Five Ethnic Groups. Final Rep USOE Project #0-0196, Contract #OEC-0-70-2673). Torrance, General Behavioral Systems, 1971.

122. GOLDBERG, L. and GUILFORD, J. Delinquent Values: Its Fun to Break the Rules. Proceedings, 80th Annual Convention, American Psychiatric Association, 1972.

123. CAMPAGNA, A. and HARTER, S. Moral Judgment in Sociopathic and Normal Children. *J. Pers. Soc. Psychol.* 31:199-205, 1975.

124. ALENEN, Y. O. The Family in the Pathogenesis of Schizophrenic and Neurotic Disorders. *Acta Psychiatr. Scand.* 42:189, 1966.

125. GOTTESMAN, I. Heritability of Personality: A Demonstration. *Psychol. Monogr.* 77:9, 1963.

126. ANTHONY, E. J. A Clinical Evaluation of Children with Psychotic Parents. *Am. J. Psychiatry* 126:177-184, 1969.

127. MEDNICK, B. R. Breakdown in High Risk Subjects: Familial and Early Environmental Factors. *J. Abnorm. Psychol.* 2:469-475, 1973.

128. REIDER, R. O. The Offspring of Schizophrenic Parents. *J. Nerv. Ment. Dis.* 157: 179-190, 1973.

129. FULLER, J. L. Genetics and Vulnerability to Experiental Deprivation. In: J. P. Scott and E. C. Senay (Eds.), *Separation and Depression: Clinical and Research Aspects.* Washington: American Association for the Advancement of Science, 1973.

130. HUSHKA, M. Psychopathological Disorders in the Mother. *J. Nerv. Ment. Dis.* 94:76, 1941.

131. LITAUER, W. *Juvenile Delinquency in Psychiatric Clinics.* London: I.S.T.D. 1957.

132. SHEPHERD, M., OPPENHEIM, A. and MITCHELL, S. Childhood Behavior Disorders and the Child Guidance Clinic: An Epidemiological Study. *J. Psychol. Psychiat.* 7:39-52, 1966.

133. LEWIS, H. *Deprived Children.* London: Oxford University Press, 1954, 132.

134. BUCK, C. and LAUGHTON, K. Family Patterns of Illness: The Effect of Psychoneurosis in the Parent Upon Illness in the Child. *Acta Psychiatr. Neurol. Scand.* 43:165-175, 1959.

135. BRANDON, S. An Epidemiological Study of Maladjustment in Childhood. M. D. Thesis, University of Durham, 1960.

136. RUTTER, M. Illness in Parents and Children. M. D. Thesis, University of Birmingham, 1962.

137. WOLFF, S. and ACTON, W. Characteristics of Parents of Disturbed Children. *Br. J. Psychiatry* 114:593-601, 1968.

138. FODOR, E. Moral Development and Parent Behavior Antecedents in Adolescent Psychopaths. *J. Genet. Psychol.* 122:37-43, 1973.

139. KALLMAN, F. J. *The Genetics of Schizophrenia.* New York: Augustin, 1938.

140. HALLGREN, and SJÖGREN, T. A Clinical and Genetico-statistical Study of Schizophrenia and Low Grade Mental Deficiency in a Large Swedish Rural Population. *Acta Psychiatr. Neurol. Scand.,* Vol. 140, 1959.

141. ROSENTHAL, D. *Genetic Theory and Abnormal Behavior.* New York: McGraw-Hill, 1970.

142. LANG, J. *Crime as Destiny.* Trans. C. Haldane, London: Allen and Univen, 1931.

143. LEGRAS, cited in ROSANOFF, A. HANDY, L. and PLESSET, I. R. Criminality and Delinquency in Twins. *J. Crim. Law Criminol.* 24:923-934, 1934.

144. CHRISTIANSEN, I. L. Crime in a Danish Twin Population. *Acta Genet. Med.* 19: 323-326, 1970.

145. CHRISTIANSEN, I. O. The Genesis of Aggressive Criminality: Implications of a Study of Crime in a Danish Twin Study. In: J. de Wit and W. Hartup (Eds.), *Determinants and Origins of Aggresssive Behavior.* The Hague: Mouton, 1974.

146. COWIE, J., COWIE, V. and SLATER, E. *Delinquency in Girls.* London: Heinemann, 1968.

147. HESTON, L. L. Psychiatric Disorders in Foster Home Reared Children of Schizophrenic Mothers. *Br. J. Psychiatry* 112:819-825, 1966.

148. KETY, S., ROSENTHAL, D., WENDER, P. and SCHULSINGER, F. The Types and Prevalence of Mental Illness in the Biological and Adoptive Families of Adopted Schizophrenics. In: D. Rosenthal and S. Kety (Eds.), *The Transmission of Schizophrenia*. London: Pergamon, 1968, 345-362.

149. ROSENTHAL, D., WENDER, P., KETY, S., SCHULSINGER, F., WELNER, J. and OSTERGAARD, L. Schizophrenics Offspring Reared in Adoptive Homes. In: D. Rosenthal and S. Kety (Eds.), *The Transmission of Schizophrenia*. London: Pergamon, 1968, 377-391.

150. SCHULSINGER, F. Psychopathy: Heredity and Environment. *Int. J. Ment. Health* 1:190-206, 1972.

151. HUTCHINGS, B. Environmental and Genetic Factors in Psychopathology and Criminality. M. Phil. Thesis, University of London, 1972.

152. HUTCHINGS, B. and MEDNICK, S. Registered Criminality in the Adoptive and Biological Parents of Registered Male Adoptees. In: S. Mednick *et al.* (Eds.), *Genetics, Environment and Psychopathology*. Amsterdam: North-Holland, 1974.

153. WINOKUR, G. Depression spectrum disease: Description and Family Study. *Compr. Psychiatry* 13:3-8, 1973.

154. SLATER, E. Zur Erbpathologic des Manisch-depressiven Irresuns. *Z. ges Neurol. Psychiat.* 163:1-47, 1938.

155. SHIELDS, J. Some Recent Developments in Psychiatric Genetics. *Arch. Psychiatr. Nervenkr.* 220-374, 1975.

156. KAY, D. The Genetics of Stuttering. In: *The Syndrome of Stuttering*: *Clinics in Developmental Medicine*. London: Heinemann, 1964.

157. CARTER, C. O. Genetics of Common Disorders. *Br. Med. Bull.* 25:52-57, 1969.

158. BAKWIN, H. Sleep Walking in Twins. *Lancet* II:446-447, 1970.

159. BAKWIN, H. Enuresis in Twins. *Am. J. Dis. Child* 121:222-225, 1971.

160. BAKWIN, H. Nail-biting in Twins. *Dev. Med. Child Neurol.* 13:304-307, 1971.

161. BAKWIN, H. Car-Sickness in Twins. *Dev. Med. Child Neurol.* 13:310-312, 1971.

162. BAKWIN, H. Reading Disability in Twins. *Dev. Med. Child Neurol.* 15:184-187, 1973.

163. HALLGREN, B. Specific Dyslexia Congenital Word-blindness: A Clinical and Genetic Study. *Acta Psychiatr. Scand.* 65:1950.

164. SHIELDS, J. Personality Differences and Neurotic Traits in Normal Twin School Children. *Eugen. Rev.* 45:213-246, 1954.

165. BIRCH, H. and DEMB, H. The Formation and Extinction of Conditioned Reflexes in "Brain-damaged" and Mongoloid Children. *J. Nerv. Ment. Dis.* 129:162-169, 1959.

166. LAUFER, M. and DENHOFF, E. Hyperkinetic Behavior Syndrome in Children. *J. Pediatr.* 50:463-474, 1957.

167. WORTIS, J. A Note on the Concept of the "Brain-injured Child." *Am. J. Ment. Defic.* 61:204-206, 1956.

168. BIRCH, H. The Problem of "Brain Damage" in Children. In: H. G. Birch (Ed.), *Brain Damage in Children*: *The Biological and Social Aspects*. Baltimore: Williams and Wilkins, 1964, 3-12.

169. VYYASOVSKII, A. On the Problem of Studying the Neuropsychic Diseases of Toxoplasmic Origin in Children. In: D. Fedoter (Ed.), *Problem Psychoneurologii Detskogo Vazrasta*, 1967, 183-190.

170. THOMPSON, G. *The Psychopathic Delinquent and Criminal*. Springfield, Ill. Thomas, 1953, 91-121.

171. THOMPSON, G. and FRIEDMAN, S. Autotopagnosia and Simultanagnosia with Organic Paranoid Reaction. *Bull. Los Angeles Neurol. Soc.* 2:172, 1946.

172. GIBLES, F. Ictal and Non-ictal Psychiatric Disorders in Temporal Lobe Epilepsy. *J. Nerv. Ment. Dis.* 113:522-528, 1951.

173. FRANZ, S. and LASHLEY, K. The Effect of Cerebral Destruction upon Habit Formation and Retention in The Albino Rat. *Psychobiology* 1:71-140, 1917.

174. LASHLEY, K. *Brain Mechanisms and Intelligence.* Chicago: University of Chicago Press, 1929.

175. GOLDSTEIN, K. The Modification of Behavior Consequent to Cerebral Lesions. *Psychiatr. Q.* 10:586-610, 1936.

176. STRAUSS, A. and LEHTINEN, L. *Psychopathology and Education of the Brain-Injured Child.* New York: Grune and Stratton, 1947.

177. GRAHAM, F., PENNOYER, M., CALDWELL, B., GRIENMAN, M. and HARTMAN, A. Relationship Between Clinical Status and Behavior Test Performance in a Newborn Group with Histories Suggesting Anoxia. *J. Pediatr.* 50:177-189, 1957.

178. KAWI, A. and PASAMANICK, B. Prenatal and Perinatal Factors in the Development of Childhood Reading Disorders. *Monogr. Soc. Res. Child Development* 24, 1959.

179. GRAHAM, F., ERNHART, C., THURSTON, D. and CROFT, M. Development Three Years After Perinatal Anoxia and Other Potentially Damaging Newborn Experiences. *Psychol. Monogr.* 26, 1962.

180. CORAH, N., ANTHONY, E., PAINTER, P., STERN, J., THURSTON, D. Effects of Perinatal Anoxia After Seven Years. *Psychol. Monogr.* 79, 1965.

181. SKEELS, H. Adult Status of Children with Contrasting Life Experiences. *Monogr. Soc. Res. Child Development* 31, 1966.

182. KAGAN, J. and MOSS, H. *Birth to Maturity: A Study in Psychological Development.* New York: Wiley, 1962.

183. BAYLEY, N. and SCHAEFER, E. Correlations of Maternal and Child Behaviors with the Development of Mental Abilities. *Monogr. Soc .Res. Child Development* 29, 1964.

184. HONZIK, M. Environmental Correlates of Mental Growth: Prediction from the Family Setting at 21 Months. *Child Dev.* 38:337-364, 1967.

185. LEMBERT, E. Primary and Secondary Deviation. In: S. Traub and C. Little (Eds.), *Theories of Deviance.* Illinois: Peacock, 1975.

186. YARROW, L., GOODWIN, M., MANHEIMER, H. and MILOWE, I. Infancy Experiences and Cognitive and Personality Development at 10 Years. In: L. Stone, H. Smith and L. Murphy (Eds.), *The Competent Infant: Research and Commentary.* New York: Basic Books, 1973, 1274-1281.

187. YARROW, L. Research in Dimensions of Early Maternal Care. *Merrill-Palmer Quart.*, 9:101-114, 1963.

188. TRAIN, G. and WINKLER, G. Homicidal Psychosis While Under ACTH. *Psychosomatics* 3:317, 1962.

189. STAFFORD-CLARKE, D. and TAYLOR, F. Clinical and EEG Studies of Prisoners Charged with Murder. *J. Neurol. Neurosurg. Psychiatry* 12:325, 1949.

190. MUNOZ-BATISTA, C. Enuresis: Clinical-electroencephalographic Correlation. *Revista de Neuro-Psiquiatria* 31:277-289, 1968.

191. PASTERNACK, S. The Explosive, Antisocial and Passive-Aggressive Personalities. In: J. R. Lion (Ed.), *Personality Disorders: Diagnosis and Management.* Baltimore: Williams and Wilkins, 1974, 45-69.

192. NEWMARKER, K., NEUMARKER, M. and POSE, U. On the Psychopathology of Psychomotor Seizures in Childhood. *Psychiatrie, Neurologie and medizinische Psychologie* 26:165-175, 1974.

193. OUNSTEAD, C. Aggression and Epilepsy-rage in Children with Temporal Lobe Epilepsy. *J. Psychosom. Res.* 13:237-242, 1969.

194. GLASER, B. H. and DIXON, M. Psychomotor Seizures in Childhood. *Neurology* 6: 646-655, 1956.

195. KILOH, L. and OSSELTON, J. *Clinical Electroencephalography.* Washington: Butterworths, 1966.

196. KNOTT, J., PLATT, E., ASHBY, M. and GOTTLIEB, J. A Familial Evaluation of the Electroencephalogram of Patients with Primary Behavior Disorder and Psychopathic Personality. *Electroencephalogr. Clin. Neurophysiol.* 5:363, 1953.

197. LEWIS, D. Delinquency, Psychomotor Epileptic Symptoms and Paranoid Ideation: A Triad. *Am. J. Psychiatry* 133:1395-1398, 1976.

198. MARK, V. and ERVIN, F. Brain Triggers for Evidence. In: *Violence and the Brain.* New York: Harper and Row, 1970, 92-110.

199. EYSENCK, H. *The Biological Basis of Personality.* Illinois: Thomas, 1967, 263-318.

200. PINKERTON, P. The Influence of Sociopathy in Childhood Asthma. *Psychother. Psychosom.* 18:231-238, 1970.

201. ZALTSMAN, E. On the Significance of Sialic Acid Examinations in the Cerebrospinal Fluid and Blood Serum in Childhood Schizophrenia. *Zhurnal Neuropatalogii i Psikhiatrii* 10:1521-1523, 1970.

202. COLEMAN, M. Serotonin and Central Nervous System Syndromes of Childhood: A Review. *J. Autism Child. Schizo.* 3:27-35, 1973.

203. COLEMAN, M. Serotonin Concentrations in Whole Blood of Hyperactive Children. *J. Pediatr.* 78:985-990, 1971.

204. GREENBERG, A. and COLEMAN, M. Depressed 5-Hydroxyindole Levels Associated with Hyperactive and Aggressive Behavior. *Arch. Gen. Psychiatr.* 33:331, 1976.

205. WHITEHILL, M., DeMEYER-GAPIN, S. and SCOTT, T. Stimulation Seeking in Antisocial Preadolescent Children. *J. Abnorm. Psychol.* 85:101-194, 1976.

206. KIEPIETZ, S., CAMP, J. and WEISSMAN, A. Reaction Time Performance of Behaviorally Deviant Childhood: Effects of Prior Preparatory Interval and Reinforcement. *J. Child Psychol. Psychiatry* 17:123-131, 1976.

207. WHITEHILL, M. The Psychopath: A Stimulation Seeker? An Examination of Research Derived from Quay's Hypothesis. Unpublished manuscript, 1974.

208. GREENBERG, D., O'DONNELL, W. and CRAWFORD, D. Complexity Levels, Habituation and Individual Differences in Early Infancy. *Child. Dev.* 44:569-574, 1973.

209. THOMAS, A., CHESS, S. and BIRCH, H. *Temperament and Behavior Disorders in Children.* New York: New York University Press, 1968.

210. LEWIS, D., BALLA, D., SHANOK, M. and SNEE, L. Delinquency, Parental Psychopathology and Parental Criminality. *J. Child Psychiatry* 15:665-677, 1976.

211. MOYER, K. E. Kinds of Aggression and Their Physiological Basis. Carnegie-Mellon University Report #67-12, Pittsburgh, 1967.

212. DOLLARD, J., MILLER, N., DOOB, L., MOWRER, O. and SEARS, R. *Frustration and Aggression.* New Haven: Yale University Press, 1963.

213. DUNCAN, P. Parental Attitudes and Interactions in Delinquency. *Child Dev.* 42:1751-1765, 1971.

214. QUAY, H. C. Personality Dimensions in Delinquent Males as Inferred from the Factor Analysis of Behavior Ratings. *J. Res. Crime Delinquency* 1:33-37, 1964.

215. HETHERINGTON, E. M., STOUWIE, R. and RIDBERG, E. Patterns of Family Interactions in Juvenile Delinquency. *J. Abnorm. Psychol.* 78:160-176, 1971.

216. HEWITT, L. and JENKINS, R. *Fundamental Patterns of Maladjustment: The Dynamics of Their Origin.* Springfield: State of Illinois, 1946.

217. COMLES, R. and HARPER, J. Effects of Labels on Attitudes of Educators Toward Handicapped Children. *Exceptional Children* 33:399-403, 1967.

218. GOLDFARB, W. Emotional and Intellectual Consequences of Psychologic Deprivation in Infancy: A Re-Evaluation. In: P. Hoch and J. Zubin (Eds.), *Psychopathology of Childhood.* New York: Grune and Stratton, 1955.

219. SKAELS, H. and HARMS, I. Children with Inferior Social Histories: Their Mental Development in Adoptive Homes. *J. Genet. Psychol.* 72:283, 1948.

220. TUNLEY, R. Kids, Crime and Chaos: A World Report on Juvenile Delinquency. New York: Harper and Row, 1962.

221. WITMER, H. L., TUFTS, E., SHAW, C. and McKAY, H. Juvenile Delinquency and Urban Areas. Chicago: University of Chicago Press, 1942.

222. CRAIG, M. and FURST, P. What Happens After Treatment? A Study of Potentially Delinquent Boys. Soc. Serv. Rev. 39:165-171, 1965.

223. ROBINS, L. Antisocial Behavior Disturbances of Childhood: Prevalence, Prognosis and Prospects. In: E. J. Anthony and C. Kaupernik (Eds.), The Child in His Family: Children at Psychiatric Risk, Vol. 3. New York: Wiley, 1974.

224. CIMA, E., MONTABBIO, E. and VENUTI, G. Psychotherapeutic Experiments in Subjects with Abnormal Behavior of "Character Disorder" Nature and with Slight Intellectual Retardation. Revista di Psichiatria 3:388-399, 1968.

225. LEVINE, W. and BRONSTEIN, P. Is the Sociopath Treatable? The Contribution of Psychiatry to a Legal Dilemma. Washington University Law Quarterly 673, 1972.

226. POWERS, E. and WITMER, H. An Experiment in the Prevention of Delinquency. New York: Columbia University Press, 1951.

227. LEVY, D. Primary Affect Hunger. Am. J. Psychiatry 94:643, 1937.

228. EISSLER, K. Ego-psychological Implications of the Psychoanalytic Treatment of Delinquents. Psychoanal. Study Child 5:97-121, 1950.

229. ZAVITZIANOS, G. Problems of Technique in the Analysis of a Juvenile Delinquent (Transference and Therapeutic Alliance). Meetings of the New York Psychoanalytic Society, 1966.

230. BURCHARD, J. and TYLER, V. The Modification of Delinquent Behavior Through Operant Conditioning. Behav. Res. Ther. 2:245-250, 1965.

231. ULETZEL, R. Use of Behavioral Techniques in a Case of Compulsive Stealing. J. Consult. Clin. Psychol. 30:367-374, 1966.

232. ALVORD, J. The Home Token Economy: A Motivational System for the Home. Corr. Psychiatry J. Soc. Ther. 17:6-13, 1971.

233. FODOR, I. The Use of Behavior Modification Techniques with Female Delinquents. Child Welfare 51:93-101, 1972.

234. SCHWITZGEBEL, R. Streetcorner Research. Cambridge: Harvard Univ. Press, 1974.

235. SCHWITZGEBEL, R. and KOLB, D. Inducing Behavior Change in Adolescent Delinquents. Behav. Res. Ther. 1:297-304, 1964.

236. SCHWITZGEBEL, R. Preliminary Socialization for Psychotherapy of Behavior-disordered Adolescents. J. Consult. Clin. Psychol. 33:71-77, 1969.

237. ALEXANDER, J. and PARSONS, B. Short Term Behavioral Intervention with Delinquent Families: Impact on Family Process and Recidivism. J. Abnorm. Psychol. 81:219-225, 1973.

238. GELINA, L., GOLOVAN, L. and KOGAN, A. Trial Application of Neuleptil in the Practice of Child Psychiatry. Zhurnal Neuropatologii i Psikatrii 67:906-911, 1967.

239. RESNICK, O. The Psychoactive Properties of Diphenylhydantoin: Experiences with Prisoners and Juvenile Delinquents. Int. J. Neuropsychiatry 3:30-48, 1967.

240. LEFKOWITZ, M. Effects of Diphenylhydantoin on Disruptive Behavior: A Study of Male Delinquents. Arch. Gen. Psychiatry 20:643-651, 1969.

241. LOCKER, A. and CONNORS, C. Diphenylhydantoin in Children with Severe Temper Tantrums. Arch. Gen. Psychiatry 23:80-89, 1970.

242. CONNORS, C. Recent Drug Studies with Hyperkinetic Children. J. Learn. Disabilities 4:476, 1971.

243. EISENBERG, L., LACHMAN, R., MOLING, P., LOCHNER, A., MIZELLE, J. and CONNERS, C. A Psychopharmacologic Experiment in a Training School for Delinquent Boys: Methods, Problems, Findings. Am. J. Orthopsychiatry, 33,3:431-447, 1963.

244. SATTERFIELD, J. and CANTWELL, D. Psychopharmacology in the Prevention of Antisocial and Delinquent Behavior. Int. J. Ment. Health 4:227-237, 1975.

The Asocial Child: A Destiny of Sociopathy?

245. MORRISON, H. The Syndrome of Competence: Contributions of Affect and Attachment. *Proc. Am. Acad. Child Psychiatry.* Toronto, 1976.
246. WITTELS, F. The Criminal Psychopath in the Psychoanalytic System. *Psychoanal. Rev.* 24, 1937.
247. FENICHEL, O. *The Psychoanalytic Theory of Neurosis.* New York: Norton, 1945.
248. SCHAFFER, H. and EMERSON, P. The Development of Social Attachments in Infancy. In: S. Scarr-Salapatek and P. Salapatek (Eds.), *Socialization.* Columbia: Merrill, 1973, 48-65.
249. LUSTMAN, S. Impulse Control, Structure and the Synthetic Function. In: *Psychoanalysis—A General Psychology: Essays in Honor of Heinz Hartmann.* New York: International Universities Press, 1966, 190-221.
250. BASCH, M. Toward a Theory That Encompasses Depression: A Review of Existing Causal Hypotheses in Psychoanalysis. In: T. Benedek and E. J. Anthony (Eds.), *Depression and Human Existence.* Boston: Little, Brown and Co., 1975.
251. ANTHONY, H. Depression, Psychopathic Personality and Attempted Suicide in a Borstal Sample. London: Her Majesty's Stationary Office, 1973.
252. DELAY, J., PICHOT, P., MERSIEZE, R. and PEYROUZET, J. La Nosologie des Etats Depressifs: Rapport Entre l'Etiologie et la Sémiologie. *L'Encephale* 52:6, 1963.
253. MELGES, F. and BOWLBY, J. Types of Hopelessness in Psychopathological Processes. *Arch. Gen. Psychiatry* 20:690-699, 1969.

4

The Psychopath in Rural Areas: Special Considerations

HOWARD C. REID, M.D.

This section will limit its discussion of the psychopath to that part of the population who live in a distinctly rural setting. Such areas are located throughout the United States, but this author's experience and study include rural Texas, New Mexico, Wisconsin, and Minnesota, with additional confirmatory work in rural Mexico, Belize, and Guatemala.

To further limit the boundaries of this chapter, there are certain general characteristics of "rural" which need to be delineated. The population density is frequently as low as three or four persons per square mile, and in general the towns are small and have limited access to metropolitan areas. The socioeconomic level of the population is frequently below the national average; open land is abundant and, in a narrow economic sense, not as productive as well organized agri-business communities. Numbers of welfare recipients may be above average. Small business, tourism, outdoor recreation, and single industry towns are common factors. Churches, clubs, commercial organizations, and families are usually tightly knit and conservative.

Distance and time are solid factors in rural living. For example, it is not uncommon for school children to spend two hours a day on a bus, nor uncommon for law enforcement personnel to travel up to 20 to 30 miles on a single call. Medical facilities are often 25 to 50 miles apart and in inclement weather isolation is a fact of life.

There are certain characteristics of the people and the interrelation-

66

ship of communities which need to be enumerated here for further understanding of rural America. Ordinarily, people know each other for miles around and they keep in touch frequently by telephone and, in our changing world, by CB radio. By these and other communication methods, gossip goes on in its never-ending leveling and testing of community standards. Interdependence is of high order. Helping a neighbor build a barn, plow a road, fight a fire, or to "sleep over" visitors is still a real part of the American rural scene.

At auctions, church and school functions, business clubs, professional societies, and public meetings, most of the people know each other. The lives of public figures and their families are well observed. Most of the towns grow slowly or not at all. The business and professional community is usually quite stable.

Often the government and community agencies have a high turnover in personnel because the young career people stay a year or two and then move on to metropolitan living. In the same way the brain drain of the young to cities creates its obvious long-term problems.

In the context of this description of rural America, let us look at the impact of the psychopath in this culture both in his internal and external manifestations.

In his search for the unattainable, the psychopath is frequently attracted to rural America. One reason for this is the myth of the frontier. Rural America is supposed to have a certain rustic freedom, with a bountiful amount of unexplored and untried environment. This fits well with the psychopath's dreams and his wish to start anew in a fresh and virgin land. It is interesting to note that such vagabondism usually follows the seasons. The migration to the north during the summer months quickly ceases when the snow and ice begin to be a factor; by the same token the migration to the south turns around when the heat of summer sets in; the psychopath is on the move again. He meets himself coming back!

Another common myth that attracts the psychopath is that with open land, trees and lakes, and not so many people, the air will be clean and life will be simple. In his internal environment the psychopath feels that there will be fewer rejections and failures in such a simple life and therefore he can "make it" more successfully. A corollary to this is the feeling that there is a "treasurer" somewhere "out there" and somehow the earth will provide a bounty which can be obtained without much diligence or intellectual effort.

Another attractive thought that the psychopath entertains toward rural America is that the country folks are nicer, more gullible, more easily persuaded, less aggressive and, therefore, more amenable to manipulation. The underlying motivation for this myth seems to be that the psychopath is attempting to revert to a previous state of security and to return to someone who loves him to relieve his internal grieving. Along with this goes the idea that there is more elbow room in the country and the psychopath is more at liberty to do what he pleases with freedom from restraint, in the hope that "I can do my own thing."

The adjusted or successful rural psychopaths are similar to their urban counterparts, with a possible exception of a certain degree of tolerance. The acting out businessman, farmer, or skilled worker frequently obtained his finances or position by windfall, primarily of a family sort. Here again, he is often avoided and tolerated and is the subject of local gossip. He frequently socializes at a lower level, which tends to make everyone concerned feel more important. The immediate family bears up or makes the usual excuses and such psychopaths become the examples against which the people in the community judge the total subculture.

It is not uncommon for these individuals to belong to the same clubs or community organizations as their relatively normal counterparts. They are often accepted because their peers and associates do not want to hurt their feelings or be accused of not having a wholesome attitude toward other people.

In the same vein, rural America is often frequented by the city psychopath who comes to the outlying forest or streams to hunt, fish, and engage in vacationing. Many times these "sportsmen" take license and, with characteristic abandon and little concern about the feelings of others, engage in all sorts of unbecoming behavior, creating a real problem for other sportsmen or vacationers. Frequently such psychopaths run afoul of the law with their violations of restrictions, and not uncommonly get drunk, cause accidents, and leave their impact behind when they depart.

The author recalls an account of a probation officer and social worker who brought a group of budding teenage psychopaths from the city into the wilds of Northern Minnesota. After two weeks of fights, destruction of property, arguments, noncomformity to rules, the probation officer reported the venture as a "total disaster."

Transient enterprises with their share of psychopaths move through rural areas taking money and leaving their trail of influence. Carnivals, fair shows, insincere religious groups, and door-to-door salesmen are examples. Such enterprises leave a few and pick up a few as they go along.

THE IMPACT OF THE PSYCHOPATH ON RURAL INSTITUTIONS

School Systems

In the grade and middle schools the budding psychopath is treated primarily as a problem child and, depending upon the manifestations, various forms of discipline, deterrent activity, and persuasion are tried. Of course, this system doesn't work, so the teacher and the psychopath go along parallel tracks, neither understanding the other. With increasing maturity, the earlier tendencies become more obvious and manifest.

One of the 23 children in the first grade, Benny was known as a "mean kid." He had only one friend, whom he abused, stole from, and frequently deserted. Through the next five years, he became a petty thief. His teachers and parents "tried everything." At 13 he was referred to the mental health center because he had shot and killed a neighbor's cow. His reason was, "Old man Barney wouldn't give me a ride to town in his pickup . . . said he wasn't going that way." A clinical opinion of character disorder, antisocial type, was made and boarding home or juvenile training center was recommended. The parents successfully resisted both alternatives. Truancy, sexual precocity, and juvenile crime quickly followed. He was placed on probation. At 18 he was arrested on charges of drug abuse and car theft. At his request, the Court and attorneys referred him again to the mental health center. This time he said, "This town is too small for me; they all have it in for me. I'll go into the Service and start over again if you can help me." He lasted six weeks, went AWOL, was discharged and moved to a large city. For the next six years he came home for money, clothes, or refuge. He served a short sentence for assault. At age 22, Benny was killed—gangland style—in a drug-related incident. His parents said, "We knew it would happen. It was just a matter of when and where."

In the high school, there is a situation similar to that of the grade school. The long bus rides, intimate relationships between and among families, and school relationships, both curricular and extracurricular, make the psychopath stand out and his behavior become common knowledge. The desertion and alienation are more firmly set as the years go by. In high school the inadequate and immature psychopath begins to show up more readily than in grade school because his peers tend to move ahead of him, producing an ever widening gulf between his antisocial behavior and that of the other young people in his environment.

In this age group the problem of differentiating between normal juvenile behavior and early psychopathic behavior becomes quite acute. When this occurs, there are a number of rationalizations which are engaged in by the adult community, such as "the child will outgrow it,"

"I was just like that when I was a kid," or "she is just going through a stage." In addition, when the behavior becomes unmistakably dysfunctional, the community tends to blame the school system or the parents. Because of the common knowledge factor throughout the rural community, the family structure tends to suffer more than it might in other environments.

As a logical outgrowth of this frustration and common knowledge, the solution to the psychopath's behavior is frequently sought in simplistic terms or by regression to a previous state of imagined security rooted in regressive thinking. For example, there may be an attempt to force the youngster into a conservative religious control pattern or, even more devastating, to expel the child from school for periods of time in the vain hope that he will reflect on his misbehavior or inadequate activities. Occasionally the school counselor or school nurse is brought into the situation as a therapist. This, of course, is a viable option but usually is fraught with the double-bind problem of such helping personnel being paid by the school system and trying to counsel the child, therefore having a divided allegiance. In addition, many of the school counselors heavily weight their activities toward vocational counseling or advice regarding higher education.

In our experience the most successful approaches to the teenage psychopath in a rural environment have been the group home, the juvenile training center, and the private boarding school for dysfunctioning teenagers. It should be stressed that such placement is sought only after careful and professional screening, which ideally should be done by third party professionals to help eliminate the bias which may be present in the small rural community. In addition to the third party screening, the teenage psychopath tends to do better if he is placed some distance from his home environment, where the old haunts and tempetations are not so readily available.

The small rural college, with its frequently lower academic standards and greater needs to sustain enrollment, attracts the psychopath. The families and parents see such schools in a socially favorable light and lean to the hope that a less stressful environment will help their relative. All too often, however, the smaller horizons, more restrictive rules, and social visibility help force the psychopath into his unrewarding behavior. The usual methods have failed again.

Eleemosynary Institutions

The impact of the psychopath on welfare systems, social rehabilitation programs, work-study programs, or job placement agencies is unique in a rural setting, again because the person is usually known in the area and has made the rounds from one agency to another. Therefore, as each agency tends to fail in meeting the psychopath's and community's expectation, there is little surprise among the agencies when the dysfunctioning again produces faliure. Occasionally a new social worker or vocational counselor will be taken in by the psychopath and devote himself to a wholehearted attempt to rehabilitate and reorganize the individual's behavior pattern. This results, of course, in a moment of success and attention for the psychopath and in valuable experience for the worker.

At the opposite end of the scale, a newly arrived psychopath in a rural area must cope with two fundamental variables. The first is that he is a stranger and therefore the so-called "stranger complex" exerts its impact. He is suspect, carefully observed, wondered about, and, in general, shunned until he has proven himself or until the community gets accustomed to him. The second is the fact that it takes social institutions a while to catch on to him and during this interim, if the psychopath is sufficiently clever, he is apt to do surprisingly well from a social point of view.

As a rule the rural service institutions have many fewer resources and personnel with which to deal with the psychopath. This produces a high frustration level among such personnel and results in considerable waste of the time and resources which are available.

Private institutions such as churches and service clubs tend to be quite conservative and traditional in rural America. The impact of the psychopath is likewise different here than upon institutions in urban areas, which may be trying to find new ways to deal with social dysfunction. In the rural area such institutions tend to polarize and are either quite gullible or extremely reluctant to become involved.

In spite of superior intelligence, Marcy barely graduated from high school. She left a trail of used up friends and teachers. Known as a carrier of tales, shoplifter, easy make, and a persistent liar, she married a carnival worker and moved away the summer following graduation. Her parents brought her home after paying some $300 to cover her bad checks on a fictitious account. The local employment agency got her a job cleaning cabins at a resort. Soon she was fired for stealing and drinking on the job. Charges were pressed and she was placed on probation. Now eligible for vocational rehabilitation, she trained as a nurse's aide, but was discharged from this program for truancy. In the meantime, she was arrested for driving while under the influence of alcohol and chose an alcoholic treatment center as an alternative to a fine. She was a model patient for two months and married an alcoholic who was in treatment with her. The next few years brought three children, fights, marginal living, divorce, and local social intervention. She could not cope with the children. She was deserting, abusive, and unloving. The children were placed in a foster home. Vocational Rehabilitation again accepted her as a client. This time she wanted to go to college to be an alcohol and drug abuse counselor, but left before completing the first semester. Neither her children nor her parents have heard from her for 10 years.

Special Professional Problems

Both the indigenous and transient psychopath offer special problems to the legal and medical professions. Rural areas are usually understaffed in health facilities. Hospitals are small and do not have the sophisticated facilities found in larger communities. The acting-out psychopath with his high rate of physical injuries and other illnesses due to his own misconduct puts an additional burden on the understaffed hospitals. The alcohol and drug abuse components of the psychopath's behavior put great stress on the meager rural facilities designed to cope with such problems.

The transient psychopath puts a special burden on the legal profession. His unreliable accounts of his difficulties, along with inadequate information concerning background history, produce considerable frustration for the rural attorney.

Law Enforcement

In recent years law enforcement in rural areas has undergone a welcome improvement and upgrading. Local officers are usually recruited from the community population and are known to their neighbors, peers, and acquaintances. The visibility of both the psychopath and the officers has interesting ramifications. One of the most common is a bias which places those psychopaths who have been offenders in a position of being watched so that their behavior is scrutinized quite frequently. The officer justifiably holds these persons suspect as he goes about his responsibilities. On the other hand, the criminal psychopath justifiably complains of harassment and borderline violations of privacy. Jails and other holding areas for dysfunctioning individuals tend to be small, inadequate, and understaffed in rural communities. If and when there is an outburst of acting out behavior, such as during a tourist season or fiesta, overcrowding and actual inhumane treatment are a logical outgrowth.

Occasionally, the psychopath will become a member of a law enforcement organization. The effect is devastating no matter where it occurs. The frequency of this sort of occurrence is probably no greater in rural than in urban America, but because of the relatively lower level of sophistication of rural law reforcement systems, the results are probably more dramatic.

Coping Systems

We have already touched on the ways in which social service systems, schools, and law enforcement agencies handle the problems of the psychopath. In addition, other organized facets of the community also make efforts in this direction.

Rural churches and religious organizations offer a visible bulwark against the psychopath's easily obtaining a following. The community conscience, bolstered by a conservative religious background, offers a real deterrent to acting out behavior and unprincipled activities.

The relatively stable family organization found in rural communities tends to polarize morality and, along with social customs, produces whatever amount of shame or guilt the psychopath is capable of. This likewise serves as some deterrent. In the same context, the watchful eye of the community acts somewhat like an alter ego which may or may not have an effect on acting out behavior and internalization of value systems.

Many communities throughout rural America now have mental health centers. These are often expected to have some sort of magic treatment for psychopaths, or at least an ability to handle them. The author knows of no successful rural mental health center program for acting out psychopaths, but such attempts are often made and the mental health center may serve as a dumping ground for community problems. When it is found that the community mental health center can do little, the community and the mental health center must reassess their goals and expectations or face the mutual anger and frustration that comes with unmet needs and unkept "promises" to the populace.

One area in which the mental health center can be of excellent value in the community with regard to the psychopath is within its function as a screening and diagnostic facility. It is beyond the scope of the rural mental health center to try therapeutically to alter the behavior of such individuals, but it is quite within the confines of its ability and expertise to furnish referring agencies or individuals with a competent opinion regarding diagnosis, prognosis and treatment recommendations.

One of the most important of the coping systems is time itself. Observers of the psychopathic scene have long realized that through the years the psychopath tends to "burn out." His/her behavior becomes less spectacular and less overtly hostile, and the inadequate or unstable components find a modicum of adjustment in some respects. It seems that the psychopath finally reaches some sort of resignation in his search for the unattainable and in his wish for a meaningful experience.

Martin has a long and checkered history of blooming success and abysmal failure. Multiple wives, get-rich schemes, travel, brushes with the law, and flamboyance have been his life. He is now 81 and in his third nursing home. He sits around the dayroom regaling all who will listen with his exploits and adventures, both real and imagined. Nowadays, he gets them mixed up because he is quite forgetful. When observed alone, he stares at the floor. His only son has no contact with him except to send the nursing home a check once a month.

Nelly G., at age 65, lives upstairs over a beer joint. She paints her face and comes down about noon to sit in a booth. Her vocabulary is coarse and vulgar. She has a tattoo on her left knee and wears multiple rings and other jewelry. Within her biography is the fact that her mother couldn't handle her and Nelly spent much of her young life traveling with what she calls "my sugar daddy." She reminisces about how she has spent her life in the pursuit of pleasures and good times and often says, "It seemed like a good idea at the time." Occasionally, Nelly gets drunk and has to be helped upstairs to her one-room flat.

RECOMMENDATIONS

Theoretical considerations, understanding, future research, and treatment of the psychopath are dealt with elsewhere in this volume. A few suggestions germane to this section are as follows:

1. A centralized facility, located in a metropolitan area, professionally staffed, with long-term treatment or modification programs is urgently needed. It is not feasible, professionally or financially, for rural communities to have therapeutic facilities for treatment of the psychopath. It is necessary, however, for such facilities to be available with close communication between the referring rural agency and the specialized facility.

2. Early diagnosis and screening are a must. Delay in recognition and management of the psychopath leads only to further individual and social problems. Such diagnoses and recommendations should be done by third party professionals.

3. Educational opportunities to understand the psychopath and his behavior should be made available to that cross-section of the rural society which is most likely to be affected. Such a program might properly be an adjunct to tertiary intervention by mental health centers or medical societies.

4. There need to be made available sufficient financial and other attractions with which to attract well-trained social service and other professional personnel to rural areas.

SUGGESTED READING

AICHHORN, A. *Wayward Youth.* New York: Viking Press, 1935.

DILLON, J. Community Mental Health in a Rural Region. In: G. Caplan (Ed.), *American Handbook of Psychiatry*, 2nd ed., Vol. II. New York: Basic Books, 1974.

DOHRENWEND, B. P. and DOHRENWEND, B. S. Psychiatric Disorders In Urban Settings. In: G. Caplan (Ed.), *American Handbook of Psychiatry*, 2nd ed., Vol. II, New York: Basic Books, 1974.

KOLB, L. C. *Modern Clinical Psychiatry*, 8th ed., Chapter 26: Personality Disorders. Philadelphia: W. B. Saunders, 1973.

PAREDES, J. A. and REID, H. C. *The Land and the People, Vol. II.* Minneapolis: University of Minnesota Press, 1970.

II

SYNDROME CORRELATES

Clinical and social characteristics which are, or have been, associated with antisocial syndromes are discussed in this section. Although the authors may at times speak in terms of causality, the term "correlates" better describes the overall purpose of this portion of the book. In Chapters 5 and 6, both traditional and Jungian psychodynamic and psychoanalytic characteristics which are found with, preceding, or otherwise in proximity to chronic antisocial behavior patterns are discussed. In Chapter 7, associations between family and social environments and eventual sociopathy are presented. Chapters 8 and 9 address to a larger extent more discrete syndromes, behaviors which co-exist to a significant degree with grossly definable central nervous system deficit. Chapter 10 summarizes a body of research which does not often find its way into the psychiatric literature. The directions of this research, and its potential linking many of the developmental, neurologic, and social hypotheses regarding core psychopathic disorders make it particularly relevant to the comprehensiveness which is a major goal of our study.

Chapters 11 and 12 address the anecdotal association of antisocial personality with chemical abuse, of both alcohol and other drugs, which is so prevalent among some mental health professionals and lay observers. The reader will find that these chapters do not examine alcohol or drug abuse at length, as these are felt to be basically different from the theme of the antisocial personality. They are designed to add a perspective for consideration of the separate problems and to point out the existence—but incompleteness—of overlap among them. Finally, Chapter 13 summarizes, in a fairly nontechnical manner, present thought with regard to genetic and familial transmission of antisocial characteristics and propensities for them.

77

5

The Antisocial Personality:
Psychodynamic Implications

LOUIS A. LEAFF, M.D.

In considering the psychodynamics of the antisocial personality, we are dealing with an area in which there have been differing opinions as to etiology, in which sociology, criminology and psychiatry interface, and in which the role of hereditary and organic factors must be considered.

The Diagnostic and Statistical Manual of the American Psychiatric Association (*DSM I*) placed the Sociopathic Personality Disturbance under the heading of a Personality Disorder primarily, and a Personality Trait Disorder secondarily (1, p. 7). Personality Disorders were defined as developmental defects or pathologic trends in the personality structure with minimal subjective anxiety and little or no sense of distress. In most instances, the disorder was manifested by a lifelong pattern of action or behavior rather than by mental or emotional symptoms. Personality Trait disturbances in sociopathic personalities were considered to be able, under stress, to regress to lower levels of personality organization and to function without development of psychosis. It was stated that patients with sociopathic personality disturbances were

> ill primarily in terms of society and of conformity with the prevailing cultural milieu, and not only in terms of personal discomfort and relations with other individuals. However, sociopathic reactions are very often symptomatic of severe underlying personality disorder, neurosis, or psychosis, or occur as the result of organic brain injury or disease. Before a definitive diagnosis in this group is employed, strict attention must be paid to the possibility of the pres-

79

ence of a more primary personality disturbance; such underlying disturbance will be diagnosed when recognized (1, p. 38).

Antisocial reaction described the individuals to whom we most commonly referred as sociopaths, namely, individuals

> always in trouble, profiting neither from experience nor punishment, and maintaining no real loyalties to any person, group or code. They are frequently callous and hedonistic, showing marked emotional immaturity, with lack of sense of responsibility, lack of judgment and an ability to rationalize their behavior so that it appears warranted, reasonable and justified (1, p. 38).

In the 1952 manual, dyssocial reactions, sexual deviations and addictions were also categorized under Sociopathic Personality Disturbances. In *DSM II* the use of Personality Trait as well as Sociopathic Personality has been dropped and listed under Personality Disorder: "Generally, these are lifelong patterns, often recognizable by the time of adolescence or earlier. Sometimes the pattern is determined primarily by malfunctioning of the brain, but such cases should be classified under one of the non-psychotic organic brain syndromes rather than here" (2, pp. 41-42). "Sociopathic Reaction" was replaced by "Antisocial Personality":

> This term is reserved for individuals who are basically unsocialized and whose behavior pattern brings them repeatedly into conflict with society. They are incapable of significant loyalty to individuals, groups, or social values. They are grossly selfish, callous, irresponsible, impulsive, and unable to feel guilt or to learn from experience and punishment. Frustration tolerance is low. They tend to blame others or offer plausible rationalizations for their behavior (2, p. 43).

Some trace the psychopathic disorder back to Pinel's observations of *manie sans délire,* and to Benjamin Rush's disorders of "will." J. C. Prichard is generally recognized as formulating the concept of "moral insanity" in 1835 (3). Despite semantic changes, psychopathy, psychopath and constitutional psychopathic inferiority remain terms which are in use among psychiatrists as well as laymen.

For decades it was assumed that the psychopath's abnormality was the result of hereditary defect. Statistical studies seemed to be indicative of such defect, although contradictions in studies with regard to the role of organic factors were frequent (e.g., whether or not there is a higher percentage of electroencephalographic abnormalities and the significance of same) (3).

Hervey Cleckley, in the early edition of his book, *The Mask of Sanity,* expressed the belief that the psychopathic personality was a psychosis (schizophrenia) concealed by an outer surface of intact function. Thirty years later, in the 1976 edition of the same book, Cleckley states:

> In the psychopath, we maintain there is also a generalized abnormality or defect of the personality that can be compared with schizophrenia, in contrast with ordinary psychoneurosis . . . It cannot be said that the disorder is that of schizophrenia, but in the whole of the patient's life, we find such inadequacy of response, such failure of the adaptation, that it seems plausible to postulate alterations more fundamental and more extensive than in classic psychoneuroses . . . in contrast [to the neurotic] this severe psychopath, like those so long called psychotic, does not show normal responses to the situation. It is offered as an opinion that a less obvious but nonetheless real pathology is general, and that in this respect the Psychopath is more closely aligned with the psychotic than with the psychoneurotic patient. The pathology may be regarded not as gross fragmentation of the personality but as a more subtle aberration. Instead of macroscopic disintegration the change could be conceived as one that seriously curtails function without obliterating form (4, p. 396).

Cleckley offers a clinical profile of the psychopathic personality which is in accord with most other characteristic profiles. The following symptoms are taken from *The Mask of Sanity* (1976): superficial charm and good intelligence; absence of delusions or other signs of irrational thinking; absence of "nervousness" or psychoneurotic manifestations; unreliability; untruthfulness and insincerity; lack of remorse or shame; inadequately motivated antisocial behavior; poor judgment and failure to learn by experience; pathologic egocentricity and incapacity for love; general poverty of major affective reactions; specific loss of insight; unresponsiveness in general interpersonal relations; fantastic and uninviting behavior with drink and sometimes without; suicide rarely carried out; sex life impersonal, trivial and poorly integrated; and failure to follow any life plan (4, p. 337).

In this present chapter we will develop and hopefully elucidate the various psychodynamic trends and constellations which may give rise to that severe personality disorder known as the antisocial or sociopathic personality. We underscore, however, that, at this time in the development of our knowledge, the interplay of the developmental-dynamic and the genetic-biologic cannot be emphatically dichotomized. I quote the section in the most recent *Comprehensive Textbook of Psychiatry:*

The evidence currently suggests that a predisposition to the disorder is inherited. This implicates a constitutional diathesis . . . in addition to biologic factors, the evidence also points to environmental influences interacting with the biological predisposition. The presence of certain forms of parental deviance in the home clearly facilitates the development of antisocial personality. Although this influence may be partly genetic, the adoption work has demonstrated that nongenetic parental influence is important also (5, p. 1290).

A related issue that needs to give us pause is that of "diagnosis" itself, which plagues psychiatric nomenclature in general. Are we in fact dealing here with a "pure" diagnostic entity? As Stoller (6) indicates, in order to make a proper diagnosis there should be: 1) an agreed upon syndrome, i.e., symptoms; 2) underlying neuropathophysiology or psychodynamics; and 3) an etiology from which the dynamics originate. The sociopath (antisocial personality) arouses strong feelings in those who are manipulated by him, who must deal with him in society, or who attempt to treat him. There may in the long run be no particular or "unitary" cause for antisocial behavior in spite of the fairly well spelled out characteristics of this syndrome. It is conceivable that the diagnosis exists because "society needs it"; i.e., society needs to group together individuals with a similar picture who may, in very important ways, be different but who share the important attributes of defiance and rebellion against certain standards and values of society. Sociopathy would then be an attribute of *behavior* as opposed to a distinct diagnostic entity. Such grouping would make it easier to reconcile, on the surface at least, antisocial behaviors of individuals in high position and esteem in our society with whom the diagnosis of psychopath seems incompatible. On the other hand, the sheer persistence of the term and concept speaks to its usefulness from a heuristic and perhaps even a classificatory sense.

In the present chapter we will use the concept of the antisocial personality or sociopath as a personality type present since childhood or adolescence. At this point in the development of our understanding of the disorder, it is probably well to separate the presenting syndrome from subsidiary syndromes also present, e.g., alcoholism, trauma or organic brain syndrome, cerebral (EEG) dysrhythmia, etc. Following Stoller (6), such a diagnostic system is descriptive rather than pretending to be totally explanatory, yet at the same time admits such information as is available. In this way, with time, needed subgroupings can be defined within the psychopathic personality diagnosis, toning down its moral implications.

There are, however, trends in the developmental and psychoanalytic writings which have over the years become increasingly focused in the area of the character neurosis, and which help us to conceptualize and understand the severe personality disorders, including the sociopath. Although differences of opinion exist with regard to etiology, as well as to treatability, we may with increasing clarity dynamically conceptualize the stuff of which the sociopath is made.

There are mainstreams in the literature which overlap, yet which are complementary and may ultimately be confluent. The first has to do with criminals, wayward youth, character perversions, etc., not thought suitable for traditional psychoanalysis. Such writings contain theories regarding the sociopath as well as treatment approaches. Others include developmental studies of delinquents and psychopaths, family studies, genetics and development of psychodynamic theory to include patients who are characterologically disordered (see Figure 1).

BACKGROUND AND LITERATURE REVIEW

Although there is a seeming leisureliness to theory building, evaluative studies, etc., those who were forced to deal with antisocial personalities were not free to select their cases in terms of suitability or compatibility with existing theoretical formulations. Communication and some degree of understanding grew out of clinical necessity. The literature selected for review is an attempt to be representative and does not attempt to be inclusive of the entire field.

In 1950, Sheldon and Eleanor Glueck (7) compared delinquents and nondelinquents on four hundred traits and factors. In *Physique and Delinquency*, the Gluecks (8) established that the traits were closely determined by heredity but not entirely so. In 1962, they reported their belief that, although they were dealing with socio-cultural influences, such traits were conditioned originally and fundamentally by inherited anatomic and physiologic factors, which responded to socio-cultural factors in a certain way. They attempted to separate traits which were more specifically constitutional from those which were more socially conditioned (9).

Aichhorn (10) actively worked with and attempted to understand deviant or psychopathic behavior from the psychoanalytic frame of reference. His formulations seemed largely oedipal in configuration, e.g., ". . . because of this repressed and unconscious antagonism and rivalry, a boy refused to go to school, and achieved unconscious revenge against his father" (10, p. 114). Aichhorn described conscious and unconscious struggles which raged within a youth when his efforts at oedipal rebellion and resolution, as well as his efforts to hold his father as a love object, failed. However, Aichhorn brought in the concept of "narcissism" and pointed out that his patients could become good and did become depressed. Acting out behaviors were seen as symbolic equivalents. Delinquency was explained partly by the unconquered pleasure principle, and also by taking into consideration the libidinal relationships which had not been dealt with adequately in earlier childhood. He felt that when a child was too strictly treated or when enough bad experiences with reality had occurred too early, he was unable at that stage of development to make the necessary adjustments. Regression then occurred and the pleasure principle achieved mastery.

Aichhorn stressed the importance of early identifications, although later oedipal identifications were felt to be paramount, particularly with regard to development of the ego ideal (superego), forcing the child to limit his instinctual satisfactions. However, he also felt that a faulty ego ideal

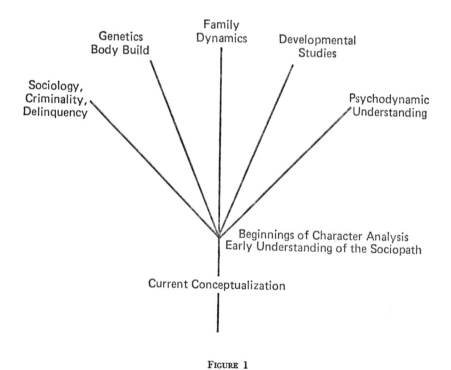

FIGURE 1

could be developed on the basis of hereditarily determined structural deficiencies or inborn defects created by an inherited lack of capacity for object cathexis (identification) of either a quantitative or qualitative nature. Even in those with inherited problems, Aichhorn asserted that such an individual could hardly be criminal from birth, and stressed the many external circumstances which make the formation of a socially acceptable ego ideal difficult or impossible—e.g., a brutal father, a weak inconsistent father, a parent who uses the child as a "plaything" of his unconscious drives, a nagging quarrelsome, abusive mother, or separated parents who can play the child against each other. A socially directed ego ideal could not develop if the nucleus of the ego ideal based on the first objects was weak or nonexistent. Following Freud (11), Aichhorn also described individuals with hypertrophied superegos who became criminals out of an unconscious sense of guilt, victims of their own morality.

Eissler (12) stated that sociopaths, in spite of their resemblance to delinquents and to neurotics, exhibit a unique and original group of disorders which cannot be reduced to a composite of others, even though some sociopaths develop apparent neurosis or psychosis when external reality interferes with their symptom formation. He drew attention to the alloplastic nature of the antisocial personality, i.e., its consisting of behavior lacking in anxiety or guilt feelings, and stressed the superficiality of the sociopath's goals and object relationships and the using, self-centered orientation of such individuals. He stated that there is an almost invariable feature of magic among delinquents that "serves to enhance or to restore an inflated feeling of omnipotence which is essentially different from the feeling of mastery . . ." (12, p. 15). When the sociopath is prevented from acting out, Eissler believed, he becomes depressed and panicky; such restraints weaken his ties to reality: "Sporadic or periodic destructiveness was an indispensable requirement for his maintaining a balanced feeling of well being and of being in contact with reality" (12, p. 15).

Eissler also pointed out that the delinquent was exposed to irrational, concrete injustices on a reality level in early life, i.e., during the pre-oedipal as well as the oedipal phases. The awareness of having suffered trauma at the hands of those with whom the child sought to identify, and who should serve as models for his later ego ideals and the origin of his conscience, interfered with appropriate identification processes and led to a predisposition toward unhampered release of aggression. In contrast with the neuroses, psychoses and sociopathies, Eissler stated that in the delinquencies there is a withdrawal from a specific sector of reality, namely from a portion of its representations and prohibitions. The ego refuses to accept the validity of certain behavioral norms, thereby permitting the corresponding impulse to maintain its full force.

Bender and Cramer (13) reviewed girls referred by courts and social agencies and commented on the frequency of delinquency centered around patterns of sexual behavior. The authors pointed out that living out sexual drives was frequent in girls from deprived homes, especially where an antisocial behavior was the family pattern. They also pointed out that such behavior was common in institutionalized children, for whom greater dependency existed. The authors stressed that prepubertal problems affected the later identifications with the "sexual mother." Szurek (14) noted that the then prevalent theories of delinquency rested on the implicit assumption, supported by clinical evidence, that the child had failed in certain essential areas of integration. This deficiency was felt to be in the realm of confidence, i.e., self-esteem, in that the person was driven to be defiant, either openly or surreptitiously. His disregard for the rights of others and lack of consideration for their feelings could result only if his earliest experiences at the hands of others were similarly characterized without much regard for, or consideration of, *his own* needs, feelings and welfare.

Melitta Schmideberg (15) reported her clinical impression that antisocial development and psychopathy were largely due to disturbances of "object relations" rather than of superego. She described such patients as excessively ambivalent and particularly unstable. She described "depersonalization" as an important defense mechanism of the criminal and emphasized the role of anxiety in the patient's antisocial activity. Adaptation and ego functions were handicapped in development, as were object relationships; attachments to parents or their substitutes were prevented, skewed or distorted. The "second step," i.e., the extension of object relationships to relationships with community, society and culture, was thus also interfered with. Internalization and identification could not proceed in the usual fashion when emotional ties were "missing," nor was it possible to form the identifications which shape the core of a strong yet flexible superego, one which, on the one hand, acts as a modifying force with regard to the instinctual impulses and, on the other hand, guides behavior in terms of internalized social standards.

Anna Freud (16) pointed out the crucial importance of the first year of life and the important transitions from primary narcissism to object love. In cases where the mother was absent, neglectful, emotionally unstable, or ambivalent and failed to be a stable or reliable source of emotional supplies—where care of the infant was lacking or where there were constant separations and/or lack of a stable mothering figure—the transformation of "narcissistic libido to object libido" was not carried out adequately (adequate identification did not occur). Freud felt that such early deprivation led to inadequate binding of aggressive impulses. Early libidinal development was deficient and aggressive impulses remained isolated, finding expression in seemingly contradictory fashion, that is, in breakthroughs of aggressiveness and destructive behavior, attitudes and behaviors which lent themselves to sociopathy. In normal development, such aggressive impulses are not isolated (split off) and so become part of the relationships to the pregenital love object, of the maternal relationship, and later part of the manifestations of the oedipus complex.

However, dyssocial or antisocial reactions do not necessarily originate from a weakening of ego functions and identifications (though secondarily their existence may harm the integrity of the ego) and social maladjustments may be closer to the neurotic. When oedipal and preoedipal attitudes and experiences are too depriving or violent, and remain unresolved, the child is not able to make the necessary differentiations between important individuals in the family constellation and those in the environment. The environment becomes an extended battleground for the acting out of such unresolved conflicts. For example, aggressive and destructive images of the oral phase, sadomasochistic fantasies of the anal phase, exhibitionistic fantasies, castration fears and family romance with feelings of being isolated and unloved are transferred to the external world where they become a hindrance to social adjustment. Such disturbances do not, in and of themselves, create sociopathy. They may lead to an anxious, resentful or withdrawn child; however, the feelings of emptiness, of being discriminated against, and of lack of meaningful relationships are important coordinates that make up part of the picture of the antisocial personality.

In essence, we are dealing with a qualitative and quantitative problem with the aggressive impulses and with their lack of integration into the emotional life of the child. For example, sadistic fantasies may be acted out with animals or younger children. Scopophilic impulses and fantasies may be verified in reality as the child is witness to sadistic scenes between the parents. Exhibitionistic fantasies may be acted out in school. The child may be seen as a disruptive element, either via his acting the buffoon or his attempting some sort of "heroic" behavior, e.g., standing up to teachers, fighting, being oblivious to realistic dangers, etc. The home environment may present not only continual battles between the parents but opportunity for sexual stimulation from the parents and/or observation of intercourse. The unmitigated aggression, already difficult to deal with, leads to the conception of intercourse as a violently aggressive, sadistic act which is continued until one or both of the partners are severely damaged. In the outside world, such children may be belligerent, troublesome, always ready to fight. Their hate relationships are most important to them, as they represent *love* relationships; the hated enemy is their unconscious representative of the sexual partner. Usually such fantasies and impulses are repressed; however, in the children we are discussing, they may not only become fixation points, but also continue to find direct expression in characterologic and aggressive behaviors which represent condensations of masochistic, sadistic, scopophilic or exhibitionistic fantasies and/or fantasies of aggressive intercourse.

Much past research on delinquency has been confined to accessible groups, such as offenders in institutions. In an outpatient group, West (17) found that boys with dull intelligence, who were mesomorphic and who scored poorly on psychomotor tests, were at least twice as frequent among the acting out categories. West found a complex of personal inadequacies and external handicaps reinforcing each other. In ranking the importance of factors in juvenile misconduct, both now and as predictors of later delinquency, this study of home background documented that socially deprived, unloving, erratic, inconsistent and careless parents tended to produce badly behaved boys. The author also studied the possible connection between brain damage and subsequent behavioral difficulties. This was considered relevant, particularly as regards the possibility that difficult behavior in some delinquents is caused by brain damage which may have occurred during the mother's pregnancy or at the time of birth, i.e., some behaviors may be secondary to minimal brain damage and dysfunction. Investigation of medical records gave no support to the theory that a significant contribution could be traced to widespread occurrence of subclinical brain damage.

The author also noted that until now delinquency has been referred to as if it were some constant homogeneous category of behavior with much the same origin in different individuals. From West's observations, this does not appear to be the case. Antisocial behavior rests upon a matrix of interrelated factors; concomitants of early misconduct were summarized as follows: 1) family income, 2) adverse environmental features, 3) height/weight ratio (this association was slight but interesting, given the assumption that body build is determined largely by heredity), 4) unpopularity among peers, 5) lower intelligence level, in conjunction with social level, 6) unfavorable parental characteristics, e.g., inconsistency between mother and father in handling the child and parental under-vigilance—lack of supervision and erratic material discipline (Parental disharmony did not hold true at the lowest level of the socioeconomic scale; in the sample as a whole, having a loving normal mother was associated with lower incidence of bad behavior but among the poor group it was the anxious overprotective mothers who had the better behaved children.), and 7) physical health of mothers and fathers (This appeared to have only a slight bearing upon behaviors but mental health, particularly that of the mother, was distinctly relevant.). There was little evidence that temporary separation from mother during infancy led to disturbed behavior; however, complete and permanent disruptions of family life and chronicaly anomalous family situations resulting from illegitimacy, bereavement, desertion, divorce, etc. appeared to be relevant to juvenile delinquency (17).

SOCIOLOGIC CONSIDERATIONS

It is important to consider the problem of antisocial behavior from the sociologic as well as the psychologic point of view; the one perspective complements and enriches the other. Cloward and Ohlin (18) differentiate three principal orientations in the formation of delinquent subcultures:

1. Criminal, which is organized primarily for material gain.
2. Conflictual, which is founded on violence.
3. Retreatist, which emphasizes the consumption of drugs (18, p. 540).

Their view of the sources of delinquent subcultures focuses on the adjustment problems that stem from the marked disparity between the goals to which lower class youths are led to aspire on the one hand, and the limited opportunities for achievement on the other. They hypothesize that when such youngsters are unable to downgrade their ambitions, they are confronted with intense frustrations which stimulate the exploration of antisocial alternatives and which may lead to orientation toward a delinquent subculture. Other theories which have been promulgated have to do with "ganging" as part of masculine identification and the forming of delinquent subcultures and delinquency as a product of the adjustment difficulties related to the transition into adolescence, given the lack of socially institutionalized means to facilitate this change. In *Family Relationships in Delinquent Behavior,* Nigh (19) pointed out that there have been hundreds of studies related to delinquency but that a general fivefold classification of these behaviors may be employed involving social disorganization, subculture, means and ends, cultural conflict, and personality maladjustment. The author's position was that delinquent behavior relating to minor or serious emotional states is comparatively rare and that most delinquent behavior is the result of inefficient social control. It was found that the father's behavior was more often significantly related to delinquent behavior than that of the mother. The author proposed that the child's identification with the parent—with indirect control—is associated with low direct delinquency and that need satisfaction through parental behavior is likewise related to low delinquency. Nigh postulates a "U" shaped correlation with delinquent behavior being at a minimum where there is moderate amount of control exercised.

Boys in Fatherless Families (20) was a study that gave support to the proposition that the father's absence is less salient than is the climate and tone of the home and the kind of supervision given to the child. Impact of the father's absence was associated chiefly with the mother's ability to maintain effective supervision in a harmonious home climate.

Kaufman and Reiner (21) believed that the majority of parents of juvenile delinquents studied in their guidance centers fell into the category of impulse-ridden character disorders. They felt that the parents of these families were not only marginal workers but marginal human beings in the sense that they live "on the edge of life." Appearing selfish and pleasure loving, they live their lives in the shadow of failure, defeat and rejection. The authors believed that the public sees only the hedonistic behavior and its results and is unaware of the misery that the behavior conceals. Their study cited the inconsistency of behavior in persons who have character disorders as a factor which has made classification difficult. They believed that the only sound classification that can be made is in relation to the primary, pregenital level of fixation which determines the individual defenses.

Persons with character disorders are constantly threatened by anxiety and unresolved depression. Much of their activity is designed to ward off such affects. Inwardly they are seething and hypersensitive. They have only a small repertoire of behavior patterns, so that the impulse-ridden character may be in a perpetual state of crisis. They must experience something that is "happening" in order to feel alive. The authors in this volume (21) found that it was useful to classify character disorders according to the level of psychosexual development.

Kaufman and Reiner's work is reviewed here because it serves more or less as a model of other writers who have used the libidinal states of development to classify character pathology. Most notable, of course, is Wilhelm Reich (22). In *Character Disorders in Parents of Delinquents,* Kaufman and Reiner described what they felt were typical features of persons with character disorders: a history of traumatic episodes, major disturbances in psychosexual development, and characteristic patterns of ego pathology. The trauma often included actual or emotional loss of parents. Patients often acted as if their parents were dead, as if they were searching for them, but denied the feeling of loss and attempted to deal with it in various substitutive ways. Kaufman and Reiner found "no overt depression" in their cases, but rather "a process of denial, and a resultant core of anxiety" which they called "a depressive nucleus" (21, p. 10; 23). The authors stated that the patients denied the affective component of loss of their parents and displaced the anxiety onto other persons. The specific choice of symptoms depended upon a variety of factors, including, especially, the level of psychosexual fixations and identifications. Having experienced loss of love and/or inconsistent nurturing themselves, they were unable as adults to provide a mature consistent type of parental care for their children and hence subjected their own children to losses and experiences that engendered similar attitudes. Often the parent himself engaged in overt delinquencies or showed defiant attitudes that counterpointed the child's behavior.

A BEGINNING PSYCHODYNAMIC FORMULATION

Different cultures stress different values and, hence, create different character patterns. From the psychoanalytic point of view, character refers to the habitual mode by which the ego acquires, and later compromises with respect to instinctual drives, the superego and the external world (24). Characteristic modes of such adaptations are called character. If the ego is relatively primitive, its habitual character will be primitive as well. In the early understanding of character, Freud (11) initially described a tripartite classification; character traits were perpetuations of the original impulses, sublimations of them, or reactions against them. Character traits of the reactive type were divided into avoidance (phobic) and reaction formations. Reactive types of character traits, by virtue of their rigidity and limited adaptive functions as compared with the sublimative type, were considered pathologic.

Wilhelm Reich (22) compared character traits to suits of armor donned by the ego as protection against both instinct and external dangers. Disguised gratification is the vital part of all characterology and, hence, character traits are not easily given up. In addition, the gratification and safety involved may relate not only to an instinctual demand but also to superego and ego ideal, as well as to pathologic behavior toward the id, i.e., to satisfaction of the instincts rather than to their suppression.

Following Fenichel (24) and Reich (22), a preliminary psychoanalytic classification of character types might include *reactive type, character defenses against anxiety, narcissistic character, anal character traits, oral character traits, phallic character traits* and *character defenses against the superego.*

The *reactive type* of character defense produces an alteration of the outward personality, so that the aims of the drive seem contradictory to the original drive (e.g., excessive humility as a defense against underlying rage and sadism). *Character defenses against anxiety* would include counterphobic attitudes, intimidation of others, identification with the aggressor, flight into activity or attempts to secure a magical protective object. *Narcissistic characters* are in conflict over very archaic oral fears. Primitive ego experiences permit an increase in self-esteem and a recapturing of the early sense of omnipotence through idealization. In such individuals a "duality" of "ideals" may be based upon a dichotomy corresponding to the original identification with parental figures into good and bad objects. This is frequently associated with ambivalence, splitting and displacement to the environment.

Persons with *anal character traits* fear their uncontrolled impulses. They are "always in a hurry." The typical anal character consists of qualities of both resistance and obedience. Traits of orderliness and propriety represent compliance, while stubbornness and provocation are used as instruments in the struggle with the superego as the person strives for a feeling of superiority. Such individuals use reaction formation, isolation and undoing against pregenital strivings and unconscious hostilities which create a "narcissistic satisfaction" so that we see less of the defense of repression. *Oral characters* are dependent upon objects and external supplies of self-esteem and narcissistic satisfaction. External forces are responsible for omnipotent protection and comfort. *Phallic or phallic narcissistic characters,* as described by Reich (22), correspond to the wish fulfilling type of reaction to castration. Phallic characters are reckless, vain and insensitive. These individuals have both castration fears and narcissistic needs and are frequently oral dependent.

Character defenses against the superego may be divided into several categories. Character defenses against guilt may produce a "collector of injustices," constantly driven by the need to prove that it is the other fellow who has done the injustice. Their obstinacy confirms their power.

"Blackmailers of affection" demonstrate their misery as proof of having been unfairly treated. Individuals who commit criminal acts because of unconscious guilt feelings—Freud's criminals out of a "sense of guilt" (11)—derive a feeling of relief when they are discovered and punished. Masochistic characters may project their superego and anticipate criticism or punishment. They may criticize others as they unconsciously feel others criticize them and as they criticize themselves, or heap punishment and self-reproach upon themselves in order to reinforce narcissistic supplies. They may become victims of unconsciously arranged accidents which are symbolic acts of rebellion on the one hand and sacrifice (as a suffering victim) on the other. They may live their entire lives suffering repeated reversals when life goals seem within reach, never attaining victory, as part of "neuroses of destiny."

Moral masochists, on the other hand, are those in whom rebellion against a severe superego is sexualized and submissive, or in whom suffering attitudes are directed toward achievement. They blackmail "forgiveness" which serves as a distorted kind of passive, sexual pleasure, frequently symbolic of the wish to be beaten by the father. This wish may be displaced toward "fate" in general. Freud also described traits of "those wrecked by success" (11), people who retain their sense of guilt with regard to their impulses, coupled with a severe superego which does not permit them to enjoy any success. The reverse of this is the overachiever whose accomplishments never seem to undo his inner sense of failure and guilt.

Finally, there is the psychopath, an individual with an apparent lack of guilt feelings who readily yields to impulses. Fenichel (24) states that analysis has not confirmed the assumption that impulsive characters are "happy narcissistic psychopaths" who have no superego and therefore gratify all their demands without any consideration of others. Such individuals have suffered a lack of a lasting object relationship in early childhood, or an oral fixation and traumatic experiences which make a complete and definite establishment of an effective superego difficult to attain.

It should be stressed that *criminality is not a psychological concept.* Criminality is action contrary to the penal code. Acts of this nature may be committed by every conceivable psychological type, normal as well as pathological. Many things that the penal code calls crimes, the criminals *do not consider outside the law* from the viewpoint of their own code, based upon their own superego structure. Criminals of this type have identified themselves with an asocial or antisocial object.

Identifications are essential for the construction of character; therefore, the influence of the social milieu as well as the parent is of importance in shaping character. Thus, antisocial behavior may mean very different things under different cultural conditions. There are, however, in all cultures, individuals whom we may call "severe character disorders" or "acting out characters" or "instinct-ridden characters" who are in constant friction with the rules of the society in which they reside. The environment is the stage in which they act out their personality as well as their internal conflicts. That stage is essential for their personal integration. They may appear restless and hyperactive or they may appear as victims of an unkind and cruel fate. Their superego is not lacking but incomplete.

Reactions of the ego to the pathologic superego reflect the ambivalences and contradictions which these persons felt toward their first objects. The typical anamnestic findings among antisocial personalities are frequent change of milieu, loveless environment and/or a very inconsistent environmental influence. The attempted resolution of the oedipus complex is correspondingly disorganized, weak and inconsistent. There is a distinct deficit in object relationships. There are various kinds of qualitative anomalies of the superego and its relation to the ego which correspond to the problem of impulsiveness; there may be a "bribing" and an "isolation" of the superego or an isolated "instinct approving" superego may be formed.

Weakness of conscience and other superego defects, therefore, have long been considered basic factors involved in the etiology of sociopathic (antisocial) behaviors. Superego disturbances in the form of deficiencies have been variously attributed to learning from and identifying with deficiencies of parental superego functioning, physical and psychological trauma during superego formation, and constitutional factors. Prior to the publication of Johnson's works (25, 26), it was common to attribute severe superego defects to "constitutional psychopathic inferiority." Although the psychopath is often described as one who lacks any capacity for inner control, closer inspection reveals that this is inaccurate in that superego defects are rarely total (27-32). When Johnson (25) introduced the term "superego lacunae" to describe Szurek's observations, she founded a useful concept for certain types of delinquency, as well as for a wide variety of other "acting out" behaviors. This concept relates more to the choice of the particular piece of behavior than to the motivational forces underlying that behavior. Such lacunae correspond to those in parents who derive unconscious gratification from their child's misbehavior.

The concept of problematic superego integration and superego lacunae, however, is only one of several factors contributing to sociopathy (33). Ego deficiencies or disturbances must of necessity be involved. The complexity of the concept of ego calls for specificity in terms of the deficiencies of which we are speaking when we talk of the antisocial disorder, as so much of the therapeutic relates to "ego support" and implies dealing with particular ego functions. Fritz Redl (34, 35) pointed to such ego deficiencies as: coping with insecurity, anxiety, and inferiority problems by means of sublimation; severe anxiety in new situations; sequelae of past traumata; and disorganization in the face of guilt and learning from experience. Clinical precision arises from consideration of the specific ego functions impaired, defensive operations used and identifications employed, adaptive as well as pathologic (i.e., ego strengths as well as weaknesses).

A CURRENT CONCEPTUALIZATION

The work of Johnson and Szurek (26) serves as a bridge linking current psychodynamic formulations with their predecessors. Much has remained relevant and has been refined and integrated into current theory. The crucial role of ego as well as superego pathology has been recognized by a number of authors, including Kernberg (26-40), Kohut (41), Giovacchini (42, 43) and Bursten (44, 45).

Johnson (25) stressed the importance of accurate understanding of the character problems involved as well as the nature of the superego and ego deficits. She described a group of antisocial adolescents in whom there was not a generalized weakness of the superego but rather a lack of superego in certain circumscribed areas of behavior, areas which she termed superego lacunae. Frequently, mild or severe neurotic conflicts accompanied such superego lacunae. The author illustrated that the parents of such individuals found vicarious gratification of their own poorly integrated forbidden impulses in the acting out of the child, due to their conscious or unconscious permissiveness or inconsistency. The child's superego lacunae corresponded to similar defects of the parents' superegos, which in turn were derived from the unconscious permissiveness of their own parents. She strongly emphasized that her successes were not with very severe cases such as highly narcissistic children with widespread superego defects. Also, with successful patients the parents had been cooperative and well enough to enter treatment themselves, or to allow the therapist to place the adolescent in a school or other residential setting.

In "The Genesis of Antisocial Acting Out in Children and Adults," Johnson and Szurek (26) stated that parental attitudes of love and warmth need definition. Such attitudes should contain firmness with respect to the form of expression of the child's impulses and such firmness optimally should be devoid of masochistic or sadistic coloring. They described "scapegoating" wherein the child holds a unique significance for the parent. Parental acting out, vacillation, guilt or unconscious hostility made firmness and fair dealing difficult and led to specific superego lacunae.

The sources of hostility from the parent are varied. The child may have unconsciously become a rival for the attention of the other parent; the child may represent a parent sibling or the child may be born and reared in times of extreme stress and tension between the parents. Sexual aberrations, promiscuity, antisocial behavior, etc., result from parents' accusations, detailed questioning, provocative suggestions and dire warnings, any of which may constitute unwitting permissions. The authors stress that, rather than producing "criminals out of a sense of guilt" (11), it is not the guilt which is at issue. Instead, it is unwitting parental prompting which causes acting out, along with the fostering of detection aimed at halting more serious future acting out by means of extreme penalties. They state that apprehension in the delinquent stems not from guilt, but from *anticipated punishment* with no guilt coloring. Although there is unconscious guilt in abundance in the cases under discussion, as in all neurotic personalities, the forbidden impulses derive from a variety of neurotic conflicts and may find expression in stealing, arson, truancy, etc., depending on the nature of the sanctions.

Ben Bursten has made significant contributions to the literature in his book *The Manipulator* (44). He traces the changes in our categorization of character types from the beginning, in which stages of libidinal development were emphasized as the basis for classification. Freud (11) and Abraham (46) stressed the instinctual underpinnings of character. With the evolution of the concept of ego and the structural theory, other bases for classifying character arose. Fenichel (24) describes sublimative and reactive character types in addition to the others we cited previously. Kernberg (28, 40) rejects the classification based on stages of libidinal development and employs a model based on levels of instinctual development. He describes three main levels of instinctual fixation which can be encountered: a "higher" level, at which genital primacy has been reached and predominates; an "intermediate" level, at which pregenital, especially oral regression and fixation points predominate; and a "lower" level, at which a pathological condensation of genital and pregenital instinctual strivings takes place with a predominance of pregenital aggression (28, p. 803).

Bursten (44, 45) suggests the importance of *aim* in the understanding of instinctual development and the vicissitudes of character. Narcissists do love objects, although the objects represent themselves, and in psychoanalysis they do form a transference along their type of object relationship. He feels that identification might be a better term than transference in this case, and uses the term "complementary relationship" to denote the other type of object choice (anaclitic), implying a sense of separateness, yet with a fitting together of mutual needs.

In order to understand the psychopathic personality, it is essential to understand the evolving conceptualizations of the narcissistic personality, since it is our opinion that *psychopathic personalities represent one form, a severe form, of a narcissistic personality structure.* Previously we talked about different types of pathology, e.g., superego pathology, which could give rise to sociopathic-type behavior. We also made reference to the sociologic and hereditary-biologic evidence. What we are postulating here is a "core" personality type, which represents the antisocial or sociopathic personality. He is an individual of narcissistic character structure with particular and severe deformations of ego, superego and instinctual integration upon which we will elaborate. He has a characteristic quality of object relations with specific intrapsychic conflicts, defenses and structure. Here, in the "Sociopathic Disease," as opposed to the "phenomena," there are primitive structuralizations within the ego and superego. Distortions arise from a chaotic mother-child relationship, with difficulties becoming evident around the *rapprochement* phase, and with a father who is an active traumatizer or an inadequate "escape valve" for the child from a traumatic maternal situation.

The reader is again referred to Bursten's excellent book *The Manipulator* (44). In it, the author deals at length with the essential features of the manipulator and elaborates on such factors as intentionality, deception and "putting something over." Bursten addresses himself to the fact that the term "sociopath" remains, and usually refers to the antisocial personality. His impression is that the descriptions in *DSM I* and *DSM II* (1, 2) demonstrate the blending of the social and psychiatric viewpoints; i.e., we diagnose such individuals both on the basis of mental processes (inability to learn from experience, callousness, rationalization), and in terms of social deviance (antisocial conflict with society and difficulties with the law) (44, p. 155). Bursten proposes that we abandon such diagnostic labels, which imply a mixture of psychological and sociological factors, and that we set up common psychological characteristics which enable us to make a truly characterologic diagnosis.

He states, for example, that it should be possible to describe a type of personality organization, characteristic of the chronic manipulator, which can serve as a diagnostic guideline even when the patient is not particularly socially deviant or criminal. Bursten views the antisocial personality psychodynamically as "putting someting over" and his manipulation as arising out of conflict of goals, containing within it a power struggle which is differentiated from other manipulations by the fact that the manipulator has little or no real interest in the other person except as a need-satisfying object. The other person is devalued and is seen essentially as an extension of the manipulator's own self; there is no true relationship in the mature sense. Bursten's expression "putting something over" is essential in these dynamics, and is tied in with feelings of contempt and devaluation that enhance and restore self-esteem. Other dynamic motives for manipulation may relate to needs for a sense of power, sadism (or its alternative, masochism), the need to control other people, and oedipal competition. There is, however, the distinct clinical impression that individuals with a "higher level" of personality organization have achieved a more mature way of relating to other individuals and that manipulation is used only occasionally. Such manipulation may be considered to have been induced by, and been adaptive in, certain reality situations. Such victories and exhilarations, though, are peripheral to the mainstream of the personality and do not serve as the central focus for this maintenance of self-esteem as they do in the impulsive sociopath. All personalities represent varying mixtures of narcissistic and "complementary" components such as these.

Since the manipulative personality is a type of narcissistic personality, we can place him into a framework of understanding, especially in light of recent advances in this area. Kohut (41) and Kernberg (36-40) have provided us not only with a framework for understanding the narcissistic personality, but with a treatment rationale as well. The superficiality, callousness, ruthlessness, lack of loyalty and manipulativeness described in the sociopath become understandable in terms of his narcissistic personality structure. He must be omnipotent, unable to invest in or depend upon others (44, p. 159). His inner world of objects is that of dark shadowy persecutors, a world of danger and paranoid fears where, as one patient stated, if he is not actively "screwing" he knows that he is "being screwed."

The narcissistic personality has the basic need to identify with an all-good, all-powerful person and hence be protected from this world of hostile persecutory images which exist within himself and which are projected outward. He attempts to control the aggression he sees in others through a variety of mechanisms. The basic need is expressed by omnipotence, perfection and a need to seek out objects who reflect this omnipotence, objects who are essentially extensions of the self. The need is to control the idealized objects, to use them, and to tame their aggression through such mechanisms as projective identification and ingratiation. Such omnipotent objects are devalued and discarded when they no longer serve such needs. Having a true object relationship exposes the sociopath to humiliation, loss and shame, with consequent rage and envy. The parental experiences of early life have taught such individuals to seek safety and omnipotence in relationships in which *they* are in control and which *they* can manipulate. Only powerful giving figures can be valued; those who are seen as worthless and those who frustrate must be revengefully destroyed.

Bursten sees the differentiation as lying in the area of early infantile orality:

> The degree of self/object differentiation is tied in with the mode of narcissistic repair. The manipulative personality repairs his narcissism by the dynamics of putting something over . . . that is, he does something to the other person. The paranoid personality and the chronic complainer . . . (handle) their wounded narcissism: they bellow with rage or cry with frustration much in the same manner as the little infant who knows only his underlying needs and who cannot well tune in to the existence of other people. They desperately *demand* things from the world; they do not seem to be clear enough about the world to *use* it in any subtle fashion. Putting something over then is the mode of narcissistic repair of the manipulative personality, and contempt is its vehicle. By purging the shameful introject in this manner, the patient is able to restore his sense of omnipotence and, thus, he is probably spared the need to regress to the more primitive rage of the paranoid personality (44, p. 160).

The author feels that this purging, with its feeling of contempt, has strong libidinal roots in anality, not only in the purging aspect but in the emphasis on shame and the need to please.

The borderline personality has a less cohesive self than the narcissistic personality and is more easily subject to fragmentation. The boundary between himself and others is less clear. The primary task of the "complementary personality" (44) is to resolve the oedipus complex. The main task of the narcissistic personality is to achieve the bliss and contentment characteristic of the primary narcissistic state. This implies a reunion of the self, which must be very grand, with an object that must be nourishing and powerful. In describing the "manipulative personality," Bursten includes some, but not all, persons known as antisocial personalities or sociopaths. He states that he finds current designations inadequate because they rely on a combination of psychological and sociological criteria, with the diagnosis being made on a record of repeated offenses and conflicts with the law. The clinical features of the manipulative personality center around manipulativeness within the context of socially approved activities, as in the case of some businessmen and administrators, or in the context of socialy disapproved activities, as in the case of "confidence men." The manipulator perceives another person's goals as conflicting with his own, and attempts to influence the other person. He employs deception and has a satisfying feeling of having put something over on the other person when the manipulation works.

The author describes four components of the manipulation: conflicts of goals, intent to influence, deception and the feeling of putting something over. He also describes the manipulative personality as characterized by a propensity for lying (deception), little guilt, transient and superficial relationships, and considerable contempt for other people. Some of these people are aggressively antisocial, repeatedly get into trouble, and do not learn by experience.

The contempt and devaluation that are prominent in the paranoid personality are also a central feature in the manipulative personality. The mode of narcissistic repair in the manipulative personality is that of putting something over on the other person. Putting something over involves contempt and a feeling of exhilaration when the deception succeeds. The instinctual component is the same as the component described for the paranoid personality—expulsion of the shameful, worthless self-image and its projection onto the victim. The exhilaration is the elation of the renewal fantasy when the cleansed self is now glorified and powerful. Thus there are both eliminative and phallic themes in the manipulative personality (44). Instinctual roots are in early orality, modified by contributions from later libidinal stages as well.

From the ego aspect, the processes of separation and individuation described by Mahler et al. (47) play a major role. Mothers of narcissists, in varying degrees, have difficulties in letting their children separate. Their own narcissism so influences the child's object relations through his infancy that the libidinal stages take on the coloration of narcissistic object relationships. The family of the manipulative personality plays out its conflicts on the stage of public image with the covert message that hidden, vicariously enjoyed activities are acceptable, as long as the public image remains "clean" (44). Even though he is a liar, the public image counts far more than the truth. The family settings and needs of the parents, upon which the issues of shame and restoration of pride are enacted, become internalized, along with the value systems that determine which narcissistic personalities will become of the sociopathic type.

Giovacchini (42) believes that a study of the various character disorders shows that such patients may not complain about discrete symptoms, but that the clinician notes confusion about identity and special problems in dealing with reality. He believes that, although we have learned a great deal about the ego structure, little progress has been made in distinguishing these cases from psychoses, and that the psychoanalytic treatment of such individuals should be reevaluated so that those patients who have been traumatized and deprived during their early development may receive meaningful treatment. Modifications of technique are necessary so that patients who have experienced traumatic, disruptive and narcissistic object relationships in their early life may experience an object relationship that compensates for or corects effects of early disruptive object relations (42, p. 211). He cites other authors as well who believe that the analyst, in some way, must make up for resulting developmental deficiencies in patients who have been so traumatized by early life experiences. Patients with severe characterologic defects could not extract necessary gratifications from parental objects in their early life experiences. Caretakers failed in terms of support and in later life the patient repeatedly gets into the same situations.

Giovacchini conceptualizes these characterologic difficulties as existing on a continuum which can be correlated with various stages of development. Early on there is no separation between mother and child. With later psychic development, there is greater structure and differentiation of ego systems associated with more highly differentiated needs, as well as with means for gratification delay and secondary process. Such development goes along with and is a prerequisite for the development of meaningful object relationships.

The author also draws some parallels and finds some distinctions between the early development of the psychotic and characterologic patient. As we have seen, these dynamics overlap with the development of that particular narcissistic personality disorder known as the sociopath. Giovacchini feels that the psychotic patient has never felt understood, i.e., there was a lack of empathy, with the mother responding to her own needs and the patient experiencing rejection or assault. As a result, his ego development is narrow and there are deficiencies not only in the instinct (need maturation) but in methods of expression as well. The same complaint that we hear from many of our severe character disorders is heard also from borderline patients; namely, they complain about not knowing what they want and experiencing hopeless dejection, feeling that the outer world is frustrating and ungiving. On the other hand, they feel a sense of emptiness and nothingness within themselves. In addition, Giovacchini feels that patients who have been diagnosed as character disorders are aware of such feelings in only a gross way, and that the sense of inner emptiness is experienced as non-existence and alienation (42).

Repression is not a major mechanism of defense in character disorders, nor is it as effective as in the psychoneuroses, because of the major ego defects; the ego is too poorly structuralized to support the function of repression. In comparing schizophrenics and character disorders, Giovacchini believes that both demonstrate ego defenses which lead to distortions of perception in various areas of the external world, severe disturbances in object relationships and a poorly integrated sense of identity. The ego defects with character disorders, however, have defensive elements which prevent the ego from undergoing a psychotic regression and are involved in relating to demands of both internal needs and the outer world. Although hypertrophied and defective, they enable the patient to deal with the traumatic features of his reality. "The traumatic reality of early childhood has become incorporated into the ego as destructive, constricting introjects which later are projected onto the outer world and defended against" (42). In comparison with borderline patients, the author feels that character disorders also manipulate with megalomanic expectations, but that the character disorders have a more stable differentiation between self and object. The borderline patient reflects the influence of primary process thinking more obviously. Giovacchini deals with the debates which have centered around supportive versus analytic therapy. He feels that the analyst must feel positively for his patients and make up for resulting developmental deficiencies. He cites "integrative interpretations" with character disorders, which expand the ego's self observing function and aid structuralization and, consequently, repression. Attempts to supply the nurturing needs of such patients inevitably lead to greater needs, frustrations and disruption. He feels that the essential, unique quality of analytic help is that it shifts the patient's energies from the search for gratification.

DEVELOPMENTAL PATTERNS

Although there are some differences of opinion, our own experience has been that the childhood histories of these patients are characteristic in their general outline (48). By and large, they come from grossly disturbed or chaotic family settings. The diagnosis of sociopathy does not preclude the presence of coexisting neurotic patterns but, generally, the adaptation to the outer world is in terms of the manipulative, impulsive behavioral patterns already described. In contrast to the neurotic and some schizophrenics, one does not find the "subtle sicknesses" which lead to primarily neurotic conflict. The severe character disorder comes from a home where disruptions, moves, job changes, failures were frequent; the parents fought often and openly and one or both left for varying periods of time; the children were shifted among relatives or foster agencies. Most striking is the presence of overt brutality from the father toward the children, and a mother who was antisocial herself in the sense of feeling deprived and much abused and who clung fearfully to her children with an almost phobic attitude toward the outside world. She may have been manipulative, may have cheated because she felt cheated, and was contradictory in her values with superego lacunae or splitting. Parental histories are frequently unreliable and little may be presented except the sorts of behavior—acting out and socially disruptive acts—which gave the parents difficulty or embarrassment. The patients recall such behaviors, as well as subjective unhappiness and great rage toward one or both parents. Such anger is expressed in subtle and not-so-subtle behavior patterns, e.g., enuresis, temper tantrums and/or thievery of parental property.

Antisocial and disruptive behaviors characteristically begin with a vengeance in adolescence. Parental concerns regarding propriety and how the child is viewed by neighborhood and school seem to depend on the parents' own conscious or unconscious value systems, as well as on their socioeconomic status. The groups chosen by the patient for identification are those adolescents who have also been in difficulty with authority and who are similarly full of rage toward their family environment. Such "acter outers" and "obstructionists" are in repeated disciplinary difficulties with school authorities. Expulsion from school, truancy, school and work failures, incorrigibility, fighting, minor (leading to major) thefts, reckless driving, drinking, drug abuse of one form or another and encounters with the police become a frequent story. The usual conflicts and separation problems of adolescence are intensified by the intense aggression carried along with latency and oedipal years. As the conflict intensifies, so do legal entanglements and antisocial behaviors which may, depending on the community, be laid at the feet of the parents.

At this point, the adolescent sees his parents as being overly controlling, intrusive, depriving, demanding and suppressive. Intertwined, however, is a sense of failure and of having let the parents down, of not having lived up to some spoken or unspoken expectation. The child, at a deeper level, feels let down and unloved. Following some major calamity, such as an arrest, expulsion from school, or repeated failure at school or job, desperate attempts at restitution by both parents or attempts at escape may surface. Overt anger and rejection come to the fore as father or mother manifestly states that he or she hates the child and wishes him out of the family (had never been born, were dead, etc.). However, attempts to remove the child from the home or enlist the family in some sort of collaborative therapeutic effort are frequently met with frustration and subtle opposition.

The child is meeting some unconscious, and possibly conscious, needs of one or both parents. His acting-out behaviors may be a source of gratification to the parent. The conflict between the parents over the child may be holding the marriage together. The mother may be clinging to the child unconsciously as a surrogate for her husband, whom she sees as unloving and unsatisfying; there may be an unconscious oral-oedipal configuration, with the child—son or daughter—providing nurturance and care to one or the other parent, that care which the parent felt deprived of in his/her own earlier life. The child may also represent an unconscious extension of parental aggression in a world in which propriety prohibits such expression of impulses. For these and other reasons, varying aspects of the separation/individuation process are incomplete (see Mahler, Kernberg); the child remains fixated, with intense rage, at a narcissistic level of development and adolescence is skewed.

In any case, when the adolescent is able to escape from the parental setting, he finds the inconsistent and intolerable authority of the parents, as well as their intolerable needs and demands, replicated in the outside world. They have been internalized. The structure and expectations of job, marital relationship, military authority and other situations lead to a reenactment of the fixations and conflicts that existed at home along lines of reparation and love seeking, recompense or otherwise restoring esteem, and the expression of primitive superego through masochistic "instinctual behaviors." According to the identifications and early patternings, as well as the vicissitudes of separation, a certain level and form of ego defensive organization is determined. The individual may respond with manipulative, possibly antisocial behavioral patterns, explosiveness, rage, temper outbursts, or with passive aggressive behaviors with underlying needs and expectations of omnipotent care and provision. Each potential "provider" must be aggressively attacked and destroyed to prove (unconsciously) that trust and reliability are not part of life's expectations. In effect, the original deprivers and frustrators are "unmasked" and destroyed with an abiding rage. One will be used and "screwed" unless he is ever vigilant and doing the "screwing."

Robins (49) set the age of the first signs of antisocial behavior as usually before 12 years. There were specific childhood antisocial symptoms which reliably predicted an adult antisocial behavior adjustment: theft, incorrigibility, truancy, running away, associates with bad reputations, staying out late, physical aggression, poor employment record, impulsiveness, reckless and irresponsible behavior, lack of guilt and pathologic lying. There were significant symptoms which did *not* predict antisocial adjustment in the same group, including enuresis, sleepwalking, sleep talking, irritability, nail biting, anorexia, oversensitiveness, withdrawal, seclusiveness, unhappiness, depression, tics, and fears.

DIAGNOSTIC CONSIDERATIONS

As I have attempted to demonstrate in the earlier portion of this chapter, literature on the antisocial (sociopathic), characterologically disturbed individual tends to be scattered, i.e., it comes from many points of view including literature, criminology, sociology, psychology and psychiatry. Although there may be overgeneralizations and oversimplifications, often with one dynamic or developmental factor being used as a global explanation, I believe there is a trend toward confluence and complementarity in terms of dynamic understanding. Various authors have focused on the hereditary/genetic aspects; others have focused on superego pathology, faulty identifications and introjections of childhood; still others have focused on the descriptive clinical picture without clear explanations of differing constellations and symptom patterns. The close approximation that some severely disturbed personality patients have to the schizophrenic has been noted by several authors. It is quite possible that genetics and heredity may predispose an individual to pathologic difficulties, to high or low stimulus barriers, levels of autonomic activity, overgeneralization of stimuli, and general quality and availability of other inborn autonomous ego functions, so that the infant may have greater difficulty extracting its needs from a less-than-optimal expectable environment.

We have, I believe, achieved a level of psychiatric sophistication where the "phenomenon" should be separated from the "disease." Individuals with characterologic and personality structures which are not sociopathic (antisocial) in nature—for example, criminals out of a sense of guilt, whose behavior may be "antisocial" in the criminal sense of the word but whose basic conflict is neurotic in ego structure and object relationships, and who are not narcissistically fixated as in the classic psychopath —can and should be differentiated. In addition, organic factors should be looked for clinically, developmentally, and in the history. Mental retardation, minimal brain dysfunction and childhood schizophrenia should be given recognition in terms of their etiologic significance. In other words, the psychopathic personality (the antisocial personality, the sociopath) needs to be transformed from a wastebasket or catch-al diagnostic classification, where diverse etiologic factors are found along with varying treatment needs, into a consistent conceptual entity.

The behavioral manifestations of the psychopathic personality—selfishness, callousness, irresponsibility, impulsivity, deficiency and guilt, difficulties in learning from experience and punishment, low frustration tolerance, tendency to project blame and rationalize behavior—have stood for decades as the phenomenological hallmarks of the antisocial personality and should remain. The dynamic core diagnosis of the "true" sociopathic personality would be reserved for those severe narcissistic personality disorders who, without apparent guilt, manipulate, exploit and control.

Superego reactions do occur in these people but because they are poorly integrated, unstructured and of uneven development they, on the one hand, are projected and, on the other hand, may be unusually harsh and masochistically color the psychopath's life-style. In terms of their narcissistic development, such individuals are charmers with a great need for attention, which may pass itself off superficially as "love," although love does not exist for them in the mature sense of the term (nor does true interest in or empathy for other individuals). Such individuals seek a steady input of narcissistic suplies in order to maintain a feeling not only of well-being and esteem, but of integrity to their inner selves. Objects are idealized and preserved; that is, they are seen as grandiose as long as they continue a steady input of narcissistic supplies (exciting activity, attention, admiration, etc.). Deprivation leads to feelings of emptiness, loneliness and isolation which are often described subjectively as depression and are usually associated with rage at the depriving, frustrating object. In spite of their extreme need for such supplies, these patients, because of their early life experiences, are not able to truly trust. They expect harm and deprivation so idealizations are temporary and fleeting in nature.

Such a diagnostic classification would also make possible the inclusion of genetic, organic and hereditary factors when they are present or suspected. An example might be as follows:

A. Clinical diagnosis: Personality disorder: Antisocial (sociopathic) type

B. Characterologic diagnosis: Narcissistic personality—low level (see Kernberg, 40)
C. Major clinical manifestations: manipulativeness, exploitiveness, passive receptive mastery
D. Predisposing factors: antisocial mother, absent father
E. Secondary and/or related syndromes: Minimal Brain Dysfunction in Childhood

The question of differential diagnosis is of major importance in dealing with severely characterologically disordered patients, particularly antisocial (sociopathic) individuals whose underlying difficulties may not be evident at first blush because of their charming (at times seductive) façades, which may arouse rescue fantasies in the therapist. The patient himself may not be aware of the true nature of his difficulties, being subjectively aware only of anxiety, depression, etc., which may be the presenting complaints which brought him to the psychiatrist. Less diagnostic difficulty (but possibly more treatment difficulty) is encountered in those individuals who are "sentenced" to therapy by judges, probation officers, or their own families after long histories of disciplinary difficulties, provocativeness, playing one individual against another, intolerance of structure, instability of job and marital relationships, repeated failures at job or college, or repeated antisocial activities of major or minor nature which create an "intolerable" situation for either the family or the community.

Of import is the differentiation from the borderline personality, whose attempts to maintain internal stability may result in antisocial behavior. The characterologically disordered patient, although he may be chaotic, reckless and impulsive at times, *does not regress to psychosis,* as does the borderline patient, nor does he lose the ability to distinguish external and internal realities. It must be remembered, however, that any patient may suffer from impaired reality testing in particular circumscribed areas (e.g., the phobic). The characterologically disordered patient also experiences distortions of reality testing to the extent that his perceptions are colored by his own needs and distorted by his own internal conflicts, particularly during times of great tension. He does not, however, lose contact with reality in the same sense as the borderline patient who regresses to psychosis.

The basic (although pathologic) integrity of his self/object relations remains intact. According to Kernberg (36-40), splitting of the self representation is characteristic of borderline patients, but not of the narcissistic patient, who is able to maintain a differentiation of self and object images; that is, a stable ego boundary is kept, but at the price of creating a pathologic internal structure in the form of a grandiose self, devalued images of self and others, intense oral sadism, and nonintegrated sadistic forerunners. Devaluation of aggressive, depriving or sadistic parents results in impaired superego structure in terms of values, value systems and ego ideal.

Deficient, distorted superego development is an issue not only for value systems but for the development of adaptive ego functions (sublimation). Object relationships and identifications are impaired, as are the constructive outlets for drive derivatives. Defenses remain of a primitive nature and affects are dealt with through primitive mechanisms such as splitting, turning against the self or permitted direct outlet (as in aggressive and emotional storms). The primitive ego and superego organization explains not only the impaired capacity for affect and repeated feelings of emptiness, but also the antisocial behaviors which may occur in this group of individuals, sometimes in seemingly isolated forms and at other times as frenetic activity which gives a sense of being "alive."

Borderline and psychotic individuals may also show antisocial patterns and should remain differentiated from that particular characterologic group whom we are designating as sociopathic (antisocial personalities). Such latter individuals are able to maintain, for practical purposes, a stable differentiation between self and object, and are able to identify the demands of reality, although they may not, for a variety of reasons, be able to adapt to or cope with them. Although this appears at times to be hairsplitting, there are practical implications. A psychiatrist may be called upon to give testimonial evaluation as to the ability of particular patients to distinguish external reality, e.g., whether or not a patient is eligible for trial or was psychotic at the time of a crime. There are also treatment implications and at times implications for financial compensation.

Psychological testing may be helpful. On testing, antisocial patients demonstrate a combination of pre-oedipal and oedipal strivings, frequently in pathologic condensation. There may be a lack of predominant heterosexual strivings, in spite of what may appear to be a frenetic sexual life. There may also occur a lack of defined sexual identity and unsuccessful attempts to deal with aggressiveness which infiltrates genitality and instinctual derivatives in general. Identity diffusion stemming from multiple fixations, usually with a predominantly oral case, may be present and represents an attempt to cope with extreme aggression and rage (40, 48). Aggression is usually one predominant feature of the test results. The early history of the borderline personality may be similar to that of the psychopath in that there may have been severe frustration and aggression directed toward the child. This aggression, however, appears clinically more subtle and covert, with the parents' own behavior not so infiltrated with antisocial behavior patterns as we see in the psychopath. The inadequate personality and the schizoid personality appear to be more closely related dynamically and genetically to the schizophrenic, and to suffer more profound ego disturbances and distortions in identifications and object relationships, as well as in superego development.

Patients in all diagnostic categories may present with complaints of "anxiety." In the psychopath this may result from the failure of some antisocial activity or imminent confrontation with an authority figure. He attempts to enlist the therapist as a "manipulative companion," a "co-conspirator" in escaping from an intolerable or dangerous situation. There is an intense underlying dread of being abandoned. The anxiety may stem from conflicting identifications or it may be the consequence of primitive superego structures which may be split off and possibly projected, so that internal dangers are seen as coming from the external environment. Indeed, life is frequently arranged so that such expectations are lived out in reality. The anxiety may stem from a sense of lack of control of the impulses as the healthier parts of the ego struggle with their preemptive nature, suffer following impulse or affect storms, or suffer from fear of abandonment and a sense of aloneness and emptiness. The emptiness or the breakdown of manipulations may in themselves be frightening and bring the patient for treatment.

Many personality structures, particularly the hysterical character, may demonstrate narcissistic, at times antisocial, qualities. Such patients also experience anxiety, but have evolved their symptomatology from later developmental phases. The need to manipulate, to be powerful, beautiful, superior, etc., stems from a personality structure in which there has been a more "normal" internalization of the superego (conscience and ego ideal). The character traits mentioned are defensive and compensatory in nature, stemming from shame and narcissistic mortification involving the early ego ideal, in this case, compensation for feelings of inadequacy deriving from intense penis envy and/or castration envy.

Obsessional personalities may be cold, isolated, narcissistic, and manipulative; however, there has been the development of an excessively harsh, demanding superego. The manipulations, superiorities, and, at times, idealistic and perfectionistic strivings stem from defensive needs against a harsh, sadistic superego and an attempt to receive "love" from an "unrealistic," harsh ego ideal. Such conflicts are traditionally related to the anal phase of development, with the idealism and "cleanliness" relating to anal sadistic conflicts structurally (see Reich, 22). The fixation of the ego ideal in the obsessive is not associated with the primitive fusion of an idealized self with the ego ideal or with devaluation of the representatives, internal and external, of the object world (40).

Depression as a chief complaint, depressive-masochistic patterns, or even purely masochistic patterns may be the presenting symptomatology of the antisocial personality whose sociopathic personality structure is only secondarily recognized. It is important to differentiate such complaints from those of the psychotic, borderline and neurotic patient who may present with similar subjective disturbances. To do so, one must look at the state of ego-superego development, identifications, and the differentiation of self and object images. Psychotics suffer from severe deficiencies in ego development, with poor differentiation between self and object images and an attendant lack of ego boundaries. Borderline patients present an ego-superego structure which is more advanced, with differentiation between self and object images and relatively firm ego boundaries in all areas except those of close interpersonal involvement; the potential for regression to psychosis (identity diffusion) is present (37). Neurotics present a strong ego organization with concomitant ego boundaries.

In other words, the better the superego integration deriving from internalization and identification with reasonable, realistic parental objects, and resulting from expectable oedipal conflicts, the more integrated will be the personality in its potential for grief and mourning (i.e., the classic picture of the depressive constellation involving loss of an object of narcissistic importance, with the ambivalent emotions, particularly aggression, becoming directed against the internalized object or objects and mediated via the superego). The emotions involved are of loss, guilt and diminished self-esteem.

Since "depression" is such a frequent complaint which brings the patient with severe characterologic problems to the psychiatrist, it is of importance to elucidate the dynamic and structural issues, not only to recognize the "depression" but to enhance the chances of establishing rapport and a therapeutic alliance. Antisocial characters whose early lives have been characterized by intense aggression and ambivalence are marked on the one hand by paranoid features (an untrusting, suspicious attitude toward the world), and on the other hand by a sense of emptiness and aloneness, so that the world appears empty, bleak and devoid of meaning. This may be described as "depression" when such patients present for treatment. Such patients do not have a continuity of stable, non-malignant objects in their early lives, a stable set of internalized identifications, or consistent integrated superego and ego ideals to protect them from a chronic sense of emptiness and/or persistent severe anxiety. Underlying is a sense of worthlessness. Kernberg (37) indicates that such emptiness stands part way along a continuum between the longing and sadness of the neurotic (that represents the hope for reestablishment of object relations) and a regressive psychotic fusion. From a therapeutic point of view, it is essential that the therapist recognize the defensive operations involved, as well as the underlying ego structure which supports the emotional experience. For example, in the neurotic, mechanisms of unconscious guilt or envy may predominate, whereas with the narcissistic psychopath, manipulation ("putting one over"), "dehumanization" of the therapist, splitting, primitive omnipotence, devaluation and the underlying internal rage may be the prime factors needing interpretation. The experience of emptiness and boredom of the psychopath is intimately connected with his/her aberrant ego-superego development and inability to experience depression. The capacity to tolerate the depression, loss and mourning is a part of the process of identification whereby a lost "good object" or a lost "ideal image" can be incorporated into one's own self representation (40).

The shallowness, lack of empathy, contempt, depreciation, coldness, ruthlessness and aggression of the psychopath must also be distinguished from the possibility of other diagnostic entities, such as the individual who presents himself as a "criminal" but whose antisocial activity is primarily in the service of his own self concept. He may be essentially depressed and/or masochistic, the concept of being antisocial being the result of intense feelings of worthlessness and self derogation deriving from a harsh superego. Such a patient may achieve a sense of worth and recognition deriving from identification with an idealized or recognized "criminal."

The ego deficits of the psychopath and hence his accessibility for treatment represent a broad spectrum of severity of pathology. The self-image is poor, although to varying degrees, and in spite of apparently successful manipulation. His behaviors repeatedly contain components which result in failure, subtle or overt destructiveness, self-harm and punishment. The poor self-image, low self-esteem and inconsistent identifications may carry him into dangerous, reckless behavior. Where enough ego strength is present, such reckless behavior and risk taking may result in gain and even recognition and success within the community. Frequently, however, it results in harm and some sort of destructiveness. The internalized image of the self is of being "bad" because of having been injured or harmed by the early parental introjects. On the other hand, he may feel that he is worth more to his family dead than alive.

But existing alongside the poor self-image are (infantile) feelings of omnipotence and entitlement, of having been injured, deprived, harmed, etc. Along with such feelings of entitlement are stated omnipotent, grandiose expectations from the environment and of his own ability to extract. His neediness, infantile expectations and poorly modulated aggressive impulses undermine the development of autonomous ego functions and distort ego-superego development, identification and object relationships. Negative expectations are not infrequently associated with aggressive outbursts and feelings of being righteously indignant. Good intentions, positive feelings, friendly behaviors and external help (therapy) are received with suspicion and are tested in a provocative fashion until hostile, destructive expectations are confirmed. With regard to object relationships, individuals are related to in terms of what they can provide and what can be extracted from them, rather than viewed as individuals in their own right. They are seen as extensions of the self and when they can no longer be manipulated, controlled, or extracted from, they are discarded and/or rage ensues, depending upon the importance of the object.

In a seemingly paradoxical fashion, someone may be selected out as a loving, "good" object—for example, a girlfriend who is maintained as good and actively clung to in spite of what appears to be overt neglect and abuse, infidelity, or even degradation from her. Hence, positive and negative feelings and attitudes toward the same object in an extreme form may not be combined; individuals are experienced in extremes. Such psychopaths are constantly envious and jealous of others whom they see as having more than they. They con their way "into the hearts" of such individuals in order to extract all the "goodies" that they have to supply, but after the bones of the "powerful one" are picked clean, or he refuses to collaborate with the psychopath and his deceptions (or after the game has been discovered), the object is abandoned and another powerful supplier is sought. Frequently, the "all good" object to which the patient may cling is a woman whose values, manipulations and narcissistic use of the patient are a replication and an extension of the patient's own relationship with his mother, and who offers symbolic protection against abandonment. It is preferable that she be wealthy and it is a prerequisite that her value system have some congruence with the patient's—namely, to exploit, control, take from, have power over.

Money is frequently a central issue in the lives of such individuals. If the underlying personality structure is not too severely disabled, they may be quite successful from the financial point of view, although suffering from an inner emptiness. Such feelings are offset, and a sense of worthiness and aliveness maintained, as long as one is deceiving, conniving, making money, etc. There exists the wish to be valued for one's own self and great rage toward the parental figure exists consciously. Hence, no matter how much money is acquired, the underlying needs never seem quite acquitted.

Anal and oedipal conflicts are not mutually exclusive; indeed, the greater the preponderance of their presence, the better the prognostic outlook. The oedipal distortions relating to preoedipal conflicts and severe aggression may result in perverse sexual trends, e.g., fetishism, transvestism, etc., which may be the presenting symptomatology. These are angry, resentful people, seeking retribution against the objects of their early childhood (see Stoller, 6). According to Kernberg (40), although superego components such as prohibitive parental demands are internalized they preserve a distorted, aggressive, primitive quality. They are not integrated with the loving aspects of the superego usually drawn from the idealized self and object representations. As a consequence, the superego is harsh and hostile expectations are the rule—the "screw or be screwed" formula described earlier. The superego is fixated at a preinternalized stage in which one lives within the law to the extent that obvious punishment will not be brought down. This is a variable, depending on the extent of the pathology involved.

The answers are certainly not all in. However, as our field continues to mature and develop, particularly as regards our understanding of the concept of the severely characterologically disturbed individual and the psychopath, there is growing congruence in terms of the psychodynamic and developmental factors involved. For example, even in a study in which parental psychopathology did not relate to antisocial patterns in childhood in any simple, clear, one-to-one relationship, and in which there were a multitude of behavioral disturbances, the author concludes that "the parents' conflict and ambivalence prevented them or interfered with their ability to help the child attain age appropriate or effective ways of managing aggressive and sexual impulses" (50).

Charles Malone (51) cited a variety of factors in the mothers of antisocial children, centering around their narcissistic needs, devalued self-image, oral and anal conflicts, impulsivity and ambivalence, which resulted in a delay in the transition from primary to secondary process, with predominant use of action rather than words. He states that it appears that these children demonstrate in their actions the failure to have experienced comfort and protection from their mothers, have not developed a stable inner attitude of self-protection, and have identified with the neglectful aspect of their mothers. Such "protection" of the ego is an important superego function and results from identification with a protecting, loving parent. The mothers of such children disregarded and devalued themselves and others, and the children seemingly identified with this devaluation.

A variety of references in the literature describe the impulsive, psychopathic character as demonstrating a retardation of language development and a predisposition to action as opposed to verbalization. Eveoleen Rexford (52) carried out a series of studies of antisocial young children, mostly boys, from six to 10 years of age, over a period of 10 years. She observed the influence of unsolved or maternal oral conflicts upon impulsive acting out; i.e., the mother's feeling that her own oral dependent wishes had not been met prevented her from meeting the needs of her children for love and affection. The young child's strong hostile feelings were not sufficiently overcome that he could move into a capacity for true object relationships, or such relationships remained predominantly hostile. These mothers felt unable to set limits or to frustrate the child in a constructive fashion. Consequently, the child could not tolerate delay and frustration, and was not forced to find substitutive formations for direct gratification. Sublimation and reality testing were limited; the child repeatedly had to resort to action to master tension and anxiety. Also, the mother, in her search for an individual who would meet her own infantile needs, was constantly changing her love object. This had the effect of preoedipal and oedipal configurations which were further confounded by the mother's unconscious sanctioning of the child's acting out behaviors, and her vicarious enjoyment of his non-conforming ways.

In this particular study, the fathers of the children did not fit our "typical story." The fathers displayed a similarity in attitude toward their sons, being passive-aggressive men with high dependency needs and confused sexual identifications.

Clinical problems in the mother-child relationship emerged during the second year of life, centered around issues of activity and control, and deteriorated further with growing self-assertion and motor skills on the part of the child (corresponding to the above-described situation of problems arising at the time of the *rapprochement* subphase between mother and child). Acting out was rooted in oral conflicts, heightened narcissism and intolerance for drive frustration, along with an inadequate grasp of reality. Although this constellation characterized chronic "acting out" individuals, it might not be obvious except under circumstances of stress or specific conflicts which shift the balance of drive and defense. The developmental history of acting-out individuals revealed early emotional disturbances, particularly problems in the second year of life when the issues of autonomy, control and self-assertion were paramount.

IMPLICATIONS FOR TREATMENT

Treatment approaches will not be explored in depth here as they are covered in subsequent chapters in this volume. However, it is important to state that such individuals may be treatable, depending on adequate developmental and structural history and analysis. Treatment modalities may range from psychoanalysis to psychotherapy of either an insight-oriented or structured supportive nature. Treatment could also require the use of institutionalization, whether in a hospital or prison setting, as well as medication.

Treatment demands with regard to such patients are great. Although over the broad spectrum much can be done to help such individuals, in most of the diagnostic spectrum which constitutes the "psychopath" the therapist is buffeted by demands from the patient and the external world, as well as by intense transference and countertransference reactions (43). The patient, as well as his family, may subvert treatment; provocativeness and acting out may bring extreme pressure to bear from the environment, or evoke inner feelings of discouragement and failure in the therapist. The patient's devaluation of and/or "picking the bones" of the therapist may lead to feelings of depletion. Covert and overt hostility may engender counterhostility. Repeated use of externalization and hostile expectations may make engaging the patient difficult. The patient's own grandiose fantasies, seductive flaunting of authority, or get-rich-quick schemes vibrate with unconscious needs on the part of the therapist and seduce or otherwise stimulate the therapist into unconscious collaboration and inclusion in the patient's acting out. Vicarious gratification may be obtained from the therapist. In such a conscious or unconscious collusion, fantasies, impulses, manipulations and hostilities of the patient may go uninterpreted in the therapy; the patient's conscious and unconscious rage toward the therapist may eventuate in termination of treatment, increased acting out or even assault upon the therapist. Alternately, the therapist's values are threatened. He may attempt to become the patient's "superego" or his own instinctual drives may be so stimulated by the patient that the therapist becomes anxious, does not function effectively, and/or withdraws from the treatment situation. Psychopathy, both as a phenomenon and as a "disease," continues to present an interesting challenge for the psychiatric profession.

REFERENCES

1. American Psychiatric Association. *Diagnostic and Statistical Manual of Mental Disorders.* American Psychiatric Association, Washington, D.C.: 1952.
2. American Psychiatric Association. *Diagnostic and Statistical Manual of Mental Disorders II.* American Psychiatric Association, Washington, D.C.: 1968.

3. ARIETI, S. (Ed.). *American Handbook of Psychiatry, Vol. 1.* New York: Basic Books, Inc., 1959.

4. CLECKLEY, H. *The Mask of Sanity.* St. Louis: C. V. Mosby Co., 1976.

5. FREEDMAN, A. M., KAPLAN, H. I. and SADOCK, B. J. (Eds.) *Comprehensive Textbook of Psychiatry*, Second Edition. Baltimore: Williams and Wilkins Co., 1975.

6. STOLLER, R. J. *Perversion, The Erotic Form of Hatred.* New York: Random House, 1975.

7. GLUECK, S. and GLUECK, E. *Unraveling Juvenile Delinquency.* New York: The Commonwealth Fund, 1950.

8. GLUECK, S. and GLUECK, E. *Physique and Delinquency.* New York: Halpern Brothers, 1954.

9. GLUECK, S. and GLUECK, E. *Family Environment in Delinquency.* Boston: Houghton, Mifflin Co., 1962.

10. AICHHORN, A. *Wayward Youth.* New York: The Viking Press, 1925.

11. FREUD, S. Some Character Types Met Within Psychoanalytic Work (1916). In: *Standard Edition of the Complete Psychological Works of Sigmund Freud, Vol. 14.* 309-33. London: Hogarth Press, 1957.

12. EISSLER, K. R. Some Problems on Delinquency. In: K. Eissler (Ed.), *Searchlights on Delinquency*, 3-25. New York: International Universities Press, 1949.

13. BENDER, L. and CRAMER, J. B. Sublimation and Gratification in the Latency Period of Girls. In: K. Eissler (Ed.), *Searchlights on Delinquency*, 53-64. New York: International Universities Press, 1949.

14. SZUREK, S. A. Some Impressions from Clinical Experience with Delinquents. In: K. Eissler (Ed.), *Searchlights on Delinquency*. 115-127. New York: International Universities Press, 1949.

15. SCHMIDEBERG, M. The Analytic Treatment of Major Criminals: Therapeutic Results and Technical Problems. In: K. Eissler (Ed.), *Searchlights on Delinquency*, 174-189. New York: International Universities Press, 1949.

16. FREUD, A. Certain Types and Stages of Social Maladjustment. In: K. Eissler (Ed.), *Searchlights on Delinquency*, 193-204. New York: International Universities Press, 1949.

17. WEST, D. J. *Present Conduct and Future Delinquency.* New York: International Universities Press, 1969.

18. CLOWARD, R. A. and OHLIN, L. E. Some Current Theories of Delinquent Subcultures. In: S. Harrison and J. McDermott (Eds.), *Child Psychopathology: An Anthology of Basic Readings*, 540-564. New York: International Universities Press, 1972.

19. NIGH, F. I. *Family Relationships in Delinquent Behavior.* New York: John Wiley and Sons, Inc., 1958.

20. HERZOG, E. and SUDIA, C. E. *Boys in Fatherless Families.* Office of Child Development, Children's Bureau, DHEW Publication No. (OCD) 72-33, U.S. Government Printing Office, Washington, D.C., 1971.

21. KAUFMAN, I. and REINER, B. S. *Character Disorders in Parents of Delinquents.* New York: Family Service Association of America, 1959.

22. REICH, W. *Character Analysis.* New York: Noonday Press, 1949.

23. KAUFMAN, I. Three Basic Sources for Pre-delinquent Behavior. *The Nervous Child*, Vol. 11, No. 1, 1955, 12-15. New York: Child Care Publications, October, 1955.

24. FENICHEL, O. *The Psychoanalytic Theory of Neurosis.* New York: W. W. Norton and Co., Inc., 1945.

25. JOHNSON, A. M. Sanctions for Superego Lacunae of Adolescents. In: K. Eissler (Ed.), *Searchlights on Delinquency*, 225-245. New York: International Universities Press, 1949.

26. JOHNSON, A. M. and SZUREK, S. A. The Genesis of Antisocial Acting out in Children

and Adults. In: D. Robinson (Ed.), *Experience, Affect, and Behavior*, 145-154. Chicago: University of Chicago Press, 1969.

27. KARPMAN, B. The Psychopathic Delinquent Child. Round table, 1959. *Amer. J. Orthopsychiat.* 20:223-265, 1950.

28. KARPMAN, B. Psychopathic Behavior in Infants and Children: A Critical Survey of the Existing Concepts, Round table, 1951. *Amer. J. Orthopsychiat.* 22:223-272, 1951.

29. KARPMAN, B. A Differential Study of Psychopathic Behavior in Infants and Children, Round table, 1951. *Amer. J. Orthopsychiat.* 22:223-267, 1952.

30. KARPMAN, B. Psychodynamics of Child Delinquency, Round table, 1952. *Amer. J. Orthopsychiat.* 26:1-69, 1953.

31. KARPMAN, B. Psychodynamics of Child Delinquency: Further Contributions, Round table, 1953. *Amer. J. Orthopsychiat.* 25:238-282, 1955.

32. LIPPMAN, H. Antisocial Acting Out: Symposium. *Amer. J. Orthopsychiatr.* 24:667-696, 1954.

33. HARRISON, S. I. and McDERMOTT, J. F. (Eds.). *Childhood Psychopathology: An Anthology of Basic Readings.* New York: International Universities Press, 1972.

34. REDL, F. and WINEMAN, D. *The Aggressive Child.* New York: The Free Press, 1957.

35. REDL, F. Ego Disturbances. In: S. Harrison and J. McDermott (Eds.), *Childhood Psychopathology: An Anthology of Basic Readings*, 532-539. New York: International Universities Press, 1972.

36. KERNBERG, O. F. Notes on Countertransference. *J. Am. Psychoanal. Assoc.* 13:38-36, 1965.

37. KERNBERG, O. F. Borderline Personality Organization. *J. Am. Psychoanal. Assoc.* 15:641-685, 1967.

38. KERNBERG, O. F. A Psychoanalytic Classification of Character Pathology. *J. Am. Psychoanal. Assoc.* 18:800-822, 1970.

39. KERNBERG, O. F. Early Ego Integration and Object Relations. *Ann. N.Y. Acad. Sci.* 193:233-247, 1972.

40. KERNBERG, O. F. *Borderline Conditions and Pathologic Narcissism.* New York: Jason Aronson, 1975.

41. KOHUT, H. *The Analysis of the Self.* New York: International Universities Press, 1971.

42. BOYER, L. B. and GIOVACCHINI, P. L. *Psychoanalytic Treatment of Characterological and Schizophrenic Disorders*, 208-335. New York: Science House, Inc., 1967.

43. GIOVACCHINI, P. L. Technical Difficulties in Treating Some Characterologic Disorders: Countertransference Problems. *Int. J. Psychoanal.* 1:112-128, 1972.

44. BURSTEN, B. *The Manipulator.* New Haven: Yale University Press, 1973.

45. BURSTEN, B. Some Narcissistic Personality Types. *Int. J. Psychoanal.* 54:287, 1973.

46. ABRAHAM, K. *Clinical Papers and Essays on Psychoanalysis.* New York: Basic Books, Inc., 1955.

47. MAHLER, M. D., PINE, F. and BERGMAN, A. *The Psychological Birth of the Human Infant.* New York: Basic Books, Inc., 1975.

48. LEAFF, L. A. Psychodynamic Aspects of Personality Disturbance. In: J. R. Lion (Ed.), *Personality Disorders, Diagnosis and Management*, Chapter 1:1-15. Baltimore: Williams and Wilkins Co., 1974.

49. ROBINS, L. H. *Deviant Children Grown Up: A Sociologic and Psychiatric Study of Sociopathic Personality.* Baltimore: Williams and Wilkins Co., 1966.

50. VAN AMERONGEN, S. T. Permission, Promotion, and Provocation of Antisocial Behavior. *J. Amer. Acad. Child Psychiat.* 2:99-117, 1963.

51. MALONE, C. Some Observations on Children of Disorganized Families and Problems of Acting Out. *J. Amer. Acad. Child Psychiatr.* 2:22-49, 1963.

52. REXFORD, E. N. A Developmental Concept of the Problems of Acting Out. *J. Amer. Acad. Child. Psychiat.* 2:6-21, 1963.

6

A Jungian Viewpoint

JOHN EDWARD TALLEY, M.D.

Psychopathy is as old as man, perhaps older. Higher animals have norms of behavior, and extreme social deviants—men as well as animals—have traditionally been removed from their societies.

REHABILITATION OF THE DEVIANT

At different periods in man's history there have been systems for rehabilitation of the deviant, all of them, until recently, religious in nature.

The Eleusinian Mysteries, which were viable in ancient Greece for 2000 years, drew their vitality in part from their essential role in integrating warriors back into home and city after their prolonged exposure to a life of killing, pillage and rape. The Mysteries were in devotion to Demeter and her daughter, Persephone. The epiphany of Persephone at the climax of the celebration of the Greater Mysteries evoked in the initiates a profoundly humanizing and civilizing experience.

In A.D. 364, a non-Greek proconsul from Rome ignored an edict from the Catholic Roman Emperor Valentinian which would have in effect prohibited the celebration of the Mysteries. Praetextatus, the proconsul, declared that

> this law would make the lives of the Greeks unlivable, if they were prevented from properly observing the most sacred Mysteries, which hold the whole human race together (1, p. 12).

In the Homeric-style "Hymn to Demeter" written in the eighth century B.C., the poet wrote:

Blessed is he among men on earth who has beheld this. Never will he who has not been initiated into these ceremonies, who has had no part in them, share in such things. He will be as a dead man in sultry darkness (1, p. 14).

And Sophocles:

Thrice-blessed are those among men who, after beholding these rites, go down to Hades. Only for them is there life; all the rest will suffer an evil lot (1, p. 14).

Pindar wrote:

Blessed is he who, after beholding this, enters upon the way beneath the earth; he knows the end of life and its bgeinning, given by Zeus (1, p. 15).

Cicero referred to the "radiance which Eleusis casts on all life." The orator Isocrates declared, "Those who take part in them possess better hopes in regard to the end of life and in regard to the whole aion" (1, p. 15).

Nearly three thousand years later, Kerenyi stated that the performance of the Mysteries "conferred on Greek existence a characteristic sense of security and, because it was able to do this, it responded to a spiritual need which formed a bond uniting the whole human race; this was the need for a bulwark against death" (1, p. 16). The facts that revealing the secrets of the Mysteries was punishable by death or banishment and that the religion maintained its vitality as long as it did attest to its effectiveness.

The Mysteries were not limited to warriors. Greek and non-Greek, man and woman, slave and master, came to be initiated. They experienced and perpetuated that which Demeter and Persephone, Mother and Daughter, signified.

But there were those who were not permitted to be initiated. No person who had committed murder, other than sanctioned killing in wars, was acceptable. Murderers were considered lost souls, forever alienated from what Demeter and Persephone signified, from the realm of the gods, and from the human condition. Perpetrators of crimes other than murder were, after release from prison, eligible for initiation into the Lesser Mysteries. After a prescribed length of time they could join the holy procession to Eleusis on what is now the 27th or 28th of September and participate in the holy night within the sanctuary (1).

If this were a Zen or a Sufi study of the psychopath one might let the descriptive intimations of the Mysteries stand alone, for the moment, to be pondered, for in it are many of the elements pertinent to the description, dilemma and treatment of the psychopath.

The functional model of the psyche which, for Jung and others, has proved to be of value in seeing relationships between certain kinds of human experience includes a structure called the collective or objective unconscious. It is this stratum of the unconscious which carries the *given* of man, the instincts already possessed when he comes into the world. These instincts are more related to the sympathetic than to the central nervous system, and probably ultimately to the four fundamental amino acids (thymine, adenine, cytosine and guanine) found in the DNA and the RNA of the chromosomes themselves (2, p. 85).

Metaphorically, one might consider the collective unconscious as nature itself. The individual experiences this natural, collective, instinctual dimension of himself in the form of behavior and of *archetypal images.*

An archetypal image is a symbol and possesses affect. Whereas an archetype is an instinct itself, physiologic, genetic, and ultimately unknowable, the archetypal image is the manifestation or intimation of a fundamental instinct in the psyche. The archetypal images are experienced in dreams, in myths, in fairy tales, in cosmologies, and in religions. Although they are clothed in the particularities of one's specific individual and cultural experience, these archetypal images are the basic universals for everyone.

Edinger has categorized four general archetypes. Each image may be placed within one of these broad categories: The Great Mother (or the feminine), The Spiritual Father (or the masculine), Transformation (which includes ego phenomena with imagery of the hero, the quest, the journey, the battle), and Wholeness (completion, totality, quaternity, mandala symbolism) (3, p. 4).

Of archetypes, Hillman says,

> the curious difficulty of explaining just what archetypes are suggests something specific to them. That is, they tend to be metaphors rather than things. . . . In fact, it is precisely as metaphors that Jung writes of them, insisting on their indefinability . . . . Imagine archetypes as the *deepest patterns of psychic functioning,* the roots governing the perspectives we have of ourselves and the world. They are the axiomatic, self-evident images to which psychic life and our theories about it ever return. They are similar to other axiomatic first principles, the models or paradigms, that we find in other fields. For "matter," "God," "energy," "life," "health," "society,"

"art" are also fundamental metaphors, archetypes perhaps themselves, which hold whole worlds together and yet can never be pointed to, accounted for, or even adequately circumscribed . . . But one thing is absolutely essential to the notion of archetypes: their emotional possessive effect, their bedazzlement of consciousness . . . By setting up a universe which tends to hold everything we do, see and say in the sway of its cosmos, an archetype is comparable with a God (4, pp. xiii-xiv).

In considering some of the archetypal phenomena associated with psychopathic behavior and the psychopathic personality, it might be well to keep in mind that archetypes are metaphors and attitudes, not substances or concrete literalisms. The archetypal mode of approaching the psyche implies movement, imagination, relationship, personification, i.e., seeing the psyche as the dynamic, living, shifting phenomenon it is.

THE PSYCHOPATH

Ben Karpman several decades ago attempted to separate various manifestations of psychopathic (sociopathic) disorders (5). Although he found the majority of these syndromes to be ultimately related to some core ("cardinal") neurotic, psychotic or affective diagnosis, there was a small group of patients in whom no other cardinal disease could be found, even after lengthy, analytically-oriented examination. These core, "true" psychopaths he called "anethopaths."

Archetypal distinctions can be made between the person with various kinds of "psychopathic personality" and the anethopath. This differentiation is important because the psychopathic personality is in some instances amenable to psychotherapy, while the anethopath is not. Behaviorally, the two are on an antisocial continuum or spectrum ranging from minimal to profound. Yet behavior alone is not the differentiating factor.

Besides their obvious value in the therapeutic situation, dreams can be helpful in diagnostically differentiating the patient with psychopathic characteristics from the true anethopath. Two dreams with similar imagery might serve as illustrations. The first is that of a young woman described by Kohut as having a narcissistic personality disturbance. (Many psychopathic personalities suffer from this problem.) In the dream

the patient is on a swing, swinging forward and backward, higher and higher . . . yet there is never a serious danger of either the patient's flying off, or of the swing uncontrollably entering a full circle (6, pp. 4-5).

Kohut states that this person was amenable to psychoanalytic treatment. In contrast is the dream reported by von Franz of

> an international criminal who had already murdered 10 or 12 people, a kind of pathological creature who committed cold-blooded murder without the slightest reaction of conscience . . . (he) killed an unknown old man in the streets of Zurich, took his money, and got caught. Dr. Guggenbuhl-Craig had to give the court the psychiatric expert's opinion and ascertain whether or not the man was responsible for his deeds. . . . (Dr. Guggenbuhl) told us the man's dreams without telling us (anything of the dreamer). He simply asked us what we thought of a man of 40 who had such dreams. Naturally I did not know that the dreamer was a pathological murderer, but I said literally, "Hands off, leave that man alone, he is a lost soul!" The dream in question was very simple. It was one which was repeated frequently and in which the murderer went to an amusement park where there were big swings. He was on such a swing, swinging up and down, higher and higher, when suddenly the swing went too high and he fell into empty space. That was the end of the dream.
>   I thought, "My God, swinging between the opposites and taking it as a pleasure with no reaction towards it, taking it as fun!" And the lysis in the end sentence of the dream was "falling into empty space," without even the reaction of "I woke up with a cry." There was no emotional reaction. I could only say that this was a lost soul. I felt, to put it into pictorial language, as if God had written off this soul. In the dream there is no attempt by nature (i.e., by the unconscious) to save the man by giving him a shock. We assume that dreams come from the unconscious instinct toward nature. His ununconscious tells him, just as cold-bloodedly as he murders, that he is lost! It speaks with his own cold-bloodedness, talking to him on his own level (7, p. 117).

The first dream might be that of a non-anethopathic psychopath. The second, without question, is that of an anethopath.

ANIMA

I would suggest that the structure within the human psyche which Jung named *anima* is possibly the crucial factor in not only differentiating the two kinds of psychopaths, but also in seeing their differences from the non-psychopath.

Simplistically, an individual's capacity for living life richly, in contrast to merely existing, is directly proportional to the degree of conscious realization of, and relation to, the anima. Anima is the feminine principle. It is variously described as soul, as the mediatrix or bridge between ego and the archetypes of the collective unconscious, between ego and the creative matrix, or between ego and what those in other times or places called the gods. She is called the unconscious itself, feeling, eros, the eternal feminine, the life principle. These are all *metaphors* for particular kinds of human experience which are different and distinct from experiences related to the masculine principle.

The masculine (*animus*) attributes of the psyche are objective, outer-directed, related to consciousness, rational, ego-oriented, focused, aggressive and goal-directed. The anima is subjective, inner-directed, related to the unconscious, irrational (or better, non-rational), and oriented toward non-ego phenomena (yet is crucial to ego development). It is diffuse, mysterious, receptive and, above all, reflective.

As an archetypal image within the collective unconscious, the anima is different and distinct from personal introjects of the feminine gender. Figures of known women in dreams, for example, are not amina figures, unless in the particular situation they have that one quality which all archetypal figures possess, i.e., numinosity (referring to light, specifically to the kind of light mankind has always attributed to the supernatural, either gods or demons).

So anima may appear as Eve, Helen of Troy, or the Virgin Mary; or as Sophia, as a film star, reigning queen, or wife of a president, each representing a unique aspect of what romantics have called the eternal feminine. When an individual experiences, within a dream, an image of her in any one of her many presences, that person is affected by her. The influence is manifest in the dreamer's mood, affect and behavior. When Jung speaks of an archetypal image as "a picture of an instinct," he means that image and its affect which cause definite reactions within the psyche of the individual experiencing the instinct, the archetype.

The effects which the anima may have on the individual (and consequently on perception and behavior) are as various as the feminine principle itself, but each image has its specific effect and its specific meaning in the immediate setting experienced.

Hillman states that anima as soul is "that unknown component in the human experience which 1) makes significance possible whether in love or in religious concerns, from its special relation with death . . . 2) refers to the deepening of events into experiences . . . and 3) is the imaginative possibility in our natures, the experiencing through reflective speculation, dream, image, and fantasy that mode which recognizes all realities as primarily symbolic and metaphorical" (4, p. x).

Writing elsewhere, Hillman states that it is the anima function which "makes consciousness possible by her reflective nature" and that "the sense of personal identification is given not *by* the ego but *to* the ego by the anima." Evidence for this is found in the clinical condition called "depersonalization" which was defined by Schilder in 1914 as "a condition in which an individual feels himself thoroughly changed in regard to his former state of being. This change encompasses both the ego and the external world and results in the individual not recognizing himself as a personality. His actions seem to be automatic. As an onlooker he observes his activities and deeds. The outer world appears alien and new and has lost its reality" (8, p. 114). Hillman amplifies:

In this condition memory, perception, association, thinking, willing . . . all ego functions are intact and working, yet there is a loss of personal sense of being, subjective interiority, the sense of "me-ness" and with this absence is lost too the sense of the world . . . It is seen as an existential "void" and "abyss."

Less extreme experiences of "depersonalization" not unfamiliar to us are moods characterized by apathy, monotony, dryness and weary resignation, the sense of not caring and not believing in one's value. This is seen characteristically at the end of a love affair, where one can experience a sense of loss of vitality, of reality in regard to oneself and the world itself. "Nothing seems real anymore." "I feel dead, empty."

Depersonalization presents a striking similarity with what anthropology has called "loss of soul." And in fact, "depersonalization" is also used as a philosophy of the universe which no longer regards the natural forces as manifestations of supernatural agents or gods. Loss of anima means both loss of internal animation and external animism.

Our sense of personality, attachment to persons, beliefs in personal immortality and our cult of personal relationships and development all rest upon *personifying*, which is the native habit of the soul, an effect of the anima archetype.

Absence of soul opens one to the soul's immeasurable depths, that primary characteristic of the psyche according to Herakleitos, revealing those depths as an abyss. Not only is the guide and the bridge gone, but so too is the possibility of a personal connection through personified representations. *For it is through anima that the autonomous systems of the psyche are experienced in personified form. Without her the depths become void.* This happens because the anima who personifies the collective unconscious is not there to mediate the depths in personified images with personal intentions. At the same time, the world outside is perceived without its depths, losing perspective, becoming a soulless flatland" (8, pp. 114-118).

This void, this abyss, this soulless flatland is the "nothing" which Karpman and others have described in their depth analyses of psychopaths (5, 9).

Fortunately, most of us are spared this fate. We are able to form relationships, love, marry, make friends, have interests and passions, and
sustain the underpinnings of the life process. We are connected with
our unconscious, even if only dimly. We possess varying degrees of awareness of our own fantasies and myths and dreams and images, our per-
sonifications, our gods.

For the psychopathic personality, however, it is this inner life which
is lost and with it the capacity for relationship. Anima development
has been arrested at some point. There is a loss of soul. "Something" was
there once, or there were the seeds of "something," but the "something,"
the soul, has disappeared. And, tragically, the anethopath, for unknown
reasons, seems utterly devoid of the psychological factor which mediates
the capacity for relationship to others and especially to oneself. The anethopath's dilemma is not loss of soul. It is *absence* of soul.

All of the antisocial behavior of the psychopath can be explained by
this loss of anima. It is a defense against facing the inner emptiness of his
life. For the anethopath this emptiness was probably present at birth.
But what dynamics in the non-anethopathic psychopath's young life
drove his soul from him?

Because what is lost pertains to the feminine, one must suspect the
parental, especially the mother, experience in some way. I would speculate that the child not only lacked nurturing, but experienced very early
life as withholding, lacking affirmation, and possibly as actually cruel,
harsh and violent. Whatever the circumstances, the world—his world—
was evil.

In normal development, at adolescence there is an activitation of
what Guggenbuhl calls "archetypal destructiveness" (Jung called it archetypal evil, the archetypal shadow). Young people suddenly become reckless, take mindless risks, vandalize, steal. Or, if they do not act it out,
they fantasize violence, arson, rape, and worse. This is a crucial time in
development. The contact with his or her own capacity for destruction
(which Jung called the "murderer and suicide within us") seems to be a
mechanism which presents a developing young person with his first
sense of moral choice. He cannot consciously choose for life if he has not
also chosen destruction and experienced it in some way. Guggenbuhl
relates the dilemma very neatly in a fairy tale called "The Devil with the
Golden Hair" in which a youth, in order to marry the princess, must
first steal three golden hairs from the devil and return with them (10,
pp. 107-115). Most of us, luckily, get our golden hairs and are able to
return.

One is no longer innocent, having eaten of the fruit of the tree of knowledge of good and evil, and thenceforth must suffer one's own temptations and darknesses. Hopefully, more often than not we choose the *yes* of life rather than the *no* of destructiveness. At the time one is flirting with, experimenting with, the inner archetypal shadow, most realize that it is "bad." One's already-formed, father-fed conscience, in both its collective aspect (human law) and its archetypal aspect (the Self, the natural ethical impulse, divine law), is active.

But what of the young person who has grown up in a harsh and ungiving world? When this person experiences this archetypal destructiveness which exists in his *own* psyche, he misreads it. Because the outer world to him has always been actually destructive, he projects his own inner destructiveness onto the world, society and its institutions, and then he rages against them (10, pp. 199-120). Thus he is never able to see that he has a choice in life, that he can say *yes* to life. He never gets the golden hairs of the devil. He never marries the princess. He loses her.

The princess is a metaphor for his own feminine aspect, the anima, the soul. As the reader will recall, we have discussed the consideration of psychopathic behavior as a defense against realizing the loss of soul, the inner void.

It is to be understood that an archetypal image, when experienced in a dream, for example, has its own particular attributes. The image itself conveys a personality which includes *physical appearance* (old, young, male, female, clothing, ornaments, weapons, etc.), *behavior* (fighting, fishing, reading, pronouncing, making love, etc.) and *style of consciousness* (independent, maternal, passive, punishing, instructive, loving, coping, etc.). The image is expressing a psychological attitude to the ego of the dreamer as a compensation to a consciously held position, as an alternative possibility, as an affirmation, or as a warning. Its presence has a compelling, numinous effect on the ego. An archetypal image is neither good nor bad. It is an expression of nature. The question of morality is related not to the archetypal image but to the ego's attitude toward that which the image conveys. At times it is essential to challenge an archetypal phenomenon in oneself; at other times it is essential to accept and integrate it. Always it is essential to pay attention to it. If the ego ignores, fails to comprehend, or represses the archetypal manifestation, the archetype itself may override the ego and act autonomously—at the core of every complex, there is an archetype. It is for this reason that an understanding of archetypal phenomena is important.

The archetypal shadow, as manifest at a particular moment in the psyche, psychopath or not, has its own personality, its own physical appearance, its own behavior, and its own style of consciousness. There are archetypal roots for psychopathic behavior evident in the psyches of everyone. These are manifestations of the archetypal shadow.

To gather examples of archetypal phenomena in general, and about the archetypal shadow in particular, one looks to fairy tales, myths, and cosmologies for universal characters, situations, and themes which express the recurring human dilemmas. A pantheon of gods and their relationships and behavior, whether Hindu, aboriginal or Greek, express this archetypal experience of man.

Because the Greek mythology is part of Western psychological history, themes from that tradition might serve as examples of archetypal shadow material and integrative material (although Judeo-Christian myths are equally rich). Each of the gods is different from all the others. And each is, as mortals are, complex and contradictory. Each god has both a beneficent and a dark negative aspect. Aphrodite, for example, brings madness as well as love.

How did the Greeks experience a particular god? When that god was invoked, worshipped or cursed, what psychological dimension was intended? The god referred to a reality, not to a formless power. Kerenyi said,

> He was something very precise, possessed a distinctly delineated personality and was contained by the definition of his own inherent meaning. No Deity can be reduced completely to color of skin, hair dressing, clothing and other attributes without something being left over. This "left over" part is precisely what is essential to understanding. We should not presume that the "something" which contributes to a God's reality must necessarily correspond to something sublime . . . The Greeks never found the primitive aspects of a God's configuration incompatible with his Godhood (11, pp. 1-3). . . .
>
> "By understanding, knowing the reality of an antique God . . . one has a different experience of the world than one would without him. Speaking mythologically, each God is the source of a world that without him remains invisible but with him reveals itself in its own light (11, pp. 54-55).

These gods, as archetypal images, exhibit the range of human attitudes and behavior. Each manifests, as part of his complex personality, a "psychopathic" dimension. Hermes, for example, while manifesting such attributes as "bearing the supreme knowledge of the Greeks, the Hermetic-spiritual aspect of knowledge which exists in friendly union with the animal divine" and as "god of exposition and interpretation," as the "masculine life (phallic) force" and as "guide of souls," "messenger of the gods," and "easer of death," is also "a child of many wiles and cunning council, a driver of kine (he stole Apollo's cattle), a captain of raiders, a watcher of the night, a thief of the gates" (11, pp. 20-21).

The Trojan War showed the gods opposed to each other—Zeus manipulating men and gods against the Trojans, and Athena lending her wiles to the Trojans against the Hellenes. Aphrodite, jealous of Psyche's beauty, schemed and plotted to make her fall hopelessly in love with her own son, Eros (Cupid), creating endless anguish for the innocent Psyche. Zeus, in his rebellion against his own father, Kronus (who, to be sure, had a penchant for eating his own children), castrated and banished him.

Each god, each myth, each encounter between gods or between gods and men, exemplifies a human psychological situation. To know the gods is to know oneself. To be alienated from the gods, from that dimension of the human psyche, is to be cut off from one's own part in humanity.

The central problem of the psychopath and of the anethopath then might be called a religious one, in the metaphorical sense which has been suggested. The loss of soul, of the anima—who serves as mediatrix and bridge to the gods, to the archetypal realm—precludes the deepening, enriching, reflecting, personifying experience which is the essence of life.

THERAPY

The therapeutic implications are apparent. In all probability, the anethopath can at best be humanely contained or managed without illusion of psychological change. As Cleckley has pointed out, at our present level of knowledge we can only protect the individual from himself, and society from him (12, pp. 119-120).*

There is always hope, however, for one who is not anethopathic but who, somewhere during his development, became locked into a course away from acceptance of the archetypal shadow and did not experience development of the feminine, soul side of his nature.

Of therapy for one who has lost soul, Hillman says, "I believe we have located the missing person in anima. How to recapture her in therapy is another matter. But where to look tells us something about how to look. By relating archetype and symptom we have an inkling at which altar to place the complaint" (8, p. 118). "There are Gods in our diseases," suggests Jung (13, p. 54). And so we can relate our diseases to them. Relating the anima archetype to the symptom could take place by revivifying images. In a somewhat similar condition in which "the patient's world has become cold, empty and grey," Jung turned to fantasy,

---

* See Chapters 14-16 for other views on the treatment and treatability of these conditions.

because "Libido can never be apprehended except in definite form: that is to say, it is identical with fantasy-images" (14, p. 345). Imagination is the particular province of the anima: "anima *is* psyche" (13, p. 75).

The revivification of images reconstructs personal belief through belief in a personified world, with personal intentions and confidence in oneself as a carrier of interior personalities. Grinnell has described this as "psychological faith" (15, p. 15). Faith in psyche and faith in oneself as personality are particular effects of anima. Anima has this effect through the presentation of images. But any therapeutic method for restoring an animated, repersonalized world must constellate in the patient, and in the therapist as well, "the sense of utter reality of the personified image" (8, p. 118; 13, p. 55; 16, p. 753).

How does a Jungian therapist approach the task of revivification of images within the psyche? Assuming that one has, through personal analysis, experienced one's own depths and consequently has "the sense of the utter reality of the personified image," it is the therapist's prime responsibility to create an atmosphere within the therapeutic relationship which not only allows, but positively respects, honors and affirms the imaginal dimension.

This requires uncommon sense. One must not judge or intellectualize or reduce a dream image or a fantasy to something else. Its vitality is best respected, not by interpretation, but by what Jung called amplification.

Working with a dream or fantasy is a joint effort between therapist and dreamer to the end that they experience together as thoroughly as possible the reality of the dream or fantasy. The dreamer describes the drama in as much detail as he can; he gives the cast (images), the problem set forth, the climax and the resolution. Emotional nuances and the effect of different aspects of the drama on the ego of the dreamer are carefully considered and the dreamer offers personal associations.

The therapist *listens,* both to what the dreamer presents and to the reactions which arise from his own unconscious. He may be reminded of a similar theme or situation in a fairy tale, a myth, or a piece of literature or biography. He may recall a fact of natural history or the model of an organic compound. Or he may become aware of a strong emotion or feeling tone or of a bodily sensation.

It is here that the art of therapy is called for. The therapist must know —intuit—which of his own associations, *if any,* are to be expressed, which will at best enhance the dreamer's living experience, and at worst not kill it. The art demands that the therapist not pronounce, not declare. He asks, "Could it be this?" or "That reminds me of . . . is there a connection?" He *rarely,* if ever, says "That image means such-and-such."

This mode of relating to emerging unconscious material is predicated on Jung's description of what psychological analysis is: "An ongoing dialectic between consciousness and the unconscious" (17, p. 4). For a dialectic to remain animated, the ego of the therapist cannot presume to know more than his own unconscious or than that of the dreamer.

Any interpretative amplification which is to remain true to the process is best served by an "as if" attitude. This, after all, realistically takes into account the fundamental subjectivity of the psychotherapeutic process.

What, besides dreams and fantasies, might be utilized to revivify images? The term "active imagination" describes a technique which aims at the expression of unconscious material in a variety of ways. Everyone is familiar with the therapeutic value which may be derived from painting or from writing a poem. In situations wherein conventional verbal therapy has become prolongedly barren, a drawing may suddenly reveal an unexpected image or emotion, which in turn may continue into a symbolic outpouring whose authenticity and meaning are verified by unmistakable psychological deepening and insight.

Effective modes of expression are individual and varied. Painting, drawing, sculpting, writing poetry or fantasy, dancing, creating sand-table dramas using miniature figures and natural objects, and recording internal dialogues are all possibilities. Any genuine expresssion of one's imaginal world in concrete form, if it is done with a minimum of conscious ego-involvement, may serve to animate the unconscious.

As with any aspect of therapy, active imagination has its dangers and pitfalls. It can be used as a defense. Its value and authenticity increase as its ego-directedness decreases. Active imagination is not the giving of expression to something which from an ego point of view the patient assumes is "good."

Again, the perceptive therapist and/or the conscientious analysand will usually know the difference between a spontaneous, authentic expression of the unconscious and something which is false and self-conscious. The first is fruitful and leads somewhere; the second is static and leads one to dead ends.

Any of these approaches might be applied specifically to help the non-anethopathic psychopath begin to reconnect with the unconscious. If— and that *if* is a large part of the problem—a psychopath can stay in the therapeutic relationship, and if the imagination can be touched, there is hope.

For everywhere man is, there is the possibility of realizing that which lived at Eleusis for 2000 years and which somewhere in each of us still lives, waiting to be quickened. It is the utterly convincing, unshakable experience of the eternal reality and value of the human soul.

REFERENCES

1. KERENYI, K. *Eleusis, Archetypal Image of Mother and Daughter.* New York: Random House for Bollingen Foundation, 1967.
2. OSTERMAN, E. The Tendency Toward Pattern and Order in Matter and in the Psyche. In: J. Wheelwright (Ed.), *The Reality of the Psyche.* New York: Putnam, 1968.
3. EDINGER, E. An Outline of Analytical Psychology. In: *Quadrant.* New York: C. G. Jung Foundation, 1968.
4. HILLMAN, J. *Revisioning Psychology.* New York: Harper and Row, 1975.
5. KARPMAN, B. On the Need of Separating Psychopathy into Two Distinct Clinical Types: The Symptomatic and the Idiopathic. *J. Crim. Psychopathol.* 3:112, 1941.
6. KOHUT, H. The Analysis of the Self. Monograph Number Four: *The Psychoanalytic Study of the Child.* New York: International Universities Press, 1971.
7. VON FRANZ, M. L. *Shadow and Evil in Fairytales.* New York: Spring Publications, 1974.
8. HILLMAN, J. Anima II. *Spring* 1974. New York: Spring Publications.
9. REID, W. H. Personal communication.
10. GUGGENBUHL-CRAIG, A. *Power in the Helping Professions.* New York: Spring Publications, 1971.
11. KERENYI, K. *Hermes, Guides of Souls.* New York: Spring Publications, 1976.
12. CLECKLEY, H. Psychopathic Personality. In: *International Encyclopaedia of the Social Sciences,* 13:119. New York: MacMillan and Company, 1968.
13. JUNG, C. G. *Alchemical Studies.* Princeton University Press for Bollingen Foundation, 1967.
14. JUNG, C. G. *Two Essays on Analytical Psychology.* New York: Random House for Bollingen Foundation, 1953.
15. GRINNELL, R. Reflections on the Archetype of Consciousness: Personality and Psychological Faith. *Spring* 1970:15. New York: Spring Publications.
16. JUNG, C. G. *Mysterium Coniunctionis.* New York: Random House for Bollingen Foundation, 1963.
17. JUNG, C. G. *Psychology and Alchemy.* Princeton: Princeton University Press for Bollingen Foundation, 1968.

7

Social and Familial Correlates
of Antisocial Disorders

DON A. ROCKWELL, M.D.

Like any individual, the psychopath emerges from and lives within a variety of systems. This chapter focuses on social systems aspects of psychopathy. By focusing on systems aspects, our attention is drawn to facets of psychopathy often overlooked and both interactional aspects and gaping holes in our understanding of the sadness of the psychopath are illuminated. The major flaws in our understanding of the psychopath are most evident from the social correlates perspective. Until very recently the diagnosis of and data about the psychopath suffered from confusion of major proportions. Value judgments were (and continue to be) major stumbling blocks. The standard criteria—"callous," "unloyal," etc.—carry strong inherent value positions; the label has a pejorative ring to it. Recently, we have begun to move beyond these flaws, yet much of what we say and believe is colored by them.

The positive side of the sociocultural systems aspect of psychopathy evolves from the confluence of many separate streams of research. For our purposes we need to attend to only a few examples from each in order to develop our theme.

FAMILIAL CORRELATES

The familial correlates of psychopathy have been examined from several major perspectives. The psychoanalytic perspective was earliest and most subject to inadvertent distortion—on the basis of both the limited data provided by psychopaths and the selective nature of analysis. Quite naturally, the earliest notions were also the most global. North American workers have, since Adolph Meyer's time, focused on psychopathy as an environmental reaction. Diagnostic limitations were severe and consensus could be reached only on the notion that psychopathy represented an outcome of faulty early childhood process—most frequently laid in the lap of an indulgent yet narcissistic mother. Greenacre's (1) concept of the importance of the superego demand for punishment retains its currency. Healy (2, 3) viewed the problem more broadly, seeing broken homes and poor parental control as antecedent conditions to delinquency. Cyril Burt (4), whose work has evoked recent interest because of evidence of psychopathy in its production, stressed the etiologic importance of the 'family drama" discussed by Aichhorn (5) and Alexander (6). Bowlby (7) described the affectionless character and developed the concept of maternal deprivation as etiologic in juvenile thieves.

Childhood loss and bereavement, especially before the age of five, are related to antisocial behavior. Some of the sadness of the psychopath relates to the high frequency of loss of parent (by death, divorce or disengagement) and its attendant deprivation (8, 9). The repeated pain of this loss is associated with both irrational guilt at having "caused the loss" and rage at the resulting deprivation (7). These affects must be defended against; both acting out behaviors (truancy, theft, etc.) and closing over behaviors (callousness, failure to form close relationships, etc.) ensue. The sense of betrayal experienced by the child and the lack of stable, dependable identification models leads to a pervasive, intense rebellion against authority (10). Such hatred contains within it its own self-destructive punishment. This process often takes place in a sociocultural milieu in which values are inconsistent or countercultural, with intermittent reinforcement, leading to consistently antisocial behavior.

There has been much debate about the relative importance of various types of parental loss *vis à vis* antisocial behavior. The data seem to suggest that loss of father has more untoward effects related to the development of sociopathy, while loss of the opposite-sexed parent is more associated with subsequent depression (11).

After Bowlby's work the focus of attention shifted. The McCords' (12), Jenkins' (13) and the Gluecks' (14) work related psychopathy to parental rejection. Johnson and Szurek (15) provided the first paper which looked at antisocial behavior arising from a specific familial context. As the first to emphasize an interactive aspect, they were the forerunners of the subsequent family system perspective. Szurek (16) points out that the psychodynamics of the psychopathic person become "no great mystery" when both parents and child are studied concurrently. The concept of the superego lacunae developed by Johnson and Szurek (15) states that the identified patient is acting out the unconscious impulse of the parent or parents. The neurotic needs of the parent are met vicariously through the child's acting out. The parents displace any self-punishment to the antisocial child through expression of hostility. The child may get some impulse gratification, while the family system is maintained through the scapegoating of the "sick" or "evil" members.

While the notion of the superego lacunae was originally developed for the family system, it can be applied to other larger systems without extensive modification. Any system ambivalent about certain impulses or societal restrictions may transmit its ambivalence by inconsistent limit-setting.

In a correctional or therapeutic facility the treatment team can reproduce the conflictual family complete with superego lacunae, thus encouraging the very acting out the program may be designed to "treat." Szurek's awareness of this possibility in treatment teams was subsequently graphically illustrated in work on psychiatric units by Caudill (17), Stanton and Schwartz (18) and Rapoport (19). The elucidation of staff communication dysfunction, the importance of therapeutic triads, ward mood oscillations, and so forth are modern contributions to the understanding of acting-out behaviors in the therapeutic context. The clear relationship of psychopathic acting out in the hospital to the staff's communication problems, and the parallel of staff dynamics to family dynamics are seen in Rockwell's work (20, 21).

Two contemporary strands of this thread are evident in the drug abuse literature. Although drug abuse is not synonymous with our primary topic, it remains a close relative. The role of familial sanctions for superego lacunae is seen in the addictor-addictee relationship. There are repeated examples in the substance abuse area in which the substance abuser is condemned for being a "drunk" or "hooked" while simultaneously being actively supported in that pursuit. The "easy rider" syndrome, in which—because of familial and interactive conditions—a male heroin addict is supported by a female partner, illustrates this perspective (22). The addictor-addictee relationship is well formulated by Little and Pearson (23) and confirmed by studies of addicts' wives (24) and parents (25) and by clinical experience with "alcoholic" couples. At an even larger systems level one can speculate that American cultural values about alcohol and drugs (ambivalence, inconsistency) are reflected in their widespread abuse (26).

We find, then, that the psychopath's behavior is inextricably bound up in a series of systems—first familial, later societal. These systems may in fact support the behaviors they condemn through social system dynamics and/or intermittent reinforcement.

The apparent role of the father in the family drama was curiously seen as a small and, at best, passive, distant one until Andry's work (27). Beginning with Andry, the father came under careful scrutiny. More recently paternal influence has assumed primacy as the result of Robins' seminal *Deviant Children Grown Up* (28). Robins' work is exemplary in both approach and depth. It goes far toward destroying much mythology about the development of antisocial behaviors and toward providing leads for further investigation. Robins is clear in her denigration of many of the characteristics used clinically to describe the antisocial character. Descriptions using words such as "callousness," "guiltlessness," "uncaring," "unloyal," etc., in others' work represent inferences and are highly value-laden. Robins and her associates have taken a more descriptive, operationally-defined behavioristic approach in order to avoid to a great extent the value-laden, the subjective, and the inferential. It is worth noting that George Vaillant's article on sociopathy (25) from a contemporary ego psychoanalytic viewpoint represents another challenge to the description of the psychopath as nonanxious, unloyal, callous, etc.

Earlier experience of working with psychopathic characters both supports and refutes Robins' and Vaillant's contentions. There are times when the psychopath illustrates the anxiety, caring and learning to which Vaillant refers. There are also times at which he elicits in the therapist a tremendous urge toward social control and punitive sanctions. The problem of a scientific *versus* a social control perspective is not a readily resolvable one, either personally or professionally.

In any case, much that has been written about psychopathy is palpably incorrect if we accept the results of Robins' careful work. This work has done for the background of the psychopath what Cleckley (29) did for his description.

It is now accepted that, contrary to what has often been said, the antisocial personality frequently has disabling neurotic symptoms. Alexander's description (6) of patients "living out their impulses" and acting out to solve conflicts now has new meaning. We know that for the psychopath the major parental influence is paternal rather than maternal. The psychopath frequently has a psychopathic paternal identification model; 65% of the fathers of psychopaths exhibit sociopathic behavior while mothers are not necessarily antisocial, although they often have other more typically psychophysiologic or neurotic symptoms.

In Robins' work, parental predictors of antisocial behavior in their adult children included antisocial behavior, arersts, desertion by either parent, father's chronic unemployment, excessive drinking and failure to support the family. Non-physically-abusing but cold fathers produced significantly fewer sociopathic children. Robins speculates that coldness is a descriptor of strict disciplinarian fathers and that this functions as a deterrent to adult sociopathy. Sociopathic fathers clearly played a strategic role in the development of sociopathic children since if the mother alone were sociopathic the children were not especially likely to develop sociopathy. Children with neither a severely antisocial father nor multiple antisocial symptoms as juveniles rarely developed into adult sociopaths. The degree of discipline and supervision exerted by parents also played a role in the development of sociopathy, with increasing frequency of sociopathy as leniency and lack of supervision increased. Furthermore, parental discord was not "an important determinant of sociopathic behavior" in Robins' work, and differential association (learning from sociopathic siblings or peers) appeared to play little role in producing sociopathic behavior.

True sociopathy never develops *de novo* in adulthood but is established prior to ages 12 to 15 and is potentially predictable by age six. Rarely, if ever, do we see severely antisocial behavior in adults arising from children growing up in "normal" families, in spite of Cleckley's view that this is not uncommon. *In the absence of childhood antisocial symptoms, things usually associated with a "bad" background—broken home, impoverishment, social disorganization, even sociopathic parenting—do not apparently lead to chronic adult antisocial behavior.*

SOCIALIZATION

Although the family is the earliest socializing agency, it is not the sole or perhaps even the most crucial one, even given the evident pathology seen in the prior section. The parameters of socialization of human behavior have been increasingly well delineated. Characteristic of human development is integration into a highly complex social organization with a high degree of specialization of both instrumental and affective function. Human development is marked by a long period of dependency in which socialization of control, conformity, and postponement of immediate gratification is prominent. Familial support for socialization into psychopathic behavior is clear-cut from Robins' works. However, in addition to the socializing agents other parameters are important.

We know that negative and positive sanctions are applied irregularly to the psychopath—both during and after early development. Rarely are sanctions immediate and clear. The experience of the psychopath is one in which legal sanctions are delayed and increasingly fuzzy. Although delinquent behavior is described as rampant (30), the cultural values about such behavior may be ambivalent; a piece of behavior seen as innocuous in one context may be strongly condemned at another time and in a different context. The young sociopath both is confused by and takes advantage of such cultural chaos. While Robins plays down the role of peer group influence in the etiology of psychopathy, it remains a reality for the clinician. The passive youth can, as a result of a deviant or subculturally enforced peer group, assume psychopathic behaviors and ultimately a psychopathic identity in the absence of other more appropriate models. Bandura's social learning theory supports this viewpoint (31).

Support for viewing psychopathy and other forms of deviance as a process of "commitments" in a progressive career is widespread in the sociologic literature. The McCords (32) elucidate this principle for the delinquent career. Primary proponents of this orientation include Becker (33), Schur (34), Goffman (35), and Erikson (36). The major drawback of this sociologic perspective is its difficulty in explaining exceptions to the rule—those persons growing up in psychopathic milieus who do not themselves become psychopaths.

Harrison Gough (37) developed a theory of deficient role-taking ability in the psychopath. From this viewpoint the antisocial character lacks the ability to take the role of the other and therefore plays roles in an "as if" way, models a social façade, or operates nearly randomly in his expectations of others' reactions to him. The McCords also see the inability to identify with others as a key problem. It seems likely that this applies to at least a small subset of psychopaths.

SOCIAL CONTEXT INFLUENCES

The early work of Stanton and Schwartz (18) and Caudill (17) focused attention on the promotion of acting out behaviors by larger systems. Expectations about given behaviors clearly tend to lead to the production of such behaviors in a self-fulfilling prophecy. Covert system conflict and blocked communication at various levels of organizational life can produce individual acting out behaviors (social deviance, poor morale, etc.) and collective disturbance at the group level. The notion originally put forth by W. I. Thomas (38) that what people perceive as real is real in its consequences was ultimately applied to the general treatment of psychiatric patients and later specifically adapted to psychopathic characters by Thomas Main (39), Maxwell Jones (40), and others via the therapeutic community. This was subsequently incorporated into the labeling perspective (discussed below) and finally into the "myth of mental illness" paradigm.

While the latter two notions may go too far, respectful attention should be paid to the social context of sociopathic behavior. Haney and Zimbardo's (41) fascinating study which turned normal college students into sadistic guards and passive-aggressive cons within a very short time is a striking example of situational behavior demand. In essence, they make a case for the plasticity (or superficiality) of individual behavior given strong contextual cues. Milgram's (42) work on authority supports the contention that humans are not nearly as firmly socialized and civilized as we would like to believe. Recent reports on contextual reinforcement for addicts' drug seeking and using behaviors (43) and even on the actual social conditioning and reinforcement of the drug experience (44) point further to the importance of environmental cues in a variety of psychopathic behaviors. Manne (45) postulates an early learned action orientation based on nonverbal communication. We shall return later to the ways in which society and subcultures may "pull" for antisocial behaviors over and above the individual or familial push for such behaviors.*

A second line of research in this area is that of the social ecologists, most prominently exemplified by Moos (46) and others (47, 48). Galle et al. indicate that asocial aggressive behavior is highly correlated with population density even when social class and ethnicity are controlled (47). Ghetto redevelopment has taught us much about psychoarchitectural influences on antisocial behavior, usually through disastrous examples. The McCords (32) note that specific crimes are related to specific home environments. In many ways, then, the social milieu, both personal and impersonal, may foster or inhibit sociopathic behavior. While this approach is too new to utilize for predictions, it is an intriguing one.

THE SOCIOPATHIC CAREER

Once an individual has embarked upon a career of sociopathic behaviors, it is striking how infrequently he will change course. Much has been written about the "burn out" of sociopathy. For the most part this refers to the decreasing aggressivity of the adult sociopath or the decreasing drug dependence of the heroin addict between 30 and 40 years of age. The sociologic perspective would suggest that this is due to adult

---

*The recent antisocial behavior during New York's blackout raises the question of whether sociopathic decompensation is only "a light bulb away" in many subcultures.

socialization while the personality perspective suggests that it represents late blooming maturity.

In all probability the "burn out" represents at least four separate avenues out of sociopathy. For the hyperaggressive or drug dependent, death —by accident, homicide, or suicide—is likely. The aggressive sociopath with increasing age becomes more passive (a change related to environmental and/or biologic influences) and hence less visible as a social problem. Frequently this means taking on a "legitimate" sick role. Other "burned out" people will have switched from an antisocial sociopathy to a prosocial sociopathy, as in going from alcoholic to AA member or from drug user to drug counselor, or in experiencing religious conversion. Finally, the normative developmental crisis of the 30s and especially the midlife crisis of the 40s may allow the sociopathic person a new perspective as well as opportunities for growth and the development of a relationship, overriding earlier fears of the potential pain of such closeness and dependency. Vaillant's work, in particular, suggests this optimistic possibility. The frequencies with which these pathways are followed remain a subject for empirical investigation.

The psychopath's career leaves a wide swath of destruction. The systems he encounters pay a price. His sadness is shared by those with whom he comes in contact. His family of origin and conjugal family bear the greatest burden. The family system trades off a pathologic homeostasis for a pervasive feeling of despair and failure, not to mention an endless chain of economic and social sorrow. Because of the interactive nature of psychopathy, the manipulator and manipulatee are often interchangeable; the "con" succeeds with the "mark" because he appeals to the "mark's" sociopathic side.

In addition, the family and larger social systems provide intermittent reinforcement. Families of origin rarely successfully "disown" their psychopathic member. Later, the psychopath must enter into a pathologic marital relationship in order to retain his brittle stability. Unless the couple succeeds in getting past the psychopath's terror of intimacy, they reproduce the cycle anew in their children. Societies' systems likewise collude to reinforce psychopathic behavior (if we accept a functionalist view of deviance). These, then, are the social and familial correlates of the psychopath's personal sadness.

SOCIOPATHY AS SOCIETY

Contemporary American culture is in a state of flux. A major element in that flux is the process of changing values. As values change many families may be caught at transition points; e.g., values prominent in parental systems may be unshared or unshareable by children. Sociopathy has been and can be construed as a value illness. The inability to identify with parental values leads to idiosyncratic narcissistic value systems. Hence, we see a growth in numbers of sociopathic symptoms.

One would be hard pressed to say that sociopathy has not become modal behavior. The evidence for white collar crime, the retreat from altruism, the emphasis on "here and now" gratification, and so on, represent palpable outcroppings in "normal" America. As is often the case in mental health we have focused on the pathologic at the expense of an understanding of the overall continuum. What about the background factors that produce the *creative* sociopath (cf. 49)? Only recently have we begun to study not only the failures of the multiproblem family but also those members who survive unscathed or even excel in spite of psychotoxic environments. Clinicians will rarely see these outcomes.

Can we say that society currently reinforces sociopathic behavior? Again, the evidence would seem to indicate that we do provide a surprising amount of intermittent reinforcement. One can well speculate that we have come out of the age of anxiety and into an age of sociopathy.

TREATMENT

In the absence of clear etiology, "treatment" of the antisocial personality is at best empirical. Considering the social and familial correlates discussed above we can infer some courses of action. Unfortunately, none of the treatment programs are "proved" from a scientific perspective. Given a "burn out" or spontaneous improvement rate of 35-40% occurring at a median age of 35, claims for therapeutic success must necessarily exceed this rate.

For each social and cultural correlate we can point to a therapeutic enthusiast. Wolfgang Lederer (50), for example, using an analytic approach, offers replacement therapy for the absent father. Vaillant (25) suggests a series of preconditions necessary for the insight oriented psychotherapy of the psychopath. Family therapists involve the family and other systems. Therapeutic communities and prisons based on therapeutic community models have their advocates. At broader social levels the elimination of poverty is proposed to eliminate much symptomatology (51). The consistent theme throughout seems to be a focus on locking the psychopath into a stable milieu in which the *therapist's countertransference* is looked at in great detail. The previous pessimism and hopelessness of therapists are unwarranted, and yet we cannot be sure that what we do can be shown to be helpful. In that sense we may unfortunately end in sharing the sadness of the psychopath.

We are in the position of psychiatry of 70 years ago. In that era much of what we now say about the treatment of the psychopath was said about treatment of the neurotic. With the very significant refinement of the definition and our understanding of the genesis of psychopathy, new treatment forms are to be anticipated.

AN ALTERNATIVE EXPLANATION

Until these new understandings and treatments evolve it is worthwhile to suggest still another paradigm. The value of a paradigm rests in its ability to foster creative thinking and research which expands our understanding in some area. We have a number of facts about psychopathy that are not explained adequately by social and familial or other correlates. These include:

1. There is a 5:1 to 10:1 preponderance of males to females in diagnosis of psychopathy. Guze et al. (52) point to close associations among male psychopathy, female "hysteria," and parental—especially paternal—psychopathy and alcoholism.
2. Core or primary psychopathy is a distinct syndrome with no proved effective treatment.
3. Much of what is written about psychopathy is value-laden description.
4. There appear to be familial and environmental predicates which are often contradictory in their proposed impact.
5. There is a "burn out" phenomenon affecting about one-third or more of persons diagnosed as psychopathic, usually between the ages of 30 and 40 (53).
6. There is a failure to explain on usual learning theory grounds the psychopath's peculiar insensitivity to learning and to generalization.
7. The psychopath is probably neuropsychologically deviant from "normals" (cf. Chapter 10).
8. One can argue for evidence of significant genetic influence (cf. Chapter 13).
9. There seems to be an increased frequency of psychopathic behavior in Western society as a whole.

In view of the apparent failure of our usual paradigms to help us understand these aspects of sociopathic behavior, an alternative paradigm might be considered. Should that paradigm offer to explain the previously unexplainable we would at least have to consider it. If, further, it offered an approach to test its validity we would be hard pressed to dismiss it.

Sociobiology (54) has recently burst, with much controversy, upon the scientific scene. Like all new ideas it has proselytes and rabid opponents. This epiphenomena, however, obscure the need to scientifically assess its value as a paradigm. Very briefly, the major tenets of sociobiology are as follows (55). Sociobiology is concerned with interpreting behavior in ultimate terms. Evolution (natural selection) influences traits in which there is a correlation between genotype and phenotype. Genotype and environment contribute in varying degrees to behavior. Even the most complex human behavior is influenced by genotype, and behavior patterns are subject to natural selection. Reproductive success is crucial to natural selection. Behaviors that improve reproductive success will be increasingly represented in the genetic pool. When any behavior reflects some component of genotype, animals should behave to maximize their inclusive fitness—usually by maximizing the production of successful (genotype success) offspring. This is the control theorem of sociobiology. The major focus then is on natural selection at a most interesting level—the level of the gene rather than the individual or species.

This brief statement significantly reduces the concept of sociobiology but does capture its essence. Not surprisingly, it has been widley attacked, usually at the *ad hominem* or political level rather than scientifically.

Let us look for a moment at sociopathic behavior in this sociobiologic context. It is widely agreed that intermediate variables representing genotypic expression have been discovered. The sociopath is neuropsychologically deviant; Hare's work is persuasive in this area. One can then argue that there is evidence for genetic influence. Sociobiologists have no difficulty acknowledging environmental influence but ask that we look beyond that. Sociobiologic explanations for the findings of Robins and others should at least give us some cause for study.

Neither psychological nor sociocultural theory explains why sociopathy is predominately a male phenomenon (and hysteria-hypochondriasis a female phenomenon). Are the phenotypic representations of sociopathy and hysteria-hypochondriasis selected for as a result of reproductive behaviors? Certainly the behaviors themselves represent primordial (or unsocialized) characteristics of maleness and femaleness. While biology is not destiny, it certainly is an influence. For ultimate survival—in an evolutionary sense—reproduction of one's genes is mandatory. Childbearing is necessarily limited to females and evolution has selected behaviors to foster reproduction. Sexual promiscuity and associated characteristics in men—failure to provide, desertion, separation—all serve to enhance the genetic presence of these males by increasing the possibility of passing on their gene pool, especially if in so doing they do not risk death of their progeny. If we now look at Robins' work we find that some anti-social behavior might be directly related to this. The marital history of 81% of male antisocial personalities reveals two or more divorces and/or repeated separations, as well as 64% who had arrests on charges pertaining to sex and/or extreme promiscuity (50+ partners) (28).

The major difficulties with current sociobiologic theorizing are that it both goes too far, speculating for example on a biologic basis for rape (56) or the "double standard" (55), and does so without adequate data. The power of the theory, however, is striking. Barash—on the basis of "divorce" in kittiwake gulls—predicts an increase in divorce among humans following the death of a young child (55). As clinicians we know this to be the case; coming from Barash, a biologist, it seems a striking prediction. Moving from the paradigm we might well discover that psychopathy carries a reproductive benefit. It does not, however, imply that this is then biologic and immutable. It would imply that a higher level of environmental intervention is necessary in order to redirect the genetic/environmental program. The approach bears examination.

LABELING AND ITS CONSEQUENCES

A final polemic on the labeling of the sociopath is in order. The labeling perspective suggests that once a behavior has been named it becomes increasingly easy to reinforce that name and very difficult for the labeled one to shed the label. Some have gone so far as to say that much deviance is really secondary to the labeling and societal reaction to the label, rather than to the behavior itself. Particularly when the label is stigmatizing or frankly pejorative we may produce what we hope to dissemble. Examples abound in both the experimental and real world. Once defined as a problem child ("retarded," "bad," "sick," etc.), a child has real difficulty being seen apart from his label and often ultimately accepts the labeled identity even in the face of overwhelming evidence to the contrary. The labeling process is understandable and useful in the short run. Nevertheless, we must recognize its potential for negative consequences. Experts in criminology and delinquency are coming to the recognition that the very system designed to eliminate sociopathic, delinquent and criminal behavior in point of fact institutionalizes and fosters it. Alternatives are by no means evident, however. Suffice to say that it is important for us to recognize several things. First, judgments about psychopathic behavior always contain a value judgment; making those values explicit is helpful. Second, the label of psychopathy—whether or not it is rephrased as "sociopathy" or "antisocial personality"—will invariably carry a pejorative meaning. Third, because of the above, the diagnosis and treatment of psychopathy always contain a social control aspect. Awareness of the degree of that element is important. It may at some times be reasonable to be in the role of a "behavior cop" but this role must be explicit in the therapist's mind. Finally, and most difficult, we need to be aware of the consequences of our labeling. "The psychopath" about *which* we so glibly write is in fact a person about *whom* we must care.

REFERENCES

1. GREENACRE, P. *Trauma, Growth and Personality.* New York: University Press, 1952.
2. HEALY, W. *The Individual Delinquent.* London: Heinemann, 1915.
3. HEALY, W. and BRONNER, A. F. *Delinquents and Criminals: Their Making and Unmaking.* New York: MacMillan, 1925.
4. BURT, C. *The Young Delinquent.* London: University of London Press, 1944.
5. AICHHORN, A. *Wayward Youth.* New York: Viking Press, 1935.
6. ALEXANDER, F. The Neurotic Character. *Int. J. Psychoanal.* 11:292-311, 1930.
7. BOWLBY, J. *Maternal Care and Mental Mealth, Monograph Series #2,* WHO, Geneva, 1951.
8. GREER, S. Study of Parental Loss in Neurotics and Sociopaths. *Arch. Gen. Psychiatry* 11:177-80, 1964.
9. OLTMAN, J. and FRIEDMAN, S. Parental Deprivation in Psychiatric Conditions. *Dis. Nerv. Syst.* 28:298-303, 1967.
10. WITMER, H. L. and KOTINSKY, R. (Eds.). *New Perspectives for Research in Juvenile Delinquency.* U. S. Child Bureau Public. #356, 1956.
11. BUNCH, J., BARRACLOUGH, B., NELSON, B. and SAINSBURY, P. Early Parental Bereavement and Suicide. *Social Psychiatry* 6:200-202, 1971.
12. McCORD, W. and McCORD, J. *Psychopathy and Delinquency.* New York: Grune and Stratton, 1956.
13. JENKINS, R. L. Psychiatric Syndromes in Children and their Relation to Family Background. *Am. J. Orthopsychiatry* 36:450-57, 1966.
14. GLUECK, S. and GLUECK, E. *Unraveling Juvenile Delinquency.* Cambridge, MA: Harvard University Press, 1950.
15. JOHNSON, A. and SZUREK, S. The Genesis of Antisocial Acting Out in Children and Adults. *Psychoanal. Q.* 21:323-43, 1952.
16. SZUREK, S. Notes on the Genesis of Psychopathic Trends. *Psychiatry* 5:1-6, 1942.
17. CADILL, W. *The Psychiatric Hospital as a Small Society.* Cambridge, MA: Harvard Press, 1958.
18. STANTON, A. and SCHWARTZ, M. *The Mental Hospital.* New York: Basic Books, 1954.
19. RAPOPORT, R. *Community as Doctor.* Springfield, IL: Charles C Thomas, 1960.
20. ROCKWELL, D. A. Some Observations on 'Living In.' *Psychiatry* 34:214-23, 1971.
21. ROCKWELL, D. A. Psychiatric Residents' Disease: Social System Contributions to Residents' Emotional Problems. *Int. J. Soc. Psychiatry* 19:226-29, 1973.
22. WELLISCH, D. K., GAY, G. R. and McENTEE, R. The Easy Rider Syndrome. *Family Process* 9:425-430, 1970.
23. LITTLE, R. and PEARSON, M. The Management of Pathologic Interdependency in Drug Addiction. *Am. J. Psychiatry* 123:554-560, 1966.
24. TAYLOR, S., WILBUR, M. and OSNOS, R. The Wives of Drug Addicts. *Am. J. Psychiatry* 123:585-591, 1966.
25. VAILLANT, G. Sociopathy as a Human Process. *Arch. Gen. Psychiatry* 32:178-183, 1975.

26. ROCKWELL, D. A. Alcohol and Marijuana—Social Problems Perspective. *Br. J. Addict.* 68:209-214, 1973.
27. ANDRY, R. G. *Delinquency and Parental Pathology.* London: Methuen & Co., 1960.
28. ROBINS, L. *Deviant Children Grown Up.* Baltimore: Williams & Wilkins, 1966.
29. CLECKLEY, H. *The Mask of Sanity.* St. Louis: C. V. Mosby, 1964.
30. RAFFERTY, F. Juvenile Delinquency and Antisocial Behavior. *Psychiatr. Annals* 6:321-24, 1976.
31. BANDURA, A. and WALTERS, R. H. *Social Learning and Personality Development.* New York: Holt, Rinehart & Wilson, 1963.
32. McCORD, W., McCORD, J. and ZOLA, I. *Origins of Crime.* New York: Columbia University Press, 1959.
33. BOCKER, H. *Outsiders.* New York: Free Press, 1963.
34. SCHUR, E. M. *Crimes Without Victims.* Englewood Cliffs, N.J.: Prentice Hall, 1965.
35. GOFFMAN, E. *Asylums.* Chicago: Aldine Press, 1961.
36. ERIKSON, K. T. *Wayward Puritans.* New York: John Wiley & Sons, 1966.
37. GOUGH, H. G. A Sociological Theory of Psychopathy. *Am. J. Sociol.* 53:359-66, 1948.
38. THOMAS, W. I. In: *On Social Organization and Social Personality. Selected Papers.* M. Janowitz (Ed.). Chicago: University of Chicago Press, 1966.
39. MAIN, T. F. The Hospital as a Therapeutic Institution. *Bull. Menninger Clin.* 10:66-70, 1964.
40. JONES, M. *The Therapeutic Community.* New York: Basic Books, 1953.
41. HANEY, C. and ZIMBARDO, P. G. The Socialization into Criminality: On Becoming a Prisoner and a Guard. In: *Legal Socialization: Issues for Psychology and Law.* J. Tapp and F. Levine (Eds.). New York: Holt, Rinehart & Wilson, 1975.
42. MILGRAM, S. *Obedience to Authority: An Experimental View.* New York: Harper & Row, 1974.
43. WIKLER, A. Dynamics of Drug Dependence. *Arch. Gen. Psychiatry* 28:611-626, 1973.
44. BEJEROT, N. A Theory of Addiction as an Artificially Induced Drive. *Am. J. Psychiatry* 128:842-846, 1972.
45. MANNE, S. H. A Communication Theory of Sociopathic Personality. *Am. J. Psychother.* XXI:797-807, 1967.
46. MOOS, R. *Evaluating Treatment Environments.* New York: Wiley, 1972.
47. GALLE, O. R., GOVE, W. R. and McPHERSON, J. M. Population Density and Pathology: What are the Relations for Man? *Science* 176:23-30, 1972.
48. BARKER, R. G. *Ecological Psychology.* Stanford, Ca.: Stanford University Press, 1968.
49. MACCOBY, M. *The Gamesman.* New York: Simon & Schuster, 1976.
50. LEDERER, W. Dragons, Delinquents and Destiny. *Psychological Issues* IV #3 Monograph 15, 1-85, 1964.
51. KENISTON, K. *All Our Children.* New York: Harcourt, Brace, Jovanovich, 1977.
52. GUZE, S., WOODRUFF, R. and CLAYTON, R. Hysteria and Antisocial Behavior: Further Evidence of an Association. *Am. J. Psychiatry* 127:957-60, 1971.
53. VAILLANT, E. E. A 20-year Followup of New York Narcotic Addicts. *Arch. Gen. Psychiatry* 29:237-241, 1973.
54. WILSON, E. O. *Sociobiology, The New Synthesis.* Cambridge, Ma.: Harvard University Press, 1975.
55. BARASH, D. *Sociobiology and Behavior.* New York: Elsevier, 1977.
56. BARASH, D. Sociobiology of Rape in Mallards: Responses of the Mated Male. *Science* 197:788-789, 1977.

8

Neurological Aspects of Antisocial Behavior

FRANK A. ELLIOTT, M.D.

It is a truism that our behavior is shaped by genetic endowment, by physical events affecting the brain from embryonic life onwards, by experience, and by what we learn from the precepts and practice of others. The purpose of this chapter is not to derogate environmental determinism or the role of psychodynamics, but to focus on neurological disorders, developmental or acquired, which contribute to psychopathic behavior.

Neurologists, of course, are apt to be biased in favor of physical explanations for such behavior, and this bias is strengthened by several considerations. First, there is the role of genetic factors as evidenced by both twin and adoption studies, and by the prevalence of abnormal EEG's in the parents of many psychopaths. Second, from 50% to 80% of psychopaths exhibit abnormal EEG's. Third, almost all of the clinical features of the psychopath can be produced by physical disorders of the brain. Fourth, despite statistical evidence linking psychopathy and emotional deprivation in early life, it is also true that not all psychopaths have been thus deprived; conversely, many—perhaps most—emotionally deprived children do not become psychopaths, though many of them bear emotional scars.

Benjamin Rush (1) shared this bias. Speaking of the "total perversion of the moral faculties" in "persons of sound understanding and some uncommon talents" who exhibited "innate preternatural moral depravity," he postulated that "there is probably an original defective organiza-

146

tion in those parts of the body which are occupied by the moral faculties of the mind." He went on to say that "Such persons are in pre-eminent degree objects of compassion, and it is the business of medicine to aid both religion and the law in preventing and curing their moral alienation of mind."

In 1835 Prichard (2), writing about "moral insanity," was more precise. He commented that "the power of self government is lost or greatly impaired in the individual, who is found to be incapable, not of talking or reasoning on any subject proposed to him, but of conducting himself in decency and propriety in the business of life," a description which often comes to mind when one is faced with a psychopath. Since then the list of symptoms has been expanded to include inadequately motivated antisocial behavior, aggression, absence of conscience (and therefore absence of neurotic anxiety), inability to distinguish between truth and falsehood or between fact and fantasy, lack of insight, lack of judgment when faced with alternative courses of action, failure to learn by experience (including punishment), imperception, lack of natural affection, impersonal response to sexual partners, absence of a normal sense of fear, capacity for ingratiation, impulsivenes, total egocentricity with constant disregard for other people's feelings and interests, inability to foresee or worry about the results of their actions, and proneness to pathological intoxication by alcohol (3-6). In consequence their lives reveal "a persistent pattern of self defeat" (3).

Such are the pieces of the mosaic; but all are not necessarily present in every case. Many marginal cases display only fragments of the mosaic, as for instance individuals who are not without conscience and who are capable of affectionate ties with others, but who are prone to episodic behavioral disorders akin to those of the psychopath—inadequately motivated aggression, lack of judgment, failure to learn by experience, imperception, and impulsiveness. *Organic disorders tend to produce a "partial" psychopath rather than the fully fledged classical picture as described above.* However, this does not exclude the possibility that physical insults in early life may delay maturation and the acquisition of adult social values and responses, thereby producing classical psychopathy.

PSYCHOPATHIC BEHAVIOR ASSOCIATED WITH

ORGANIC DISEASE OF THE BRAIN

Perhaps the most dramatic example of the link between organic disease and psychopathic behavior was provided by the epidemic of encephalitis lethargica in the second and third decades of this century. Psychological disorders appeared in at least 30% of the children it attacked. After the acute phase had passed, disturbances of behavior developed, sometimes in the absence of intellectual impairment or nuerological defects. Kinnier Wilson (7) described it thus: "The moral and social sense of the patient suffers eclipse, a feature impressing itself on even the most casual observer. His misdemeanors range over the whole gamut of juvenile depravity from lying and petty pilfering to offenses against the person. Such changes in conduct seem always to be for the worse and might be taken to lend evidential support to the doctrine of original sin; a child of previous responsible character may be so transformed as actually to seem a different person. Impish, cruel, destructive, abusive, indecent, he may become guilty of any offense from naughtiness to crime . . . a creature of impulse, the child's opportunist policy of social offense thrives on the material he finds at hand . . . when taken to task, some at least of these juvenile delinquents show genuine regret."

On the same subject, Bender (8) reports, "These children are destructive and impulsive. Impulses are immediately translated into action. Inhibitions and fear of consequences are lacking. They steal, lie, destroy property, set fires, and commit sex offenses. They do not try to avoid detection and claim that they cannot help their conduct. They are indifferent to punishment. When they express remorse, this does not modify their behavior." Kanner (9) notes that these children "lose any feelings of empathy, are cruel, hit their playmates, parents, and teachers, use profanity, lie, steal, wander away from home, and drive their environment to despair. Threats, punishment, rewards and admonitions have, at best, only temporary results. Some children do for the moment regret their behavior, apologize, and make promises, and are sincere in what they say. They often feel that they could not help it, that some irresistible force had driven them to act as they did. Any regret, however, is transitory and impulsive behavior continues."

In commenting on the post-encephalitic psychopathic personality, Craft suggests that the damage to the personality might have been the result of adverse environmental circumstances in early life, which would predispose them to develop psychopathic characteristics later on. He points out that those who observed these children did not investigate this possibility and that the types of encephalitis which occur today do not seem to produce psychopathic personalities (4). There are several objections to this argument. The pathology of encephalitis lethargica differs from that of other forms of viral encephalitis. Secondly, psychopathic behavior *can* follow viral encephalitis in children who have not been subjected to emotional or other deprivation prior to the encephalitis; the author has three such cases in treatment. Third, psychological aftereffects occurred in no less than one-third of the children who suffered from encephalitis lethargica; it is unlikely that environmental stress could have been responsible for gross departures from normality in so many individuals.

Trauma to the brain can convert a normal child into the facsimile of a psychopath; this can also occur in adults. As a cause of psychopathic behavior, head injury should not be underrated. Caveness (10) estimated that, in 1974, 1.9 million people in the United States suffered from head trauma. Behavioral sequelae of some of these injuries are a common part of any psychiatric or neurologic practice.

The American Crowbar Case of 1868 is an early example of what a frontal injury can do to a man's personality:

> Phineas Gage was an efficient and capable foreman until an accidental explosion forced an iron bar nearly 4 feet long and 1¼ inches thick through his head, damaging the left temporal and both frontal lobes. He was stunned for a short period and then walked, with help, to see a doctor. Thereafter he became unreliable, irreverent, profane, lacking consideration for his fellows, impatient of discipline or advice, and capricious. He devised many plans for the future but they were no sooner arranged than he abandoned them for others. He completely lacked control over his own behavior (11).

The most common sites of contusion in closed head injuries are the anterior temporal and prefrontal lobes, areas of the brain which are particularly concerned with social behavior patterns. Personality changes can also result from multiple minor injuries—as in the punch-drunk syndrome of pugilists—but are more commonly seen following severe injuries with prolonged post-traumatic amnesia. The patient may be apathetic or belligerent, or both. He or she may become shameless, careless as to appearance, irresponsible in domestic and financial matters, without natural affection for spouse or children, and unscrupulous. In most cases there is also evidence of intellectual impairment—memory suffers, thinking is slow, and the capacity for abstract thought is blunted.

Explosive rage in response to minimal provocation is common. Blau described this result of head trauma in children in 1936: "Common antisocial trends include unrestrained aggressiveness, destructiveness, quarrelsomeness, cruelty to younger children and animals, lying and stealing. Their whole personality is essentially egocentric and self-interested, with total disregard for the welfare of others" (12). Black and his colleagues later studied the extent to which behavioral disorders before trauma predisposed to similar disorders after head injury. This is a particularly valuable study because children ranging in age from birth to

14 years were registered for prospective study when they entered the hospital for treatment of their acute injury. Of those who had had pretraumatic symptoms, 36% acquired new symptoms or exhibited severe aggravation of premorbid traits. Approximately one-fifth of the whole group developed behavioral problems attributable to the injury (13).

A third example of psychopathic behavior associated with developmental or acquired disorders of the brain is provided by some of the children affected with the syndrome of minimal brain dysfunction (14-18). These children may be of normal or above average intelligence, but do not live up to their intelligence when it comes to performance. Hyperkinesis is common. Attention span is often poor and they are easily distracted. Sometimes there is perseveration. Memory may be poor or exceptionally good. Perception is often blunted and as a result the child's responses to social situations may be inappropriate, because he does not perceive the cues which are so important to interpersonal relationships. Specific learning difficulties are common and may involve speech, reading, writing, mathematics, left-right orientation, or the capacity to learn geographical relationships. Because of the last, these children tend to get lost easily. Some have no fear of heights or other hazards. Their thinking tends to be concrete and their judgment poor. Lacking foresight, they are unable to foresee the results of their actions. Many are apt to talk a good deal, but not to listen. They are impulsive and some are aggressive. Their emotions are labile and they are given to temper trantrums. Their stress threshold is low. Affect is often shallow. Lacking in insight, they are not embarrassed by their own behavior and as they grow older they are at a loss to know why they generate antipathy, tending then to project blame. Cruelty to animals is not uncommon. They often run away from school or home and some of them display little capacity for spontaneous affectionate behavior. Many do not respond to punishment (19).

Minor neurological defects are common. Some of these children are clumsy. The child may not learn to skip, to run, to hop, or to ride a bicycle at the expected age, and manual clumsiness may be noticed in his/ her manipulation of toys. Some do well in one form of activity and badly in another—for instance, manual dexterity may be good for everything except writing. A child, who can run perfectly well, may fail to ride a bicycle. Dyspraxia is common, especially in bimanual tasks ("He didn't learn to do up his shoelaces until he was 16.") Activities requiring visuospatial organization are often badly performed; thus a child who is able to walk normally on flat surfaces may have difficulty in going up and down stairs. Minor involuntary movements are not uncommon—action tremor of the hands or mild choreiform movements. Synkinesia may be excessive. Some signs, such as astereognosis or impaired graphesthesia or two-point discrimination will escape notice unless the child happens to have had a careful neurological examination.

Such defects handicap the child in many ways. Not only do they impair the individual's capacity to learn and adjust to circumstances but, in some families, they create emotional problems by evoking antipathy on the part of the parents, siblings, and peers, thus contributing to a vicious circle of alienation and hostility. Neurotic patterns of behavior are particularly likely to arise in children with learning disabilities if the nature of the defect is not recognized by teachers and parents and is incorrectly attributed to laziness or naughtiness. In some cases emotional dyscontrol is very marked and recurring temper tantrums in response to minor frustrations create problems both at home and at school. In others, *this dyscontrol is itself a product of the fundamental organic defect of cerebral function*:

A man of 28 was referred because of attacks of explosive rage during which he attacked people, his mother in particular. The attacks were abrupt in onset and termination and were very dangerous. He professed amnesia for what he said and did during these "spells." Most of the time he was a pleasant and rather passive individual. His mother said that he had always been normal in a physical sense; but when pressed on this point, she recalled that he had been rather a clumsy child, and that even now, as an adult, "When he runs, he gallops like a horse." There were no other abnormal neurological signs but the accuracy of his mother's description was confirmed when he was instructed to run down the corridor. A CAT scan disclosed extensive dilatation of the lateral, third and fourth ventricles, without cortical atrophy. This was clearly a case of arrested hydrocephalus dating from very early life. So far as could be judged from the parent's account, he had not been subjected to emotional deprivation. A sleep EEG with nasopharyngeal electrodes disclosed nothing amiss. Nevertheless, because of the explosive nature of his rage, and because of the evidence of organic damage to the brain, 400 mg. daily of Phenytoin was prescribed for the seizure behavior. He has had no further attacks since medication was started two years ago.

In many cases the individual either outgrows or learns to circumvent his defects; but some persons do not and psychopathic behavior persists into adolescence and adult life (14, 20-26). A history of minimal brain dysfunction in childhood was obtained in one-third of a personal series of 124 adolescents and adults with "explosive personality" (p. 162). The symptoms and signs are often subtle and are either missed or attributed to emotional factors. The patient may not remember them but the parents (when available) can often supply pertinent information.

Epilepsy

Another disorder to be looked for in the background of people exhibiting psychopathic behavior is temporal lobe epilepsy. Behavioral disturbances have been found in from 15 to 60% of these cases, depending upon the source of reference material, but few are truly psychopathic because temporal lobe epileptics usually relate well to other people and their episodes of aggressive behavior are usually followed by remorse. This is not always so, however, as in the case of a 30-year-old man who at intervals of several years had been guilty of four savage homicides, all without obvious motivation or real remorse:

> Intellectually, Mr. J. was bright but he had always been in trouble at school for a variety of foolish delinquencies, including absenteeism. As a small boy he had attempted to set fire to a favorite cat. At 14 he had a single convulsion while asleep. A routine EEG was normal, but a spike focus in the left temporal region was elicited by an injection of pentylenetrazol. Phenytoin was prescribed but he was in a reform school at the time and never received it. While in prison, he embarked upon the writing of an autobiography and wrote some poems, but his writing was marred by confused thinking. For the past two years he has taken 400 mg. of phenytoin daily. He has had no further attacks of violent behavior. Moreover, his literary capacity has improved dramatically and he commented that he is now able to think—in his own words—"consecutively and accurately." It is likely that subclinical epileptic activity was interfering with both his behavior and his thinking.

Temporal lobe epilepsy assumes subtle forms, far removed from conventional convulsive seizures; many individuals suffer from it and have behavioral problems for many years, without diagnosis or treatment. Even when it is suspected, a normal EEG is too often accepted as evidence against a diagnosis of epilepsy. EEG results are improved by the use of chemical activation. Even these may prove negative and depth electrodes may be required to identify epileptic focus. When this is not practicable —and it rarely is—the response to anticonvulsant treatment is the only way to confirm the diagnosis.

Sporadic examples of psychopathic behavior starting in middle age as a result of brain disease emphasize the fact that "moral insanity" occasionally occurs as the sole indication of such disease. Dixon and Hargreaves, in 1942, studied 248 cases of cerebral cysticerocosis: 10 previously normal individuals with good Service records had become psychopathic; no details were given (27). In the days when dementia paralytica was common, behavior which fully earned the term psychopathic sometimes occurred in the early phase of the illness, before dementia supervened. A personal case:

> A much respected business woman, age 48, began to steal small sums of money (which she did not need) from the cash register of the hotel which she managed. She became sexually promiscuous for the first time in her life and when admonished, she exhibited a blithe indifference to the situation. She left home for three days and on her return said she had been to see her dying mother, which was palpably untrue. She fabricated stories about her past life. Neurological examination revealed nothing amiss, but examination of the blood and spinal fluid revealed evidence of neurosyphilis. Following a course of penicillin she reverted to her former rather prim self.

Occasionally a stroke may have comparable effects on personality, in addition to a neurological deficit:

> A successful business man who enjoyed a warm family life was a changed character after a subarachnoid hemorrhage which caused a left hemiplegia. He wrote checks that bounced and was unconcerned when he was found out. He was physically and verbally brutal to his wife and projected the blame on her. He made casual sexual advances to a complete stranger, a woman who shared his compartment in a suburban train. Despite all this, he was rational in planning the changes he would have to make in his manner of life by virtue of his hemiplegia.

THE NEUROLOGY OF INDIVIDUAL SYMPTOMS

Most of the symptoms displayed by the classical psychopath can be reproduced by physical disorders, notably those which affect the prefrontal lobes and/or the limbic system. An exception is the apathy or lack of incentive and initiative, which is a common early symptom of tumors involving deep midline structures (28) and of injuries and tumors of the frontal lobes. One point of difference is that organic cases do not usually display the capacity for ingratiation and persuasiveness which is seen in most psychopaths.

Impulsiveness

This is seen in some cases of minimal brain dysfunction, temporal lobe epilepsy, tumors involving the orbital surface of the frontal lobe and as a sequel of encephalitis lethargica and head injuries. In animals it is common following experimental damage to the prefrontal lobes (29). In man the impulse may be to lie, to steal, to run away, to burn down a barn, to injure an animal or fellow human being, or to have sex. There may well be psychodynamic reasons for the choice of offense but it seems to be carried out because of faulty inhibition. The impulse of the moment is paramount and must be satisfied at whatever cost. In these organic cases, there is no obvious reason for the act so far as the outside observer is concerned, or at best the reason may appear inadequate.

Lack of Foresight

Inability to foresee the results of an act compounds impulsiveness and explains why, in so many cases, little or no attempt is made to avoid discovery. This is all the more remarkable when it occurs against a background of good general intelligence. In experimental animals damage to the prefrontal lobes renders the animals unable to anticipate the consequences of their behavior in relation to other animals (29-31); they appear puzzled when taking food from another animal results in an attack. The same inability to visualize the consequences of an act has been seen following prefrontal lobotomy in man (32). This defect is regarded by Denny-Brown as central to the behavioral disturbances resulting from prefrontal lesions (31).

Lack of Insight

Lack of a critical attitude to self, so obvious in many psychopaths, is seen in disease affecting the prefrontal lobes (29) and after prefrontal lobotomy (29, 32). It is often seen in dementia paralytica, after head injuries, and in minimal brain dysfunction. As a result of lack of insight, the patient is unable to acecpt blame, which he projects onto others, and he is unable to see himself as others see him. Clearly, this symptom is closely related to the denial of physical illness which is so common after prefrontal leukotomy and frontal lobectomy. Such anosognosia is a prominent result of damage to the parietal lobe of the non-dominant hemisphere, and also occurs in lesions of the diencephalon, midbrain, and posterior fossa. Weinstein and Kahn consider that in cases of tumor and stroke, the occurrence of anosognosia is more related to the premorbid personality than to the site of the lesion. They postulate that in individuals who are insecure, but who possess a drive for superiority and perfection, the anosognosia is an attempt to deny the physical evidence of imperfection (33).

Absence of Conscience

The classical psychopath lacks capacity for shame and remorse, albeit to a variable extent, but as Craft points out, some "normal" subjects display even more pronounced egocentricity and lack of guilt feelings than some psychopaths (4). Moreover, in assessing conscience it is necessary to take into account the ethical standard in the individual's past and present environment. In *The Courage of His Convictions*, Parker and Allerton describe a habitual criminal who states that "Violence is in a way like bad language, something that a person like me is brought up with, something I got used to very early as part of the daily scene of childhood as you might say. I don't at all recoil from the idea. And I don't have an inborn dislike of the thing, like you do. As long as I can remember I have seen violence in use all around me—my mother hitting the children, my brothers and sisters all whacking their mother or other children, the man downstairs bashing his wife, and so on" (34). This was in England. The same unhappy situation was brought out by Davis, who writes about the American scene: "The lower class does not uncommonly teach their children and adolescents to strike out with their fists or knives and to be certain to hit first. Boys and girls engage in free-for-all family encounters." A young woman who was a member of a gang in New York stated on television that if she had a child, she would teach it to lie and steal and use a knife. Individuals reared in such surroundings cannot be expected to have a sense of guilt about violent delinquent behavior when such behavior is the accepted pattern of their subculture (35).

A further difficulty in assessing the factor of conscience is that some psychopaths and many patients with brain damage will agree that their actions were wrong and may even appear to be sincere about what they say; but this does not prevent them from continuing with their delinquencies. Following a prefrontal leukotomy, a patient said, "Now that I have done it, I see that it was wrong, but I did not think so at the time" (32).

In patients with organic neurological disease, conscience is sometimes an early casualty. This is often seen in early dementia paralytica and following head injuries both in children and adults. It was frequently observed in children following encephalitis lethargica, and is encountered in some cases of minimal brain dysfunction.

A lifelong absence of conscience was a prominent feature of an 18-year-old boy. He showed no affection for his family, and consistently denied that there was anything wrong with him. He stole and told unnecessary lies. He was often physically aggressive. However, he had had occasional attacks of "absence" since the age of five and an EEG showed focal spikes in the left fronto-temporal area. He refused to take anticonvulsants and his parents were afraid to enforce their authority because he was too big, too strong, and too aggressive. His troubles continued until he was sent to a correctional institution because of his delinquencies. There he apparently decided that the best way of getting out of the place was to conform and he agreed to take phenytoin regularly. Within 10 days it was noticed that he was no longer hostile and aggressive. For the first time he admitted that there was something wrong with him and he began to feel what seemed to be genuine remorse over his previous activities. His father remarked that for the first time his son appeared to have developed a conscience. He appears to have undergone a change of character, but it remains to be seen whether this change persists when he regains his freedom.

A possible explanation for his gain in insight is that the subclinical epileptic activity in the temporo-frontal area was interfering with perception, including apperception of self. There is ample evidence that an individual may lose the capacity to recognize his own defects following prefrontal lobectomy (32).

Defective Affect

Inability to relate affectionately to other people is a familiar feature of the psychopath, who displays a ruthless disregard for the feelings and interests of spouse, children, and associates (3, 6). It is also seen in some children with minimal brain dysfunction (14, 19) and after head injuries in both children and adults. Moreover, it can appear for the first time following a stroke. Bianchi, in 1922, summarizing the results of prefrontal lobectomy in monkeys, reported loss or modification of "the higher sentiments of friendship, gratitude, and jealousy, maternity, protection, dominion, authority, self-esteem, ridicule, and above all, that of sociality" (30). Pavlov noted that following frontal lobotomy dogs became totally "degenerate" and no longer recognized their master.

Inability to Learn from Experience

This feature of many psychopaths is sometimes seen in the syndrome of minimal brain dysfunction (19) and it was a common feature following encephalitis lethargica (9). It is occasionally encountered following severe head injuries in both adults and children (9, 12, 19). Experimental removal of the prefrontal lobes renders the animal unable to learn from previous experience (29, 36). Inability to learn from experience includes unresponsiveness to punishment; the situation is compounded by the individual's inability to imagine the consequences of his actions.

Diminished Sense of Fear

Some of the most intrepid pilots in World War II were psychopaths who lacked a sense of fear (6). Further, some children with minimal brain dysfunction display the same characteristic. Thus,

> An adolescent who was well aware of the risks he ran skiing down precipitous slopes at reckless speed, and who acknowledged that he might be seriously injured, showed no sense of fear and could not understand the fears of others. As a child he had been hyperkinetic and his scholastic record displayed the patchy performance which is so characteristic of minimal brain dysfunction.

In man a feeling of fear or apprehension can be produced by stimulation of the amygdala, while bilateral temporal lobectomy in monkeys produces the Kluver-Bucy syndrome characterized by, among other things, absence of fear of natural enemies.

Inadequate Motivation

The inadequately motivated antisocial behavior of the psychopath, which is so self-defeating, is often seen in minimal brain dysfunction and after head injuries in both children and adults. It was common following encephalitis lethargica and is seen from time to time in temporal lobe epileptics, in patients with tumors affecting the limbic system, and in the early stages of dementia paralytica.

Poor Judgment

The psychopath is notoriously liable to errors of judgment and the same applies to many individuals with minimal brain dysfunction. It sometimes occurs as the first sign of dementia and has been reported following prefrontal lobectomy. Judgment of an external situation can be affected by faulty perception of the situation, by inability to mobilize memories of similar situations in the past, and by incapacity for direct association and abstract thought. Another factor in organic cases is the patient's difficulty in distinguishing between figure and ground, i.e., between what is important and what is irrelevant. Inability to get to the heart of the matter, to grasp the essential point of the problem, is often seen after severe head injuries. In the early stages of organic dementia it contributes to the inefficiency in business and social affairs which sometimes precedes more easily recognizable features of mental dilapidation. In minimal brain dysfunction, difficulty in distinguishing between the essential and the inessential can occur even in the presence of a high IQ (14). Inability to make the right choice when faced with alternatives also occurs in monkeys following prefrontal lobotomy (29).

Absence of Depression and Neurotic Anxiety

"Lacking insight and the ability to see himself as others see him, the psychopath is often poised and at ease in situations where the average person would be tense and apprehensive" (3). Most psychopaths do not progress emotionally to the stage of being able to experience depression. If they feel hostile, their feelings are directed outwards rather than inwards. On the other hand, when antisocial behavior is a result of structural disease or developmental defect, anxiety, remorse, and reactive depression are common. Depression and lack of self-esteem are common in children and adolescents with minimal brain dysfunction (15) but this is by no means always the case. One of the most poised and self-satisfied individuals the writer has ever known suffered from non-familial dyslexia, dysgraphia, left-right disorientation, explosive rage, and an almost total lack of empathy for other human beings.

Lies and Fantasies

Anderson (4) remarks that the sincerity of persons with MBD is usually no pose, for they really believe what they are telling. The same is true of many psychopaths. A similar failure to distinguish between truth and falsehood and fact and fancy is sometimes seen after a severe head injury, following encephalitis, and in the early stages of dementia paralytica.

The Effects of Alcohol

Many classical psychopaths and most individuals who exhibit psychopathic behavior as a result of organic disease are liable to inappropriate behavior when under the influence of alcohol, even in small amounts. A curious feature of such pathological intoxication is that it cannot be produced in the laboratory, even in patients who exhibit it elsewhere. The social setting appears to be important.

Aggressive Behavior

Aggression in the psychopath is more often cold-blooded and predatory than the result of rage. Storr likens it to the violence of an unthinking child: "They treat other people as the rest of us would treat a wasp" (6). If violence is necessary for the satisfaction of a whim or in the execution of a crime, so be it. However, punishment evokes anger and hostility. A violent criminal, discussing corporal punishment, said, "What it does is to produce anger and resentment, and most of all, a determination somehow to get your own back. But being deterred? The idea never gets a look in" (34).

In organic disorders violence is more often affective than predatory and it commonly takes the form of explosive rage with little or no provocation. However, this is not true of all children with minimal brain dysfunction. The pyschopathic type of predatory behavior is also seen following encephalitis lethargica and may appear for the first time after a head injury. The organic dyscontrol syndrome is characterized by attacks of explosive rage and violence which are usually followed by remorse. It will be discussed separately, at the end of this chapter.

Self-defeating Pattern

As Cleckley has said, "One of the really remarkable features of this life pattern is that a person who shows so concretely the ability to succeed, will throw away all he has gained and apparently what he desires for no reason comprehensible to others. . . . The intricate pattern of gratuitous folly, nonsensical failure and unprovoked social aggression, repeated over and over again, may, indeed, impress one as an expression of madness" (3). A similar pattern of self-defeat is seen in many cases of minimal brain dysfunction in children, and, as previously stated, some of them display psychopathic behavior in adolescence and adult life.

THE MATURATIONAL LAG HYPOTHESES

While it is true that organic disease can give rise to psychopathic behavior, it is also true that in many psychopaths there is no evidence of trauma or physical disorder, either in the history or on clinical examination. The question arises as to whether psychopathic behavior can reflect a maturational lag in brain development, as suggested by Mangun (37) and by Hill and Watterson (40). Many psychopathic traits are infantile in character and tend to become less obtrusive in middle life (6, 21, 37-39).

The notion of delayed maturity is supported by EEG studies. Bilateral theta activity, notably in the temporal and frontal areas, is found in some normal chlidren but is uncommon in the second and third decades. However, it is found in many adult sociopaths (40-44). In them it becomes less prevalent as middle age approaches. Williams has advanced the cogent argument that the type and distribution of the EEG abnormality in these cases point to a disturbance of function in the diencephalic and mesencephalic components of the reticular activating or "limbic" mechanisms, which have their densest projections to the anterior temporal and frontal cortex. This fits in with psychophysiological evidence provided by Hare and others of cortical hypoarousal in psychopaths (45; Chapter 10).

It is usually stated that myelination, one index of physical maturation, is incomplete in the human brain until the second decade (46-48). Different areas of the brain myelinate at different rates. In the reticular activating system it continues well into the second decade, thus lagging behind the rest of the brain with the exception of the intracortical association areas, in which myelination is completed last. Kaes (46) found that it continued in the anterior temporal and prefrontal cortex until the age of 45.

A second factor in the process of maturation is the development of dendrites, which connect the neurons. Their branching patterns become more elaborate after birth (49) but it is not known how long this aspect of the maturational process continues.

Is there a lag in the maturation of the prefrontal cortex in the psychopath? There are so many similarities between the symptoms of the psychopath and those which result from bilateral prefrontal damage in both man and other primates that this notion deserves consideration.

In man prefrontal leukotomy or lobotomy is inconsistent in its effects on the personality, as is to be expected because of the many variables which are involved. Postmortem examination has shown that the extent and position of the cut vary considerably from case to case. In some cases vascular lesions have been found at a considerable distance from the line of the cut. Moreover, the most posterior cuts involve not only the prefrontal lobe, but also pass through the anterior portion of the cingulate gyri, thus involving the limbic system. Also, in assessing the results of psychosurgery, the nature and severity of the mental disorder for which the operation was carried out have to be considered, as well as the premorbid personality of the patient.

Studies of the effects of frontal lobotomy on monkeys and dogs have the advantage of more precise surgical interference, which can be checked by postmortem examination, and of the presumed absence of mental illness prior to operation; but they labor under the disadvantage that since the animal cannot speak the changes produced by the operation can only be inferred by the animal's behavior. In primates other than man, and in dogs, the effects of prefrontal lobectomy include emotional indifference, lack of natural affection (29, 30), impulsiveness, inability to ignore irrelevant stimuli, inability to make a correct decision in the face of alternatives, inability to solve problems which depend on past experience (36), apathy or irritability, and inability to direct actions in accordance with a general plan directed at a specific goal.

Prefrontal lesions in man produce a variety of symptoms, not all of which are seen in any single case. They include impaired moral and social sense, lack of conscience and anxiety, lack of foresight, inability to learn by experience, lack of natural affection, little sense of fear, inability to direct and sustain activities according to a general plan, inadequately motivated behavior, untruthfulness, imperception of other people's feelings, indifference to threatening situations, difficulty in distinguishing between figure and ground and between essential and inessential, lack of drive, lack of self-control, and absence of self-criticism (29, 31, 32, 50, 51).

There are, of course, several obvious differences between prefrontal cases and the classical psychopath. The latter does not display the apathy, the impairment of memory, or the facetious jocularity which is often seen in the former. The prefrontal case shows bad judgment both in his own affairs and in the affairs of others, whereas the psychopath often demonstrates good judgment in assessing theoretical situations concerning other people, but fails in his own practical affairs. Further, whereas the prefrontal case is consistently abnormal, the psychopath may tread the path of virtue and show considerable skill in the management of his affairs for prolonged periods before committing some egregious folly or senseless crime. (Such episodicity is, however, not limited to psychopaths; it may be seen in individuals with organically determined disorders such as temporal lobe epilepsy and in the explosive rage or dyscontrol syndrome following head injuries.) The capacity of many psychopaths to ingratiate themselves with others and to lie with every appearance of sincerity is not conspicuous in prefrontal cases.

The behavioral disturbances which accompany massive lesions of the temporal and parietal lobes have little in common with those which follow prefrontal damage.

The hypothesis of a physical maturational lag in the prefrontal cortex or in the reticular activating projections which it receives (or in both) is not necessarily inconsistent with the observation that emotional deprivation and personal adversity in early life contribute to psychopathy;

the functional development of the nervous system after birth depends to some extent on environmental stimuli. This is illustrated by observations of what happens if one eye of a kitten is occluded for a few days between the fourth and seventh week after birth. When the occlusion is removed, there is visual impairment in that eye and histological changes are found in the portion of the geniculate bodies which receive fibers from the occluded eye. In the adult cat, temporary occlusion of the eye does not produce permanent visual impairment, but in kittens (and in young monkeys) there appears to be a period of critical susceptibility to the physical effects of sensory deprivation (52). Is it possible that an adverse emotional environment in early infancy can retard the maturation of the limbic and prefrontal structures?

THE NEUROLOGY OF EXPLOSIVE RAGE*

Explosive rage is part of the organic dyscontrol syndrome as defined by Mark and Ervin (53). It is one of the causes of wife and child battery, apparently motiveless homicide, unprovoked assault on friends or strangers, sexual assault, dangerously aggressive driving, and senseless destruction of property. Even when the violence is only verbal, it can disrupt marriages and spoil careers, and has a harmful effect on children who are exposed to it in the home.

It is important, but not always easy, to distinguish between psychopathic aggression, explosive rage associated with neurological organic disease, and the "acting out" of emotional turmoil in psychoses and neuroses. Marginal cases are not uncommon. In contrast to the psychopath, most individuals who suffer from organic explosive rage have a warm personality and suffer remorse after the attack. Their outbursts of rage can usually be prevented by appropriate medication.

Neurological Findings in 124 Cases

This account is based on cases seen in private neurological practice over a period of five years. Aggressive psychopaths and psychotics were excluded. The age of the patients ranged from 7 to 70; 80 were under the age of 30. There were 76 males and 48 females. Three were black and 121 were white. The majority came from middle and upper socioeconomic classes. Only 2 were prisoners.

---

* This section is part of a paper which appeared in the *Bulletin of the American Academy of Psychiatry and the Law*, May, 1977, and is reproduced by permission of the editor.

TABLE 1

Causes of Dyscontrol Syndrome in 124 Cases.

More than one-third were referred for symptoms other than emotional dyscontrol or violence, the existence of which was a carefully preserved family secret which was uncovered only by direct questioning.

Diagnosis	*Number*
Epilepsy (temporal lobe)	37
Epilepsy (other)	4
Minimal brain dysfunction (by history)	31
Head injury	23
Brain tumor (post operative)	5
Brain tumor (pre-operative)	1
Encephalitis	4
Multiple sclerosis	4
Stroke	6
Cardiac arrest	2
Arrested hydrocephalus	1
Alzheimer's Disease	2
Organic brain syndrome, cause not established	4
	124

Kaplan, in 1899, described what he called the explosive diasthesis in these words: "Following the most trivial and most impersonal causes, there is the effect of rage with its motor accompaniments. There may be the most grotesque gesticulations, excessive movements of the face, and a quick sharp explosiveness of speech; there may be cursing and outbreaks of violence which are often directed towards things; there may or may not be amnesia for those events afterwards. These outbursts may terminate in an epileptic fit. There is an excess of reaction, with inadequate adaptation to the situation which is so remote from a well considered and purposeful act that it approaches a pure psychic reflex" (54). An earlier description is that of Benjamin Rush; he, too, remarked that the attack could end in a convulsion (1).

Some patients report that explosive rage differs in quality, as well as in degree, from ordinary anger aroused by adequate provocation: "Something comes over me and takes charge of my brain." The intensity of the fury bears little relationship to conventional anger and there seems to be a total transformation of the personality during these attacks. Occasionally the term dyscontrol cannot be applied because, although the patient feels a catastrophic sense of fury, he or she is able to control it.

A young man, who developed mild temporal lobe seizures and some intellectual blunting as a result of a head injury, reported that when faced with a difficult intellectual task or an irritating social situation, he would experience a sense of rage, but was able to contain it—sometimes by abruptly walking out of the room.

Kinnier Wilson provides an example of the same phenomenon in a young woman who had survived encephalitis lethargica:

> She used suddenly to become conscious of a rising surge within her, a seemingly physical wave which flooded her brain and caused her to clench her fists, set her jaws, and glare in frenzy at her mother; "Had my mother said anything then to cross me, I would have killed her." The attacks were followed by tears (7).

The explosion may be preceded by a premonitory sense of mounting tension, or a sense of helplessness and depression, but in other cases the onset is abrupt and without any warning. The attack can last minutes to hours and is followed in most cases by remorse. A frequent comment is, "How could I do a thing like that?" So great is their remorse that suicide or attempted suicide is not at all uncommon (53), in which respect they differ from psychopaths.

In most cases, the patients remember what they did or said; in others there is partial or complete amnesia either because the patients suppress the memory or because the rage was an ictal (i.e., epileptic) event.

The violence which accompanies the rage may be verbal or physical; in the former, unwonted obscenity and profanity are common. Physical violence often has a primitive quality—biting, gouging, spitting, and so on.

Mark and Ervin point out that patients who suffer from episodic dyscontrol are frequently guilty of dangerously aggressive driving and have had repeated convictions for traffic violations or a record of serious accidents (53). Three patients in the present series said that they were afraid to drive.

Impulsive sexual misbehavior in the home or outside is less common than temper dyscontrol in organic cases, perhaps because libidinous activities tend to be reduced by organic lesions of the brain. This is especially evident in temporal lobe epilepsy (55). However, there are exceptions. Mohan and his colleagues describe an example, and quote others, of hypersexuality in disease of the limbic system (56).

Sexual offenses are not necessarily accompanied by anger; a literary example is that of Jacques in Zola's *La Bête Humaine,* a psychomotor epileptic who was not always able to control his urge to kill women to whom he was sexually attracted (57). It is tempting to speculate that Zola got the idea from the writings of his contemporary, Falret, who, in 1861, described epileptics who were the helpless victims of violent impulses (58).

Many suffer from pathological intoxication in the sense that a small amount of alcohol triggers either rage or drunkenness. Dr. Rada's chapter in this volume addresses this issue in more detail.

An attack of rage may terminate in a seizure, but this is rare:

> A young woman who suffered from infrequent temporal lobe seizures reported such an event. She was trying to get a tablet of aspirin out of a bottle when the cap stuck. She found herself screaming with rage and actually "saw red." She then fell to the ground and had a generalized convulsion.

Such chromatopsia is an occasional feature of seizures arising in the temporal lobe. Another woman reported that she became incontinent of urine and feces at the end of two of her attacks of rage.

In addition to poor impulse control the patient may exhibit symptoms and signs appropriate to the underlying condition, whatever it may be. While this is obvious in some cases, there are many in whom defects are not disclosed by conventional neurological examination because the signs are "soft" and are only revealed by diligent inquiry or by psychometric tests designed to identify organic disorders. This applies particularly to the cognitive, affective, and somatic disturbances of the syndrome of minimal brain dysfunction (14, 17, 59). There is often an early history of such defects, which the patient may have outgrown. Indeed, the striking thing about many of these patients is that they appear so normal when encountered on the witness stand or on a social occasion.

Many of the studies of violence have been conducted on prison populations or in mental institutions or neurosurgical institutes to which the most serious cases gravitate. These reports emphasize the prevalence of a low IQ and an adverse domestic environment in early life—parental dissension and violence, lack of ordinary affection, poverty, and alcoholism. None of these features was conspicuous in the present series. Only one person was mentally retarded. Three patients with temporal lobe epilepsy exhibited schizophrenia-like symptoms. The remainder were neither psychotic nor chronically malevolent and were earning a living, running a home, or going to school. Yet members of this group of otherwise pleasant people had been responsible for wife and child battery, sexual assault, senseless destruction of property and other such actions.

Prevalence

There is relatively little information on this point. Homicide excepted, there are no statistics as to the prevalence of aggression in the family circle, where most of it occurs, but it is generally agreed that the cases which come to official notice represent only the tip of the iceberg. This was the opinion of a British Government Committee report on wife battery (60), which expressed its concern about the problem in the United Kingdom to the extent of advising that refuges for battered wives and their children should be provided to the tune of one refuge per 10,000 population. It is estimated that there are over one million cases of child battery in the United States every year but nothing is known as to what proportion of these cases is due to organic disorders.

There are many reasons why the dyscontrol syndrome is underreported. In the first place, a violent temper is often regarded as a quirk of personality rather than a matter for medical concern, especially in strata of society in which violence is so common that it excites little comment. Secondly, few people are willing to admit to an uncontrollable temper, whether from a sense of shame, a fear of commitment, or a fear of legal penalties; and the family often helps in the coverup. Euphemisms are common. One man who admitted only that he had a "short fuse" assaulted his wife and children on several occasions and had broken furniture during his rages. To uncover this kind of thing it is necessary for the physician to ask the right questions: "Do you have difficulty in controlling your temper? Have you been charged with traffic violations or dangerous driving? Are you especially sensitive to alcohol?" It is also necessary to inquire, preferably at a later interview, about the more delicate question of inability to control inappropriate sexual impulses.

A third cause of underreporting is that the violent patient is unpopular with physicians. We try to avoid both the patient and the subject; we seek a legal remedy as a means of evading the issue; or we attribute the violence to cultural factors. Like the patient, we use euphemisms such as "irritability," "explosive personality," "the hyper-responsive syndrome," and so on.

THE PATHOPHYSIOLOGY OF THE ORGANIC DYSCONTROL SYNDROME

Clinical and experimental evidence indicates that explosive rage often results from disorders which affect the limbic system, a phylogenetically ancient portion of the brain which is interposed between the diencephalon and the neocortex. There has been much discussion as to the anatomical limits of the system but the portions of it which are pertinent to the study of rage are the amygdala and the hippocampus in the temporal lobe, the hypothalamus, the cingulate gyri and the cingulum, the septum pellucidum and septal area, and related portions of the thalamus, basal ganglia, orbital region of the frontal lobe and mid-brain (Figure 1). This system is intimately concerned not only with the expression of emotion, but also with the neural control of visceral functions and chemical homeostasis (61, 62).

An early hint of the link between the limbic system and rage was unwittingly furnished by Boerhaave, who, in 1715, spoke of patients "gnashing their teeth and snarling like a dog" when suffering from rabies (63) which attacks (*inter alia*) the hippocampus and brain stem. In his description of this disorder, Gowers (1892) spoke of the patient being "exhausted by attacks of fury" (64).

In 1892, Goltz reported that removal of portions of the cerebral hemispheres in dogs produced a phenomenon which later came to be called sham rage. These animals are liable to periodic attacks of rage, and also snarl and bite in response to minor provocation.

Other workers confirmed these studies. By carrying out a series of systematic ablations in cats, Bard found, in 1928, that the posterior hypothalamus had to be intact if sham rage was to appear (65). Many years

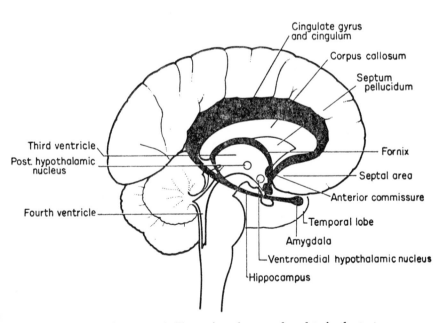

Figure I. Diagrammatic illustration of areas referred to in the text.

later Sano et al. showed that in man explosive rage could be abolished by bilateral lesions in the posterior hypothalamus (66).

Although the literature on this subject speaks of the "decorticate" animal, this term is misleading because in most cases a good deal more than the cortex was removed. Indeed, Bard and Mountcastle found that, in cats, removal of the neocortex only, leaving the limbic cortex intact, produced placidity. "Even with the most painful stimulus, these animals could not be made to show the slightest signs of anger, nor did they show any of the autonomic responses; no pupilary dilatation, no increase in cardiac rate, no increase in cardiac output, no sweating, not even a rise of blood sugar. These passive animals had all the hypothalamus and the whole limbic system intact and showed not the slightest reaction of agression or rage" (67). This observation is in accord with clinical evidence that explosive rage is far more common in disorders involving the limbic system than it is in disease of the neocortex.

Experiments with animals and man show that the limbic system contains within itself both excitatory and suppressive mechanisms. Electrical stimulation of the central and medial portions of the amygdala complex *usually* induces rage, whereas the animal is pacified by stimulation of the lateral group of nuclei. Bilateral amygdalotomy usually reduces the ferocity of the Rhesus monkey, the lynx and other animals. In man, this operation usually abolishes the explosive rage of the dyscontrol syndrome.

In the cat, destruction of the ventro-medial nucleus of the hypothalamus produces—after a delay of weeks—a chronically savage animal. Possible reasons for this delay are discussed by Glusman (68). A more prolonged delay is sometimes seen in the development of explosive rage in man following the removal of brain tumors involving the limbic system, after head injuries, and after encephalitis.

In man, electrical stimulation of limbic structures can produce both pleasant and unpleasant sensations. A sense of fear and apprehension is perhaps the most common. Violence is rarely induced in the operating room (69), but this may be due to the social setting for, as we all know, fear can provoke anger. In a 1955 case described by Heath, Monroe, and Mickle, stimulation in the region of the amygdala produced fear on some occasions and anger on others (70). Mark, Sweet, and Ervin found that stimulation of the medial amygdala could produce the prodomata of attack behavior without the attack itself on some days, whereas if the patient had been disturbed by a prior argument with the family, stimulation at the same point could trigger an attack of uncontrolled violence (71). Again, stimulation of the central gray matter of the brain stem in Gibbon monkeys carried out in the laboratory caused attacks on other animals, but if the stimulation was carried out when the animal was running free in its natural habitat, it did not attack other monkeys but might attack the experimenter (72).

Clearly, the limbic system does not act in a vacuum as an autonomous center for aggressive behavior, but interacts with other portions of the brain. This is illustrated at the electrophysiological level by the fact that stimulation of midline structures of the cerebellum can inhibit sham rage and stimulation of the caudate nucleus has a pacifying effect (72). Nevertheless, the explosive rage of the organic dyscontrol syndrome is usually the product of a damaged limbic system and it has been controlled in a large number of children and adults by stereotaxic operations on the amygdala, posteromedial hypothalamus, the cingulate gyri and underlying cingulate bundle, and the anterior thalamus, and also by unilateral temporal lobectomy, bilateral temporal lobotomy, and orbito-frontal tractotomy (73).

Predatory aggression in animals (for instance, the lion in search of a meal) involves other circuits which need not concern us here. In man, predatory violence is cold and calculated, and is carried out for profit. It is properly viewed as originating in the neocortex. Sometimes the distinction between predatory and affective aggression is blurred, as in the case of an individual who plans a crime of violence in cold blood and carries it out under the influence of alcohol or drugs which are taken to accentuate the aggressive drive.

Etiology of the Organic Dyscontrol Syndrome

This syndrome can occur at any age, but is most common in adolescence and early adult life. In general, aggression declines with advancing age; however, the syndrome can develop for the first time in old age when the brain is assailed by organic disease such as a stroke or Alzheimer's disease, or after a head injury.

Males are more affected than females, at all ages. Aggressive behavior is sometimes associated with high androgen levels in the plasma, and in most animals, male castration, which lowers androgen levels, has a taming effect. This is illustrated by the difference between "the raging bull and the peaceful steer" (74). Bremer found, in 1959, that in man castration did not inhibit aggression except in relation to sexual crime (75), but this observation ignores the possible psychodynamic effects of castration.

The family background is important. An uncontrollable temper sometimes runs in families, involving several generations and affecting about half of the progeny of a violent parent, according to Davenport's 1915 study (75). The writer has encountered several pedigrees in which typical explosive rage appeared in two or three generations, affecting about half the sibship in each generation. Hill and Watterson (1942) report that aggressive behavior was found nearly three times as frequently among first-degree relatives of aggressive psychopaths as amongst those of "inadequate" psychopaths, but they did not distinguish between explosive rage and other types of aggression (40).

There is a high incidence of EEG abnormalities in the families of patients showing episodic aggressive behavior (40, 77). A genetic factor is also evident in temporal lobe epilepsy (78), although structural lesions are present in the majority of cases—sclerosis of Ammon's horn, porencephalic cysts, hamartomas, benign glial tumors, and so on (79). Possibly it is the genetic factor which determines whether such lesions will produce epilepsy and/or the dyscontrol syndrome. Thus, sclerosis of the hippocampus is the most common cause of temporal lobe seizures (80). It is likely that while the convulsive response to pyrexia is genetically determined, the subsequent development of temporal lobe seizures is due to sclerosis of Ammon's horn produced by the original convulsions.

Most observers agree that some, but not all, children reared in an atmosphere of uncontrollable temper, parental dissension or separation, and emotional deprivation become violent themselves; it is not always easy to decide whether the effect is due to heredity, emotional trauma, bad example, or a mixture of all three. Nevertheless, many children brought up in this atmosphere do *not* become violent.

Patients with organic dyscontrol syndrome fall into two groups. In the first, there is a history of temper tantrums in infancy and childhood which has persisted as more formidable explosions of rage in adolescence and adult life. In the second group, formerly normal individuals become subject to explosive rage as a sequel to a brain insult or metabolic disorder.

In the first group, the emotional dyscontrol dates from early life and can often be traced to prenatal, natal, or postnatal events. These include birth trauma, fetal anoxia, infantile convulsions, head injury, encephalopathy complicating infectious diseases, and encephalitis. These infants are difficult to rear, often reach the milestones of development late, and are marked in childhood by seizures or the protean manifestation of minimal brain dysfunction, including hyperkinesis. Explosive rage also occurs in more severely affected individuals with cerebral palsy and mental retardation. It is often difficult to identify the precise cause of the disability because infants with congenital defects are often premature and are therefore particularly liable to birth injury. A prolonged and difficult labor at term is not uncommon in the history of individuals with epilepsy, minimal brain dysfunction or cerebral palsy. Psychoanalysts have sought a link between a violent birth and a violent child; an alternative explanation is that violent birth damages the brain in a structural sense.

Head Injury

Some of the behavioral effects of head injuries have already been discussed. Explosive rage can be a sequel, in both children and adults. Hooper et al., in 1945, identified 12 such cases in 2,000 men who had suffered a serious brain injury in World War II (81); but the figure might have been larger had the follow-up been longer, because explosive rage sometimes develops one to two years after the initial trauma. The *contre coup* lesions of closed head injuries show a predilection for the tip and orbital surface of the frontal lobe and the anterior portion of the temporal lobe; Crompton (82) has found histological evidence of damage to the hypothalamus. Multiple minor head injuries can have a cumulative effect, as in the "punch-drunk syndrome" in which explosive rage is not uncommon. In other words, portions of the limbic system which are known to be concerned with the production of affective aggression are particularly vulnerable to severe closed head injuries.

Minimal Brain Dysfunction

Children with minor brain dysfunction are prone to develop neurotic reactions, including aggressive behavior. Critchely, writing about the dyslexic child, says that, "It is a commonplace observation that once a dyslexic child is diagnosed as being the victim of a genuine inherited disability and is not an ordinary stupid, lazy, or neurotic youngster, its self respect is immediately enhanced and any bad behavior he has shown improves without intervention on the part of child psychiatry" (83). This is often true, but not always. Some patients, notably those who suffered a natal or postnatal brain insult, have temper tantrums in their earliest years which may persist through adolescence and adult life even if the patient has outgrown his other handicaps. The fact that, in some of these individuals, explosive rage does not respond to psychotherapy but does respond to anticonvulsant medication suggests that the dyscontrol is organic in origin rather than simply a response to frustration.

Epilepsy

Temporal lobe epileptics are more prone to behavioral disorders than are patients with centrencephalic epilepsy; but the reported prevalence varies with the source of cases (84). As is to be expected, it is higher in epileptics who have been committed to institutions than in those who can live at home. It is also high in those admitted to neurosurgical clinics because they are a selected group of intractable cases. Rodin (85) reported pathological aggression in only 4.8% of 700 cases from the Michigan Epilepsy Center. Currie and his colleagues (86) at the London Hospital found it in 7% of 666 patients with temporal lobe epilepsy of mixed etiology and type. Bingley (87), who drew his material from the neurological and neurosurgical services of a general hospital in Sweden, found aggressive behavior in 17% of 90 cases of temporal lobe epilepsy. Gastaut et al. (88) reported paroxysmal rages in 50% of their temporal lobe epileptics. Falconer found pathological aggressiveness, occurring in outbursts in otherwise well adjusted individuals, in 38% of 50 cases of temporal lobe epilepsy with a predominately unilateral spike focus; another 15% had a milder or more persistent aggressiveness associated with a paranoid outlook (80). This useful distinction between explosive rage in an otherwise well adjusted personality, and aggression resulting from a paranoid outlook, is not always made in the literature; moreover, it is often difficult to know whether the term "aggressive behavior" refers to affective or predatory aggression.

In the present series, one or more seizures had occurred at some time in the patient's life in 58 cases; in 45 of these, there was clinical and/or EEG evidence that they originated in a temporal lobe. In most cases they were mild and infrequent. Analysis of the EEG findings will be presented elsewhere. Suffice to say, in the present context, that bilateral temporofrontal theta activity, so common in psychopaths, was found in only five cases, whereas abnormalities consistent with a seizure disorder were present in 54.

In epileptics episodic rage occurs under three circumstances. It can occur when attempts are made to restrain the patient during post-epileptic automatism. Secondly, patients with temporal lobe lesions, epileptic or otherwise, often have inter-ictal explosions of rage on trivial provocation. Thirdly, there is ictal rage. Many believe that rage can be part of a seizure but Gloor believes that it is a very uncommon manifestation of an epileptic discharge, though he agrees that the association of aggressive behavior and temporal lobe epilepsy is a real one—conclusions based on hundreds of cases of epilepsy examined at the Montreal Neurological Institute (69). The fact that ictal rage is rarely evoked by electrical stimulation of the brain in conscious patients emphasizes the role of the social setting in experimental work, to which attention has already been directed. In his analysis of 100 cases of temporal lobe epilepsy, Williams

(89) identified 17 cases of ictal aggression. In the present series seven cases were subject to attacks of violence which came on abruptly, lasted a few miuntes, and were followed by amnesia, exhaustion and headache. All were controlled by anticonvulsant medication.

Inter-ictal rage is more common. In some the attacks of violence are preceded by a period of mounting tension which may be obvious to others if not to the patient. In others, however, the onset is abrupt and without warning and it is difficult to know whether they should be regarded as ictal or inter-ictal. The presence or absence of amnesia is not decisive, since many patients with temporal lobe seizures can describe what happened during the attack. The attacks occur in response to seemingly minor provocation. The word "seemingly" is used advisedly because provocation which appears trivial to the observer may have psychodynamic significance for the patient. Thus, one temporal lobe epileptic attempted to strangle his wife because a remark she made reminded him of his mother, whom he had hated. The wife was a surrogate victim. The patient usually remembers most of what he did or said during these attacks, unless it is advantageous to forget it, and remorse usually follows. Occasionally the patient insists that his behavior is appropriate.

Precisely similar episodes occur in people who have never had a seizure, but whose EEG displays evidence of a seizure disorder. It is important to recognize these cases for what they are, because the dyscontrol usually responds favorably to anticonvulsant medication. These patients have to be distinguished from the larger group of sociopathic individuals who are given to recurrent violence, who are not epileptic, and whose EEG's may display bilateral paroxysmal slow waves, predominately in the anterior temporal and frontal regions. This theta (4-7 HZ) activity is frequently seen in the resting record, but the number of positive results is greatly increased by activation techniques, notably by using alpha chloralose (42). Theta activity is found in apparently normal children and becomes progressively less prevalent in early adult life; it may well represent a maturational lag. Williams studied the EEG's of a large group of patients who were habitually aggressive. After those who were mentally retarded, had epilepsy, or who had had a major head injury were removed from the series, the EEG was abnormal in 57%, whereas an abnormal EEG was found in only 12% of apparently normal people who had committed a solitary major violent crime—the same as in the population at large. Bilateral theta activity was the most common finding in the aggressive group. He concludes that "the distribution and type of the EEG abnormalities suggest that the primary disturbance of function responsible for them is in the diencephalic and mesencephalic components of the reticular activating or 'limbic' mechanisms which have their densest projections to the anterior temporal and frontal cortex" (44).

It must be emphasized that ictal aggression plays a negligible role in criminal violence. The notion that a premeditated crime carried out for gain or revenge can be attributed to ictal discharges or post-ictal automatism is inconsistent with all that is known about epilepsy. Ictal, post-ictal and inter-ictal aggression is almost without exception poorly organized, senseless, and out of character.

Explosive rage is only one of a number of disturbances which may be associated with temporal lobe epilepsy. Intermittent symptoms include depersonalization, depression, free-floating anxiety, and hallucinations. These patients, unlike most psychotics, usually describe their symptoms objectively and accurately.

More persistent symptoms include personality disorders and a schizo-phrenia-like syndrome. In an important paper, Slater, Beard, and Glithero (90) reported—as had other before them—the development of acute psychotic episodes closely resembling schizophrenia many years after the onset of temporal lobe seizures. The mental symptoms often appear at a time when the frequency and severity of the seizures are waning. The mode of onset can be acute, subacute, or insidious, and the disorder tends to be episodic. Psychiatric examination shows a high incidence of personality changes with an organic complexion, but these patients differ from true schizophrenics in that the personality usually remains warm and outgoing. As Rodin has pointed out, "The temporal lobe patient can be brought to tears or to be made to laugh gaily within a matter of minutes by a skillful interviewer. . . . This cannot be done with patients with what one calls primary schizophrenia" (91). Moreover, they are not chronically irritable or malevolent and the attacks of rage constitute a break in the life-style of the patient. In the patients described by Slater and his colleagues, pneumoencephalography disclosed the presence of an atrophic process of the brain in 37 out of 56 cases.

A personal case illustrates some of these features:

An intelligent woman of 38, with a warm and pleasant personality, developed temporal lobe attacks. In only two of these did she lose consciousness. Most of the attacks consisted of a momentary dreamy state during which external objects appeared unfamiliar. Over the same period she became subject to attacks of what she called insane rage. She was unaware of any external or internal reason for her anger. She might go down to the cellar and start breaking things or she would scream at her children or her husband for no reason at all. These attacks disturbed her greatly and she had been under psychotherapy for eight years without benefit. She complained of episodes of depersonalization. Sometimes she felt that "my head is in one position, my mind in another, and my body in a third." Occasionally when she would reach for an object it would seem to move slightly. She achieved good grades in school except in mathematics; even the simplest calculation was, and is, beyond her capacity. She suffers from pathological intolerance for alcohol which had not troubled her in her earlier years. An electroencephalogram three years after the onset of the seizures showed epileptic spikes in all leads, especially in the left temporal area. More recent tests show diffuse slowing without any focal or paroxysmal activity. The seizures, the attacks of explosive rage, and her schizoid symptoms disappeared entirely when she was given 400 mg. of phenytoin daily but a new symptom developed. She had been aware for most of her life that she was devoid of an ordinary sense of fear such as other people have. It did not disturb her to go out alone at night in a bad neighborhood. With phenytoin, she developed a normal sense of fear and apprehension under such circumstances.

The therapeutic response in this case supports Symonds' suggestion (92) that the schizophrenic features encountered in some temporal lobe epileptics are the result of interference with thought and perception by persistent subclinical seizure activity in the temporal lobe. The same inference may be drawn from the remarkable decrease of both seizures and personality disorders, including aggression, which follows hemisphelrectomy in children with infantile hemiplegia. In children who have suffered a major unilateral cerebral insult such as a severe infarction, seizures become less frequent and inter-seizure behavior improves when the damaged cerebral hemisphere is removed surgically (93).

BRAIN TUMORS

Tumors involving the limbic system and colloid cysts of the third vertricle are apt to produce apathy even before intracranial pressure has risen (28). They can also give rise to angry aggressive behavior. This occurred in 6% of 250 cases of temporal lobe glioma studied by Bingley (87) and in seven out of 17 cases of tumors in limbic structures reported by Malamud (94). It has been reported in a case with a dermoid cyst of the third vertricle (95) and in hypothalamic tumors, sub-frontal meningiomas, tumors involving the cingulate gyri, tumors and cysts of the septum pellucidum, and glioma of the optic chiasm. A personal case:

An intellectually precocious boy of 14 with undescended testes and an infantile penis gave a two-month history of episodic rage in which he became violent. Between attacks he was frightened and remorseful. There were no abnormal signs on neurological examination or pneumoencephalography but a CAT scan showed a cyst lying between the hypothalamus and the pituitary fossa. It contained an oily fluid.

Explosive rage sometimes occurs for the first time *after* the removal of a cerebral tumor. This occured in five cases in the present series—a glioma of the temporal lobe, three parasaggital meningiomas and a sphenoid ridge meningioma.

INFECTIONS

Viral and bacterial invasions of the brain are occasional causes of explosive rage and aggressive behavior, which usually appear *after* the acute phase is over. Such behaviors can also occur in the acute stage of cerebral malaria and rabies. Episodes of rage and destructiveness may occur in the early stage of general paresis and are sometimes seen following severe bacterial meningitis and cerebral abscess.

Viral encephalitis has provided some of the most dramatic examples of post-infective episodic rage. It occasionally occurs as a sequel to herpes simplex encephalitis, which has a predilection for the temporal lobes. Herpes encephalitis can also produce extreme placidity, the reverse of hyper-irritability. Corsellis and his colleagues have reported on the anatomical findings in three patients who died after prolonged survival from this disease. During life they presented a Kluver-Bucy syndrome—extreme placidity, inability to retain memories for even a minute, and a marked oral tendency. At autopsy they were found to have almost complete destruction of the anterior portion of both temporal lobes, including the amygdala (96). It has already ben pointed out that encephalitis lethargica provided many examples of the dyscontrol syndrome.

CEREBRAL VASCULAR DISEASE

A stroke or subarachnoid hemorrhage occasionally causes explosive rage either as the patient emerges from the coma or as a delayed phenomenon. In the present series it occurred in a man who had a subarachnoid hemorrhage accompanied by left hemiparesis, and in another man who had multiple transient ischemic attacks involving both the carotid and vertebral basilar systems. The writer has also seen the reverse situation:

A physician had been prone to severe temper outbursts throughout his life. He often assaulted his wife. He was hypertensive and diabetic, and developed a mild hemiparesis as a result of a cerebral infarct. This incident increased his violence. One evening, however, he complained of unaccustomed dizziness and appeared a little confused. The next morning his wife noticed a striking change in his temperament. He had suddenly become benign and remained so for a year until his death from a myocardial infarction. During this period he never lost his temper and was kind and considerate; he was also rather irresponsible and facetious. Autopsy revealed so many small infarcts in both hemispheres and in the brain stem that it was impossible to draw any conclusions as to which was responsible for his change of behavior.

MISCELLANEOUS NEUROLOGICAL DISEASES

Paroxysmal rage is sometimes seen in presenile and senile dementia. It is not uncommon, with or without schizophrenic-like symptoms, in Huntington's chorea, a disease in which there is degeneration of the caudate nucleus and putamen. These structures are not usually considered to be part of the limbic system, but electrical stimulation of the caudate nucleus has a pacifying effect on Rhesus monkeys. Episodic dyscontrol has also been reported in normal pressure hydrocephalus and in the present series it was the sole symptom of arrested internal hydrocephalus in a young man. Multiple sclerosis of late onset appeared to be responsible for the development of temporal lobe seizures and the dyscontrol syndrome in four personal cases; it was present in 1% of 666 cases of temporal lobe epilepsy studied by Currie and his colleagues (86). However, the association betwen multiple sclerosis and seizures is sometimes fortuitous, postmortem examination revealing the presence of some other disease in addition to the multiple sclerosis.

In Down's syndrome (mongolism), children are generally passive and happy, but if they survive to the third or fourth decade, some develop a pre-senile dementia akin to Alzheimer's disease, together with aggressive behavior and seizures. In these cases neurofibrillary degeneration is especially marked in the hippocampal gyrus, the cortex of the temporal lobe, and the cingulate gyrus (97). Aggressive behavior is also characteristic of certain rare metabolic disorders involving the nervous system— the San Filippo syndrome, phenylketonuria, and the Spielmeyer-Vogt disease.

Diseases which involve the hippocampus do not *necessarily* produce either seizures or disordered behavior. The same inconsistency is seen in tumors involving the limbic system. All the evidence derived from experimental procedures in animals and psychosurgical operations in man points to the fact that both the production of rage and its control depend to some extent on the precise position of lesions within the limbic system. Even within the amygdala complex alone, the exact locus of the lesion may determine whether rage or placidity is to be the result. Moreover, in man heredity appears to play a part in determining whether a given lesion will or will not give rise to seizures; the same may be true of episodic rage.

ENDOCRINE AND METABOLIC DISORDERS

Of the metabolic disorders that can trigger explosive rage, hypoglycemia is the most common, whether it be functional, iatrogenic, or due to an insulinoma.

Wilder (98, 99) assembled a formidable bibliography in the 1940s of violent behavior triggered by hypoglycemia, including references to many instances of intrafamilial strife. Hill and Sargant described a case of matricide caused by hypoglycemia in a man who had suffered brain damage at birth or in infancy (100). A modest fall of blood sugar induced by intravenous tolbutamide activates epileptic discharges in the EEG in some patients with seizures (101). Since hypoglycemia is usually marked by sweating, early flushing of the face and a sense of weakness, rather than violence, the question arises as to whether the occurrence of explosive rage under these circumstances should suggest the presence of epilepsy or structural disease, as in Hill and Sargant's case. By way of analogy, hypoglycemia can produce hemiparesis, monoparesis, or aphasia when it occurs in individuals with carotid stenosis.

The fact that rage does not appear during the hypoglycemia induced by a five-hour glucose tolerance test, even in people who suffer from hypoglycemic anger outside the laboratory, emphasizes the role of the social setting. It has already been noted that the same applies to pathological intoxication and to the results of electrical stimulation of the brain.

Angry aggressive behavior is seen from time to time in Cushing's disease and in the Cushing syndrome. It can also occur acutely, along with other symptoms of a toxic psychosis, as a result of hypocalcemia induced by parathyroidectomy.

Premenstrual tension in women provides another example of the effects of metabolic and chemical factors on the rage threshold, a circumstance which is familiar to many. Morton and his colleagues found from a 1953 study of the records of women prisoners that 62% of their violent crimes were committed during the premenstrual week and 2% at the end of menstruation (102). This trend is confirmed by Dalton (103). The premenstrual syndrome is accompanied by depression, irritability, and feelings of futility and paranoia; presumably in individuals with inadequate controls, these feelings generate aggressive behavior. More information is needed as to whether premenstrual tension can evoke episodic rage in the absence of psychological or neurological disorders.

DIAGNOSTIC AIDS

The study of patients suffering from the dyscontrol syndrome requires a complete medical history which must go all the way back to the womb. Precise details are desirable as to prenatal, natal, and postnatal events, and subsequent illnesses and injuries. Evidence of postnatal hypoxia and infantile convulsions is important because these are frequent precursors of temporal lobe epilepsy. It must also be remembered that repeated minor head injuries have a cumulative effect on the brain, both in childhood and in adult life. A careful historical search must be conducted to detect failure to reach the physical and mental milestones of development at an appropriate age and a search must also be made for evidence of minimal brain dysfunction in childhood.

The family history must be scrutinized for evidence of epilepsy; heredity plays a part not only in the centrencephalic form of grand mal and petit mal, but also in temporal lobe epilepsy, despite the fact that a structural lesion is present in a great majority of the latter. Bray and Wiser (78) found that 30% of their patients with temporal lobe spikes and sharp waves, who had had seizures, had a family history of epilepsy. Other things to be looked for include mental illness, personality disorders, an ungovernable temper, alcoholism, intrafamilial strife, abandonment by a parent, lack of affection in infancy, and brutal treatment in infancy and childhood.

Psychiatric examination is desirable not only to throw light on personal and intrafamilial psychodynamics, but also for the assessment of the patient's personality before the brain injury occurred. Psychological tests designed to identify physical disorders are useful when there is no overt evidence of organic disease. A routine neurological examination itself seldom discloses anything amiss, but a search for evidence of specific learning deficiencies often proves fruitful.

Laboratory investigation starts with electroencephalography. A normal result from a single test with scalp electrodes has little value. There is an appreciable increase in the yield of positive findings on the second or third test; this may be due in part to the fact that the patient has become more relaxed about the procedure. Sleep records with nasopharyngeal electrodes, which can pick up discharges from the medial aspect of the temporal lobes, are essential. The yield is still further improved by activation techniques—hyperventilation, photic stimulation, and the use of pharmacological agents. Even when all these methods fail, and even when recordings taken from the surface of the brain prove negative, seizure activity may be found in deep subcortical structures by using depth electrodes. Most clinicians have to make a diagnosis without these sophisticated techniques; they are mentioned only to emphasize the limitations of the scalp-electrode EEG and the danger of concluding that because a scalp EEG is normal, all is well within the brain.

Plain x-rays of the skull should always include half-axial views to display the base, because in patients with temporal lobe seizures the middle fossa on one side may be smaller than the other, signifying that something has happened in early life to stunt the growth of the temporal lobe on that side.

Computerized axial tomography (the CAT scan) makes it possible to identify morphological abnormalities such as focal dilatations of the ventricular system (notably the temporal horn), porencephalic cysts, cortical atrophy, tumors, angiomatous malformations, and internal hydrocephalus. This non-invasive outpatient procedure is proving valuable in identifying organic pathology in cases suffering from explosive rage, even when pneumoencephalography and arteriography have failed to reveal anything amiss; but it is necessary to remember that small lesions such as the all-important medial temporal lobe sclerosis may escape detection or may be obscured by artifacts.

A five-hour glucose tolerance test should be carried out if there is the slightest suggestion of hypoglycemia.

TREATMENT

Explosive rage is a symptom of many disorders, psychological and physical, structural and metabolic, congenital and acquired, and in many cases it has multiple roots. The presence of organic disease, for instance, does not preclude the development of a functional psychosis, and vice versa. Moreover, the sense of guilt caused by an organic dyscontrol syndrome often gives rise to a train of secondary emotional disorders. The brain damage which is causing the attacks of rage can itself produce disorders of thought, emotion, and behavior. These circumstances give rise to problems in the management and treatment of the patient.

Should he/she be in the hands of the psychiatrist or the neurologist? Rodin, from his great experience with epileptics, says

> I have tried in a number of these difficult treatment problems to restrict my role to the management of the seizure disorder itself and to have the psychiatrist take care of the mental and emotional

problems. It has never been successful. Direction in the total management was lacking and a characteristic question was: "Is this a symptom I should be talking to you about, or to Dr. X?" The neurologist has been played against the psychiatrist in the same way as children tend to play one parent against the other to obtain their gratifications. Unless the neurologist and the psychiatrist consult constantly with each other after each patient's visit, they cannot achieve anything worthwhile (91).

The same point has been made by Monroe (42). This problem also arises in dealing with the dyscontrol syndrome in non-epileptic subjects. There is no easy solution. It is essential for one doctor to take charge and there should be agreement, not only as to the general strategy of treatment, but also as to the identity and dose of medications to be used. Even this *detente* often fails to bridge the gap between psychodynamics and neurology. As one bewildered patient put it, "After 10 years of psychiatric treatment I have come to believe that my troubles are due to a sexual hangup. Now *you* tell me that it is all due to minor brain damage. Whom am I to believe?"

The social, psychological, and pharmacological management of the dyscontrol syndrome has been reviewed by Moyer (74) and discussed at some length by Monroe (42), Lion (104), and Lion and Monroe (105). Their writings should be consulted, including their chapters in this volume. There can be no doubt that the lives of these patients, and of their families, can be transformed by appropriate treatment.

The patient can often be taught to recognize a premonitory dysphoria and to take evasive action by walking away from irritating confrontations, by calling his physician, or by going to a clinic. A "hot-line" similar to that used for suicide prevention is desirable in any clinic that deals with violent patients (104), because whether the patient's impending rage is psychogenic or organic, or a mixture of the two, it can often be averted by a discussion with somebody outside the family circle.

In the organic type of dyscontrol it helps to explain that the attacks are largely physical in origin and will almost certainly respond to treatment. Reassurance is sorely needed, particularly by those who have vainly sought help in the past. The fact that their physician understands and is willing to help does much to allay the hostility and skepticism of these reluctant patients.

Alcohol must be avoided if it triggers attacks of rage.

It is prudent to point out to the patient and his family that it may take time to find the right drug and the correct dose. Paradoxical drug reactions are not uncommon and the writer has seen cases in which the attacks of rage were aggravated by phenytoin, primidone, diazepam, the phenothiazines, and meprobamate. It is therefore desirable to proceed cautiously, starting with a small dose and working up to the limits of tolerance, bearing in mind the fact that if the first drug prescribed does not work at once or has undesirable side-effects, these impulsive individuals are apt to go elsewhere. There are two types of intolerance. The first is indicated by the appearance of conventional toxic symptoms and signs; the second takes the form of an increase of the symptoms for which the drug is being given.

An occasional reason for therapeutic failure is that the patient does not take his medication regularly, or is not taking it at all. This may be because he lacks insight and sees no need for treatment or because the attacks bring him secondary gain such as avoidance of responsibility or the domination of others in the household. Attacks of rage may also afford welcome relief from emotional tension. Some forget to take their medication; others who are unemployed and penurious are disinclined to spend money on expensive drugs.

The attacks can usually be reduced and sometimes abolished by pharmacological agents. These should be given on a maintenance basis when the attacks come on without warning, but can be taken intermittently, at times of mounting tension, in patients who are aware of their prodromal symptoms. Women whose attacks are mainly premenstrual may fall into this latter group.

If there is clinical or EEG evidence of epilepsy, anticonvulsant medication is the first choice, preference being given to the hydantoinates or carbamazepine. The hydantoinates sometimes prevent explosive rage even in the absence of clinical or EEG evidence of epilepsy (42; personal observation), and the same is true of carbamazepine (106). Primidone has been less useful in the author's experience, though others recommend it (107). It often reduces the seizures, but sometimes aggravates the aggression; moreover, the dose needed to suppress seizures may cause an unacceptable degree of sedation. The same applies to barbiturates. Phenobarbital and secobarbital, whether alone or with alcohol, are recognized by young addicts as the drugs most likely to induce aggressive behavior (108). On the other hand, several patients have told me that smoking marihuana is the most effective and rapid method of dissipating explosive rage.

If anticonvulsants fail, meprobamate (which has a special effect on the amygdala and thalamus) should be added in doses of 400 mg. b.i.d., or one of the benzodiazapines can be used, e.g., oxazpam, diazepam, or chlordiazepoxide. Phenothiazines, so useful in the control of psychotic hostility, sometimes aggravate the organic dyscontrol syndrome. This may be because they lower the seizure thresholdi They can be used in conjunction with anticonvulsants.

The amphetamines and methylphenidate are effective in some aggressive hyperkinetic children and in some immature adults who have outgrown their hyperkinesis but remain subject to explosive rage (109).

Two careful studies have shown haloperidol to be effective in the treatment of children suffering from the hyperactive aggressive syndrome (110, 111). It has also proved useful in some adults suffering from the organic brain syndrome, but effective doses sometimes induce undue sedation.

The association between explosive rage and predatory aggression, on the one hand, and "maleness," on the other, has led to an extensive search for androgen antagonists (74). Stilbesterol has been used successfully in selected cases but its side-effects are unpopular.

In women whose attacks of explosive rage occur predominately in the premenstrual week, small doses of meprobamate can be used to advantage. Progesterones may or may not help. Diuretics make the patient feel more comfortable in a physical sense but do not seem to alter the rage threshold.

Propranolol, an adrenergic receptor blocking agent which in mice and rats has anticonvulsant properties and which also reduces the fighting behavior produced in rats by septal lesions (112, 113), has proved effective in abolishing the belligerence of patients who are emerging from coma induced by head injury or stroke, in abolishing the irritability of the post-concussion syndrome, and in preventing the less common attack of explosive rage which may persist as a chronic relic of brain injury (114). I have also found it useful, in conjunction with anticonvulsants, in preventing aggressive behavior in some individuals with psychomotor epilepsy. The value of the drug is enhanced by the fact that it does not sedate the patient in a general sense. Its central psychotropic effect appears to have nothing to do with its adrenergic blocking properties. The *dextro-* isomer of propranolol blocks aggressive behavior in animals, though it has little beta blocking capacity (115). A possibility which requires further study is that the central effects of the drug may be due to the action of its metabolites, several of which have been identified in man and dogs. Saelens and his associates (116) have found that one of these metabolites, propranolol glycol, which is present in the brain of treated animals, gives mice more protection against strychnine-induced convulsions than propranolol itself. Moreover, maximal anticonvulsant activity for propranolol glycol is obtained immediately following its injection, whereas the full effect of propranolol is delayed for about 10 minutes.*

The treatment of hypoglycemias depends on the underlying cause. When rage attacks occur as a result of functional hypoglycemia, it is best treated with frequent high protein meals, reduction of carbohydrate intake, and the regular administration of phenytoin. Phenformin hydrochloride is also advised by some authorities to inhibit the secretion of insulin.

Further discussion of pharmacotherapy, especially of psychotropic medications and functional sociopathic syndromes, may be found in chapter 16, which is devoted to drug treatment of these disorders.

Psychosurgical treatment should be limited to severe cases of dyscontrol which have not responded satisfactorily to conservative treatment, and it should only be carried out after careful psychological and physiological studies. The procedures which may be useful include unilateral temporal lobectomy, bilateral anterior temporal lobotomy, unilateral or bilateral stereotaxic amygdalotomy, stereotaxic posteromedial hypothalamotomy, anterior and posterior cingulotomy, anterior thalamotomy, and orbitofrontal tractotomy. These techniques, and their results, are discussed in two books, one edited by Hitchcock, Laitinen, and Vaernet (73), the other by Fields and Sweet (117). The results vary from good to indifferent, but the catastrophic disasters which in the past sometimes resulted from frontal lobotomy are avoided by these selective procedures. It is to be hoped that the search for still greater refinements will be pursued despite the recent irrational, emotional, and ill-informed public opposition which brought such research virtually to a standstill in the United States in the early 1970s. Fortunately the National Commission for the Protection of Human Subjects of Biomedical and Behavioral Research has recently approved research in psychosurgery provided it is carried out under well defined and stringent rules (118).

REFERENCES

1. Rush, Benjamin. Medical Inquiries and Observations upon the Diseases of the Mind (1812). New York: Hafner Publishing Company, 1962. Published under the auspices of the New York Academy of Medicine.
2. Prichard, J. D. Treatise on Insanity. London: Sherwood, Gilbert and Piper, 1835.
3. Cleckley, H. The Mask of Sanity. 4th ed. St. Louis: C. V. Mosby, Co., 1964.
4. Craft, M. Ten Studies into Psychopathic Personality. Baltimore: Williams and Wilkins, 1965.

---

* Further propranolol research, completed too late for inclusion herein, is also encouraging.

5. McCORD, W. and McCORD, J. *Psychopathy and Delinquency*. New York: Grune, 1956.
6. STORR, A. *Human Aggression*. New York: Atheneum, 1968.
7. WILSON, S. A. K. *Neurology*. Vol. 1. London: Edward Arnold and Co., 1940.
8. BENDER, L. In: J. B. Neal (ed.), *Encephalitis—A Clinical Study*. Grune and Stratton, 1962.
9. KANNER, L. *Child Psychiatry*. Springfield: Charles C Thomas, 1968.
10. CAVENESS, W. F. Epilepsy, a Product of Trauma in Our Time. *Epilepsia* 17 (2): 207-217, 1976.
11. HARLOW, J. Recovery from the Passage of an Iron Bar Through the Head. *Publ. Mass. Med. Soc.* 2:329-332, 1868.
12. BLAU, A. Mental Changes Following Head Trauma in Children. *Arch. Neurol.* 35:723-730, 1936.
13. BLACK, P., JEFFRIES, J. J., BLUMER, D., WELLNER, A., and WALKER, A. E. The Posttraumatic Syndrome in Children. In: A. E. Walker, W. F. Caveness, and M. Critchley (Eds.), *The Late Effects of Head Injury*. Springfield: Charles C Thomas, 1969.
14. ANDERSON, C. *Society Pays. The High Cost of Minimal Brain Damage in America*. New York: Walker and Company, 1972.
15. CANTWELL, D. P. *The Hyperactive Child. Diagnosis, Management, Current Research*. New York: Spectrum Publications, Inc., 1975.
16. CLEMENTS, S. D. and PETERS, J. E. Minimal Brain Dysfunction in the School Age Child. *Arch. Gen. Psychiatry* 6:185-197, 1962.
17. GUBBAY, S. S. *The Clumsy Child*. Philadelphia: W. B. Saunders, Co., 1975.
18. MYKLEBUST, H. R. Learning Disabilities in Minimal Brain Dysfunction in Children. In: D. B. Tower (Ed.), *The Nervous System*. New York: Raven Press, 1975.
19. PINCUS, J. H. and TUCKER, G. *Behavioral Neurology*. New York: Oxford University Press, 1974.
20. CANTWELL, D. P. Psychiatric Illness in Families of Hyperactive Children. *Arch. Gen. Psychiatry* 27:919-977, 1972.
21. GLUECK, S. and GLUECK, E. *Criminal Careers in Retrospect*. New York: The Commonwealth Fund, Harvard University Press, 1963.
22. MORRISON, J. R. and MINKOFF, K. Explosive Personality as a Sequel to the Hyperactive Child Syndrome. *Comp. Psychiatry* 16:343-348, 1975.
23. O'NEILL, P. and ROBINS, L. N. The Relationship of Childhood Behavior Problems and Adult Psychiatric Status: A 30 Year Followup of 150 Patients. *Am. J. Psychiatry* 114:961-969, 1958.
24. ROBINS, L. N. *Deviant Children Grown Up: Sociological and Psychiatric Study of the Sociopathic Personality*. Baltimore: Williams and Wilkins, 1966.
25. THOMPSON, B. M. *The Psychopathic Delinquent and Criminal*. Springfield: Charles C Thomas, 1953.
26. WOOD, D. R., REIMHERR, F. W., WENDER, P. H., and JOHNSON, B. E. Diagnosis and Treatment of Minimal Brain Dysfunction in Adults. *Arch. Gen. Psychiatry* 33:1453-1460, 1976.
27. DIXON, H. B. F. and HARGREAVES, W. H. Cycticercocosis (Taenia Solium): A Further 10 Year Clinical Study Covering 268 Cases. *Q. J. Med.* 13:107-121, 1969.
28. ELLIOTT, F. A. Midline Syndromes. In: P. J. Vinken and G. W. Bruyn (Eds.), *Handbook of Clinical Neurology*. Amsterdam: North Holland Publishing Company, 1969.
29. LURIA, A. R. Frontal Lobe Syndromes. In: P. J. Vinken and G. W. Boyn (Eds.), *Handbook in Neurology*. Vol. 2. Amsterdam: North Holland Publishing House, 1969.

30. BIANCHI, L. *The Mechanisms of the Brain and the Functions of the Frontal Lobe.* Translation by J. H. McDonald. Edinburgh and New York: Wood, 1922.
31. DENNY-BROWN, D. The Frontal Lobes and Their Functions. In: A. Feiling (Ed.), *Modern Trends in Neurology.* New York: Paul Hoeber, Inc., 1951.
32. FREEMAN, W. and WATTS, J. W. *Psychosurgery.* Springfield: Charles C Thomas, 1947.
33. WEINSTEIN, E. A. and KAHN, L. R. The Syndrome of Anosognosia. *Arch. Neurol. Psychiatry* 65:772-791, 1950.
34. PARKER, T. and ALLERTON, R. *The Courage of His Convictions.* London: Hutchinson, 1962.
35. DAVIS, W. A. Child Rearing in the Class Structure of American Society. In: M. S. Sussman (Ed.), *Source Book of Marriage and the Family.* Boston: Houghton Mifflin, 1963.
36. PRIBRAM, H. Comparative Neurology and the Evolution of Behavior. In: A. Roe and G. G. Simpson (Eds.), *Behavior and Evolution.* New Haven: 1958.
37. MANGUN, C. W. The Psychopathic Criminal. *J. Crim. Psychopathol.* 4:117-127, 1942.
38. GIBBENS, T. C. N., POND, D. A., and STAFFORD-CLARK, D. A Followup Study of Criminal Psychopaths. *J. Mental Sci.* 105:108-115, 1959.
39. DETRE, T. The Nosology of Violence. In: W. S. Fields and W. H. Sweet (Eds.), *Neural Bases of Violence and Aggression.* St. Louis: Warren H. Green, 1975.
40. HILL, J. D. and WATTERSON, D. EEG Studies of Psychopathic Personalities. *J. Neurol. Neurosurg. Psychiatry* 5:47-65, 1942.
41. KNOTT, J. R. and GOTTLIEB, J. S. The Electroencephalograph in Psychopathic Personalities. *Psychosom. Med.* 5:139-141, 1943.
42. MONROE, R. R. *Episodic Behavioral Disorders.* Cambridge, Mass.: Harvard University Press, 1970.
43. SILVERMAN, D. The EEG of Criminals. *Arch. Neurol.* 52:38-42, 1944.
44. WILLIAMS, D. Neural Factors Related to Habitual Aggression. *Brain* 92:503-520, 1969.
45. HARE, R. D. Psychopathy. In: P. Venables and S. M. Christie (Eds.), *Psychophysiology.* New York: Wiley, 1975.
46. KAES, T. Die Grosshirnrinoe des Menschen und in Ihren Wassen und in Ihren Fassengehalt. Ein Gehirnanatomische Atlas Jena. Fischer. 1907.
47. NORTON, W. T. Myelin: Structure and Biochemistry. In: D. B. Tower (Ed.), *The Basic Neurosciences.* New York: Raven Press, 1975.
48. YAKOVLEV and LECOURS. In: A. Minkowski (Ed.), *Regional Development of the Brain in Early Life,* 1967.
49. PURPURA, D. P. and SCHADE, J. P. (Eds.). *Progress in Brain Research.* Vol. 4. Amsterdam: Elsevier, 1969.
50. RYLANDER, G. Personality Changes after Operation on the Frontal Lobe in a Clinical Study of 32 Cases. *Acta Psychiat. Scand.* (Suppl.) 20:1-327, 1939.
51. SMYTHIES, T. R. *The Neurological Foundations of Psychiatry.* New York: Oxford University Press, 1966.
52. HUBEL, D. H. and WIESEL, T. The Period of Susceptibility and the Physiological Effects of Unilateral Eye Closure in Kittens. *J. Psysiol.* 200:919-936, 1970.
53. MARK, V. H. and ERVIN, F. R. *Violence and the Brain.* New York: Harper and Row, 1970.
54. KAPLAN, O. Kopftrauma und Psychosen. *Alleg. Z. Psychiat.* 56:292-296, 1899.
55. WALKER, A. E. and BLUMER, D. Long Term Effects of Temporal Lobe Lesions on Sexual Behavior and Aggression. In: W. S. Fields and W. H. Sweet (Eds.), *Neural Bases of Violence and Aggression.* St. Louis: Warren H. Green, 1975.
56. MOHAN, K. F., SALO, M. W., and NAGASWAMI, S. A Case of Limbic System Dysfunction with Hypersexuality and Rugue State. *Dis. Nerv. Syst.* 36:621-624, 1975.

57. ZOLA, E. *La Bête Humaine* (The Beast in Man). London: Elek Books, 1969.
58. FALRET, J. De l'état mental des épileptiques. *Arch. Gen. Med.* 16:666, 17:461, 18: 423. 1860, 1861.
59. PINCUS, J. H. and GLASER, G. H. The Syndrome of "Minimal Brain Damage" in Childhood. *N. Engl. J. Med.* 275:27-30, 1966.
60. British Report on Violence in Marriage. Select Committee, Vol. 1 Report. London: Her Majesty's Stationary Office, 1974-1975.
61. ISAACSON, R. L. *The Limbic System.* New York: Plenum Press, 1974.
62. MACLEAN, P. W. The Hypothalamus and Emotional Behavior. In: W. Haymaker, E. Anderson, and W. S. H. Nauta (Eds.), *The Hypothalamus.* Springfield: Charles C Thomas, 1969.
63. BOERHAAVE, O. *The Aphorisms of Boerhaave,* translated by Delacoste, 1715.
64. GOWERS, W. R. *Diseases of the Nervous System.* Vol. 2. London: Churchill, 1893.
65. BARD, P. Diencephalic Mechanism for the Expression of Rage, with Special Reference to the Sympathetic Nervous System. *Am. J. Physiol.* 89:490-515, 1928.
66. SANO, K., YOSKIOKA, M., OGASHIWA, A., ISHIJIMA, B., and OHYE, C. Postero-medial Hypothalamotomy in the Treatment of Aggressive Behavior. *Confin. Neurol.* 27:164-167, 1966.
67. BARD, P. and MOUNTCASTLE, V. The Hypothalamic "Savage Syndrome." *Res. Publ. Assoc. Res. Nerv. Ment. Dis.* 52:91, 1974.
68. GLUSMAN, M. The Hypothalamic "Savage Syndrome." *Res. Publ. Assoc. Res. Nerv. Ment. Dis.* 52:87, 1974.
69. GLOOR, P. Electrophysiological Studies of the Amygdala. In: W. S. Fields and W. H. Sweet (Eds.), *Neural Bases of Violence and Aggression.* St. Louis: Warren H. Green, 1975.
70. HEATH, R. G., MONROE, R. R., and MICKLE, W. Stimulation of the Amygdala in a Schizophrenic Patient. *Am. J. Psychiatry* 111:862-863, 1955.
71. MARK, V. H., SWEET, W., and ERVIN, F. R. Deep Temporal Lobe Stimulation and Destructive Lesions in Episodically Violent Temporal Lobe Patients. In: W. S. Fields and W. H. Sweet (Eds.), *Neural Bases of Violence and Aggression.* St. Louis: Warren H. Green, 1975.
72. DELGADO, J. M. R. *Physical Control of the Mind.* New York: Harper and Row, 1969.
73. HITCHCOCK, E., LAITINEN, L., and VAERNET, K. (Eds.). *Psychosurgery.* Springfield: Charles C Thomas, 1972.
74. MOYER, K. E. Physiology of Aggression and the Implications for Aggression Control. In: J. L. Singer (Ed.), *The Control of Aggression and Violence.* New York: Academic Press, 1971.
75. BREMER, J. *Asexualisation: A Followup Study of 244 Cases.* New York: Macmillan, 1959.
76. DAVENPORT, C. B. The Feebly Inhibited. 1. Violent Temper and Its Inheritance. *J. Nerv. Ment. Dis.* 42:593-628, 1915.
77. MITSUDA, H. *Clinical Genetics in Psychiatry.* Tokyo: Ogaku Shoin, 1967.
78. BRAY, P. F. and WISER, W. C. Evidence of a Genetic Etiology of Temporal—Central Abnormalities in Focal Epilepsy. *New Engl. J. Med.* 271:926-933, 1964.
79. MATHIESON, G. Pathology of Temporal Lobe Foci. In: J. K. Penry and D. D. Daly (Eds.), *Advances in Neurology.* Vol. 11. New York: Raven Press, 1975.
80. FALCONER, M. A., SERAFETINIDES, E. A., and CORSELLIS, J. A. N. Etiology and Pathogenesis of Temporal Lobe Epilepsy. *Arch. Neurol.* 10:233-248.
81. HOOPER, R. F., McGREGOR, J. R., and NATHAN, P. Explosive Rage After Head Injuries. *J. Mental Sci.* 91:458-464, 1965.
82. CROMPTON, M. R. Hypothalamic Lesions Following Closed Head Injury. *Brain* 94:165-172, 1971.

83. CRITCHELY, M. *The Dyslexic Child.* 2nd Ed. London: Heinemann Medical Books, 1970.
84. STEVENS, J. R. Interictal Clinical Complication of Complex Partial Seizures. In: J. K. Penry and D. D. Daly (Eds.), *Advances in Neurology.* Vol. 11. New York: Raven Press, 1975.
85. RODIN, E. A. Psychomotor Epilepsy and Aggressive Behavior. *Arch. Gen. Psychiatry,* 28:210-213, 1973.
86. CURRIE, S., HEATHFIELD, K. W., HENSON, R. A., and SCOTT, D. F. Clinical Course and Prognosis of Temporal Lobe Epilepsy; a Survey of 666 Patients. *Brain* 94:173-190, 1971.
87. BINGLEY, T. Mental Symptoms in Temporal Lobe Epilepsy and Temporal Lobe Glioma. *Acta Psychiatr. Scand.* 33 (Suppl. 120):1-151, 1958.
88. GASTAUT, G., MORIN, G., and LESEVRE, N. Etude du comportement des épileptiques psychomoteurs dans l'intervalle de leurs crises. *Ann. Med. Psychol.* 113:1-29, 1955.
89. WILLIAMS, D. The Structure of Emotions Reflected in Epileptic Experiences. *Brain* 79:29-67, 1956.
90. SLATER, E., BEARD, A. W., and GLITHERO, E. The Schizophrenia-like Psychoses of Epilepsy. *Br. J. Psychiatry* 109:95-150, 1963.
91. RODIN, E. A. Psychosocial Management of Patients with Complex Partial Seizures. In: J. K. Penry and D. D. Daly (Eds.), *Advances in Neurology.* Vol. 11. New York: Raven Press, 1975.
92. HILL, J. D., POND, D., and SYMONDS, C. P. The Schizophrenia-like Psychoses of Epilepsy. *Proc. R. Soc. Med.* 55:311, 1962.
93. WHITE, H. H. Cerebral Hemispherectomy in the Treatment of Infantile Hemiplegia. *Confin. Neurol.* 21:1-50, 1961.
94. MALAMUD, N. Psychiatric Disorders in Intracranial Tumors of the Limbic System. *Arch. Neurol.* 17:113-123, 1967.
95. ALPERS, B. J. Relation of the Hypothalamus to Disorders of Personality. Report of a Case. *J. Neurol. Psychiatry* 38:291-303, 1937.
96. CORSELLIS, J. A. N., JANOTA, I., and HIERONS, R. A Clinico-Pathological Study of Long Standing Cases of Limbic Encephalitis. Paper read before the Association of British Neurologists, London, 1975.
97. JERVIS, G. S. Early Senile Dementia in Mongoloid Idiocy. *Am. J. Psychiatry* 105: 102-106, 1948.
98. WILDER, J. Problems of Criminal Psychology Related to Hypoglycemic States. *J. Crim. Psychopathol.* 1:219, 1940.
99. WILDER, J. Sugar Metabolism in Its Relation to Criminology. In: R. W. Lindner and R. V. Seliger (Eds.), *Handbook of Criminal Psychology.* New York: Philosophical Library, 1947.
100. HILL, D., and SARGANT, W. A. A Case of Matricide. *Lancet* 1:526-529, 1943.
101. GREEN, J. B. The Activation of EEG Abnormalities by Tolbutamide-induced Hypoglycemia. *Neurology* 12:192-200, 1963.
102. MORTON, J. H., ADDITON, H., ADDISON, R. G., HUNT, L., and SULLIVAN, H. A Clinical Study of Premenstrual Tension. *Am. J. Obstet. Gynecol.* 65:1182-1191, 1953.
103. DALTON, K. *The Premenstrual Syndrome.* Springfield: Charles C Thomas, 1964.
104. LION, J. R. *Evaluation and Management of the Violent Patient.* Springfield: Charles C Thomas, 1972.
105. LION, J. R., MONROE, R. R. Drugs in the Treatment of Human Aggression. *J. Nerv. Ment. Dis.* 160:75-80, 1975.
106. DALBY, M. A. Behavioral Effects of Carbamazepine. In: J. K. Penry and D. D. Daly (Eds.), *Advances in Neurology,* Vol. 11. New York: Raven Press, 1975.
107. MONROE, R. R. and WISE, S. Combined Phenothiazines, Chlordiazoxide and

Primidone Therapy for Uncontrolled Psychotic Patients. *Am. J. Psychiatry* 122: 694-698, 1965.

108. TINKLENBERG, J. R. and WOODROW, K. M. Drug Use Among Youthful Assaultative Offenders. *Res. Publ. Assoc. Res. Nerv. Ment. Dis.* 52:Chapter 10, 1974.

109. BAN, T. A. *Psychopharmacology.* Baltimore: Williams and Wilkins, 1969.

110. BARKER, P. and FRAZIER, I. A. A Controlled Trial of Haloperidol. *Br. J. Psychiatry* 114:855-857, 1968.

111. CUNNINGHAM, M. A., PILLAI, V., and ROGERS, W. J. B. Haloperidol in the Treatment of Children with Severe Behavioral Disorders. *Br. J. Psychiatry* 114:512-512, 1968.

112. GREENBLATT, D. J. and SHADER, R. I. On the Psychopharmacology of Beta-adrenergic Blockade. *Curr. Ther. Res.* 14:615-617, 1972.

113. MURMANN, W., ALMITANTE, L., and SACCANI-GUELFI, M. Central Nervous System Effects of Beta-Adrenergic Receptor Blocking Agents. *J. Pharm. Pharmacol.* 18:317-318, 1966.

114. ELLIOTT, F. A. Propranolol for the Control of Belligerent Behavior Following Acute Brain Damage. *Annals of Neurology* 1:489-492, 1977.

115. BAINBRIDGE, J. E. and GREENWOOD, D. T. Tranquilizing Effects of Propranolol Demonstrated in Rats. *Neuropharmacology* 10:453-458, 1971.

116. SAELENS, D. A., WALLE, T., and PRIVITERA, B. J. Central Nervous System Effects and Metabolic Disposition of a Glycol Metabolite of Propanolol. *J. Pharmacol. Exp. Ther.* 188:86-92, 1974.

117. FIELDS, W. S. and SWEET, W. H. *Neural Bases of Violence and Aggression.* St. Louis: Warren H. Green, 1975.

118. National Commission Report, *Science* 194:299-301, 1976.

FURTHER SUGGESTED READING

ALPERS, B. J. Personality and Emotional Disorders Associated with Hypothalamic Lesions. *Psychosom. Med.* 2:283-303, 1940.

BACH-Y-RITA, G., LION, J. R., CLIMENT, C. F., and ERVIN, F. R. Episodic Dyscontrol: A Study of 130 Violent Patients. *Am. J. Psychiatry* 127:1473-1478, 1971.

BRICKNER, R. M. Bilateral Frontal Lobectomy: Followup Report of a Case. *Arch. Neurol. Psychiatry* 41:580-584, 1939.

BRICKNER, R. M., ROSNER, A. A., and MUNROE, R. Physiological Aspects of the Obsessive State. *Psychosom. Med.* 2:309-383, 1960.

ELLIOTT, F. A. The Neurology of Explosive Rage. *Practitioner* 217:51-60, 1976.

GLASER, G. H. The Problem of Psychosis in Temporal Lobe Epileptics. *Epilepsia* 5:271-278, 1964.

HILL, J. D. The EEG in Psychiatry. In: J. D. Hill and G. Parr (Eds.), *Electroencephalography.* New York: Macmillan, 1963.

LINDSAY, J. M. M. Genetic Epilepsy. *Epilepsia* 12:47-59, 1971.

NARABAYASHI, H. and UNO, M. Long Range Results of Stereotaxic Amygdalatomy for Behavioral Disorders. *Confin. Psychiatr.* 27:168-172, 1966.

PAMPIGLIONE, P. The Effect of Metabolic Disorders on Brain Activity. *J. R. Coll. Physicians Lond.* 7:347-364, 1973.

STEVENS, J. R. Psychiatric Implications of Psychosomatic Epilepsy. *Arch. Gen. Psychiatry* 14:461-471, 1966.

9

The Medical Model in Psychopathy and Dyscontrol Syndromes

RUSSELL R. MONROE, M.D.

The neuropsychiatric model for criminality has been in disrepute for years. In fact, the label of the "constitutional psychopathic inferior" is hardly remembered by current professionals. This is certainly justified in terms of 18th and 19th century views of Gall and Lambrosia that criminality could be identified through phrenology or the 19th century point of view that all disordered behavior simply reflected a genetic taint, degeneration of the nervous system or both. However, recent analysis of criminality gives some clues as to the multifactorial—that is, social, personal, and medical—contributions to such behavior, indicating interactive effects which predispose one to antisocial acts.

This suggests that an important research strategy will be careful phenomenological analysis of antisocial behavior with an attempt at development of subtypes of this all-too-inclusive label. Such strategy is paying off in the area of affective disorders and schizophrenia. Subtypes of these two broad diagnostic categories have clinical relevance in predicting response to psychopharmacologic agents and perhaps ultimately to psychotherapeutic or sociologic regimens. We need to be able to predict treatability and to determine proper treatment regimens on the basis of identifiable subtypes within broad diagnostic groups. It is time to again explore the usefulness of the medical model for psychopaths as well.

Figures 1, 3, 4, 5 and 6 and Tables 1 and 2 are reprinted with permission from *Brain Dysfunction in Aggressive Criminals*, by Russell R. Monroe, Lexington Books, Lexington, MA., 1978. Tables 3 and 4 are from are from "Neurologic Findings in Recidivist Aggressors," by Russell R. Monroe et al., in *Psychopathology and Brain Dysfunction*, edited by C. Shagass, S. Gershon, and A. J. Friedhoff, Raven Press, New York, 1977.

Even if a small subgroup of psychopaths would respond to a medical regimen, this could be a highly significant contribution to the fields of psychiatry and criminology.

To illustrate this point let us refer to Wolfgang's (1) cohort of 9,946 boys reared in a ghetto area of Philadelphia. Thirty-five percent had at least one contact with the police before the age of 18. Only 6.3% of this group were chronic offenders, however, as defined by having had five or more offenses. This small latter group of 627 boys were responsible for 5,305 delinquent acts, 52% of the total committed by the entire birth cohort. If there is a subgroup of delinquents that fit the medical model it might well be represented by these boys. Almost certainly, an effective treatment for this group would significantly reduce crime.

This was one of the issues which led us to investigate a group of recidivist aggressors incarcerated at the Patuxent Institution in Maryland. These were individuals who had a mean of 4.2 previous incarcerations and were adjudged "defective delinquents"; that is, for intellectual or emotional reasons they were incapable of existing in society without committing further crimes. They were incarcerated by the courts for an indeterminant sentence until they were felt to be reasonably safe for release to society. A detailed report of this study is in preparation but a brief summary follows.*

Ninety-three subjects were randomly selected, except for the fact that they had volunteered for and eventually completed the six-month study as the research population. Overt neurologic disorders (one epileptic) and overtly psychotic individuals (one simple schizophrenic) had been eliminated by preliminary screening processes before admission to the Institution; nevertheless, a significant number of the volunteers showed evidence for a central nervous system dysfunction on the basis of neurologic evaluation and electroencephalographic analysis. This suggested that the population, which was homogeneous from the points of view of the criminal justice system and demographic data, included a subgroup or groups that might fit the medical model. Broadly speaking, the hypothesis was as follows: Limbic system dysfunction in the form of circumscribed or focal excessive neuronal discharges may result in recurring violent acts of dyscontrol, leading to repeated arrests, convictions, and incarcerations.

Mark and Ervin (2), in their study *Violence and the Brain*, suggested

---

* The investigators on this project are all on the faculty of the Department of Psychiatry, University of Maryland School of Medicine. They are Drs. George U. Balis, J. David Barcik, Barbara Hulfish, John R. Lion, Matthew McDonald, Russell R. Monroe, and Mr. Jeffrey S. Rubin.

that violent dyscontrol acts were not only associated with this limbic system dysfunction but were also common among temporal lobe epileptics. They pointed out that not all temporal lobe epileptics are violent, however, and our data would indicate that very few recidivist aggressors have either the symptoms or the signs of temporal lobe epilepsy. None of our 93 subjects described symptoms typical of simple automatisms. Furthermore, the EEG findings on these subjects revealed only two with temporal spikes and four more with focal temporal slow activity, showing only 6% of our population to have had the slightest indication of temporal lobe foci. The concept of temporal lobe epilepsy as a cause of crime would thus seem to be a simplistic inaccuracy.

On the other hand, data reported previously (3) suggested that generalized paroxysmal theta activity reflecting central nervous instability—conceived either as a maturational lag (4) or as a reflection of an episodic focal ictal response within the limbic system (3, 5)—seemed to correlate with impulsive dyscontrol behavior. This author pointed out that such generalized paroxysmal theta activity was not in itself a sufficient cause for dyscontrol behavior; however, if an individual was destined for other reasons to become neurotic, psychotic, or psychopathic, symptoms were more likely to be episodic with associated dyscontrol behavior if such an EEG pattern could be elicited. I also pointed out that dyscontrol acts could occur in some individuals as purely learned responses having "hysteroid" characteristics, suggesting that psychodynamic factors were preeminently important. In these cases impulsive actions would be likely to be predominantly symbolic in nature, usually reflecting unconscious, unresolved conflicts (3).

Each of the 93 subjects had two EEG's which included awake, sleep, and hyperventilation recordings, both baseline and with drug (alpha chloralose)-induced activation. Eighty-two percent of the subjects on the first EEG and 88% on the second had at least borderline abnormalities whereas in previously studied control groups with no medical, neurologic or psychiatric history less than 20% had similar abnormalities (3). Thirty-eight of the 93 subjects had a significant period of high amplitude paroxysmal theta activity after drug activation in the pre- and post-hyperventilation records and almost continuous such activity during the hyperventilation period (6).

In the same group episodic symptoms were determined on a self-rating scale (Monroe Scale) which was developed by Plutchik (7) on the basis of my monograph on episodic behavioral disorders (3). This consisted of the following 18 statements rated on a 4 point scale as never ("0"), rarely ("1"), sometimes ("2"), and often ("3").

1. I have acted on a whim or impulse.
2. I have had sudden changes in my moods.
3. I have had the experience of feeling confused even in a familiar place.
4. I do not feel totally responsible for what I do.
5. I have lost control of myself even though I did not want to.
6. I have been surprised by my actions.
7. I have lost control of myself and hurt other people.
8. My speech has been slurred.
9. I have had "blackouts."
10. I have become wild and uncontrollable after one or two drinks.
11. I have become so angry that I smashed things.
12. I have frightened other people with my temper.
13. I have "come to" without knowing where I was or how I got there.
14. I have had indescribable frightening feelings.
15. I have been so tense I would like to scream.
16. I have had the impulse to kill myself.
17. I have been angry enough to kill somebody.
18. I have physically attacked and hurt another person.

The mean score for our sample was 20. This was similar to what Plutchik found in male prisoners while male college students scored an average of 12. Fifty-three, or 57% of our population, scored higher than this mean and hence were considered to show a high dyscontrol symptom.

Figure 1 summarizes four possible subgroups within our population of recidivist aggressors identifiable by two independent criterion variables as follows:

Group 1—with high paroxysmal theta suggesting CNS instability, presumably a low limbic system threshold for excessive neuronal discharge and high episodic symptoms. This group was tentatively referred to as "epileptoid" dyscontrol, a label selected to indicate the potential for an anticonvulsant therapeutic regimen.

Group 2—with low paroxysmal theta but equally high dyscontrol behavior, indicating a learned or motivated pattern determined more by experiential factors than by faulty functioning of the central nervous system. The dyscontrol behavior was assumed to reflect repressed conflicts; hence the acts were more likely to have unconscious symbolic meaning. This group was tentatively labelled "hysteroid," the label implying that a therapeutic regimen of an uncovering, psychotherapeutic nature would be the treatment of choice.

Figure 1
Predicted Characteristics in Monroe Episodic Disorders in Four Groups

	High	EEG Theta	Low

	1. "Epileptoid" Dyscontrol	2. "Hysteroid" Dyscontrol
High	Confusion and partial amnesia Accepts responsibility Diffuse affects Undisguised goals Uncoordinated or indiscriminate action "Alloplastic readiness" No premeditation Tension release or direct gratification Projective tests do not indicate impulsivity	Clear sensorium-complete amnesia Denies responsibility Discrete affects Disguised symbolic goals Sophisticated action Normally inhibited action Premeditation: Conscious or unconscious Indirect or symbolic gratification Projective tests indicate impulsivity
Low	3. "Inadequate" Psychopaths	4. "Pure" Psychopaths

(left axis label: Dyscontrol Scale)

Non-dyscontrol Criminality
(Life-style Antisocial)

? ←— Differences —→ ?

The differential characteristics of Groups 1 and 2, as predicted by the author on the basis of his clinical studies, are summarized in Figure 1. It was pointed out in my original monograph that dyscontrol acts are motivated by intense primitive affects, particularly those of fear and rage. The intensity of the affects—or of the intellectual confusion associated with them—overwhelms the usual control or inhibitory mechanisms, resulting in explosive behavior which lacks foresight, perhaps to the extent of commission of heinous crimes. It is not surprising then that many such individuals end up in prisons rather than in hospitals. This seems to be reflected in the fact that 57% of our population were rated as "high dyscontrol" individuals. Other differential characteristics between the epileptoid and hysteroid dyscontrol behavior, as predicted on the basis of my studies of 700 such subjects, have been previously reported (3).

The author also pointed out that in some individuals impulsiveness had become a way of life occurring so frequently that it was not an episodic characteristic. This group was characterized by Shapiro (8) as follows: "To these individuals the world appears a series of opportunities, temptations, frustrations, sensuous experiences and fragmented impressions," and these individuals immediately and repeatedly act on these impressions. Such behavior is commonly an antisocial or a psychopathic act. It is presumed that such individuals would appear in Groups 3 and 4 (Figure 1), but on the basis of previous studies there were no data to predict what differences might exist between these two syndromes, both of which show low dyscontrol behavior but high and low EEG theta activity respectively.

Tables 1 and 2 summarize correlations at the $p < 0.05$ level of significance for approximately 200 psychiatric, psychometric and neurologic variables for the two criterion variables. We see that the Monroe Dyscontrol Scale seems to be weighted somewhat toward epileptoid dyscontrol (Table 1). This is reflected in the correlations with both the psychiatrist's and the neurologist's predictions of an epileptoid mechanism, as well as in correlations with other symptoms which suggest a possibly prodromal or even ictal phenomenon, such as somatic concern, psychophysiologic reaction, prodromal restlessness, depression and anger. There are correlations, as predicted, with lack of premeditation, aggressiveness during the dyscontrol act, severity of symptoms, verbal hostility in the therapeutic situation and current belligerence and negativism, as well as with amnesia, fugue, and dissociative states. The correlations with agitation/excitement and early dropout from school were not predicted beforehand.

In Table 2 we see the correlation with the clinical rating of theta waves. What dominates these correlations is the antisocial behavior, aimlessness, drug abuse, poor intellectual capacity, and stubbornness in the psychiatric history, the guilt, fear, and panic during the dyscontrol acts, and current physical hostility in the therapeutic setting. Although it was expected that this EEG characteristic would show more correlation with "epileptoid" symptoms, it would seem that the theta pattern correlates more frequently with characterologic traits.

We next looked at inter-group differences based on the least-squared differences in an analysis of variance. The MMPI Profiles of the four groups are presented in Figure 2. Notice that Groups 1 and 2, and 3 and 4 as pairs show remarkable similarities, but that the difference between these two pairs is marked. In all groups, as would be expected, the height of the Psychopathic Deviate scale was significantly elevated. It is startling that Group 1 is significantly different from Groups 3 and 4 on not only

TABLE 1

Product-Moment Correlations with the
Monroe Dyscontrol Scale
$(p < .05)$

Variable Description	Coefficient
Global Ratings	
Primary Dyscontrol/secondary dyscontrol	.18
Predict non-epileptoid	—.34
Neurological Exam	
Epilepsy suspect	.34
Photophobia	.18
Impaired sensation	—.17
Mental Status	
Somatic concerns	.21
Psychophysiological reactions	.21
Anxiety	.22
Depression	.26
Belligerence-Negativism	.27
Agitation-Excitement	.32
Dyscontrol Behavior	
Severity	.19
Premeditation	—.27
Specificity of affect	.24
Aggressive affect	.35
Prodromal restlessness	.18
Prodromal depression	.21
Prodromal anger	.18
Psychiatric History	
Early school dropout	.20
Amnesia, fugue, dissociative state	.22
Hypochondriasis	.18
Insomnia	.22
Response to Group Therapy	
Verbal hostility to therapist	.21
Psychometrics	
Bender-BIP	
No. of positives	.19
BIP difference score	.22
Class	.25
Holtzman: Abstract	—.22
WAIS Arithmetic Subtest	—.20

TABLE 2

Product-Moment Correlations with
Clinical Rating of Theta Waves
$(p < .05)$

Variable Description	Coefficient
Neurologic	
Head injury	.21
Motor strength	.19
Coordination	—.21
Psychiatric History	
Antisocial traits in childhood	.21
Outpatient treatments	.25
Aimless	.24
Narcotics-drugs	.22
Stubborn	.24
Lack of responsibility	.19
Poor intellectual capacity	.18
Mental Status	
Somatic concerns	—.20
Psychophysiological reactions	—.20
Guilt	.19
Social isolation	—.18
Dyscontrol Behavior	
Specificity of affect	.21
Fear-panic affect during act	.21
Prodromal motor restlessness	.26
Prodromal anger	.29
Mood	
Fatigue-inertia	—.26
Response to Group Therapy	
Physical hostility	.22
EEG Activation Data	
EEG other sharp	.29
EEG spike slow	.18
Psychometrics	
Memory for designs	.17
WAIS digit span	—.22
Holtzman abstract	—.18

Figure 2

Mean MMPI Profile Scales for the 4 EEG Activation—Monroe
Dyscontrol Scale Group

GROUPS 1 & 2 PROFILES

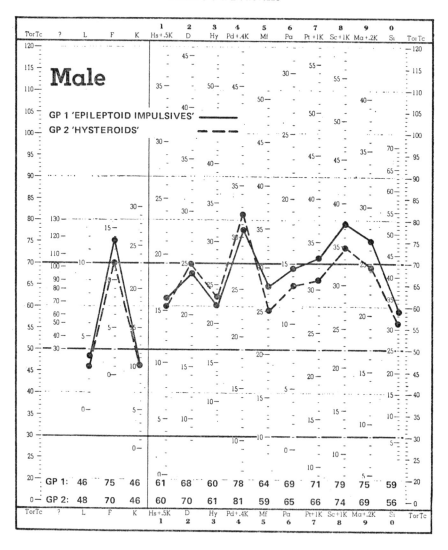

Figure 2 (continued)

GROUPS 3 & 4 PROFILES

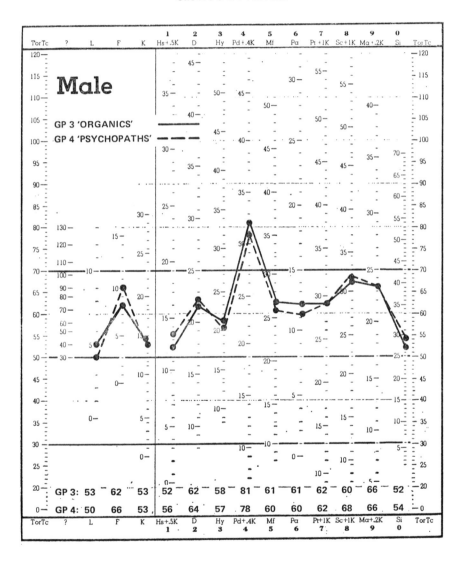

the F and K scales, but also on the Pt and Sc. Group 1 was also significantly different from 3 and 4 on the Ma scale at the 0.05 level and from Group 2 at the 0.1 level. This latter finding, in addition to other data, suggests that the epileptoid group is a "hyperactive" one. One wonders whether it might represent a residual group of hyperactive children who have carried symptoms into adulthood.

Lawrence Donner* interprets the profile of Group 1 as follows:

> the clinical picture is one of individuals with the most severe impulse control problems . . . they should be considered extremely dangerous as a group. These individuals lack basic sensitivity to, compassion for, and ability to empathize with others. They are, as a result, low in social compliance and social attachment. Of the four groups, these individuals are the most likely to suffer some form of thought disorder and, although many are not overtly psychotic, their thinking is quite peculiar, strange and autistic. As a group these individuals are more erratic and unpredictable than the other groups. They are more quick to explode into verbal rage and/or physical violence with the least provocation. They generally also show the highest level of irritability, restlessness, tension, and negativism and thus are the most agitated of the groups. In interpersonal interaction they are likely to be aggressive, moody and provocative, leaving others feeling quite uneasy and intimidated when having to deal with them. As a group they are the least trusting and most suspicious of the motivation of others. They tend to move too fast to use good judgment. Self-aggrandizing, they also have grandiose notions. Hallucinations at times are evident in individuals with this profile and projection is one of their major mechanisms of defense. It is these individuals who are capable of the most bizarre and heinous crimes of violence.

We devised a neurologic scale that also differentiated the epileptoid group from all other groups. This included the following factors:

1. Congenital stigmata including small head, small ears, pectus excavatum, extra toes or fingers, large birthmarks, amblyopic eyes, strabismus and/or hyperactivity during the examination.
2. Hyperacusis rated on the basis of distractibility, intolerance for high pitched notes or cacophony, distractibility by extraneous noise.
3. Photophobia.
4. Apraxia evaluated on the basis of fine motor dexterity.
5. Differences in motor strength in the extremities.
6. Motor incoordination.
7. Altered sensation for pain, vibration, and proprioception.

---

* Associate Professor of Psychiatry (Psychology), Department of Psychiatry, University of Maryland School of Medicine.

The last two factors proved to correlate negatively with symptoms of dyscontrol behavior; that is, the individuals in the dyscontrol group were rated as less impaired in terms of gross coordination and sensation than other groups.

Historical information that was significant included the following:

1. Evidence of birth trauma.
2. Evidence of head injury.

TABLE 3

Product-Moment Correlations with the Neurological Scale
(Items from the Modified Current and Past Psychopathology Scales)
$(p < .05)$

Data Source	Variable Description	Coefficient
PAST HISTORY (psychiatrist)	Neurotic traits in childhood	.18
	Antisocial traits in childhood	.31
	Adolescent friendship patterns	.21
	Outpatient treatment	.23
	Received treatment for psychopathology	.25
	Efforts to improve	.17
	Physical health	.17
	Amnesia, fugue, dissociative state	.22
	Hypochondriasis	.17
	Overreact emotionally	.27
	Anger	.31
	Violent	.28
	Impulsivity	.39
	Judgment (poor)	.27
	Self-defeating	.20
	Fluctuation of feeling	.21
	Lack of responsibility	.22
	Grandiosity	.24
	Overall severity	.19
CURRENT BEHAVIOR (psychiatrist)	Conversion reaction	.22
	Psychophysiological reactions	.18
	Grandiosity	.27
	Belligerence-negativism	.26
DYSCONTROL CHARACTERISTICS (psychiatrist)	Premeditated acts	—.18
	Specificity of affect during act	.18
	Prodromal anger	.20
	Prodromal autonomic symptoms	.17
GLOBAL ESTIMATE (psychiatrist)	Non-epileptoid mechanism	—.40

3. Symptoms suggesting possible epilepsy.
4. Other central nervous system insult such as CNS infection, drug toxicity, etc.

Details of this neurologic data have been reported elsewhere (5). Correlations with this neurologic scale are presented in Tables 3 and 4. Again, the correlations strongly implicate the epileptoid dyscontrol group; it is not surprising that an analysis of variance found this scale a potent distinguishing measure between Group 1 and all other groups.

Whereas Group 1 seems to be identified by neurologic signs and symptoms, Group 3 seems to be distinguished from all other groups in terms of psychiatric history. For Group 3 (Figure 3) there were two single items

TABLE 4

Product-Moment Correlations with the Neurological Scale
(Items from the Psychological and Clinical Variables)
$(p < .05)$

Data Source	Variable Description	Coefficient
MOOD SCALE (psychiatrist)	Fatigue-inertia	—.17
AFFECT SCALE (psychiatrist)	Level of tension	.19
	Emotional lability	.25
	Impulsiveness	.27
MONROE SCALE (self-rating)	Dyscontrol Score	.31
INFRACTION RATING (custodial staff)	Prison infraction rating	.21
EEG (clinical)	Chloralose induced paroxysmal theta	.33
BENDER BIP (psychologist)	Distractibility	.18
	Degree of organicity	.19
HOLTZMAN (psychologist)	Form definitiveness (FD)	.18
	Animal (A)	.17
	Anatomy (At)	.21
	Abstract (Ab)	—.18
DRAW-A-LINE (psychologist)	Distance estimation	.—29
GROUP BEHAVIOR QUESTIONNAIRE (staff therapist)	Participation	—.25
	Wide range of emotions	.34
	Verbal hostility to therapist	.23

Figure 3

Group Differences in "Inadequate" Psychopath

```
GP 3 "Inadequate" Psychopath
    Less epilepsy suspect
    Less repetitive dreams
    Less hyperacusis
    Less photophobia
    Less neurologic abnormalities
    Poorer adult friendship patterns
    More sensitive                                 vs.   GP1  "Epileptoid"
    More painful relations (gps 1 & 4)                        Dyscontrol
    More fluctuation of feelings
    More alcohol abuse (gps 1 & 4)
    More brooding
    More agitation
    Less belligerence-negativism
    Less agitation-excitement
    Poorer adaption to stress (gps 1, 2, & 4)
    Greater lack of responsibility (gps 1, 2, & 4)
    Older
```

```
GP 3 "Inadequate" Psychopath
    Poorer judgment (gps 2 & 4)
    More overall severity (gps 2 & 4)
    More outpatient treatment (gps 2 & 4)
    More aimless behavior (gps 2 & 4)              vs.   GP2  "Hysteroid"
    Poorer adolescent sexual adjustment                      Dyscontrol
    Less somatic concern
    Less fatigue-inertia
    More emotional responsiveness
    Poorer adaptation to stress (gps 2, 1 & 4)
    Greater lack of responsibility (gps 2, 1, & 4)
```

```
GP 3 "Inadequate" Psychopath
    More stubborn
    Poorer judgment (gps 4 & 2)
    More emotionally distant
    More painful relations (gps 4 & 1)
    More grandiosity
    More overall severity (gps 4 & 2)              vs.   GP4  "Pure"
    More outpatient treatment (gps 4 & 2)                    Psychopath
    More aimless (gps 4 & 2)
    More alcohol abuse (gps 4 & 1)
    More fear-panic affect during act
    More prodromal anger
    Poorer adaptation to stress (gps 4, 2, & 1)
    Greater lack of responsibility (gps 4, 2, & 1)
```

Figure 4

Group Differences in "Epileptoid" Dyscontrol

GP 1 "Epileptoid" Dyscontrol
More neurologic abnormalities (gps 2, 3, & 4)
More neurologic stigmata
More neurologic hyperacusis (gps 2 & 3)
Less passive-aggressive
More emotional responsiveness   vs.   GP2 "Hysteroid"
More perversion   Dyscontrol
More guilt
More CNS impairment
Less amnesia for act
More prodromal motor restlessness
More prodromal autonomic symptoms
Higher infraction rating

GP 1 "Epileptoid" Dyscontrol
More neurologic abnormalities (gps 3, 2, & 4)
More epilepsy suspect (gps 3 & 4)
More repetitive dreams
More neurologic hyperacusis (gps 3 & 2)
More photophobia
Better adaptation to stress
More friends   vs.   GP3 "Inadequate"
Less sensitive   Psychopath
Less painful relations
Less fluctuation of feelings
More responsibility
Less alcohol abuse
Less brooding
Less agitation
More belligerence-negativism
More agitation-excitement
Younger

GP 1 "Epileptoid" Dyscontrol
Higher estimated epileptoid mechanism
    (psychiatrist)
More neurologic abnormalities (gps 4, 3, & 2)
More epilepsy suspect (gps 4 & 3)
More photophobia
More stubborn
Lower completed school grade   vs.   GP4 "Pure"
More insomnia   Psychopath
More aggressive affect during act
More fear-panic affect during act
More prodromal anger
Speech or action is more impulsive
    in group therapy
More verbal hostility to group therapist

on the Psychiatric Rating Scale (CAPPS) which distinguished this group from all others. The first was *adapting to stress*, described as "characteristically has tended to be ineffectual when confronted with stress or had difficulty adapting himself to changes in his life circumstances." The second, *lack of responsibility*, was described as "in his dealing with family, friends or associates he has felt no obligation to carry out actions necessitated by his relationship to these people or to avoid actions harmful to them." Other common distinguishing features of this group relative to one or more of the other groups were painful relations with others, alcohol abuse, poor judgment, more severe symptomatology, and aimless behavior. It is interesting that this group was more likely to have re-

Figure 5

Group Differences in "Hysteroid" Dyscontrol

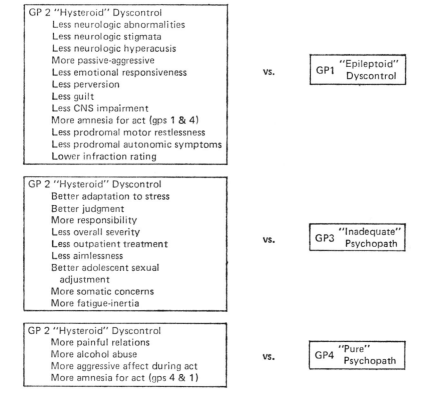

ceived some form of psychotherapy and that its members show a number
of other symptoms, suggesting the old "inadequate psychopath" diagnosis
(poor friendship patterns, sensitivity, brooding, agitation, emotional
distance, grandiosity, etc.).

Figures 4, 5 and 6 list group differences for the epileptoid, hysteroid,
and psychopathic groups. The latter two did not have any distinguishing
characteristics which delineated them from all other groups. In essence
the intergroup differences were often as predicted (see Figure 1) and

Figure 6

Group Differences in "Pure" Psychopath

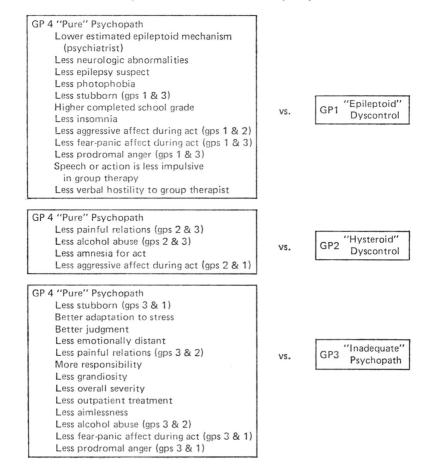

seem to lend credence to the labels originally proposed. For example, the hysteroid group showed fewer neurologic disorders than did the epileptoid group. Also, as was predicted, members of the hysteroid group were more likely to have had amnesia for their antisocial acts. The psychopathic group were more effective socially and showed on psychologic tests a tendency for greater concentration and abstractive ability. Finally, there was one totally unexpected finding that appeared in these data, both within the prison and prior to prison: subjects in Group 1, the epileptoid group, were more likely to act out sexually in terms of perversion or aggressive sexual acts.

As already mentioned, the population of subjects within which we developed our four groups of recidivist aggressors was surprisingly homogeneous from the point of view of the criminal justice system. There was no significant difference among groups in the number of convictions, length of incarcerations, violence of crimes, or pre-study diagnoses found. There was no significant difference in IQ, either full-scale or on any subtest of the WAIS. Other psychometric tests, particularly those which might show organicity, revealed no differences. Our data did not address itself to demographic differences but it is our distinct impression that the overall group was homogeneous in this area too. To separate subjects into the diagnostic subgroups required self-rating projective tests, neurologic examinations, and careful phenomenologic analysis of their antisocial acts, as well as the usual psychiatric history and mental status examinations.

The therapeutic implications of this subgrouping suggest that the most dangerous group (epileptoid dyscontrol) and the most severely disturbed group (the inadequate psychopaths) might benefit most from a psychopharmacologic regimen and thus be treatable. Certainly, in view of the severity of their behavioral deviations, they will need the limit setting and the psychotherapeutic programs necessary for the other two groups ("hysteroid" and "pure" psychopathic), but with the combination of drugs and psychotherapy these epileptoid and inadequate patients might have a better prognosis than they have at present. Indeed, they might even have a better prognosis than those who are without evidence for central nervous system dysfunction.

Evidence for the effectiveness of pharmacologic therapy, particularly for Groups 1 and 3 (with activated electroencephalographic abnormalities), is still tenuous; nevertheless, it offers hope that predictions of "treatability" can be further developed. The reader is referred to Chapter 16 for a discussion of pharmacologic treatment of sociopathic/antisocial syndromes.

REFERENCES

1. WOLFGANG, M. W. Delinquency and Violence from the Viewpoint of Criminology. In: W. S. Fields and W. D. Sweet (Eds.), *Neural Bases of Violence and Aggression*. St. Louis, Missouri: Warren H. Green, Inc., 1975.
2. MARK, V. H. and ERVIN, F. R. *Violence and the Brain*. New York: Harper and Row Publishers, Medical Department, 1970.
3. MONROE, R. R. *Episodic Behavioral Disorders*. Cambridge, MA.: Harvard University Press, 1970.
4. MONROE, R. R. Maturational Lag in Central Nervous System Development as a Partial Explanation of Episodic Violent Behavior. In: J. DeWitt and W. W. Hartup (Eds.), *Determinants and Origins of Aggressive Behavior* 337-344. The Hague, Netherlands: Mouton Publishers, 1974.
5. MONROE, R. R. et al. Neurologic Findings in Recidivist Aggressors. In: C. Shagass, A. J. Friedhoff and S. Gershon (Eds.), *Psychopathology and Brain Dysfunction*. New York: Raven Press, 1977.
6. MONROE, R. R. et al. Neuropsychiatric Correlations with Antisocial Behavior. In: Biological Model (Part I); Proceedings of the Second International Symposium on Criminology, Sao Paulo, Brazil, 1975.
7. PLUTCHIK, R., CLIMENT, C., and ERVIN, F. R. Research Strategies for the Study of Human Violence. Presented at the Fifth Annual Cerebral Function Symposium. Coronado, California, 1974.
8. SHAPIRO, D. *Neurotic Styles*. New York: Basic Books, 1965.

10

Psychophysiological Research on Psychopathy

ROBERT D. HARE, PH.D.
and
DAVID N. COX, PH.D.

This chapter presents brief overviews of 1) the procedures and problems associated with the selection of subjects for research on psychopathy, and 2) current psychophysiological theory and research concerning psychopathy, with emphasis upon autonomic correlates. To a large extent, the material to be covered is based upon recent reviews by Hare (1) and Hare and Cox (2). Extensive discussions of related topics can be found in Hare and Schalling (3).

SELECTION OF SUBJECTS FOR RESEARCH

Global Assessments

The basis for many clinical assessments of psychopathy is the American Psychiatric Association (APA) category 301.7, *antisocial personality*. However, the description of this category in the 1968 version of the APA's *Diagnostic and Statistical Manual of Mental Disorders* (*DSM II*) (4) is too sparse for research purposes. Much more detail is contained in the 1977 draft version of the proposed DSM III category 301.70, *antisocial personality disorder* (5), and its adoption will probably increase the reliability of diagnosis.

While the APA category provides the bare bones of a description of

Preparation of this chapter and some of the research reported were supported by Grant MA-4511 from the Medical Research Council of Canada.

psychopathy, Cleckley (6) provides the flesh. His rich clinical accounts of the disorder and its manifestations form the basis for an increasing amount of research by behavioral scientists. As Hare and Cox (2) point out in their extensive review of the topic, global assessments that rely heavily upon Cleckley's conceptualization of psychopathy can be extremely reliable, providing extensive case history data are available, particularly in situations in which the subjects are prison inmates. In most cases a seven-point rating scale is used. When the raters are experienced, it is not uncommon to obtain inter-judge reliabilities of well over 0.8. While interview data are generally used in making these global assessments, primary importance is placed upon evidence of a consistent pattern of behavior over a long period of time.

Research Diagnostic Criteria

The antisocial personality disorder described in the draft version of *DSM III* is based upon the Research Diagnostic Criteria (RDC) for antisocial personality outlined by Spitzer, Endicott and Robins (7). The criteria are generally quite explicit, and diagnosis is based upon the presence of each of the following conditions: (a) behavior problems in childhood; (b) poor occupational performance; (c) repeated antisocial acts; and (d) evidence of impaired capacity to sustain lasting, close, warm, and responsible relationships with others. Examples of (a) through (c) are given in the manual, but it is evident that (d) involves the same sort of clinical judgment used in making global assessments.

While the RDC procedure should facilitate the selection of subjects, there is no assurance that individuals so identified will closely fit the clinical concept of psychopathy. Moreover, it is possible that inmates who are clearly psychopathic in the strictest clinical sense could fail to meet all of the RDC conditions, particularly when they are quite young. To illustrate the point, and because the RDC and the proposed *DSM III* are likely to be used by many investigators, it may be useful to compare diagnoses using this procedure with those made using global assessments.

As part of a larger study we had two researchers rate 76 prison inmates on a seven-point scale of psychopathy. The two ratings for each subject were added together, with the result that the rating score for any given subject could range from two (low psychopathy) to 14 (high psychopathy). We also determined the extent to which the RDC conditions for the diagnosis of antisocial personality were met by each subject. Since there are four such conditions, a score ranging from 0 (no conditions met) to four (all conditions met) was obtained for each inmate. For convenience, we assumed that inmates who met 0-2, 3, or all 4 RDC conditions would receive the diagnoses of, respectively, not, probably, and definitely antisocial personality. Similarly, inmates with global ratings of 2-6 and 12-14 were considered to be nonpsychopaths and psychopaths, respectively. On this basis, there were 17 inmates who would be considered to be definitely nonpsychopathic by both the RDC and our ratings, while nine inmates would be considered to be psychopaths by both procedures. Looking at it another way, of the 21 inmates that were considered to be psychopaths by the rating procedure, the RDC procedure classified nine definitely, ten, probably, and two not, antisocial personality. Similarly, of the 22 inmates classified by the RDC as definitely antisocial personality, the rating procedure considered nine to be psychopaths, 12 in between, and one a nonpsychopath.

The two procedures agreed exactly on 38 (50%) of the inmates, were only one step apart on 35, and were in complete disagreement on only three inmates. The degree of association between the two assessment procedures was highly significant ($\chi^2 = 23.6$, $df = 2$, $p < .001$) but it is clear that they are not *equivalent* measures of the same construct. One problem is that the RDC classifications are age-dependent to a certain extent; young inmates may not have had enough time to do many of the things (especially in conditions b and c) considered by the RDC to be indicative of antisocial personality. Many of the inmates in our study were 18-20 years old; although we had enough information to classify them reliably, the RDC would perhaps be more successful at doing so when they are older. It should be noted, however, that part of the agreement between the two selection procedures reflects the fact that condition (d) of the RDC—"evidence of an impaired capacity to sustain lasting, close, warm, and responsible relationships with others"—also enters into the global assessments that we make. When condition (d) was excluded from the RDC procedure, the degree of association between the RDC and our global assessments decreased, though it remained significant ($\chi^2 = 17.0$, $df = 4$, $p < .01$). There was exact agreement on only 33 (43%) of the inmates and complete disagreement on four inmates. Only nine of the 27 inmates that received an RDC diagnosis of antisocial personality were considered to be psychopaths by our criteria. Our impression so far is that the RDC by itself may not be particularly useful in differentiating between psychopathic and nonpsychopathic criminals.

Behavior Rating Scales

Several investigators have used checklists and behavior rating scales for the selection of psychopathic subjects (see (2) for details). For example, Quay and his associates (8, 9) have developed a set of scales for the assessment of juvenile and adult offenders on the psychopathic, neurotic, and subcultural aspects of antisocial behavior. One disadvantage of these measures is that the correlations between like-named scales (e.g., those purporting to measure psychopathy) are quite low.

Self-Report Inventories

Although several self-report inventories have been used in an attempt to make the selection of psychopathic subjects more objective, most have not been very successful. The most frequently used test is the Minnesota Multiphasic Personality Inventory or MMPI (10); in general, selection is based primarily upon elevated scores on the Psychopathic Deviate (*Pd*) and Hypomania (*Ma*) scales. Unfortunately, subjects so selected are very often not psychopaths in the strict clinical sense. Moreover, there is some evidence that ratings of psychopathy are often not appreciably correlated with scores on the *Pd* and *Ma* scores.

Somewhat more encouraging is the Socialization (*So*) scale from the California Psychological Inventory (11). The scale is based upon a role-taking theory of psychopathy (12) and has been used with some success, particularly as a supplement to clinical assessments of psychopathy (1). There is also some evidence that it may be useful in studying the construct of psychopathy in noncriminal populations (1, 13).

There are several major problems in attempting to use self-report inventories to select psychopathic subjects. For one thing, given the nature of the psychopath, there is little reason to believe his responses to what are often self-incriminating questions. For another, most inventories were not developed with the use of well-defined criterion groups, and their ability to discriminate between psychopathic and other subjects is not constantly evaluated. Because of these and related problems it is unlikely that any self-report inventory could capture the full flavor of psychopathy. Nevertheless, there would be some advantage in having an easily administered, objective, and conceptually meaningful measure of psychopathy. Accordingly, we are attempting to develop a self-report inventory that is closely related to the clinical concept of psychopathy. A pool of items was written to tap what we considered to be the most salient and important features of psychopathy. These items were then given to well-defined groups of prison inmates who fell at the opposite ends of the psychopathy dimension, and those items that discriminated between the criterion groups (psychopaths and nonpsychopaths) were kept for further testing. The correlation between ratings of psychopathy and scores on an early form of the test was around 0.60. Although a great deal of work remains to be done, the initial results are very encouraging. Further details can be obtained from the senior author of this chapter.

PSYCHOPHYSIOLOGY

Details on the principles and procedures of human psychophysiology can be found in Brown (14), Greenfield and Sternbach (15), Venables and Martin (16), and Venables and Christie (17, 18).

Although the following sections are concerned with the psychophysiological correlates of adult psychopathy, the recent theory and research on hyperactive child syndrome—e.g., Satterfield's work (19)—should also be kept in mind. The two disorders may be developmentally related, appear to have some similar psychophysiological correlates, and have been interpreted in terms of similar biological models. Reference should also be made to discussions of the neurology (see Chapter 8 by Elliott) and neuropsychology (20) of psychopathy.

Electrocortical Activity

EEG Studies

In most of the published research on brain-wave activity in psychopathic patients, electroencephalographic (EEG) recordings were obtained as part of routine medical and psychiatric procedures. In many cases experimental control, quantification of data, and the diagnosis of the patients were inadequate. Nevertheless, some fairly consistent findings have been reported over the years, the most frequent being the presence of "abnormal" amounts of slow-wave activity in the EEG (21). Several interpretations have been offered for this finding. The similarity of the adult psychopath's slow-wave activity to that of a normal child has led to the suggestion that psychopathy may be related to delayed cortical maturation (22; Chapter 8). Another interpretation is that the slow-wave activity reflects some underlying cortical or subcortical dysfunction. A third possibility is that slow-wave activity in psychopaths reflects low cortical arousal and/or a proneness to become bored and drowsy during routine EEG examinations (21, 23).

A recent review by Syndulko (24) has been critical of much of the research in this area. He concludes that it has yet to be firmly established that psychopaths are in fact characterized by amounts of slow-wave activity that could be considered abnormal.

Cortical Evoked Potentials

Very little research has been done on the relationship between psychopathy and cortical evoked potentials. The recent review by Syndulko (24) concludes that significant differences between psychopathic and other subjects have not been consistently demonstrated.

Contingent Negative Variation

McCallum and Walter reported that the contingent negative variation (CNV) during the foreperiod of a reaction-time study was absent or only very small in psychopaths (25); however, there is some concern about their definition of psychopathy. Moreover, more recent research has failed to demonstrate consistent CNV differences between psychopathic and other subjects (24).

Low CNS Arousal

Even if subsequent research manages to establish the existence of electrocortical differences between psychopaths and other subjects, these differences by themselves would not necessarily indicate the presence of some underlying structural anomalies. They may, for example, reflect differences in motivational, attentional, and cognitive processes. To illustrate, if an unusual amount of slow-wave activity is observed in psychopaths, it could be associated with a lowered state of central nervous system (CNS) arousal in a situation that is not as exciting as it could be. Several investigators (21, 26, etc.) have in fact argued that much of the psychopath's behavior is the result of cortical under-arousal and a pathological need for stimulation. Psychophysiological evidence in support of a low cortical arousal hypothesis, as well as some of the implications for the psychopath's behavior, are reviewed in a recent work (21). Zuckerman (27) and Cox (28) have discussed the psychopath as a stimulation seeker. In many respects, Eysenck's theory relating extraversion to biological processes (29) is relevant here.

In spite of the methodological problems associated with much of the electrocortical research on psychopathy, well controlled research with a conceptually similar disorder, the hyperactive child syndrome, has found evidence of excessive slow-wave activity in the EEG. Satterfield notes that the data can be interpreted in terms of delayed cortical maturation or low CNS arousal, although he prefers the latter (19). The implications of the low CNS arousal model for the behavior of both the hyperactive child and the adult psychopath are also discussed by Satterfield.

Autonomic Correlates

Most of the research on the autonomic correlates of psychopathy has involved electrodermal and cardiovascular activity, generally in response to simple stimuli or in classical conditioning paradigms. Extensive discussions of this research are available elsewhere (1, 13, 21, 30-32); only a brief summary is presented here.

Electrodermal Activity

Palmar electrodermal activity has been the most frequently used index of autonomic activity in psychopaths.

a. Skin Conductance. Several investigators have recorded tonic electrodermal activity (palmar skin conductance and nonspecific fluctuations in skin conductance) during a variety of experimental procedures. The results have been inconsistent, perhaps partly because of the use of different subject selection procedures and different tasks (1). A frequent finding has been that the tonic skin conductance of psychopathic inmates is lower than that of other inmates during the initial "rest" period of an experiment. While these differences are not always significant, they are usually in the same direction. In order to remove the effects of different subject selection procedures, we recently combined the results of eight of our own experiments, two of which had obtained significant differences between groups, and six of which were in the direction of lower skin conductance for the psychopaths. The combined analysis yielded a highly significant difference between psychopathic and nonpsychopathic inmates. There is thus reasonable support for the hypothesis that the resting skin conductance of psychopathic inmates is lower than that of other inmates, at least during the sorts of laboratory procedures generally used. The difference between groups may increase during the course of experiments that are boring and tedious, with the palmar skin conductance of psychopaths decreasing more than that of the other subjects. Similarly, it appears that when the procedure is unpleasant or threatening, the palmar skin conductance of psychopaths does not increase as much as does that of nonpsychopaths.

It is difficult to interpret these findings, since tonic skin conductance is affected by so many different things. In view of the clinical symptoms seen in psychopathy, one hypothesis would be that the psychopath's low level of tonic skin conductance during experiments with aversive or unpleasant features reflects a relative lack of fear, anxiety, or apprehension. Other interpretations are possible, especially for situations in which the procedures are not particularly stressful or aversive. In these cases, the low tonic skin conductance of psychopaths may be related to motivational or cognitive factors rather than to emotional ones (e.g., 33, 34).

b. Fluctuations in Skin Conductance. "Spontaneous" or nonspecific fluctuations in electrodermal activity have also been related to psychopathy. A recent review indicates that group differences during the initial "resting" period of various experiments have been small and inconsistent. The difference between groups sometimes increases throughout the experiment, with psychopathic inmates tending to show progressively fewer nonspecific tonic fluctuations in skin conductance than do other inmates (1).

The interpretation of these data also presents problems. It has been suggested that nonspecific fluctuations in skin conductance reflect the operation of mechanisms which have excitatory effects upon the cortex (35, 36) or which help to maintain an optimal level of cortical arousal (37). Szpiler and Epstein have argued that fluctuations in skin conductance are a measure of physiological instability which reflect a state of diffuse, unchanneled arousal (or anxiety) induced by the perception of threat in the absence of a suitable coping response (38). Thus, the relatively small number of electrodermal fluctuations sometimes observed in psychopathic subjects as the experiment progresses could be related to drowsiness, boredom, lowered cortical arousal, or to a lowered level of anxiety or stress. These interpretations are not necessarily incompatible, and it may be that each helps to account for portions of the data in a complementary fashion.

c. Skin Conductance Responses. Perhaps of more significance than tonic electrodermal activity are skin conductance responses to specific stimuli, both signaled and unsignaled. For example, there is reasonably good evidence that with weak or low-intensity stimuli (e.g., tones) presented without warning, psychopathic and nonpsychopathic inmates do not differ very much in the size of the skin conductance response elicited (1). However, with more intense or aversive stimuli, psychopaths give smaller skin conductance responses than do other subjects. That is, psychopaths appear to be electrodermally hyporesponsive only to strong stimuli. This seems to apply to responses recorded from both left and right hands.

d. Recovery Limb. Recently, interest has developed in the recovery limb of the skin conductance response tracing. It has been reported that psychopaths show abnormally slow recovery to baseline levels, while schizophrenics show fast recovery (1, 39). The interpretation of electrodermal recovery rates is currently uncertain (40), but it has been suggested that fast recovery reflects "openness" to the environment and slow recovery, "closedness" (39). Whatever the correct interpretation(s) of recovery rate, recent research suggests that abnormally slow recovery in psychopaths is more apt to occur in the left hand and when the stimuli are very intense and startling (1). Until these findings have been replicated they are difficult to evaluate; however, it is interesting that Venables has recently found that the 11-to-12-year-old children of parents who are criminal, psychopathic, or character-disordered show slower electrodermal recovery than do the children of normal parents, but only in the left hand (41). Since there is some very weak evidence that cortical control of electrodermal data may be ipsilateral to the response organ (e.g., palm) (42), both sets of findings may have some bearing on Flor-Henry's theory that psychopathy is associated with dysfunction of the temporal-frontal lobes of the left hemisphere (43, see 20). Further speculation along these lines must await the accumulation of more substantial data.

e. Anticipatory Responses. Perhaps the most consistent electrodermal finding in psychopaths is that of only relatively small increases in electrodermal activity when the subject is anticipating an aversive stimulus. This applies to the traditional classical conditioning procedure (in which a warning signal—e.g., a weak tone—is repeatedly followed by an aversive stimulus—e.g., an electric shock or very loud tone) and to a quasi-conditioning procedure (in which the subject is told that he will receive an aversive stimulus after a specified period of time). In each case, psychopathic subjects show smaller increases in skin conductance and fewer nonspecific fluctuations in skin conductance in anticipation of the aversive stimulus than do nonpsychopathic subjects. That is, they appear to be poor electrodermal conditioners (1).

Since the awaited stimuli in experiments of this sort are usually painful and highly aversive, these findings have been interpreted to mean that psychopaths experience little apprehension or anticipatory fear, an interpretation that is in agreement with clinical reports. This apparent failure to experience anticipatory fear has in turn been used to account for the psychopath's relative inability to look ahead to and/or avoid punishment and to keep out of trouble. For a thoughtful discussion of this and related theories, reference should be made to the paper by Trasler (44).

f. Electrodermal Activity in the Hyperactive Child. As a final point, there is some evidence that the hyperactive child syndrome, like adult psychopathy, may be characterized by relatively low tonic skin conductance levels and electrodermal hyporesponsiveness (19). There is thus some consistency of electrodermal findings between two disorders that may be developmentally related.

Cardiovascular Activity

a. Heart Rate and Pulse Amplitude. Psychopathy does not appear to be related in any consistent way to tonic heart rate or peripheral pulse amplitude during initial "rest" periods or throughout the rather limited experimental procedures generally used. Reports that the cardiovascular system of psychopaths is unusually sensitive to injections of epinephrine (45, 46) were based upon inadequate research procedures and questionable data, and have not been supported by more recent research (47, 48). No good data are available concerning relationships between psychopathy and other cardiovascular variables, including blood pressure.

b. Heart Rate Responses. The results of research on the cardiovascular responses of psychopaths to nonsignal stimuli have been equivocal. Hare found that psychopathic inmates responded to novel 70 and 80dB tones with smaller decreases in heart rate than did other inmates (30). Heart rate deceleration is one component of the "orienting response" (49, 50) and is generally associated with sensory intake (52). The smaller cardiac orienting responses given by the psychopaths could thus have been indicative of relative insensitivity to changes in environmental stimulation. However, more recent research, using tones ranging from 80 to 120dB, failed to find any significant differences between the heart rate responses of psychopathic and other inmates (1). At the higher intensities, the heart rate response usually shifts from deceleration to acceleration (a defensive response) and may be associated with sensory rejection (51). Although there are theoretical reasons for expecting that this shift from an orienting to a defensive pattern should occur at a higher intensity in psychopaths than in nonpsychopaths, results so far do not support this prediction.

c. Anticipatory Responses. The most dramatic cardiovascular correlate of psychopathy observed thus far occurs during *anticipation* of a painful or aversive stimulus. If psychopaths can be said to be poor electrodermal conditioners, they can also be said to be unusually good *cardiovascular* conditioners. Thus, while awaiting delivery of an aversive stimulus, psychopathic inmates show much larger increases in heart rate than do other inmates (2, 52).

Interpretation of Anticipatory Responses

It could be argued that the anticipatory increases in heart rate found in psychopaths indicate fear of an impending stressor. However, the electrodermal data would imply the opposite conclusion.

The psychopathic's pattern of large increases in heart rate and small increases in electrodermal activity prior to an anticipated aversive stimulus can be interpreted in another way (1, 31). This latter interpretation rests upon the argument that cardiac acceleration is associated with sensory rejection and decreased cortical arousal (35, 51), and also upon evidence that acceleration is part of a defensive response serving to reduce sensitivity to environmental stimulation (49, 50). Cardiac responses may influence or at least reflect the way in which aversive sensory input is modulated; Hare and Blevings have suggested that this may be particularly important when such responses are anticipatory in nature (53). According to this model, anticipatory heart rate acceleration is part of an adaptive response which helps the individual to cope with, "tune-out," or reduce the impact of premonitory cues and the impending aversive stimulus.

The psychopath's pattern of heart rate acceleration and small increases in electrodermal activity is hypothesized to reflect the operation of an active, efficient coping process, and the inhibition of fear arousal. As a result, many situations that have great emotional impact for most people would be of little consequence to the psychopath, because he is better able to attenuate aversive inputs and to inhibit anticipatory fear. As indicated elsewhere (1), however, this very efficient "coping" process would be adaptive for survival only when the psychopath could not make use of the premonitory cues and anticipatory fear to facilitate avoidance behavior. To a certain extent, this may help to account for the psychopath's difficulty in avoiding punishment. That is, the cues that would help him to do so are "tuned out" and the mediating effects of anticipatory fear are reduced.

REFERENCES

1. HARE, R. D. Electrodermal and Cardiovascular Correlates of Psychopathy. In: R. D. Hare and D. Schalling (Eds.), *Psychopathic Behavior: Approaches to Research.* London: Wiley, 1978, 107-143.

2. HARE, R. D. and COX, D. Clinical and Empirical Conceptions of Psychopathy, and the Selection of Subjects for Research. In: R. D. Hare and D. Schalling (Eds.), *Psychopathic Behavior: Approaches to Research*. London: Wiley, 1978, 1-21.

3. HARE, R. D. and SCHALLING, D. (Eds.). *Psychopathic Behavior: Approaches to Research*. London: Wiley, 1978.

4. American Psychiatric Association *Diagnostic and Statistical Manual of Mental Disorders II*. Washington, D.C., 1968.

5. SPITZER, R. Personal Communication, June, 1977.

6. CLECKLEY, H. *The Mask of Sanity* (5th Ed.), St. Louis: Mosby, 1976.

7. SPITZER, R., ENDICOTT, J., and ROBINS, E. *Research Diagnostic Criteria*. New York: Biometrics Research, New York State Department of Health, 1975.

8. QUAY, H. C. The Differential Behavioral Classification of the Adult Male Offender. Unpublished manuscript. Philadelphia: Temple University, 1974.

9. QUAY, H. C. and PARSONS, L. *The Differential Classification of the Juvenile Offender*. Washington, D.C.: Bureau of Prisons, 1971.

10. DAHLSTROM, W. G. and WELSH, G. S. *An MMPI Handbook*. Minneapolis: University of Minnesota Press, 1960.

11. GOUGH, H. C. *Manual for the California Psychological Inventory*. Palo Alto, California: Consulting Psychologists Press, 1969.

12. GOUGH, H. C. A Sociological Theory of Sociopathy. *Amer. J. Sociology* 53:356-366, 1948.

13. SCHALLING, D. Psychopathy-related Personality Variables and the Psychophysiology of Socialization. In: R. D. Hare and D. Schalling (Eds.), *Psychopathic Behavior: Approaches to Research*. London: Wiley, 1978, 85-106.

14. BROWN, C. (Ed.), *Methods in Psychophysiology*. Baltimore: Williams and Wilkins, 1967.

15. GREENFIELD, N. S. and STERNBACH, R. (Eds.), *Handbook of Psychophysiology*. New York: Holt, Rinehart and Winston, 1972.

16. VENABLES, P. and MARTIN, I. *A Manual of Psychophysiological Methods*. New York: Wiley, 1967.

17. VENABLES, P. and CHRISTIE, M. Mechanisms, Instrumentation, Recording Techniques, and Quantification of Responses. In: W. F. Prokasy and D. C. Raskin (Eds.), *Electrodermal Activity in Psychological Research*. New York: Academic Press, 1973, 1-124.

18. VENABLES, P. and CHRISTIE, M. (Eds.), *Research in Psychophysiology*. New York: Wiley, 1975.

19. SATTERFIELD, J. H. The Hyperactive Child Syndrome: A Precursor of Adult Psychopathy? In: R. D. Hare and D. Schalling (Eds.), *Psychopathic Behavior: Approaches to Research*. London: Wiley, 1978, 329-346.

20. YEUDALL, L. Neuropsychological Assessment of Forensic Disorders. *Canada's Mental Health* 25:7-15, 1977.

21. HARE, R. D. *Psychopathy: Theory and Research*. New York: Wiley, 1970.

22. KILOH, L. and OSSELTON, J. *Clinical Electroencephalography*. Washington: Butterworth, 1966.

23. FORSSMAN, H. and FREY, T. S. Electroencephalograms of Boys with Behavior Disorders. *Acta Psychiat. Neurol. Scand.* 28:61-73, 1953.

24. SYNDULKO, K. Electrocortical Investigations of Sociopathy. In: R. D. Hare and D. Schalling (Eds.), *Psychopathic Behavior: Approaches to Research*. London: Wiley, 1978, 145-155.

25. McCALLUM, W. C. and WALTER, W. G. The Effects of Attention and Distraction on the Contingent Negative Variation in Normal and Neurotic Subjects. *Electroencephalography and Clinical Neurophysiology* 25:319-329, 1968.

26. QUAY, H. Psychopathic Personality as Pathological Stimulation Seeking. *Amer. J. Psychiatry* 122:180-183, 1965.

27. ZUCKERMAN, M. Sensation Seeking and Psychopathy. In: R. D. Hare and D. Schalling (Eds.), *Psychopathic Behavior: Approaches to Research*. London: Wiley, 1978, 165-185.
28. COX, D. *Psychophysiological Correlates of Sensation Seeking and Socialization During Reduced Stimulation*. Doctoral dissertation, Vancouver, Canada: University of British Columbia, 1977.
29. EYSENCK, H. J. *The Biological Basis of Personality*. Springfield, Illinois: Charles C Thomas, 1967.
30. HARE, R. D. Psychopathy, Autonomic Functioning, and the Orienting Response. *J. Abnorm. Psychol.* Monograph Supplement 73:3, Pt. 2, 1968.
31. HARE, R. D. Psychopathy. In: P. Venables and M. Christie (Eds.), *Research in Psychophysiology*. New York: Wiley, 1975, 325-348.
32. SIDDLE, D. Electrodermal Activity and Psychopathy. In: S. A. Mednick and K. O. Christiansen (Eds.), *Biosocial Bases of Criminal Behavior*. New York: Gardner Press, 1977.
33. ELLIOTT, R. Tonic Heart Rate: Experiments on the Effects of Collative Variables Lead to a Hypothesis about its Motivational Significance. *J. Personality and Social Psychol.* 12:211-228, 1969.
34. KILPATRICK, D. G. Differential Responsiveness of Two Electrodermal Indices to Psychological Stress and Performance of a Complex Cognitive Task. *Psychophysiology* 9:218-226, 1972.
35. LACEY, B. and LACEY, J. Studies of Heart Rate and Other Bodily Processes in Sensorimotor Behavior. In: P. Obrist, A. Black, J. Brener, and L. Dicara (Eds.), *Cardiovascular Psychophysiology*. Chicago: Aldine, 1974, 538-569.
36. LADER, M. H. The Effects of Cyclobarbitone on Spontaneous Autonomic Activity. *J. Psychosomatic Research* 9:201-207, 1965.
37. VENABLES, P. H. Partial Failure of Cortical-Subcortical Integration as a Factor Underlying Schizophrenic Behavior. In: *The Origins of Schizophrenia*. Amsterdam: Exerpta Medica International Congress Series No. 151, 1967, 42-53.
38. SZPILER, J. A. and EPSTEIN, S. Availability of an Avoidance Response as Related to Autonomic Arousal. *J. Abnorm. Psychol.* 85:73-82, 1976.
39. VENABLES, P. H. Progress in Psychophysiology: Some Applications in a Field of Abnormal Psychology. In: P. Venables and M. Christie (Eds.), *Research in Psychophysiology*. New York: Wiley, 1975, 418-434.
40. EDELBERG, R. and MULLER, M. The Status of the Electrodermal Recovery Measure. Philadelphia: Presented at the Annual Meeting of the Society for Psychophysiological Research, October, 1977.
41. VENABLES, P. H. Personal Communication, October, 1976.
42. GRUZELIER, J. H. and VENABLES, P. H. Bimodality and Lateral Asymmetry of Skin Conductance Orienting Activity in Schizophrenics. *Biological Psychiatry* 8:55-73, 1974.
43. FLOR-HENRY, P. Psychosis, Neurosis, and Epilepsy: Developmental and Gender-related Effects and Their Etiological Contributions. *British J. Psychiatry* 124:144-150, 1974.
44. TRASLER, G. Relations Between Psychopathy and Persistent Criminality: Methodological and Theoretical Issues. In: R. D. Hare and D. Schalling (Eds.), *Psychopathic Behavior: Approaches to Research*. London: Wiley, 1978, 273-298.
45. LINDNER, L., GOLDMAN, H., DINITZ, S., and ALLEN, H. Antisocial Personality Type with Cardiac Lability. *Arch. Gen. Psychiatry* 23:260-267, 1970.
46. SCHACHTER, S. and LATANE, B. Crime, Cognition and the Autonomic Nervous System. In: M. R. Jones (Ed.), *Nebraska Symposium on Motivation*. Lincoln: University of Nebraska Press, 1964, 221-275.
47. HARE, R. D. Psychopathy and Sensitivity to Adrenalin. *J. Abnorm. Psychol.* 79:138-147, 1972.

48. HARE, R. D. The Origins of Confusion. *J. Abnorm. Psychol.* 82:535-536, 1973.
49. GRAHAM, F. K. and CLIFTON, R. K. Heart Rate Change as a Component of the Orienting Response. *Psychological Bulletin* 65:305-320, 1966.
50. SOKOLOV, E. H. *Perception and the Conditioned Reflex.* New York: Macmillan, 1963.
51. LACEY, J. I. Somatic Response Patterning and Stress: Some Revisions of Activation Theory. In: M. H. Appley and R. Trumbell (Eds.), *Psychological Stress: Issues in Research.* New York: Appleton-Century-Crofts, 1967, 14-44.
52. HARE, R. D. and CRAIGEN, D. Psychopathy and Physiological Activity in a Mixed-motive Game Situation. *Psychophysiology*, 11:197-206, 1974.
53. HARE, R. D. and BLEVINGS, G. Conditioned Orienting and Defensive Responses. *Psychophysiology* 12:289-297, 1975.

11

Sociopathy and Alcohol Abuse

RICHARD T. RADA, M.D.

INTRODUCTION

It is a generally accepted belief that sociopathy is related in some major way to heavy drinking, alcoholism, and crime. This belief is supported in part by the growing evidence of an association between alcohol, alcoholism, and criminal acts, especially violent acts. However, not all sociopaths drink, are alcoholic, or commit crimes. The purpose of this chapter is to discuss the ways in which sociopathy and alcohol may be related, as well as the importance of distinguishing the diagnostic categories of sociopathy and alcoholism.

SOCIOPATHY AND ALCOHOL

Genetics and Familial Patterning

The strongest evidence indicating an association between sociopathy and alcoholism comes from studies of the genetic and familial associations of the two. The clustering of alcoholism in families is generally recognized. Likewise, sociopathy and criminality run in families. However, the relative importance of heredity in such familial clustering is debated. A number of recent studies suggest an hereditary component in alcoholism (1-3) and in sociopathy (4-6).

Several reports indicate a familial association between alcoholism and sociopathy. Robins, Bates and O'Neal (7) reported a 30-year follow-up study on 502 children who had been seen in a child guidance clinic, and compared this group to untreated matched controls. A significantly larger percentage of the ex-child guidance clinic patients developed alcoholism,

223

as compared to the matched controls. Factors in the childhood history of the clinic patients significantly related to alcoholism in later life inincluded very low family social status, parental inadequacy (particularly antisocial behavior on the part of the fathers), and serious antisocial behavior of the patients themselves. Amark (8) reported a high rate of criminal behavior and alcoholism in the brothers of alcoholics and some evidence that the fathers also had a high rate of criminal activity. Guze et al. (9) and Cloninger and Guze (10) found a greater frequency of alcoholism, sociopathy and drug addiction among both male and female first degree relatives of a group of male felons.

More recently a number of studies indicate that alcoholism and sociopathy may be associated with a third condition, the hyperactive child syndrome. Follow-up studies indicate that some hyperactive children become sociopaths (11-13) or alcoholics (14, 15) as adults. Goodwin et al. (16) recently compared alcoholics and nonalcoholics in a sample of Danish adoptees and found that the adult alcoholics as children were more often hyperactive, truant, antisocial, shy, aggressive, disobedient, and friendless. Wood et al. (17) have recently reported that minimal brain dysfunction in childhood may not terminate with adolescence but may persist into adulthood, concealed by a number of different diagnostic labels. Although they present no specific data, the authors suggest that sociopathy and alcoholism may be among the types of psychopathology which persist.

Thus, there is growing evidence of a familial association between sociopathy and alcoholism, but whether this association is genetically determined is not certain.

Personality Characteristics

During the 1940s and 1950s there was considerable interest in developing psychological test profiles diagnostic of specific mental disorders, using such tests as the MMPI, the Rorschach, and others. It was hoped that on the basis of test findings subjects would cluster into more or less homogeneous subgroups. Dahlstrom and Welsh (18) point out that one of the most persistent findings among the MMPI studies on diagnosed alcoholics is the appearance of a strong psychopathic trend. Thus, investigators tended to label alcoholics as psychopaths. Although alcoholics were found to differ from psychopaths in certain important characteristics, e.g., guilt, these differences were not seen as sufficient to form separate diagnostic categories but rather as differentiated traits of the same basic character structure.

During this same period clinicians investigating both groups began to formulate lists of personality traits characteristic of each. Cleckley (19) presented a clinical profile of the antisocial personality comprised of 16 basic characteristics. Likewise, Catanzaro (20) cites 13 characteristics of the typical alcoholic. Some of the characteristics of the alcoholic, e.g., ambivalence toward authority, emotional immaturity, and low frustration tolerance, appear similar to those of the sociopath. More credence was given to the association between antisocial personality and alcoholism when, in 1952, the first *Diagnostic and Statistical Manual* of the American Psychiatric Association listed alcoholism under the general category of sociopathic disorder (21).

In recent years, the assumption that alcoholics are primarily sociopathic personality types has been disputed. It is now generally recognized that there is no typical alcoholic personality profile. Furthermore, a comparison of the lists of personality characteristics, such as those by Cleckley and Catanzaro, suggests more differences than similarities in the personality traits of the two groups. Frame and Osmond (22) administered the MMPI to a group of alcoholics entering an alcoholic treatment program and found the prevalence of profiles with strong psychopathic traits was significantly higher on admission than on follow-up examination, a change not generally noted in sociopaths.

These additional findings may have been responsible, in part, for the fact that alcoholism is listed as a separate mental disorder, not specifically associated with antisocial personality, in the *Diagnostic and Statistical Manual-II* (23). Although it would appear that sociopaths and alcoholics do share a number of similar personality characteristics, as well as a tendency to abuse alcohol, they do not share the same basic personality structure.

Sociopathy, Criminal Activity, and Alcohol

Many studies have shown high associations among alcohol intake, crime, antisocial behavior (24-26), and violent acts, including homicide (27, 28) and sexual crimes (29). Other studies indicate a high frequency of alcoholism among certain types of criminal offenders (30-32). Some studies indicate that over 50% of certain offenders were drinking at the time of the commission of the offense, and that 30-40% of the offenders were alcoholic by history (29, 31). Since criminal acts are often committed by sociopaths, it is understandable that the association of alcohol and crime has further tended to establish a linkage between alcohol and sociopathy.

This association is not, however, adequately understood, nor is it clear that the association goes beyond drinking and crime to drinking and sociopathy. First, although many criminals are sociopaths, not all of the crimes associated with alcoholism are committed primarily by sociopathic personality types. For example, homicide, except for gangland slayings, is not clearly associated with sociopathy. Homicide is frequently committed by family members, and elevated blood alcohol levels are often found in both the victim and the offender (33, 34). Similarly, rape is highly associated with drinking and alcoholism, but it has not been established that convicted rapists are predominantly sociopathic personality types. Glueck (35) has compared personality characteristics of rapists with Cleckley's list of personality characteristics of sociopaths and finds the two groups quite dissimilar. Rada (36) has presented a classification system of rapists, including the sociopathic type, but suggests that sociopathic rapists do not constitute the majority of convicted offenders. Furthermore, many studies of criminals do not use stringent diagnostic criteria and tend to assume a sociopathic diagnosis based primarily on a chronic history of arrests and difficulty with the law.

There are other factors which tend to obscure the true significance of the reported relationships among alcohol, crime, and sociopathy. It is possible that alcohol abusers are more likely to be apprehended than are non-alcohol abusing criminals. Thus, studies of convicted offenders may tend to be skewed in the direction of high associations among alcohol, alcoholism, and sociopathy.

A significant factor which is frequently overlooked is differentiation between drinking at the time of the commission of the offense and a history of alcoholism in the offender. In a recent study of rapists (37), it was found that a disproportionately high number of the alcoholic rapists were drinking at the time of the commission of the offense, whereas a relatively smaller percentage of nonalcoholic rapists were drinking at the time of the commission of the offense. Thus, it is important to establish whether the offender drinking at the time of the commission of the offense is alcoholic or nonalcoholic. When the offender is nonalcoholic by history, the likelihood of his abusing alcohol at the time of the commission of the offense is significantly decreased. This research finding is bolstered by the clinical observation that the professional sociopathic criminal does not drink when he is engaging in criminal behavior. The successful criminal, like the successful professional in any field, understands that one does not combine alcohol and work.

In conclusion, the present data indicate an association between drinking and certain crimes, and between drinking by alcoholics and certain crimes, but whether these data can be extended to establish an association between drinking, alcoholism, and criminal behavior is not clear.

Of course, the association between drinking, alcoholism, and criminal behavior does not establish a cause and effect relationship among these factors (38). If one were to compare all people drinking on a Friday night with nondrinkers, the association between the drinkers and crimes committed that evening would be high, but the percentage of those drinkers who actually commit crimes would be very low.

SOCIOPATHY VERSUS ALCOHOLISM

Many sociopaths drink or abuse alcohol. Likewise, some alcoholics develop difficulties with the law. But Schuckit (39) has recently noted the importance of adequately differentiating between the diagnostic categories of alcoholism and sociopathy. Primary alcoholism is characterized by alcohol abuse with no prior history of major psychiatric problems. Secondary alcoholism, on the other hand, is found as a complication of some other psychiatric illness, e.g., depression (40) or sociopathy. Furthermore, although alcohol abuse often complicates the life history of the sociopath, some sociopaths have no history of abuse of alcohol or other drugs.

Clinical evidence and some research findings suggest the subclassification of sociopaths and alcoholics into four different types: the drinking sociopath, the alcoholic sociopath, the sociopathic alcoholic, and the primary alcoholic. What follows is a brief description of each type.

The Drinking Sociopath

The true prevalence of sociopathy is undetermined (41) and the percentage of sociopaths who drink or abuse alcohol is not yet known. Most clinicians would agree that sociopaths frequently abuse alcohol and that their pattern of drinking further complicates an already immature and self-destructive life-style.

People drink for many reasons, among them are the desire to alleviate fear, to relieve depression, to overcome boredom, and simply to produce a "high." However, the drinking episodes of the sociopath and the behavior which results often do not appear to be motivated by reasons with which most people can identify. Drinking by alcoholics and others tends to be motivated by the pleasure principle, even when the result of such drinking is not positive. Most psychological theories of alcoholism are based at least in part on the premise that intoxication favorably alters affect (42-47). Cleckley (19), however, notes that the sociopath's drinking "seldom drives at anything that looks very much like pleasure or necessary analgesia." His drinking is like many other characteristics considered typical of his personality, i.e., impulsive, self-destructive, and without guilt or insight. When treating a sociopath who appears to be doing well, it is not uncommon to one day discover that he has gone out on a binge, has acted in a bizarre, hostile, and crazy manner, and has ended up in serious trouble with the law. Unlike the alcoholic who may have been responding to developing personal stress, the sociopath is unable to give reasons for beginning the spree. His only response may be "I felt like it" or "I had nothing better to do," and the therapist is usually frustrated when he tries to find a "hidden" motive.

The sociopath's manner and behavior when drinking are often equally inexplicable. Alcoholics frequently feel more sociable when drinking, but this is not typical of the sociopath. Although he may drink in bars for days, he does not dance, carouse, or develop new friendships; rather, he remains mostly to himself. Fights frequently occur where people are drinking heavily but the altercations are usually preceded by some provocative interchange. In contrast, one sociopath admitted that when he drinks he sometimes hits people for no apparent reason. On one occasion, after drinking in a bar for several hours and without being aware of any particular negative feelings, he decided to leave. As he reached the door, another customer walked in. Without provocation he hit the man in the face and inflicted a severe injury. He had acted similarly on other occasions, had never understood why, and never seemed particularly guilty or upset by this kind of behavior. Certainly it had not prevented him from engaging in the same type of drinking on numerous other occasions.

Unlike the alcoholic who expresses remorse when he has fallen off the wagon, the sociopath often shows no concern even though his excessive drinking has caused serious harm to himself and others, particularly to members of his family.

The point to be emphasized is that the sociopath's drinking and alcohol abuse are not inconsistent with other aspects of his personality and behavior—aspects which seem foreign and inexplicable to others. This may be another of the reasons why some authorities have suggested that sociopathy is really a psychosis underneath a veneer of sanity.

Despite occasional episodes of binge drinking, the drinking sociopath does not usually drink on a daily basis and rarely if ever develops any of the medical complications of a true alcohol addiction (delirium tremens, alcoholic cirrhosis, and the like). This fact, coupled with his general lack of insight, makes him particularly unwilling to accept his alcohol abuse as a problem which requires treatment.

The Alcoholic Sociopath

The basic feature which distinguishes this group from the sociopathic alcoholic or the primary alcoholic is the onset of characteristic behavioral symptoms before the alcohol abuse. These subjects have the typical early life history of the sociopath, including truancy, fighting, difficulty with school authorities, conflict with the law, and running away from home, usually commencing before the age of 15. The alcoholic sociopath can be classified into two groups: those with early onset alcohol abuse, and those with late onset alcohol abuse. One generalization can be made for both groups: They are by and large "unsuccessful" sociopaths. They have not found a niche among the criminal element nor among those who make it in the "straight" world.

The early onset alcoholic sociopath usually begins his abuse in adolescence (48). Ethanol intake in particular is associated with criminal activity, although there will often be a history of excessive use of alcohol without antisocial behavior. The transition from heavy drinking in adolescence to alcoholism in early adulthood is unusually rapid. For example, in our study of incarcerated rapists (29) we found, using stringent criteria, that 35% were alcoholic. Of particular interest is that the average age of the alcoholic rapist was 27 years, indicating severe alcoholism at quite an early age. Although not all alcoholic rapists have a sociopathic history, a significant percentage have the typical early life history, including early abuse of alcohol.

The combination of serious sociopathic behavior and addiction to alcohol is particularly pernicious. By adulthood, the early onset alcoholic sociopath has often been confined in penal institutions for extensive periods of time. If he is discharged, he readily returns to heavy drinking, which leads to further complications with the law, reincarceration, and the vicious revolving door cycle.

The late onset alcoholic sociopath is characterized by a biphasic criminal career pattern (49). Prior to the age of 35 the majority of his arrests are not alcohol-related and include offenses such as burglary, theft, and armed robbery. Beginning in his thirties, his arrests become more clearly alcohol-related and include vagrancy, disorderly conduct, and public intoxication. His criminal career is marked by a progression of institutionalization, first in reform schools, county jails, and penitentiaries and eventually in typical sheltered milieus for chronic alcoholics such as halfway houses, residential treatment centers for chronic inebriates, and the like. For some as yet unclear reason, possibly related to his growing addiction, the late onset alcoholic sociopath seems to "burn out" in terms of his criminal activity after the age of 30 and then follows a relatively progressive downhill course which frequently ends on skid row.

The Sociopathic Alcoholic

The sociopathic alcoholic does not have the history of sociopathic behavior prior to the age of 15. He does, however, possess certain personality features of the sociopath, particularly impulsivity and lack of insight. He is more likely than the alcoholic sociopath to experience a sense of guilt about his behavior, which makes the prognosis for treatment somewhat better. He differs from the primary alcoholic in that his antisocial activities are often more serious and occur at a younger age. His criminal activity is not the result of social deterioration secondary to alcohol. In the typical case, heavy drinking begins in early adolescence. During military service the heavy drinking, coupled with ambivalence and disrespect for discipline and authority, may lead to frequent fines and even an early discharge. Following this discharge, the alcoholism causes continued pronounced difficulties in his work and personal life. As a result, he begins to frequent bars where a "rough crowd" hangs out, including many who would be classified as alcoholic sociopaths. He is an easy target for those who engage in criminal activity and soon becomes a part of the "group." He feels that he "never had a chance," but unfortunately rarely acknowledges any personal responsibility for his problems.

Schuckit et al. (50) reported on antisocial traits in male alcoholics. Those with no definite personality disorder and onset of alcoholism before age 20 showed significantly more antisocial behavior than those who became alcoholic after age 30. If this type is properly diagnosed before antisocial difficulties become too severe, control of the addiction is usually followed by cessation of antisocial behavior. Even under the best of treatment conditions, however, he is quite susceptible to temptation to drink. When he returns to drink he is frequently abusive toward his family, particularly his wife. However, because he often experiences or professes profound guilt following each episode of wife beating, and because of the wife's reluctance to report the offense, the sociopathic alcoholic may continue for years to disrupt the stability of his family and unwittingly contribute to the next generation of self-destructive sociopathic alcoholics.

The Primary Alcoholic

The primary alcoholic differs from the other types in that he does not have the typical early life history and few, if any, of the personality traits of the sociopath. The antisocial behavior of the primary alcoholic is the result of social deterioration secondary to his addiction. It is well known that alcohol dulls judgment and numbs the social conscience, factors which contribute to the commission of antisocial acts.

Although most alcoholics do not engage in antisocial or criminal behavior, certain offenses seem to be disproportionately committed by those with a drinking problem. One such offense is child molestation. From our studies of sex offenders it would appear that abuse of alcohol may often be more directly influential in the commission of child molestation than in the commission of rape. Alcoholism and drinking at the time of the commission of the offense are extremely high among child molesters (31). Also, the average age of the child molester is considerably higher than that of the rapist. However, many alcoholic child molesters do not profess pedophilic tendencies when sober. Thus, when the chronic alcoholic loses his sexual potency as a direct result of the toxic biological effects of alcohol (51), and as his possibilties for adult sexual contacts are lessened by social deterioration related to his alcohol abuse, he may turn to a child for sexual gratification, especially when drinking heavily. Such offenses are often followed by guilt and shame; thus the prognosis in these cases is good if the offender can be engaged in a program of combined treatment for both his addiction and his sexual offenses.

Finally, as with all classification systems, the diagnostic picture of an individual subject may be confusing and there may be considerable overlapping within these groups. But the distinction between alcoholism and sociopathy has considerable relevance for treatment planning and disposition. Not only are all types admitted to both alcoholic treatment programs and penal institutions, but professionals are now frequently asked to render opinions and give testimony in court regarding disposition of various offenders, especially those whose offense is alcohol-related.

More than the other types of alcoholics, the drinking sociopath is most likely to deny any problem with alcohol abuse. Adequate treatment requires a closely monitored, consistent, well organized program such as the one recently described by Yochelson and Samenow (52). Excluding the primary alcoholic, few treatment strategies have been regularly successful with this patient population. In each instance, an individualized treatment program must be planned, with the recognition that sociopathy in combination with alcoholism is exceedingly difficult to treat.

REFERENCES

1. SCHUCKIT, M., GOODWIN, D., and WINOKUR, G. A Study of Alcoholism in Half Siblings. *Am. J. Psychiatry* 128:1132-1136, 1972.
2. GOODWIN, D., SCHULSINGER, F., HERMANSEN, L., GUZE, S. B., and WINOKUR, G. Alco-

hol Problems in Adoptees Raised Apart from Alcoholic Biological Parents. *Arch. Gen. Psychiatry* 28:238-243, 1973.

3. GOODWIN, D., SCHULSINGER, F., MOLLER, N., HERMANSEN, L., WINOKUR, G., and GUZE, S. B. Drinking Problems in Adopted and Non-adopted Sons of Alcoholics. *Arch. Gen. Psychiatry* 31:164-169, 1974.

4. CROWE, R. An Adoption Study of Antisocial Personality. *Arch. Gen. Psychiatry* 31:785-791, 1974.

5. HUTCHINGS, B. and MEDNICK, S. A. Registered Criminality in the Adoptive and Biological Parents of Registered Male Criminal Adoptees. In: R. Fieve, H. Brill, and D. Rosenthal (Eds.), *Genetic Research in Psychiatry*. Baltimore: Johns Hopkins University Press, 1975.

6. SCHULSINGER, F. Psychopathy: Heredity and Environment. *Int. J. Ment. Health* 1:190-206, 1972.

7. ROBINS, L. N., BATES, W., and O'NEAL, P. Adult Drinking Patterns of Former Problem Children. In: D. J. Pittman, C. R. Snyder (Eds.), *Society, Culture, and Drinking Patterns*. New York: John Wiley and Sons, 1962.

8. AMARK, C. A. *Study in Alcoholism*. Copenhagen: Ejnar Munchsgaard, 1951.

9. GUZE, S. B., WOLFGRAM, E. D., McKINNEY, J. K., and CANTWELL, D. P. Psychiatric Illness in the Families of Convicted Criminals: A Study of 519 First-Degree Relatives. *Dis. Nerv. Syst.* 28:651-659, 1967.

10. CLONINGER, C. R. and GUZE, S. B. Psychiatric Illness in the Families of Female Criminals: A Study of 288 First-Degree Relatives. *Br. J. Psychiatry* 122:697-703, 1973.

11. MENKES, M. M., ROWE, J. S., and MENKES, J. H. A Twenty-five Year Follow-up Study on the Hyperkinetic Child with Minimal Brain Dysfunction. *Pediatrics* 39:393-399, 1967.

12. STEWART, M. A. Hyperactive Children. *Sci. Am.* 222:94-98, 1970.

13. WEISS, G., MINDE, K., WERRY, J. S., DOUGLAS, V., and NEMETH, E. Studies on the Hyperactive Child: VIII. Five-year Follow-up. *Arch. Gen. Psychiatry* 24:409-414, 1971.

14. MORRISON, J. R. and STEWART, M. A. A Family Study of the Hyperactive Child Syndrome. *Biol. Psychiatry* 3:189-195, 1971.

15. CANTWELL, D. P. Psychiatric Illness in the Families of Hyperactive Children. *Arch. Gen. Psychiatry* 70:414-417, 1972.

16. GOODWIN, D. W., SCHULSINGER, F., HERMANSEN, L., GUZE, S. B., and WINOKUR, G. Alcoholism and the Hyperactive Child Syndrome. *J. Nerv. Ment. Dis.* 160:349-353, 1975.

17. WOOD, D. R., REIMHERR, F. W., WENDER, P. H., and JOHNSON, G. E Diagnosis and Treatment of Minimal Brain Dysfunction in Adults. *Arch. Gen. Psychiatry* 33:1453-1460, 1976.

18. DAHLSTROM, W. G. and WELSH, G. S. *An MMPI Handbook*. Minneapolis: University of Minnesota Press, 1960.

19. CLECKLEY, H. *The Mask of Sanity*, Ed. IV. St. Louis: C. V. Mosby, 1964.

20. CATANZARO, R. J. Psychiatric Aspects of Alcoholism. In: D. J. Pittman, (Ed.), *Alcoholism*. New York: Harper & Row, 1967.

21. American Psychiatric Association: *Diagnostic and Statistical Manual of Mental Disorders, (DSM-I)*, Ed. I. Washington: American Psychiatric Association, 1952.

22. FRAME, M. C. and OSMOND, W. M. C. Alcoholism, Psychopathic Personality, and Psychopathic Reaction Type. *Med. Proc. Johannesburg* 2:257-261, 1956.

23. American Psychiatric Association: *Diagnostic and Statistical Manual of Mental Disorders, (DSM-II)*, Ed. II. Washington: American Psychiatric Association, 1968.

24. BANAY, R. S. Alcoholism and Crime. *Quart. J. Stud. Alc.* 2:686-716, 1942.

25. SHUPE, L. M. Alcohol and Crime. *J. Crim. Law, Crimol. and Police Sci.* 44:661-664, 1954.

26. MAYFIELD, D. Alcoholism, Alcohol, Intoxication and Assaultive Behavior. *Dis. Nerv. Syst.* 37:288-291, 1976.
27. VIRKKUNEN, M. Alcohol as a Factor Precipitating Aggression and Conflict Behavior Leading to Homicide. *Brit. J. Addict.* 69:149-154, 1974.
28. HOLLIS, W. S. On the Etiology of Criminal Homicides—the Alcohol Factor. *J. Police Sci. Admin.* 2:50-53, 1974.
29. RADA, R. T. Alcoholism and Forcible Rape. *Am. J. Psychiatry* 132:444-446, 1975.
30. GUZE, S. B., TUASON, V. B., STEWART, M. A., GATFIELD, P. D., and PICKEN, B. A Study of Check Offenders. *Dis. Nerv. Syst.* 24:752-754, 1963.
31. RADA, R. T. Alcoholism and the Child Molester. *Ann. N.Y. Acad. Sci.* 273:492-496, 1976.
32. PIOTROWSKI, K. W., LOSACCO, D., and GUZE, S. B. Psychiatric Disorders and Crime: A Study of Pretrial Psychiatric Examinations. *Dis. Nerv. Syst.* 37:309-311, 1976.
33. WILENTZ, W. C. and BRADY, J. P. The Alcohol Factor in Violent Deaths. *Am. Practit. Dig. Treatm.* 12:829-835, 1961.
34. LE ROUX, L. C. and SMITH, L. S. Violent Deaths and Alcoholic Intoxication. *J. Forens. Med.* 11:131-147, 1964.
35. GLUECK, B. C. Psychodynamic Patterns in the Sex Offender. *Psychiatr. Q.* 28:1-21, 1954.
36. RADA, R. T. Classification of the Rapist. In: R. T. Rada (Ed.), *Clinical Aspects of the Rapist.* New York: Grune & Stratton, 1978.
37. RADA, R. T., LAWS, D. R., and KELLNER, R. Plasma Testosterone Levels in the Rapist. *Psychosom. Med.* 38:257-268, 1976.
38. WOLFGANG, M. E. and STROHM, R. B. The Relationship Between Alcohol and Criminal Homicide. *Quart. J. Stud. Alc.* 17:411-425, 1956.
39. SCHUCKIT, M. A. Alcoholism and Sociopathy—Diagnostic Confusion. *Quart. J. Stud. Alc.* 34:157-164, 1973.
40. SCHUCKIT, M. A. and MORRISSEY, E. R. Alcoholism in Women: Some Clinical and Social Perspectives with an Emphasis on Possible Subtypes. In: M. Greenblatt and M. A. Schuckit (Eds.), *Alcoholism Problems in Women and Children.* New York: Grune and Stratton, 1976.
41. WINOKUR, G. and CROWE, R. R. Personality Disorders. In A. M. Freedman, H. I. Kaplan, and B. J. Sadock, (Eds.), *Comprehensive Textbook of Psychiatry II,* Ed. II. Baltimore: Williams and Wilkins, 1975.
42. REICHARD, J. D. Addiction: Some Theoretical Considerations as to its Nature, Cause, Prevention and Treatment. *Am. J. Psychiatry* 103:721-730, 1947.
43. ULLMAN, A. D. The Psychological Mechanism of Alcohol Addiction. *Quart. J. Stud. Alc.* 13:602-608, 1952.
44. HIGGINS, J. W. Psychodynamics in the Excessive Drinking of Alcohol. *AMA Arch. Neurol. Psychiatry* 69:713-726, 1953.
45. RADO, S. Narcotic Bondage: A General Theory of the Dependence on Drugs. *Am. J. Psychiatry* 114:165-170, 1957.
46. MAYFIELD, D. and ALLEN, D. Alcohol and Affect: A Psychopharmacological Study. *Am. J. Psychiatry* 123:1346-1351, 1967.
47. MAYFIELD, D. Psychopharmacology of Alcohol. *J. Nerv. Ment. Dis.* 146:314-321, 1968.
48. WINOKUR, G., RIMMER, J., and REICH, T. Alcoholism IV: Is There More Than One Type of Alcoholism? *Brit. J. Psychiatry* 118:525-531, 1971.
49. PITTMAN, D. J. and GORDON, C. W. Criminal Careers of the Chronic Police Case Inebriate. *Quart. J. Stud. Alc.* 19:255-268, 1958.
50. SCHUCKIT, M., RIMMER, J., REICH, T., and WINOKUR, G. Alcoholism: Anti-social Traits in Male Alcoholics. *Brit. J. Psychiatry* 117:575-576, 1970.
51. LEMERE, F. and SMITH, J. W. Alcohol-Induced Sexual Impotence. *Am. J. Psychiatry* 130:212-213, 1973.
52. YOCHELSON, S. and SAMENOW, S. E. *The Criminal Personality,* Vol. II. New York: Jason Aronson, 1977.

12

Drug Abuse, Crime, and the Antisocial Personality: Some Conceptual Issues

LESTER GRINSPOON, M.D.
and
JAMES B. BAKALAR

We will consider three aspects of the relationships among crime, antisocial personality and drug use, abuse, or dependence: 1) The problems of defining "antisocial personality" and "drug abuse" or "drug dependence," especially the confusion or ambiguity between clinical diagnosis and legal or moral judgment that plagues all these terms and complicates the problem of their relationship to crime. 2) The related issue of interdefinability: "Drug abuse" and "antisocial personality" may be defined in such a way that many of their clinical or social symptoms are the same; in that case discourse about the connection between the two categories becomes almost tautologous. 3) Finally, the problem of causation, with its notorious methodological difficulties. Writers on all these subjects often seem to be hacking their way through a semantic jungle or else pointing to "facts"—for example, about drug use and crime—that shift greatly in meaning with the observer's stance. Our Ariadne's thread in the labyrinth should be the social and medical purpose of the concepts we are using.

The definition, diagnosis, and etiology of the antisocial personality are discussed elsewhere in this volume. We will assume that there is such a character type (or personality disorder), exemplified by the case histories in Cleckley's *Mask of Sanity* (1), that some indeterminate combination of heredity and environment produces the type, and that people identifiable as antisocial personalities constitute a small part of the total population and a considerably larger percentage of convicted criminals. This is where the first problem arises. As one observer points out (2), it should be theoretically possible to diagnose antisocial personality without a history of criminal offenses, but that almost never happens. Antisocial personalities are usually diagnosed only after they have been in trouble with the law, because psychiatrists otherwise rarely come into contact with them professionally. One can almost state that only people who are first socially defined as criminals on account of their acts come to be psychiatrically diagnosed as antisocial on account of their personalities. Therefore, in effect, if not in theory, the antisocial personality becomes a subclass of the class of criminals or lawbreakers. In fact, some psychiatrists concerned with civil liberties are unwilling to admit the diagnosis at all, regarding it as simply another word for what used to be called "the criminal element" (3). Many of us have known people whose behavior we would be willing to call, loosely, "antisocial" or "psychopathic," yet who have never been arrested for a crime. In these cases the term "antisocial," however reasonably used, achieves only the status of name-calling—the equivalent of "son-of-a-bitch" or "con-man"—rather than that of a diagnosis. By in effect reserving the diagnosis for those who are caught breaking the law, we are leaving out some of the most interesting cases and distorting our picture of the character type.

This problem arises whenever a diagnostic category combines a clinical judgment with a legal one. If too many of the same acts that define criminality are used to establish the diagnosis, the association becomes easy to demonstrate, but meaningless. The categories of drug abuse and drug dependence easily fall into this trap, since they are less clearly defined and more loaded with questionable connotations than "antisocial personality." In the diagnostic manuals drug dependence (along with alcoholism) has been classed as a personality disorder, yet there is no single addictive or dependence-prone (or alcoholic) personality type and no accepted etiology or predictable course and outcome. The concept of drug dependence is in any case confused and ambiguous, mixing pharmacological, psychiatric, social, and metaphysical judgments in a way that is more often misleading than helpful. It is not clear where to draw the line between dependence on a drug and simply wanting to use it or habitually using it. The attempt to avoid these problems by speaking of drug abuse rather than drug dependence also runs into difficulties. No one can state with any precision how much of which drug, taken by which route, over what period of time, constitutes abuse; ideas about drug abuse vary with time, place, and culture. For example, at one time marijuana was legally and morally acceptable in the Near East and India but alcohol was not; the situation has changed recently. A few years ago, in the United States, someone who smoked marijuana once or twice a week would have been regarded as a drug abuser and someone who took amphetamines every day to combat fatigue and work longer would not have been; today many people would reverse those judgments.

The clinical diagnosis and moral (or legal) judgments united in the term "antisocial personality" are at least partly separated in the two phrases about drugs: "Dependence" implies a psychiatric disorder, and "abuse" implies a moral or social evil. At the same time, a great deal of moralism (sometimes of a rather parochial kind) goes into definitions of drug dependence, and drug abuse is often assimilated to psychiatric disorders. The way in which we shift from "dependence" to "abuse" and back in talking about drugs indicates our unease about the mixture of psychiatric and social judgments involved but does nothing to resolve it.

The inadequacy and confusion of the terminology we use for drug problems are indicated by the different kinds of definitions considered appropriate for alcoholism and dependence on illicit drugs. In one typical recent study of criminality and psychiatric disorders (4), for example, alcoholism is defined by a complex group of features, mostly involving harm done by the alcoholic to himself or others; drug dependence is defined simply as "recurrent and prolonged use of [illicit] drugs," withdrawal symptoms, or hospitalization for addiction. No one would contemplate diagnosing a personality disorder simply on account of recurrent and prolonged use of alcohol, and yet there is no evidence that it is qualitatively distinct from recurrent and prolonged use of other drugs.* We define alcoholism differently and more strictly than we define drug dependence simply because we do not want to label most of the population with a diagnosis of personality disorder. In this way social judgments invade psychiatric categories. Recurrent and prolonged use of alcohol is statistically normal in a descriptive sense and therefore judged psychiatrically normal in a prescriptive sense. Recurrent and prolonged use of illicit drugs is not statistically normal because it is not legal and therefore not socially acceptable; so it is regarded as psychiatrically abnormal and given a diagnostic label. For a diagnosis of alcoholism we require evidence of alcohol *abuse,* and we take some trouble to define that carefully. For a diagnosis of drug dependence we require

---

* For more on this issue, see Chapter 11 in this volume.

only evidence of use; we take it for granted that any habitual use is misuse or abuse, because that is what the law assumes.

At this point it can be argued that social facts create psychiatric facts: Given the present legal and social status of, say, heroin, most people who develop the habit of using it must be psychologically disturbed in some way. That is possible, but this concept provides no hint of what disturbances are involved. Diagnosing heroin dependence itself as a personality disorder simply evades the issue by a circular maneuver. That will always be so as long as use of the drug alone, rather than some harmful consequence of it, is the basis for diagnosis.

We have pointed out that since many of the acts that constitute evidence of antisocial personality are crimes, there is an automatic connection between the disorder and criminality. This is even more obviously and tautologically true of illicit drug use, since the illicit drug user is a criminal by definition. Of course, that is not the whole story. Although the 13 million people in the United States who smoke marijuana regularly are in formal terms habitual criminals, we do not treat them that way in practice. That is because the association (not causal connection) between marijuana use and an otherwise criminal milieu no longer exists. Nevertheless, it is clear that by making a drug illegal we tend to restrict its use to those who have little respect for the law. We also make it profitable for criminals to sell the drug, so they become familiar with it. As a result illicit drug use becomes closely associated even with crime that does not involve the possession and sale of drugs; criminals use these drugs more than the rest of us because they are more easily available in a criminal milieu. Another important and familiar aspect of the socially imposed relationship between criminality and illicit drugs is the artificially high price that forces people who want or need them to commit crimes to obtain the money. For all these reasons the connection between criminal behavior and drug abuse as it is usually defined tends to become self-proving, like the connection between criminal behavior and antisocial personality.

We might speak of drug abuse or drug dependence in the same strict sense implied by a diagnosis of alcoholism, demanding evidence of harm to self or others directly caused by the drug instead of treating the drug itself as harmful by definition. This is more sensible, but it does not resolve the basic problem. What we call alcoholism or habitual alcohol abuse is so often associated with crime partly because someone who commits crimes under the influence of alcohol is by definition abusing it rather than using it as it should be used. The same would be true of drug dependence or drug abuse defined in a way parallel to alcoholism.

To the extent, then, that our use of the terms "antisocial personality" and "drug abuse" is determined by moral reactions and the criminal law as well as by clinical judgment, these diagnoses will be automatically associated with criminal behavior. Therefore studies finding them to be connected or correlated with crime prove less than they seem to prove. The conclusion that "sociopathy, alcoholism, and drug dependence are the only principal psychiatric disorders associated with serious crime" (4) is at least partly an artifact of the definitions. For the same reason that these diagnoses tend to become largely interdefinable with criminality, they tend to become partly interdefinable with each other—our second problem. The difficulty in distinguishing antisocial personality from alcoholism is notorious.* Before the diagnosis of antisocial personality took its present form, the conditions were often included together in studies of "psychopaths" (5). One still comes upon remarks like the statement that it is impossible to distinguish alcoholics from antisocial personalities in the written records of criminals' families (6).

What is true of alcoholism is even more true of illicit drug dependence or abuse as it is now defined, for the reasons given above. In its crudest form, the diagnosis of antisocial personality can become nothing more than a disguised moral judgment of the user of a drug considered socially unacceptable for some historical or cultural reason. But even where more subtlety and sensitivity are displayed (as in discussions of alcoholism) the problem is unavoidable. Our point is that the diagnostic confusion is not simply a matter of deficient empirical data or psychiatrists' limitations and prejudices: It has a large purely conceptual, logical element.

Here the question of dyssocial behavior enters into the relationship between antisocial personality and drug abuse. Dyssocial behavior is the term now often applied to the actions of certain people who belong to groups that reject or ignore some of the moral and legal standards of the dominant culture: hippies, gypsies, organized crime bosses, gamblers, prostitutes, street gangs, and so on—sometimes career criminals in general are included. In the current standard diagnostic manuals, dyssocial behavior is classified under the heading "conditions without manifest psychiatric disorder and non-specific conditions"; it is supposedly distinguished from personality disorders like antisocial personality by an absence of definite onset, clinical features, and prognosis. The dyssocial person is said to be able to control his impulses and pursue a long-range

---

* See Chapter 11.

goal in a way the antisocial personality cannot; unlike the antisocial personality, he is said to have a more or less intact capacity for deep feeling, love, loyalty, shame, and guilt, within the limits imposed by the hostility between his own group and the dominant culture—everything implied by the phrase "honor among thieves."

From what we have said about the cultural aspect of definitions of drug abuse it is obvious that many illicit drug users might be described this way instead of being called drug-dependent or antisocial personalities. Habitual marijuana smokers in the 1940s or habitual LSD users in the 1960s, for example, could be called "dyssocial" in this sense; some moonshiners and illicit drug dealers might also fit the description.

Reference to dyssocial behavior at first seems to provide a way out of the difficulties created by the overlapping definitions of antisocial personality, criminality, and drug abuse. A few illicit drug users and other criminals can be diagnosed as antisocial personalities, and the rest can be said to belong to "dyssocial" groups whose behavior is judged wrong or inappropriate by the standards of the dominant culture. The illegal acts by which dyssocial behavior is identified will often be the same as those that justify the diagnosis of antisocial personality, but their pattern and the circumstances will be different enough for a separate classification. For example, the observed associations among membership in slum gangs, illicit drug use, and crime (7) can be explained this way. We can also speak of an "addict culture" consisting of the 30% of heroin addicts estimated to be street hustlers (8). The drug dealer, like the pimp, can be regarded as a tempting role model ("Superfly") for boys and men who have no chance of success by the dominant culture's standards.

But "dyssocial" may be merely another terminological evasion of the same kind implied in the usual criteria for antisocial personality and for drug abuse or drug dependence. The difference is that now, instead of mixing moral judgment and psychiatric diagnosis, we have created a vague, neutral term that seems to imply neither and in effect simply suspends judgment. The hard choice we are avoiding is this: Do we want to attribute the condition of these people to a psychiatric disorder, or do we want to make an adverse moral judgment of them. Or do we want to judge the dominant culture adversely for stigmatizing them as morally evil or psychiatrically disturbed and making their lives difficult?

Those who have no hesitation about making the choice are usually willing to brush aside the psychiatric distinctions as meaningless. For example, the labeling theory of deviance in sociology unequivocally blames the dominant culture: The accusation is that it not only makes people into criminals and drug abusers but creates categories like dyssocial, antisocial, and drug abuse by socially defining and patterning certain acts that would otherwise be ambiguous. Another way to lay the blame on society is Marxist: Conditions in the labor market created by the inadequacies of the capitalist economic system are said to cause the kind of behavior defined as antisocial, dyssocial, or drug abuse. In these sociological approaches, both moral judgment on individuals and psychiatric diagnoses are regarded as irrelevant and misleading; the distinctions between drug dependence/abuse and simply using drugs are said to reflect not fundamental personality differences but the distorting definitions imposed on certain acts by the operation of larger social mechanisms.

It is also possible to reject the distinction between antisocial and dyssocial by making the opposite choice and placing personality unequivocally at the center. Some observers consider it wrong to class gamblers, street addicts, prostitutes, and armed robbers as members of a subculture, a criminal fraternity; rather, most of them qualify for the diagnosis of antisocial personality by their shallow hedonism, callousness, and inability to form permanent emotional attachments: There is no criminal fraternity and very little honor among thieves (2). One recent study, for example, describes 78% of its male criminal subjects as sociopaths (4). In this approach, unlike the purely sociological one, the psychiatric diagnosis is accepted as legitimate and primary; questions of whom or what to blame are secondary causal ones.

Criticizing psychiatric categories like antisocial personality, dyssocial reaction, and drug dependence as ideologically biased or morally evasive is of no practical value in dealing with individual cases as long as the only alternatives offered are blank moral condemnation of the individual or a demand for global social reforms. But such criticisms do force us to recognize that these categories are often both confused internally and hard to distinguish conceptually from one another.

This makes our third problem, the causal one, especially difficult. Causal questions in social science are notoriously intractable because of methodological problems, but the difficulties are compounded by imprecision in the definition of the causes and effects being evaluated. We would like to be able to study the causal relationships among easily distinguishable character types or classes of behavior—antisocial personality, criminality, drug abuse, drug dependence—but in reality there are no such clear distinctions. We must proceed with vague and variable working definitions, recognizing how uncertain this makes all causal identifications.

The two main causal questions, then, are whether drug abuse can produce an antisocial personality and whether antisocial personalities are inclined to drug abuse. It is easy to answer the first question "no" if we assume that antisocial personality is simply a clinical syndrome with an onset in childhood identified by features like truancy, bedwetting, and fire-setting. But if adult criminal behavior is also included in the definition of antisocial personality (rather than merely used as evidence of its existence) it may make sense to say that in some cases drug abuse aggravates a predisposition and creates an antisocial personality. On the other hand, antisocial behavior under the influence of drugs or following a diagnosis of drug dependence can be regarded as no different from antisocial behavior under the influence of paranoia or a manic episode: It is not in itself evidence of antisocial personality. In that case crimes and delinquencies caused by the use of alcohol, barbiturates, and amphetamines or by the unavailability of needed heroin would not indicate a change in the personality of the drug abuser. Here again the problem of definition arises: Since abuse of drugs is often a form of antisocial behavior, it becomes attached to the diagnosis of antisocial personality, and this in turn is then treated as a causal relationship.

More often and more plausibly, it is proposed that the antisocial personality tends to misuse drugs and thereby aggravates the consequences of his disorder. Chronologically, the behavior associated with antisocial personality often precedes any drug abuse or even drug use; it sometimes starts in childhood. The antisocial character does not feel the internal constraints that impose moderation in the use of drugs on most of us. He does not learn from the disastrous effects of his misuse of drugs because it is disastrous mainly for other people; he takes no responsibility, feels no genuine regret, and cannot be made to understand why he should not do it again. Besides, in a person already so uninhibited, any loosening of residual inhibitions by drugs is likely to be socially undesirable. An abnormal neurological organization, affected in a peculiarly unfortunate way by drugs, may also be involved.

On the other hand, many antisocial personalities do not suffer from drug abuse problems. It is hard to determine just how many do, since the definitions are so vague and variable. One recent estimate is that 15% have drug problems (including alcoholism) (6), a figure that is higher than the average for the population but not spectacularly so. Of course, a broader or narrower conception of the infinitely elastic term "drug abuse" would presumably change the figure substantially. Whatever statistics may show, reasons are sometimes given why a true anti-social personality should not ordinarily be a drug abuser; for example, it is argued that he is too narcissistic to allow himself to become dependent on a drug (5), or so uninhibited that he needs no drug to release his dangerous impulses, or unlikely to suffer from the kind of anxiety and depression that leads many people to abuse drugs. The antisocial personality might also be said to be too improvident and short-sighted for the elaborate planning that, say, a heroin addict requires to obtain his next fix. A point not made as often as it should be is that drugs provide the antisocial personality with one more item in his impressive repertory of excuses and rationalizations. Knowing that drugs are supposed to lessen one's responsibility for one's acts, he will make free use of the claim that he was not himself because he was under their influence. His laments about his abuse of drugs or alcohol should therefore be regarded with suspicion, like everything else he says. The vagueness and latitude in our social definitions of drug abuse and his awareness of our willingness to blame drugs for all kinds of misbehavior make it particularly easy for him to use them as an excuse.

Finally, there is a problem related to the fact that most people diagnosed as antisocial personalities are petty criminals. The kind of ineffectual and unsuccessful person who becames a petty criminal is also likely to be the kind of person who uses drugs in a self-destructive way and therefore becomes defined as a drug abuser. Furthermore, he may keep coming to the attention of the police, and therefore psychiatrists, partly because of his behavior under the influence of drugs and alcohol. There may be antisocial personalities who are relatively effective in (or against) society and successful in escaping the consequences of their acts; however, they would never be diagnosed as antisocial (although their acquaintances would have plenty of equivalent unflattering terms for them), and they would not often lose control under the influence of drugs or be caught using them illegally. If such people were included in the definition of antisocial personality, its association with drug abuse would seem weaker. Whether they should be included is another matter. Perhaps ineffectuality and social failure are an essential part of what we mean by antisocial personality; maybe using the term more broadly amounts to passing off moral judgment and name-calling as diagnosis. But then that has always been a danger with this diagnostic category.

It seems reasonable to say that drug problems are not at the center of the antisocial character's life but on its periphery. He does not permit all his acts to be conditioned by the effects of a drug or his need for it, as does the severe alcoholic or heroin addict. The usual way of putting it, which unfortunately has many misleading connotations, is to say that he is not likely to become truly drug-dependent. As Cleckley points out, when an antisocial personality joins Alcoholics Anonymous he is not serious; he simply uses it as a stage to get what he can out of playing the role of repentant alcoholic as long as it is useful to him. He has no conception of saving himself from alcohol because he does not feel himself to be in bondage to it. On the other hand, the antisocial character certainly abuses or misuses drugs, but mostly in the same way that he misuses firearms, his fists, his signature, or other people's money. Drugs are just one of his instruments. His antisocial behavior under the influence of drugs sometimes resembles the antisocial behavior of alcoholics and illicit drug users just as it sometimes resembles the antisocial behavior of paranoids or manic persons, but the pattern and the reasons are not the same.

We raised the question earlier whether the use of terms like antisocial, dyssocial, drug abuse, and drug dependence is a way of avoiding decisions about how to distribute our judgments between moral condemnation (of the individual or society) and psychiatric diagnosis. Even if that is so, the vagueness of the terminology may be functional. We cannot await the resolution of grand theoretical issues when we need to act in individual cases; we have to muddle through with knowledge that is not only empirically but conceptually deficient. In defining conditions like antisocial personality or drug abuse and trying to establish their causes and the causal connections among them, we are far from being able to attain a ruthless consistency and total lack of ambiguity; but that at least protects us from intellectual arrogance and moral dogmatism where human lives are at stake.

REFERENCES

1. CLECKLEY, HERVEY. *The Mask of Sanity.* St. Louis: C. V. Mosby, 1964.
2. STOJANOVICK, K. Antisocial and Dyssocial: Entities or Shibboleths? *Arch. Gen. Psychiat.* 21:561-567, 1969.
3. STONE, ALAN A. *Mental Health and Law: A System of Transition.* Rockville, MD.: National Institute of Mental Health, 1975.
4. GUZE, SAMUEL, B. *Criminality and Psychiatric Disorders.* New York: Oxford University Press, 1976.
5. RAPPEPORT, J. R. Antisocial Behavior. In: S. Arieti and Eugene B. Brody (Eds.), *American Handbook of Psychiatry.* New York: Basic Books, 1974.
6. ROBINS, L. R. *Deviant Children Grown Up: A Social and Psychiatric Study of Sociopathic Personality.* Baltimore: Williams and Wilkins, 1966.
7. FRIEDMAN, C. JACK and FRIEDMAN, ALFRED S. Drug Abuse and Delinquency. *Drug Use in America: Problem in Perspective.* Appendix Vol. 1, Washington, D.C.: Government Printing Office, 1973.
8. FREEDMAN, ALFRED M. Opiate Dependence. In: Alfred M. Freedman, Harold I. Kaplan, and Benjamin J. Sadock (Eds.), *Comprehensive Textbook of Psychiatry.* Baltimore: Williams and Wilkins, 1975.

13

Genetic Correlates of Antisocial Syndromes

WILLIAM H. REID, M.D., M.P.H.

A chapter on genetics, especially one which purports to discuss "heredity" as well, might properly be expected to concern itself with those ways of transmitting characteristics from generation to generation which are limited to physical means, particularly the orderly exchange and perpetuation of intranuclear genetic material—chromosomes and their genes—in which is encoded the manifestation of, or predisposition for, such characteristics. Barring certain special cases of outside interference (karyotype change, radiation, laboratory recombination), this portion of heredity is quite stable and predictable, provided we understand the principles involved and, perhaps more importantly, provided we have a valid, reliable method of recognizing and evaluating the endpoint (in this case a disease or syndrome) of our experiments.

Although the present chapter will address some of these "genetic" issues, it seems of vital importance to examine the *overall* concept of familial transmission of sociopathic disorders. From a practical point of view, for the clinician, social scientist and for most researchers, the issue is one of predicting incidence and prevalence as well as of formulating methods for alleviation of social and individual symptoms. Even when research does not lead to genetic "answers," data concerning familial and familio-cultural transmission may be of great use. It is with this in mind that the principles of a recently refined method of study—the "Multifactorial Model of Disease Transmission" (1)—will be considered. This model, developed primarily by Reich, Cloninger and Guze, uses the principles of quantitative genetics, along with sophisticated statistical techniques, to assess the *balance* of influences from genetic heredity, family environment and social/learning milieu. It helps us to understand from a more comprehensive viewpoint some of the principles of syndrome transmission in psychiatry. In addition, it adds some manner of tested quantification to an area previously unaddressed except in esoteric, relatively impractical papers (2).

As mentioned above, a prerequisite for the usefulness of any method of determination of transmission, even when one understands the biogenetics involved, is a valid, reliable means of recognizing and evaluating the endpoint. In order to be valid, such a procedure must be accurate with respect to that which it measures. In order to be called reliable, results using similar subjects and instruments must be consistent with each other ("replication" of a sort). There must be agreement of criteria and results from study to study—*and from research study to clinical/social application*—especially regarding the dependent variable(s) involved.

As one reviews the literature in psychiatry, one is struck by the difficulty, now being seriously addressed in the better papers, with agreement of diagnosis. The area of sociopathy, with its broad differences in interpretation from person to person, from discipline to discipline and from decade to decade, is a glaring example of this problem, which is, perhaps, the greatest stumbling block to progressive, reliable research in the field.

The most common difficulty in otherwise well-controlled genetic/familial studies is the equating of certain behaviors with a diagnosis of sociopath or antisocial personality. Since one aim of this book is to differentiate the many antisocial and sometimes aggressive behaviors and syndromes, only one or two of which might properly be termed characterologic, it is fitting that we criticize, from this differential viewpoint, the various criteria for sociopathy in the genetic/familial literature. This is done not only for the sake of clarity of interpretation of results given, but also as part of an effort to separate disparate syndromes. In this way, future studies may be designed which examine "purer" data, less contaminated by spurious, non-sociopath "sociopaths."

Criminality, usually defined as either illegal or aggressive-illegal activity, has often been used as a marker for sociopathy. Early studies, more than recent ones, often examined only criminal or delinquent individuals, sometimes separating "aggressive" from "inadequate" individuals. In the discussion which follows, I will try to point out the extent to which criminality and other "markers" are used stereotypically, in lieu of more objective measures. Of course, the hereditary factors involved in crime are important in themselves, so long as the subject is labeled as a socio-legal offender (3-5), rather than confusing criminal offense with sociopathy *per se* (6, 7).

Attempts are often made to use large prison populations for studies of character disorder and to objectively test inmates for diagnostic criteria (8, 9). Although this method has been refined and is quite reliable, the questions of skewed population must be raised: Are these "psychopaths" representative of all psychopaths? Attempts to use non-incarcerated populations as control groups are only partially successful, since the same test criteria are used (giving a measure of reliability), but the comparison is in the direction of the control population (raising a question of skew).

Again, these factors do not affect one's ability to report reliable and significant data as "results." Rather, the difficulty lies in the "conclusion" or "discussion" portion of a given study, in which the authors may try to extend their data beyond the definitions and populations to which they really apply.

Other social and cultural behaviors, including alcohol abuse, drug abuse, geographic mobility, and job instability, may become confused with character diagnosis. Each of these may represent an antisocial behavior, depending upon one's definition, but may well not be a characterologic marker unless carefully analyzed with a number of other factors.

Certain noncharacterologic cardinal psychiatric diagnoses have genetic —or at least familial—associations and may show great quantities of antisocial behavior. Schizophrenia and affective disorders have been examined in this context (10) and some evidence for increased "sociopathy" has been found in the families of patients. Because of methodologic problems (see below), it is difficult to tease out the true sociopath from the acting-out or primarily neurotic person with antisocial behavior.

Some childhood behaviors are called sociopathic, although there is no such recognized diagnosis in the child psychiatry literature (11). The many carefully documented correlations of family and child behavior with adult antisocial life-style point toward a real transmission, genetic or otherwise, of such values and behaviors (11, 12). Much of this work indicates a number of parameters of antisocial life-style, connoting a chronicity which may be reminiscent of character disorder, but which may also reflect only learned social coping patterns.

Neurologic correlates of childhood behavior disorders and of normal childhood behavior point to possible hereditary determinants. Hyperkinesis (13), delayed myelination and "maturational lag" (14, Chapter

8), "immature" EEG findings (14, 15), even the similarity between some sociopathic characteristics and normal puerile behavior (16)—each has some relationship to the syndromes under study and each is plausibly related to genetic factors.

Chronic hysterical life-styles have been studied in familial—and perhaps genetic—relation to sociopathy. Cloninger, Guze and Reich (17, 18) used the Multifactorial Model to demonstrate increased familial incidence of the two diagnoses—hysteria in women and sociopathy in men—and to take a well-controlled look at both the relationship and transmission of the syndromes. This perspective becomes all the more fascinating when considered in light of recent psychodynamic formulations by Tupin (19, 20), which postulate hysterical diagnoses in some males who exhibit sociopathic behaviors and life-styles.

How then might one arrive at acceptable criteria for "core psychopathy," a character diagnosis, avoiding contamination from social, neurotic, psychotic and organic factors, and then approximate a normal population from which to objectively draw experimental and control subjects with sufficient compliance to satisfy those critics who would like to see truly hard data? The question is usefully addressed by Hare and Cox (21). They suggest a variety of selection processes, measures, control methods, and the like which expand the concerns voiced earlier herein. The reader is referred to their reference for details; however, it does seem possible to design good studies. Interestingly, Hare and Cox make the point that the agreement which has already been found among several groups of investigators, even given the marked methodological problems, probably indicates the "salience of the concept of psychopathy" as a replicable, even biologic diagnosis.

It should be reiterated that the absence of perfect studies does not mean that the present literature is not useful when the various limitations are considered. Although dangerous to extrapolate to individual diagnosis and treatment, data which address chronic behavior, regardless of primary cause, may contribute significantly to our pool of understanding. In addition, the concepts of multiple causation, penetrance, loading, etc., make purely genetic hypotheses impractical for current use.

STUDIES

As in the cases of other medical genetic problems, twin studies and adoption studies have been most popular as ways around sampling and control issues. Both have inherent difficulties, such as the increasingly prominent problem of determining zygosity (22) and the difficulty achieving comparable reliability of information from/about biological and adoptive parents (23); however, a number of findings should be considered.

Twin Studies

Early twin studies were of a simple concordance type, concentrating upon criminals with mono- and dizygotic twins. A group of nine such studies recently summarized by Eysenck and Eysenck (2) showed 55% monozygotic (MZ) concordance for criminal antisocial behavior and 13% dizygotic (DZ) concordance for some 766 twin pairs.

Cloninger, Reich and Guze (24) estimate the correlation of MZ heritability of criminality at 0.70 and of DZ heritability at 0.28. A simple statistical manipulation after Smith (25) extends the heritability overall of criminality to about 0.84 (24). Cloninger et al. also summarize twin and adoption data presented at the NATO Advanced Study Institute of Psychopathic Behavior in 1975, which are highly supportive of genetic factors, especially with respect to criminality and delinquency (26).

Consistent with their past work, and relevant to concerns mentioned earlier in this chapter, Cloninger, Reich and Guze postulate three possible mechanisms of genotype-environment interaction, none of which is yet convincingly supported or eliminated in the literature: independent ("additive") actions, genotype dependent action (i.e., the genotype determines or predisposes one to a particular environment), and variable penetrance (in which a given genotype reacts differently in varying environments and *vice versa*).

Shields (27), in a recent review of psychiatric genetics, suggests that although twin studies support genetic influence on criminality, the same influence on juvenile delinquency is much harder to find in the literature. Shields also summarizes concordance data regarding childhood behavior deviations (enuresis, dyslexia, sleepwalking, etc.), along with sex ratios. These data are interesting, partly because of the frequently found association of childhood difficulties with adult antisocial behavior, but must be viewed with caution since no information is offered about controls, separate rearing, and the like.

Trunnell (28) reports a case of identical twins, both with evidence of sociopathic character, within a set of triplets. The third member of the set apparently shows no such symptoms and is dizygotic with respect to the other two. Although this is suggestive of a genetic hypothesis, differential treatment of the twins by the mother is clear, some diagnostic criteria are suspect (e.g., military separation diagnoses), and control methods are obviously not possible.

Adoption Studies

Studies of adoptive and biological families of early-adopted persons, when carefully controlled, offer perhaps the best opportunity to separate nature and nurture, at least from the point at which development is interrupted by separation from the parents. Of course, significant development affecting later character and behavior may take place very early, even *in utero,* so that age and circumstance of separation must be considered. In addition, duration and circumstances of time spent between biological and adoptive families (e.g., in foster or foundling home) are most important.

Among the many studies of this type, Kety et al. (29) found an increased prevalence of psychopathy among biological relatives of schizophrenics. Hutchings and Mednick (3), studying police and adoption records, using the proband method, found that almost 50% of biological fathers of adopted criminals were criminal, compared to 28% of fathers of noncriminal controls. Index biological fathers were not only more *often* criminal, but were more recidivistic and committed "worse" crimes. Although results in a similar direction were found for the adoptive fathers, the magnitude was lower, indicating proportionately greater influence from heredity. Similar results were seen among mothers of index and control cases.

Schulsinger (30), in another large Danish study, looked at psychopathy in various biological and adoptive relatives of psychopaths. His results tended strongly to support hereditary factors in transmission, especially since he addressed the issue of psychiatric diagnosis in addition to social behavior (criminality, etc.).

Crowe (6, 7) studied offspring who were eventually adopted after being born to female prisoners. Although early life experiences were skewed for both index and control cases, the two groups were matched as closely as possible. A significantly higher rate of sociopathic behavior was found in initial and follow-up studies among index cases. Some effort was made by the author to bridge the diagnostic issue between criminality and sociopathy. A review by the same author of other studies (31) indicates similar trends and makes the point that the adding of a deviant parent to genetic predisposition, at least for criminal behavior, increases the likelihood of such behavior still further.

Further review (2, 24, 27) indicates more evidence for hereditary influence at least on criminal forms of sociopathic behavior and life-style, and probably on other forms as well. Methodological problems are sufficient, however, to make one consider Bohman's 1971 study of children in adoptive, foster and biologic homes. Although fraught with unavoidable confounding variables, Bohman's results tend to show less antisocial behavior—especially among boys—associated with most groups of children of criminal fathers than with controls (32).

In utero and perinatal environmental contributions are indirectly evaluated both in the Schulsinger study (30) and in a thesis by Hutchings (33). In these studies it was noted that paternal heredity was a predictor of criminality (and perhaps of psychopathy). In addition, there was no difference shown in difficulty of pregnancy or delivery between index and control cases.

Sex Differences

Sex differences in sociopathic diagnosis are difficult to evaluate. A number of studies purport to show ratios of four to eight men per female sociopath (24, 34), sometimes citing androgenization as a possible genetically-related factor (24). However, the sex differences become far less certain if one takes into consideration (a) the possibly different presentations of sociopathic behavior in women (not solely the criminal or severely antisocial presentation) (see Robins, 12); (b) the likelihood that these behaviors may not be recognized clinically or socially as pathologic; and (c) the possibility that hysterical and sociopathic characters may be very closely related (17-20, 35). Indeed, even the direction of such a hypothetical difference is in doubt. There is likewise very little evidence for racial difference *per se* (12, 34).

Chromosomal Studies

Let us now address specific questions on the chromosomal and genetic levels. The most important issue for this section is whether or not there is a hard scientific basis for determining whether—and if so, how—sociopathic character and sociopathic behavior patterns are genetically transmitted. Indirect evidence is cited above, but what of specifically chromosomal studies?

Again, we are faced with the methodological problems already mentioned. Even though the technology necessary for accurate karyotyping examination of individual chromosomal deviations, and even study of particular gene loci is rapidly becoming available, very few good studies utilizing these techniques exist in the present field of study.

One example of possibilities for the future, fairly well controlled and using state-of-the-art karyotype analysis, is that of Say, Carpenter, et al. (36), who visualized chromosomal variants among two of two "personality disordered" children and among five of 15 children with "behavior disorder." The subjects with these two diagnoses were all under 16 years of age, but the study does not specify further, except to say that among all patients studied (several psychiatric diagnoses) there were 40 boys and eight girls, all between the ages of four and 16.

The outstanding example of use of modern genetic technique, direct and indirect, to study a field related to (but not the same as) antisocial personality is the large literature which addresses sex chromosomes and possible aggression: the XXY/XYY controversy.

Some years ago a few preliminary reports from Scottish maximum security prisons thrust into the public and political limelight the finding that inmates convicted of violently antisocial behavior had an increased prevalence of extra Y chromosome complement, the XYY genotype. The world was anxious to accept this finding, since it conceivably represented some sort of physical difference between "them" (criminally aberrant persons) and the rest of us. In addition, the carrot of predictive value was again dangled before our noses. The political/legal world started at the possibility of genuine assistance in their problems with the violent social misfit.

Unfortunately for all concerned, the progress of the idea of a genetic determinant for antisocial behavior, fueled by public need for simple explanations for complex phenomena, outstripped the progress of careful thought and research for many years. Much premature interest was stimulated, even among professional sectors.

A number of recent developments in laboratory technique have given us increasingly sophisticated methods for determination of X/Y anomalies. Some of these are quite simple, including dermatoglyphic analysis (especially fingerprinting), Barr body visualization and polymorphonucleocyte examination. Others, such as the tritiated thymidine technique for differentiating X from Y chromosomes, are more complicated. Robins (35) points out that, although these techniques are useful, studies in other fields have established the presence of several problem areas for anyone seeking to establish clear-cut genotypes: mosaicism, possible changes in karyotype over time, differences in abnormalities among various tissue samples within the same person, etc. Some of these are quite rare, but the issues involved are of such importance and controversy that definitive studies must be as well designed and complete as possible.

In 1972, Baker (37) authored an extensive review of the then available data regarding XXY, XYY, and several rarer genotypes. After careful evaluation and critique of over 260 references, he concluded that, although further study was clearly indicated and although chromosome imbalance may set up physiological conditions predisposing one to abnormal behavior, there existed at the time no clear evidence to causally link either XYY or XXY with aggressive behavior or major crimes *per se*. Baker noted the well-known association of XYY with tallness and with mental subnormality, pointing out the possible status of the genotype as an intervening variable statistically associated with social class, development and the like. Robins (35) mentions these same points, as well as the association with temporal lobe epilepsy. Robins' paper, published in 1975 and drawing from his own work and that of others from the St. Louis group, agrees that "the evidence for the role of XYY or XXY chromosome complement in aggression is still flimsy."

An extensive and carefully controlled study done in 1976 with a Danish population seems to further clarify the issue (38). Witkin et al. performed an extraordinarily complete genotyping and social review of over 4,000 tall men, identifying 12 XYY's and 16 XXY's. Their results clearly indicated an increased conviction rate among XYY's, but no statistically significant increase among XXY's, over the tall population as a whole. However, this review of the kinds of crimes involved, lengths of sentences, number of convictions, and time since release from incarceration shows a definite predilection among XYY's for non-aggressive, non-serious crimes and no chronic pattern in criminal behavior by and large. XYY's also showed *less* agressive behavior while in prison than did ordinary XY prisoners. In addition, the authors found that height alone was not confirmed as an intervening variable.

Intellectual functioning, clearly one factor important in development, in socioeconomic milieu, and even in probability of being apprehended for crimes, was seen as an important but insufficiently explained intervening variable. XYY's (and XXY's) had significantly lower individual and mean scores on measures of intelligence. Further, in the common XY sample criminality showed a "substantial relation" to level of intellectual functioning (38).

Recent Reviews

Eysenck and Eysenck have studied character disorders for many years, often approaching the subject in ways different from the usual clinical and social conceptualizations. Their recent chapter in the summary of the 1975 NATO Advanced Study Institute attempts to place these concepts in a genetic framework (2). After carefully explaining their diagnostic criteria, which involve a three-dimensional continuum of extraversion, neuroticism, and "psychoticism," the Eysencks critically review the pertinent literature and conclude that at least 50% of total variance between psychopathy and controls is due to genetic factors. Using complex statistical measures for calculating heritability (39), they cite fairly good evidence that ". . . individual differences in the personality variables which have been shown to be associated with psychopathic behavior are determined to a large extent by genetic causes" (2, p. 21).

The Eysencks' model, with its psychoticism dimension, is consistent with the correlation of psychopathy and schizophrenia in families cited above and elsewhere. Conclusions are given from some of their earlier work: "1. There are genetic connections between the various functional psychoses. . . . 2. Within the genetic *Erbkreis* of the psychoses, there is an abundant display of psychopathic behaviour" (2, p. 22).

These concepts would support the considerable body of evidence for a genetic basis for schizophrenia and, more importantly, take up some of the "slack" left by non-schizophrenic siblings and offspring which is now explained in terms of incomplete penetrance. In other words, given specific polygenic loci which may appear in various combinations, two dizygous twins (for example) might both be schizophrenic *or* might carry two separate psychotic diagnoses *or* might be separately psychotic and psychopathic, without the investigator's having to look to concepts of penetrance or environmental variables in order to explain all of what was formerly termed variance.

This genetic link is also felt by the Eysencks to support the hypothesis that "primary psychopathy"—similar to Karpman's anethopathy and to this writer's concept of core sociopathic disorder—is underlaid with genetic predisposition to functional psychosis. "Secondary psychopathy"—similar to many of the non-characterologic syndromes mentioned herein—is related by the Eysencks to other genetically determined factors (e.g., low cortical arousal and high autonomic excitability).

Cloninger, Reich and Guze, writing for the same 1975 NATO Advanced Study Institute as were the Eysencks, addressed genetic-environmental interactions with respect to antisocial personality, hysteria, alcoholism and criminality (24). The three former syndromes, seen by the authors as "clinical" ones, were carefully diagnosed using "explicit . . . validated . . . reliab(le)" criteria. Using the above-cited Multifactorial Model of Disease Transmission, the authors were able to examine non-Mendelian transmission patterns, as well as to study genetic and environmental contributions without prior knowledge of their relative relevance (24, p. 2).

Heritability estimates derived from this study are cited above (see p. 000), as are some possible mechanisms of gene-environment interaction. The good "fit" of the multifactorial model to family and twin data provides support for an additive mechanism; i.e., genetic and environmental factors act independently of each other rather than being primarily interdependent in some way. The authors suggest multiple, simultaneous research designs for future refinement of our understanding of mechanisms and heritability.

The same study finds, in a review of adoption studies, evidence for separation of the syndromes of sociopathy and alcoholism on a genetic basis. They suggest that any clinical or familial overlap must be related to experiential factors (see Chapter 11). Also of note is the fact that environmental factors become more significant, no matter what the measured trait (so long as it is not represented by 100% penetrance), as a population approaches genotypic homogeneity.

Mednick and Hutchings have summarized and criticized a number of twin and adoption studies (40). They studied primarily "asocial" (criminal) behavior and, like many of us, interpret even careful studies with caution *vis à vis* intrauterine environment and perinatal conditions. Haphazard sampling is also cited, as is increased prominence (detectability) of monozygous twins over dizygous and the possible inappropriateness of extrapolating the many Danish population studies to other societies.

Autonomic markers (and possible causes) of psychopathic disorders are also discussed, including recent preliminary work by the authors which tests the hypothesis that such organic traits point to increased probability of genetic transmission. Among electrodermal responses, several are in the predicted (genetic transmission) direction, but only recovery time (EDRec) was significantly heritable ($H = 0.89$ as estimated by the usual $(V_{DZ} - V_{MZ})/V_{DZ}$). This characteristic was "not disconfirmed" as transmissible from father to son ($p \leq 0.05$ for mean half EDRec and 0.01 for minimum half EDRec). Some of the other commonly tested characteristics of electrodermal response were also apparently transmissible at about the same significance levels. However, the EDRec trait, in addition to its *correlation* with psychopathy, is also one of the more interesting traits with regard to *cause* of the character disorder, since decreased autonomic recovery time implies defects in conditioning ability (40).

CONCLUSIONS

Although the evidence for genetic influence seems on the surface convincing, especially with the available large populations, convenient Scandinavian archives and multigeneration studies, no firm conclusions can yet be drawn on the basis of twin and adoption studies. Continuing work on the heritability of organic markers (e.g., autonomic characteristics) of personality disorders seems the most likely way to clarify the issues at hand. For the present though, we are hampered by a number of deficits which are difficult to solve:

1. Purely study problems, including sampling, agreement upon diagnostic criteria, measurement of variance and recognition of endpoints.
2. Paucity of availability and/or application of chromosomal and genetic microtechniques to psychiatry in general and sociopathy in particular.
3. Failure to adequately separate different sources for overtly similar psychopathic behaviors and syndromes (neurologic, episodic, neurotic, social, etc.), which contribute to the mass of confounding information and cloud data about one syndrome (e.g., episodic aggression) with "noise" from others (e.g., criminality, sociopathy, culturally-based deviance).
4. Paucity of attempts to address the issue of core psychopathy rather than more accessible (but "noisier") subjects of criminality and social deviance.

It is easy, however, to criticize. As a friend has said, "If you can find a better study, let's hear it." From the point of view of *transmission* (genetic and/or otherwise) of certain behaviors, some of them chronic and antisocial, some useful things can be stated with considerable assurance:

1. Many of the significant differences cited above and elsewhere, taken together, indicate a very high probability of influence at least prior to the first few days of life and likely prior to birth. Some of these data make it most tempting to say that much of this influence is genetic.
2. Environmental factors must be considered, even if we accept close relationships among psychosis, hysteria and sociopathy. For practical purposes related to social behaviors of groups, studies of such behaviors, and prediction and disposition of large numbers of cases, the multifactorial approach seems most useful. Etiologic and predictive factors include, but should not be limited to, genetic loading, condition of the nuclear family, early models, peer and social learning, institutionalized cultural norms, and organic experience (illness, injury, etc.).

It should be noted that each of these factors in the development of sociopathic behaviors and syndromes, whether or not related to the core character disorder, is discussed in detail elsewhere in this book. The reader is advised to consider this overall approach to the understanding of the issue and not to assume this or any other chapter to be as useful in isolation as it might be as a complement to the other chapters.

REFERENCES

1. REICH, T., CLONINGER, C. R., and GUZE, S. B. The Multifactorial Model of Disease Transmission: I. Description of the Model and Its Use in Psychiatry. *Br. J. Psychiat.* 127:1-10, 1975.
2. EYSENCK, H. J. and EYSENCK, S. B. G. Psychopathy, Personality and Genetics. In: R. D. Hare and D. Schalling (Eds.), *Psychopathic Behavior: Approaches to Research.* London: Wiley, in press.
3. HUTCHINGS, B. and MEDNICK, S. A. Registered Criminality in Adoptive and Biologic Parents of Registered Male Criminal Adoptees. *Proc. Am. Psychopathol. Assoc.* 63, 1975.
4. MAUGHS, S. B. Criminal Psychopathology. *Prog. Neurol. Psychiatry* 23:448-453, 1968.
5. SPAULDING, E. R. and HEALY, W. Inheritance as a Factor in Criminality. *J. Am. Inst. Criminol. Chicago* 4:837-858, 1913-14.
6. CROWE, R. R. An Adoptive Study of Psychopathy: Preliminary Results from Arrest Records and Psychiatric Hospital Records. *Proc. Am. Psychopathol. Assoc.* 63: 95-103, 1974.
7. CROWE, R. R. An Adoption Study of Antisocial Personality. *Arch. Gen. Psychiatry* 31:785-791, Dec., 1974.
8. CLONINGER, C. R. and GUZE, S. B. Psychiatric Illnesses in the Families of Female Criminals: A Study of 288 First-Degree Relatives. *Br. J. Psychiat.* 122:697-703, 1973.
9. HARE, R. D. Psychopathy. In: P. Venables and M. Christie (Eds.), *Research in Psychophysiology.* New York: Wiley, 1975.
10. FOWLER, R. C., TSUANG, M. T., and MONNELLY, E. Non-Psychotic Disorders in the Families of Process Schizophrenics. *Acta Psychiatrica Scand.* 51:153-160, 1975.
11. MORRISON, H. L. Personal Communication.
12. ROBINS, L. *Deviant Children Grown Up.* Baltimore: Williams & Wilkins, 1966.
13. MORRISON, J. R. Hereditary Factors in Hyperkinesis (Ltr). *Am. J. Psychiatry* 131: 4, April, 1974.
14. ELLIOTT, F. A. Personal Communication.
15. WHITELEY, J. S. The Psychopath and His Treatment. *Br. J. Psychiat.* (Special Issue), 9:159-169, 1975.
16. TALLEY, J. E. Personal Communication.
17. CLONINGER, C. R., REICH, T., and GUZE, S. B. The Multifactorial Model of Disease Transmission: III. Familial Relationship between Sociopathy and Hysteria (Briquet's Syndrome). *Br. J. Psychiat.* 127:23-32, 1975.
18. CLONINGER, C. R. and GUZE, S. B. Hysteria and Parental Psychiatric Illness. *Psychological Med.* 5:27-31, 1975.
19. TUPIN, J. P. In: M. Horowitz (Ed.), *The Hysterical Personality.* New York: Jason Aronson, in press.
20. TUPIN, J. P. Personal Communication.
21. HARE, R. D. and COX, D. N. Clinical and Empirical Conceptions of Psychopathy, and the Selection of Subjects for Research. In: R. D. Hare and D. Schalling (Eds.), *Psychopathic Behavior: Approaches to Research.* London: Wiley, in press.
22. COHEN, D. J., DIBBLE, E., GRAWE, J. M., and POLLIN, W. Reliably Separating Identical from Fraternal Twins. *Arch. Gen. Psychiatry* 32:1371-1375, 1975.
23. HORN, J. M., GREEN, M., CARNEY, R., and ERICKSON, M. T. Bias Against Genetic Hypotheses in Adoption Studies. *Arch. Gen. Psychiatry* 32:1365-1367, 1975.
24. CLONINGER, C. R., REICH, T., and GUZE, S. B. Genetic-Environmental Interactions and Antisocial Behavior. In: R. D. Hare and D. Schalling (Eds.), *Psychopathic Behavior: Approaches to Research.* London: Wiley, in press.
25. SMITH, C. Concordance in Twins: Methods and Interpretation. *Am. J. Hum. Genet.* 26:454-466, 1974.

26. HARE, R. D. and SCHALLING, D. *Psychopathic Behavior: Approaches to Research.* London: Wiley, in press.
27. SHIELDS, J. Some Recent Developments in Psychiatric Genetics. *Arch. Psychiat. Nervenkr.* 220:347-360, 1975.
28. TRUNNELL, T. L. Sociopathic Personality in Identical Twins in a Set of Dizygotic Triplets. *Am. J. Psychiatry* 124:43-52, 1967.
29. KETY, S., ROSENTHAL, D., WENDER, P., and SCHULSINGER, F. The Types and Prevalence of Mental Illness in Biological and Adoptive Families of Adopted Schizophrenics. In: D. Rosenthal and S. Kety (Eds.), *The Transmission of Schizophrenia.* London: Pergamon, 1968.
30. SCHULSINGER, F. Psychopathy: Heredity and Environment. *Int. J. Ment. Health* 1:190-206, 1972.
31. CROWE, R. R. Adoption Studies in Psychiatry. *Biological Psychiatry* 10(3):353-371, 1975.
32. BOHMAN, M. A. Comparative Study of Adopted Children, Foster Children, and Children in their Biological Environment Born after Undesired Pregnancies. *Acta Paediat. Scand.* Supplement, 1971.
33. HUTCHINGS, B. Environmental and Genetic Factors in Psychopathology and Criminality. Doctoral Thesis, University of London, 1972.
34. CLONINGER, C. R., REICH, T., and GUZE, S. B. The Multifactorial Model of Disease Transmission: II. Sex Differences in the Familial Transmission of Sociopathy (Antisocial Personality). *Br. J. Psychiat.* 127:11-22, 1975.
35. ROBINS, L. N. Discussion of Genetic Studies of Criminality and Psychopathy. *Proc. Am. Psychopathol. Assoc.* 63:117-122, 1975.
36. SAY, B., CARPENTER, N. J., LANIER, P. R., et al. Chromosome Variants in Children with Psychiatric Disorders. *Am. J. Psychiatry* 134(4):424-426, April, 1977.
37. BAKER, D. Chromosome Errors and Antisocial Behavior. *CRC Critical Reviews in Clinical Laboratory Sciences* 3:41-101, January, 1972.
38. WITKIN, A. A., MEDNICK, S. A., SCHULSINGER, F., et al. Criminality in XYY and XXY Men. *Science* 193:547-555, 13 August, 1976.
39. MATHER, K. and JINKS, J. L. *Biometrical Genetics.* London: Chapman & Hall, 1971.
40. MEDNICK, S. A. and HUTCHINGS, B. Genetic and Psychophysiological Factors in Asocial Behavior. Early Manuscript for: S. A. Mednick and K. O. Christiansen (Eds.), *Biosocial Bases of Criminality.* New York: Gardner Press, 1977.

III

TREATMENT

This section addresses the issue which is likely to be uppermost in the minds of our readers. For a number of reasons, including the fact that we expect the outcome of our ongoing studies of antisocial disorders to assist us in the future of choice treatment methods, we have chosen to concentrate on three primary, commonly encountered treatment modalities. In Chapter 14, the broad subject of long-term, residential treatment programs for persons whom society has deemed unacceptable is discussed. Although much of the content of this chapter is drawn from the experience of one institution, its principles are widely applicable. Chapter 15 addresses the needs of both patients for whom outpatient treatment is indicated and the clinicians who treat them. It is a discussion of classical psychotherapy, with some modifications, and does not report on the wide variety of other outpatient therapies which may be advocated by some. Chapter 16 speaks to the physician in us who looks for, and sometimes finds, a medicinal answer for what may be, at least in part, an organic problem. We do not limit ourselves to "cures" in these investigations but, as in other areas of medicine, seek palliatives and postponements as well. Brief reference to some other psychotherapeutic and organic treatment modalities is found in Chapters 3, 6 and 8.

As implied above, the reader will not find in this section major references to other forms of treatment. Some of these are indeed promising, such as "wilderness programs" similar to that of Dr. Matthews in New Mexico, but are too recent to be properly evaluated here. Others are directed more at specific symptoms than at syndromes of antisocial behavior or core sociopathy. Still others, such as comprehensive family intervention, have been omitted because they were either beyond the scope of this volume or would require too many additional pages for comprehensive treatment. A separate volume, devoted entirely to treatment of antisocial syndromes, is planned.

259

14

Inpatient Treatment Programs

FRANCIS L. CARNEY, PH.D.

The treatment of sociopathy is generally approached with gloom and pessimism. No less an authority than Cleckley (1) has claimed that sociopaths are untreatable, and experience over the years has tended to make this a psychiatric "fact." Nonetheless, attempts have been made to treat a wide variety of personality disorders in a number of settings, and the results, actually, are not all that discouraging.

In the discussion that follows I will consider the treatment of the "personality disorders"—not just "sociopaths." There are several reasons for this, the most important perhaps being the fact that there is no universally accepted definition of sociopathy. The treatment center, in a sense, tends to define the disorder: Outpatient centers and therapists in private practice tend to treat the less violent, less criminal and more neurotic-like of the personality disorders; psychiatric hospitals tend to treat those who act out more persistently and irrationally; prisons are more likely to treat those who are criminal, violent and dangerous. A review of the literature (2) suggests that one can treat a personality disorder without being too concerned about specific diagnosis—sociopath, passive-aggressive personality, and so on. There seem to be enough commonalities among the dynamics of the personality disorders to make them all amenable to the same basic therapeutic approach. Let me briefly review certain of these constants, at the same time indicating how the treatment setting itself can facilitate or hinder the resolution of therapeutic problems.

The Psychopath

The Inability to Trust

This seems to be the core issue in the treatment of personality disorders. It arises mainly from a lack of ego, or, put another way, from the lack of a stable self-concept which endures from situation to situation. It includes not only the inability to trust other people, but also the inability to trust in structure within one's world. These people are afraid of interpersonal relationships and are unable to lower their guard enough to give in any meaningful way; they also assume that the basic institutions of society—from the family to the government and all its agencies—are corrupt and uncaring. Undoubtedly, when we look at their backgrounds, which tend to include massive deprivation at every level, they have good reason not to trust. However, the etiology of the behavior cannot at first be the main concern of the therapy; treatment of these patients tends to become an uncovering process only in its later stages. Initially it is more a matter of dealing with the immediate consequences of the behavior revealed.

At the same time, therapy with sociopaths is like every other therapy in that success depends ultimately on the formation of a trusting relationship, which might also be called transference. The most difficult therapeutic task with these patients is, thus, the most essential task. In the formation of a trusting relationship the treatment setting plays an important role. For example, the security of prisons says to the prisoners that they aren't trustworthy human beings; their keepers regard them with suspicion and they regard a therapist as just another of their keepers. To a slightly lesser extent the same conditions exist when there is involuntary psychiatric hospitalization. Although involuntary commitment to a prison or hospital may hinder treatment, society often has no choice but to place affirmative restraints on individuals who act out persistently and violently.

One might anticipate that the trusting relationship would be formed more quickly if the therapy were voluntary, but this is not true. An expressed willingness to enter psychotherapy is most often part of a "con," an attempt to gain some immediate advantage by playing the "patient" or "sick" role. The necessity of playing a wide variety of roles is a consequence of ego deficit. The same person can be the repentant son, the street-wise thug or the motivated patient, but none of these roles is the real person. In truth, there is no real person, for to be real is to be hurt; also, it is likely that the role-playing has endured for so long that even the patient has lost any sense of true self, if he ever had one. Role-playing, too, is exacerbated in prison: Given the realities of prison conditions, one no longer has to fantasize a hostile environment; further, physical survival—never mind psychological survival—requires adherence to artificial codes and finding one's own place in the looking-glass structure of the prisoner society.

The Inability to Feel

Persons with personality disorders, particularly sociopaths, are often described as being free from depression and anxiety, as being callous and unrepentant. It is axiomatic that punishment has no effect on them; that they are incapable of experiencing psychic discomfort. However, when we look more closely, we see that this is a façade: It is not that these patients *cannot* feel; they *will not* feel because the pain is too great. They protect themselves from inner stress as much as they protect themselves from the perceived threat all around them.

They use two basic mechanisms to do this. The first is acting-out, for as long as they are doing *something* they don't have to feel *anything*. Secondly, rather than experience pain themselves, they attempt to elicit the feeling from some other in their environment; for example, a man can appear to be unconcerned about going to prison if his mother is feeling guilty and weeping. Obviously, a task of psychotherapy is to help the patient to feel and to take responsibility for his own feelings. Just as obviously, some environments militate against this. In prisons, particularly, and in some hospitals, the administration frowns upon the expression of feelings of anger and hostility and encourages unquestioning acceptance of rules and regulations. From an inmate viewpoint, the expression of passive feelings could lead to abuse and ridicule from fellow inmates. On the other hand, since to feel is to hurt, some form of coercion is virtually required to keep the patients in therapy. Outpatient treatment, therefore, is generally unsuccessful.

The Inability to Fantasize

Fantasy, as a normal function, helps the individual to relieve tensions and to anticipate future events. This deficit among the personality disorders leads to an increased tendency to act out and an inability to plan, contributing to these people being called impulsive and their judgment being seen as poor. This deficit is also closely connected to their inability to empathize and their real inability to understand how their actions could actually hurt others. A technique of therapy that has been used successfully is that of teaching patients to fantasize, to make them consider a variety of responses to a variety of situations, and to insist that they set goals for themselves and then work toward them. Among the techniques used, psychodrama has been particularly effective with acting-out adolescents, with role-playing, as a part of the more typical group psychotherapy, being more effective with older patients.

Fantasy as one technique in a total battery is particularly valuable in an institutional setting, for it can lead to some immediate self-control, as well as give some direction to the treatment; also, it is a technique which is not likely to lead to problems for either the patients or the administration. However, as a single technique it is also not likely to lead to any lasting change, for the ability to fantasize, even among "cured" patients, tends to remain at a very rudimentary level. There is also a danger in putting too much emphasis on fantasy: Over the years many people have suggested that there is a close link between the severe personality disorders and schizophrenia; it has been hypothesized that acting out may serve as a defense against a psychotic break.

The Inability to Learn

Personality disordered patients are able to learn role expectations very quickly but they are unable to generalize from one situation to another. It is this inability to generalize which suggests that they are unable to learn from experience. That no transfer of learning takes place perhaps accounts for the failure of most behavior modification programs with patients with personality disorders. The literature suggests that these programs help the institutional administration far more than they help the patients in that such programs are often designed to reward such things as good housekeeping, personal hygiene and a variety of behaviors which are relevant within the social structure of the institution. That is the very weakness of these programs, because what is relevant within the institution need not be relevant within society. The literature suggests that one cannot ignore the milieu in which behavior modification takes place: The inappropriate behavior was learned in society, not in an institution, so the appropriate behavior has to be learned in that same society, not in an institution. At best, the institution can prepare the patients for new learning, but then the treatment must follow them back out into the community.

This technique—new learning and aftercare combined with psychotherapy—tends to lead to the best success rates. The inability to learn is a consequence of the other ego deficits; it is an important part of the "now orientation" of these patients. They attack each experience as if it were new and unique, with no awareness of the past or expectancy for the future. They require satisfaction of their needs in the here and now;

the more distant a goal, the less likely they are ever to attain it. The prisoner with years to serve is not likely to be motivated to enter therapy by some vague promise that it will lead to a better life in some nebulous future; he is too concerned with daily survival. The short-timer may enter therapy to impress a parole board and the probationer may see a psychiatrist to satisfy a judge, but it is unlikely that these patients and their therapists will enter into psychotherapy with the same goals and expectations. It is even less likely that any insights generated will transfer beyond the immediate situation.

TREATMENT

General Considerations

Twenty years ago McCord and McCord (3) reviewed treatment of psychopathy to that point in time and reached the following conclusions: "Thus psychotherapy offers a little hope but no assurance of success. Other approaches to the problem seem even less promising: incarceration alone, while temporarily protecting society, does not seem to change basic personality trends; organic treatment (with drugs, shock or lobotomy) has shown few, if any, beneficial results." About this time Cleckley (4) repeated his generally pessimistic view of psychotherapy and suggested that what was really needed was a treatment institution which specialized in the treatment of psychopaths. A few years later Gunn (5) reviewed forensic psychiatry in Great Britain and concluded that psychiatric hospitals were generally unsuitable places in which to treat psychopaths; he felt that special centers for their treatment were needed, centers which would provide for a continuity of treatment from inpatient to outpatient status and where differential treatment would be provided according to dangerousness.

In actual practice dangerousness does become the key consideration, not as a matter of legislation but as a matter of practicality. To a certain extent the argument over "the prediction of dangerousness" is specious because the personality disorders very quickly sort themselves into groups which do or do not act out against society; those who do are restrained by either the criminal or civil law whether or not this is the "best" treatment. Steadman's (6) review of "dangerousness" suggests that not only can it not be predicted with any degree of statistical certainty, but it cannot even be defined in any generally accepted way. The literature in general suggests that the best predictor of dangerous behavior is a history of dangerous behavior.

So the question is not so much "Who is dangerous?" as "What do you do with the person who has behaved in a dangerous way?" and "How do you tell when he is no longer dangerous?" These decisions are not usually made by those who practice psychotherapy; they are more likely to be made by the judiciary or administrators within the criminal justice system. The therapist, generally, will enter the lives of these patients only after significant decisions about their treatment have already been made and the psychotherapy he practices will be constrained by forces over which he has little control. The treatment setting is one such force. Limits are placed upon the therapist, as well as on the patients, as one moves along the continuum from "voluntary" therapy, through outpatient therapy with probationers, through psychiatric hospitalization and on to imprisonment.

Among the true personality disorders, I suspect there is no such thing as "voluntary" psychotherapy. Those who have written on the subject, Esmiol (7) for example, generally indicate that these patients have a large psychoneurotic component. More commonly, these "voluntary" patients have been in some conflict with their families, schools, employers or the law and there is some pressure from someone to "get treatment." The success of treatment is questionable, at least if success is measured by real personality change. If measured by increased ability to cope, then one can speak of success. Lion and associates (8) report on their experience with a violence clinic. They find that few of their patients remain in treatment for any length of time but many of them return to treatment periodically "when the going gets rough." We can assume that patients like this, those who are troublesome but not "in trouble," represent the least severe and least dangerous of the personality disorders. With these kinds of patients—not too different from the general outpatient psychiatric population—the therapist is more or less free to practice any kind of therapy he chooses.

As we take one step up the ladder of severity the situation changes. We now deal with patients who are on probation; consequently, the criminal justice system becomes a partner in the treatment process. At this level the partnership can be valuable; indeed, probation becomes an important therapeutic tool. These patients have no motivation to remain in therapy, no desire to change any part of their life-style. They are most likely to perceive themselves as society's victims; they are not aware that they bring trouble on themselves and they have little sense of anxiety or personal suffering. The only thing that keeps them in treatment is the order of the court. I have elsewhere discussed a Special Offenders Clinic (9) which provides outpatient psychotherapy to violent offenders who are on probation. Experience suggested that these offenders did not differ markedly from an even more antisocial group who were imprisoned: The same personality characteristics existed in both groups but the outpatients had better behavioral control; the techniques of psychotherapy did not differ but it took longer with the inpatients; and for both groups limit-setting was an important part of the treatment.

Patients who have difficulty with impulse control, as much as they may verbally protest the imposition of external controls, are relieved when such controls are imposed. Their frequent testing of the limits is not so much an attempt to break away as it is a demand for reassurance that the limits are firm. The therapist who has a good working relationship with the courts and the probation officer can set limits which will be meaningful in the total therapy and which will help the patient to survive as an outpatient until internal controls are established. There is no place here for the kind of total permissiveness which characterizes some therapies; the therapist is an authority figure who must at times act in an authoritarian way. In addition, he is at times an agent of the court.

Moving from the outpatient to the inpatient setting, there are two common choices: the psychiatric hospital and the prison. The personality disorders in hospitals are a nuance. They are demanding, belligerent and manipulative; they are uninterested in treatment; and they leave the hospital long before any treatment can take hold. Whitely (10) makes the point that these disorders do not fit the medical model of illness and that physicians are frustrated by them. Medication has no long-term benefits and, in fact, the patients are likely to abuse medication; surgery is rarely necessary; and psychotherapy tends not to touch the basic disorder which is a defective awareness of social behavior. Whitely suggests that group therapy in a therapeutic community setting may offer the best hope, and that traditional hospitalization, at best, is little more than crisis intervention.

No one can say for sure just what part of the prison population represents persons with primary personality disorders. It is known that the incidence of mental illness among prisoners is significantly higher than in the general population. Roth and Erwin (11), for example, found that of 1200 Federal prisoners, 31% suffered from one of the personality disorders, but they also found that an additional 29% carried a diagnosis of alcoholism and another 25% a diagnosis of drug addiction. In fact, considering the many problems of differential diagnosis, the actual incidence of personality disorder in their sample could range from 31% to 85%. Prisoners in general have not been diagnosed more specifically. Estimates of the incidence of sociopathy *per se* in prison populations have ranged from 5% to 75% (12). In any event, we can assume that large numbers of sociopaths do go to prison, particularly those who are most antisocial, and for many of them imprisonment becomes the only treatment.

Commenting on corrections in the United States, Halleck (13) says, "Sometimes the system seems diabolically conceived to create mental illness. It does not allow offenders to find intimacy; it does not allow them to express aggression; it does not allow them to be independent, and it does not allow them to be responsible. As a matter of fact, it comes down hard on people when they begin to search for values." Also forceful is a statement by Fink and Martin (14): "In our opinion, based on experience, no total program for rehabilitation of offenders can be successful unless it is under the direction and guidance of psychiatrists. . . . The only thing that has come from totalitarian dictatorship of the correctional facilities is the dehumanization of the individual and reinforcement of the prisoners' feelings of bitterness." And somewhat melodramatically, Ramsey Clark (15), in *Crime in America,* points out that corrections is that part of the criminal justice system which receives the least moral and financial support from the public, with the result that "prisons in the United States today are more often than not manufacturers of crime . . . (they) are usually little more than places to keep people—warehouses of human degradation."

Yet, as we begin to deal with the more severe of the personality disorders, the more dangerous human beings, we reach a point where society has no choice but to protect itself by imposing affirmative restraints. But the restraints in and of themselves are no cure; the same people, over and over again, continue their antisocial ways and return to the same hospitals and prisons. In these last few paragraphs I have mentioned several treatment suggestions that have been made by various people at various times: specialized treatment facilities, a therapeutic community concept, continuity of treatment, and direction by mental health professionals. Such facilities do exist, though they are few and far between. Perhaps the best known is Herstaedvester in Denmark, which Sturup (16) describes as having a total treatment approach to the rehabilitation of an essentially sociopathic population. In the United States the Patuxent Institution perhaps serves as a model of what can be done.

The Patuxent Institution

Article 31B of the Annotated Code of the Public General Laws of Maryland brought Patuxent into existence to treat the "defective delinquent," who was defined as a person "who by the demonstration of persistent aggravated antisocial or criminal behavior evidences a propensity toward criminal activity, and who is found to have either such intellectual deficiency or emotional unbalance, or both, so as to clearly demonstrate an actual danger to society so as to require such confinement and treatment, when appropriate, as may make it reasonably safe for society to terminate the confinement and treatment." Men are referred to Patuxent only after they have been convicted and sentenced for certain categories of crimes. If, after a complete diagnostic workup, the staff feels that they meet the definitions of a defective delinquent, they are committed to Patuxent for an indeterminate period of time. (For a more complete description of the Defective Delinquency Law, see Carney (17).)

The Institution itself looks like any other maximum security prison, with fences and guard towers and cells and locks; its security is entrusted to custodial officers. It differs physically from most prisons in that its population is rarely greater than 500; there are no more than 33 men to a tier, and each man has his own cell. It is dramatically different from most prisons in that it has a large staff of psychiatrists, psychologists and social workers; about 95% of the committed men are in psychotherapy; every phase of treatment and rehabilitation is under the direction of mental health professionals; the Institution is its own paroling authority, and "parole officers" tend to be the same psychotherapists the men had in the Institution. Two aspects of this program are particularly important: the indeterminate sentence and the parole situation.

Time is a vital factor in any psychotherapy; it becomes particularly important in the treatment of the personality disorders because these patients have little anxiety or motivation to change. Should psychotherapy awaken in them real feelings of anxiety—should they begin to experience any psychic discomfort—their tendency is to act out or otherwise escape from the discomforting situation. For real change to occur, they must somehow be held in psychotherapy. The indeterminate sentence is one way to accomplish this but as a single tool it isn't enough.

California once had an indeterminate sentence law; the medical facility at Vacaville was responsible for much of the treatment prisoners received while incarcerated, including psychotherapy. But, under California law, when these prisoners were released back into the community, they fell under the supervision of the State paroling authority. In order to assess the effects of psychotherapy, Jew et al. (18), compared the recidivism rate of a group of treated prisoners with a matched control of non-treated prisoners. They found that during the first year of parole the treated group maintained a significantly better adjustment rate than the untreated group; but beginning in the second year, the gap between the two groups started to close. By the fourth year of follow-up there was a negligible difference between the groups.

The experience at Patuxent, where therapists are "parole officers," suggests why this might be so: Prerelease patients, those who have reached new plateaus of awareness through psychotherapy, have almost magical expectations of the society beyond the walls and their place in it; they literally set themselves up for parole failure. It requires careful monitoring by the therapist who knows them best to get them through the frustrations they find. It also requires the parolees' continued willingness to trust some other person in their lives. The usual parole officer, no matter how good he is, needs time to get to know his man and establish a relationship; the Patuxent "parole officer" has worked through the whole issue of trust before his man ever "hits the streets."

Treatment at Patuxent has many of the features of a therapeutic milieu as described by Liebman and Hedlund (19): "1) acceptance—the milieu should allow some regression and recapitulation of maladaptive behavior; 2) control—the milieu should provide enough control to allow the emergence of feelings that underlie the maladaptive behavior; 3) support—the milieu should provide enough support to enable the patients to endure the emergence of those underlying feelings—to do so long enough to make sense out of them and find another way to get their needs met without using the maladaptive behavior patterns; 4) learning—the milieu should offer the means whereby patients and staff can learn about their characteristic ways of behavior, thinking, and feeling, and possibly, more adaptive responses. . . ."

Liebman and Hedlund were speaking of a therapeutic community in an expensive, private psychiatric hospital, one which had the staff-to-patient ratio necessary for successful milieu therapy. So does Patuxent, and like a private psychiatric hospital, Patuxent is an expensive place to operate. We must ask if the cost to the taxpayer is justified. Patuxent reports that its recidivism rates are significantly lower than those reported by virtually every other prison system in the United States—7% for fully treated groups—an astonishing figure when one considers that Patuxent screens its admissions and accepts for treatment men who already have a history of recidivism and who are generally considered "untreatable." Of course, beyond the cost, Patuxent raises other questions—legal and ethical questions having to do with the constitutionality of an indeterminate sentence and the right of the State to coerce an individual into psychotherapy. For many reasons Patuxent has been increasingly criticized and, at this writing, Article 31B has been revised.

Later we shall consider the Patuxent program in more detail. For now, whether or not the Patuxent concept is valid—and that may be more a matter of law than of psychiatry—the Patuxent experience has led to some observations on the process of psychotherapy with an essentially sociopathic population, particularly as that therapy is practiced in a prison-like setting. Let us take a closer look at this setting.

The Prisoner Society

If Patuxent is unlike most prisons in most ways, it is like all prisons in some ways. The patient population is composed of jail-wise men who attempt to create in Patuxent a prisoner society no different from the society they knew in other correctional institutions. The custodial force also is bound to the traditional practices of the correctional establishment, which place more emphasis on punishment than on sound mental hygiene. Between professional staff and custody staff there is a conflict over the best treatment, which might be characterized as "uncovering *versus* repression"; both forces work on the patients, who sooner or later find themselves caught between the value systems of their therapists and those of the prisoner society.

The prisoner society, as it exists in a maximum security prison, was described by Sykes (20). His comments on the forms of interaction between the keepers and the kept are particularly revealing. Nothing can destroy any prison program more quickly than the opposition of the custodial force and nothing can more facilitate it than their support. It is also true that "custody" (as the custodial staff is known) is conservative and has to be convinced before it will try anything new. Sykes illustrates how prisoners and custody work together to keep the prison a relatively happy place for both sides; how there are "gentlemen's agreements" which provide for territoriality and which establish a hierarchical social structure, all of which are designed to perpetuate prisons as they have always been. Within this structure there occur behaviors which do not make sense from any conventional point of view but which offer glimpses into institutional dynamics.

For example, prisons promote drabness and sameness; it becomes important for every man to somehow establish his own uniqueness. He might do this by acquiring some article of clothing, such as a hat, which is completely different from every other hat in the institution, and wearing it all the time or by having an unusual hair style or sporting a particular medallion—something—anything—so long as it says, "This is me and no one else." Guenther (21) analyzed the functions of contraband in one prison, coming to the conclusion that it served largely as a compensation for the deprivations of prison life, citing not the actual attainment so much as the process of attainment, the ingenuity required to subvert the system. And in every prison there is "the hustle," which can take many forms, such as stealing food from the kitchen to sell on the tiers, stealing and selling pills from the hospital, gambling or running a book, loan-sharking, giving one kind of a haircut free and another kind for a price, prostitution, smuggling something into or out of the institution, and on and on. The inmates will tell you that they do it for the money, that their institutional jobs simply don't pay enough to meet basic needs, but even more basic is their need to relieve the tedium of incarceration.

In prisons role-playing runs rampant. In the sixties, for example, we saw the emergence of the "political prisoner." Brody (22) describes how prisoners are quick to take new roles, how they were "poor unfortunates" when it was fashionable to be poor unfortunates, how they were "sick" when it was fashionable to be sick, and how they became "political prisoners" when society itself became more revolutionary. In prisons we find an increased incidence of suicidal behavior, particularly self-mutilation by cutting, but a number of people, including Toch (23) and Bach-y-Rita (24), point out that this behavior is not so much related to true depression as it is to a displacement of hostility and to the frustrations and boredom of prison life.

Homosexual behavior, which is prevalent in all prisons, is also a kind of game-playing. It is rarely a matter of the stronger taking advantage of the weaker; it is more likely an adaptation to the prison environment. Men who are in and out of prison regularly easily make the shift between homosexual and heterosexual behavior. The sex object, inside or outside of prison, rarely is as important as the hedonistic delight in the sex act. That which we usually call love, the caring of one person for another, is missing in either case. To be a "pretty boy" in prison, thereby receiving protection and various other benefits, is not ego-shattering— not if one is young, good-looking, and charming, traits which have already been well used in the outside world to fool people and gain advantages. Homosexual acts are simply another, essentially meaningless, parameter of the role. To be the possessor of a "pretty boy" is to have status among one's peers, to hold a prison possession which has about the same significance as a Cadillac in the outside world.

There are dangerous games, to be sure, but most games are nuisance games. Custodians are as much caught up in the game-playing behavior as the prisoners. What all fail to recognize is the artificiality of the situation—neither the actions nor the responses tend to relate directly to life in the real world. The learning that takes place prepares the prisoner only to live in prisons. It is perhaps not accurate to say that prisons manufacture criminals, but they do manufacture prisoners, and that may be why so many ex-convicts come "home" again and again.

To intervene, therefore, requires more than any dynamic psychotherapy; it requires a direct assault on the forms and functions of the society itself. The world that exists within prison walls, where violence is encouraged and reason reproved, where criminality and perversion are accepted ways of life, bears scant resemblance to the real world beyond the walls. Unfortunately, in most prisons mental health professionals do not have any great input into prison administration. Psychotherapy is an extra that does not touch the daily lives of the majority of prisoners. It is the rare prisoner who benefits from psychotherapeutic treatment. Study after study (see Maier (25), for example) indicates that prison psychotherapy is a waste of time.

The total treatment approach and milieu therapy do intervene in the pathological processes of the prisoner society; a little later we shall look at that in more detail. For now, let us look at the psychotherapeutic process itself, since formal psychotherapy may form a part of treatment in many prisons. Of particular interest in this regard is the problem of countertransference.

The Psychotherapeutic Process

Much has been made of "fear of the patient" as an important countertransference dynamic in the treatment of aggressive patients. How the therapist handles his own fears and anxieties has a direct effect on the course of treatment. Since this has been discussed at some length elsewhere (2, 26), I should like here to examine the other side of the passive-aggressive coin.

Personality disordered individuals are almost always described as immature and as having passive-dependent needs and needs for security. A fact of institutional life is that these needs are met to a large extent and people who have spent many years in institutions are often more at "home" in institutions than they are in society. The structure of prisons, particularly, in which confined people are dependent on their keepers for the satisfaction of virtually every need, in which adult human beings are rewarded and punished in much the same way as parents reward and punish children, reinforces immature behaviors and promotes ego regression. Sargent (27) examined this ego regression in one prison and found that it had these components: increased dependency on authority, diffuse rage, increased susceptibility to suggestion, a tendency toward magical thinking, anxiety and impulsivity, and a tendency to cling to and perpetuate the restrictions originally imposed from the outside. As a consequence, many prisoners, no matter how eager they say they are for release, suffer the pangs of separation anxiety as the day of their release approaches. Often, quite unconsciously, they seek to perpetuate their stay.

It is likely, therefore, that the passivity of the patients, rather than their aggression, will become the ultimate therapeutic issue. However, in all probability aggression will be the initial focus of the therapy, because no therapy will get far as long as the patients are acting out; also, aggression is usually the continuing focus of the institutional administration, which tends to see a "cure" when the aggression stops. There are thus many forces arrayed against the aggressive impulses of the patients, which lead them, in time, to suppress, repress or otherwise disguise their aggressivity.

Perhaps the psychotherapy of no other group requires quite so much personal involvement of the therapist. Virtually all authorities on the treatment of the personality disorders agree that traditional methods are useless, that the therapist cannot remain aloof from his patients, that he must engage them in an intense and intimate relationship. Vaillant (28), particularly, speaks of the human process, indicating that from the very beginning the therapist must seize control of the relationship, must structure it and define its limitations, at the same time placing external controls on the acting out of the patients. They cannot set their own limits so the therapist originally assumes the role of the wise parent. The therapist goes on to help the patients overcome their fear of intimacy, encouraging their trust, helping them to understand the difference between control and punishment. He helps them to deal with their feelings by sharing with them their joys and sorrows, not interpreting, simply recognizing and accepting with them their own humanity. Psychotherapy of this sort could go on in any setting and contribute to the development of intense therapist-patient relationships. In the prison setting where there is a large reality component to the dependency relationship that is formed, countertransference problems become more pronounced.

We have patients who are immature to begin with and who have massive dependency needs; we have a structure which encourages their regression; and we have a therapeutic technique which promotes their dependency. It is no wonder that they do indeed become dependent. Nor is it any wonder that the concerned therapist at this point feels greatly responsible for them. The problem now is that the patients have regressed to a level at which they are quite comfortable and they don't want any further change.

But successful therapy requires that the patients now begin to grow, that they learn how to express aggressive feelings in more appropriate ways, that they begin to take on responsibility for themselves, and that they begin to see the relationship with the therapist in a more realistic and adult light. They are very adept at resisting these changes and at thrusting upon the therapist responsibilities which he does not have to take. The harsh realities of prison life are such that by this time the therapist is too often the protector and champion of his patients rather than their guide.

The humanistic therapist is concerned by what he sees: the inequalities of justice, the overuse of punishment, and the oppression in the correctional system. He no longer sees his patients as "criminals"; they are distinct human beings who may have suffered long before their criminal careers began. He becomes aware of society's antagonism toward them and of their powerlessness in the whole criminal justice system. He may become keenly aware that he is one of the few who really care and that he is virtually powerless, too. It is easy at that point for the therapist to lose sight of the treatment, to turn the whole thing into a *cause,* and to do battle with the system as represented by the prison administration or the paroling authority. Certainly, this is the course that his patients encourage as they feed his ego with their dependence and a magical belief in his omnipotence.

If the therapist does take on the role of champion, he is almost doomed to frustration and failure. Therapists leave prison work because of the intransigence of the system, not because the patients can't be helped. This countertransference reaction is a far greater threat to successful therapy than "fear of the patient."

Here, at what is essentially the midpoint of therapy, we find those ego-regressed behaviors that Sargent (27) describes: The patients go to the therapist for everything, apparently unable to make even the most innocuous decisions in their lives, and toward custodial personnel they are likely to be alternately obsequious and demanding; their moods are labile, their concentration span short, and when possible they flit from job to job or stop and start school several times in one semester; they are likely to be involved in minor mischief, seeking discipline as a reassurance of both structure and caring; they invest their therapist with great powers and they believe that he will somehow magically free and heal them; and they stubbornly resist any changes in procedure, making rules and regulations almost sacrosanct. Each of these behaviors must be worked through and in the process the therapist slowly withdraws his support from the patients until, as much as possible in the situation, the patients are functioning as reasonably mature and responsible human beings. How much actual growing the patients have done depends in part on how many opportunities they have had. The more repressive the prison, the fewer the opportunities and the less likely that psychotherapy will make any appreciable difference in the lives of the prisoners.

In the ideal situation psychotherapy will continue while the patients are on parole. In even the most advanced prison, the society inside the walls is quite different from the society outside. The coping behaviors that worked for the prisoner may not work for the free man. Leaving the rigid structure of the prison for the more relaxed structure of free society provokes anxiety and, particularly in the initial phase of parole, the patients need the support of their therapist. Throughout their parole the continuing therapeutic experience can help patients solidify the gains made while incarcerated.

THE TOTAL TREATMENT APPROACH

Liebman and Hedlund (19) have reviewed the history and development of the therapeutic community concept, particularly as it relates to the work of Harry Stack Sullivan and August Aichhorn. They describe in detail their work at the Sheppard and Enoch Pratt Hospital in Baltimore, a private, voluntary hospital. The basic principles of milieu therapy can be observed in many settings; psychiatric hospitals have been using the therapeutic community idea for years and it is an idea that guides a number of self-help groups such as Alcoholics Anonymous and Synanon. The basic principles continue to apply as we move from voluntary to involuntary treatment. Therapeutic communities have been established within prisons, for example at the Clinton Prison in Dannemora, New York, and they have been established to treat particular kinds of offenders, e.g., the Center for the Diagnosis and Treatment of Dangerous Persons at Bridgewater, Massachusetts, which treats sex offenders.

Out of this experience—public and private, penal and non-penal—four elements tend to emerge which are an essential part of a total treatment program for the severe personality disorders: *acceptance, control, support* and *learning*. Let us look more closely at what they mean, particularly as they apply to the program at Patuxent.

Acceptance

As patients enter the Institution they tend to assume those roles which have always assured their survival in prison—anything from the callous "tough guy" who's afraid of nothing to the passive "punk" who curries favor among the inmates to the fawning "nice guy" who curries favor from the staff. Initially, the staff members simply observe the behavior, getting some idea of the characteristic ways in which the patient behaves. This observation period has value to the staff as we learn what we have to deal with. It is also valuable to the patient, who can use his old familiar patterns to adapt to the new situation, and can begin to relate to staff in the role in which he is most comfortable. Even in this early stage of treatment, however, the milieu of the Institution begins to work on the patients.

For example, even while the patients are on diagnostic status they have already started to have sustained contact with professional staff, a staff that accepts and respects them as total human beings irrespective of the role they play. But acceptance of their role does not mean approval of their behavior. Time and again, particularly as the staff exercises a disciplinary function, the effort is made to help the patients distinguish between the unacceptable behavior and the acceptable human being. The custodial force, too, though more repressive than staff, is not the punitive force these men have known in other prisons and, to a large extent, it is not as corrupt and bribable, not as committed to the perpetuation of the prisoner society, as are other groups of guards the patients have known. Also, a subtle pressure is placed on the newer patients by the older patients, those who are fully involved in treatment, who are sympathetic to the problems of the new men but simply don't become involved in their schemes and machinations. In short, for all the personal acceptance, these new patients find that their traditional roles do not bring the expected rewards.

Of course, the need for acceptance is neverending. We start by accepting role-playing but we go on to accept the emergence of real feelings. The hostile, violent patient may literally not know that a man is permitted to have tender and passive feelings, until he can see that someone can accept this side of his character without denigrating him as a man. There is an ongoing effort to help the patients make the distinction between the experiencing of feelings and the expression of feelings, to show them that there is a difference between having destructive thoughts and behaving in destructive ways. As the patients come to know this they begin to establish internal controls. Eventually, we accept their fear of returning to a free society and their dependence upon the Institution, letting them know that this is a part of their total growth and that even a failure or two does not mean that they have failed as a person.

Control

Acceptance cannot be carried to the point of permissiveness—not with individuals with severe personality disorders and accompanying poor impulse control. Treatment virtually requires some degree of authoritarianism. The problem generally is not how much control to impose initially, since dangerousness tends to dictate that, but at what point and to what degree the controls should be relaxed. Most in-house programs—including prison systems—rely on behavior observation: A man is initially placed in some maximum security setting, observed, and when his behavior warrants it, is moved on to a minimum security or open setting, then to an honor ward or tier, and so on to parole. Patuxent operates in a similar fashion, but with a difference. Patuxent has a "four level" system which is very like the graded tier system in prisons or the open/closed ward systems in psychiatric hospitals, but movement between the levels depends ultimately on something more than behavioral control.

Men newly admitted to Patuxent are placed on first level tiers. The cells here are the old-fashioned variety, very like cages, open to constant observation. The movement of the men within the Institution is severely curtailed. External control is the only "therapy" at this point in time; we are dealing with the unknown, men who have histories of violence, and the safety and security of the Institution almost requires that we get to know these men a little bit before giving them more freedom. Also, the men come to us from other maximum security facilities, some even more repressive than first level, and they need a chance to make the readjustment with controls upon which they can depend. They cannot depend on their own. This holds true in any setting that treats the severe personality disorders; whatever the strength of the initial external controls, to relax them too quickly is to promote acting out.

The patients move to the second level in about 30 days. From here on the cells are all constructed so that the men have more privacy; the tiers are larger and offer more recreational opportunities; privileges gradually increase. From second level the patients can take part in educational and vocational programs; they may be assigned to some of the jobs within the Institution. Though not at first in formal psychotherapy, they have the opportunity to take part in tier counseling and they have ready access to the staff who will be working with them. Although the external controls have been relaxed, this is still a maximum security tier. Acting-out behavior may result in the man being demoted to first level.

In order to get to third level a man must maintain good behavior and be in formal psychotherapy. At this point we are not concerned about his progress in therapy, only that he attend. There have been patients who have stayed on second level for many months because they refused to attend therapy, and patients who have remained on third level for many months because they attended but did not participate. In both cases, the behavior of the patients may have been excellent; however, at Patuxent good behavior is not enough. Further, patients who continue to act out, however well they are doing in psychotherapy, cannot remain on third level. It is at this point that we begin to make the real distinction between internal and external controls.

The third level is furnished a little more comfortably than the second and has a few more privileges; also, the better jobs in the Institution become available to the men when they reach the third level. However, it is not so different from second level that the men find it particularly desirable; its real value to them is that it is a necessary step to fourth level, where they really want to be. To get there they must maintain behavioral control and, while they still have external structure to rely upon, they must also begin to deal with ever mounting frustrations. Characteristically, these men have brought their games to therapy; they have worked their "con," and they have done all the things that any prison ever required them to do. But time goes on and they find themselves no closer to parole than on the day they first entered the Institution. It is usually at this point that they truly realize that their sentence is indeterminate. Now for the first time they may begin to experience real anxiety. It might be that not until now have they recognized the futility of their role-playing. In a sense, every fiber of their being calls for them to act out—that's how they have always handled previous frustration—and some of them do. Most of them take the problems to therapy, and the real work begins. Third levels are neurotic tiers; they hold the men most in the process of change.

Perhaps a word should be said here about the use of psychotropic medications, since they can be looked upon as controlling agents. These are used in Patuxent but not to the same extent that they are used (abused?) in prisons. They are rarely used to help third level men deal with their anxiety because the therapy is aimed at establishing internal controls, not substituting one kind of external control for another.

It is the rare man, generally the psychotic, who is on any form of psychotropic medication when he leaves the Institution on parole.

Once the staff is convinced that internal controls have been established, however tenuously, the man is moved on to a fourth level tier. This is a self-governing tier; the cells are open at all times and there is no officer on the tier. There are many additional privileges, including unlimited visits, no curfew, and lawn picnics with families in the summer. Supervision of the men is so minimal that there are unlimited opportunities to act out, but by this time the therapy is largely concerned with strengthening internal controls, reinforcing a positive self-concept, and planning ahead for a future in free society.

The step to the outside of the Institution is also taken slowly, perhaps through a leave or work-release program before there is outright parole. Many men spend some time in the pre-release center—a building on the grounds of the Institution which is more like a college dormitory than a jail—visiting their homes several times a month while making final plans for parole. Some men live for a time in a half-way house located in Baltimore, not necessarily because they have no place else to go, but because some men continue to need reassurance that the external controls are still there.

Generally, when we think about controlling the behavior of others, we think of suppression, something that is done more for our benefit than for theirs. There is present that aspect of control; few will deny that society needs prisons to keep it safe from the behavior of some people. but there is another way to look at external control; one can look upon it as a need that some people have, a need that they will go out of their way to fulfill. Control, in the therapeutic sense, meets not only our needs for safety but also the patients' needs for security.

Support

The psychotherapy of the severe personality disorders is often directive. We start with people who have no sense of self and whose choices are most likely to be based on expediency or magical thinking, rather than on good reality testing. In the initial phases of treatment, particularly, it may be necessary to order patients into a specific vocational or educational program or to place them on a particular job in spite of their protests. Given a free choice they would take the easiest route, involving themselves in programs which would be meaningless in terms of their abilities and goals, applying for "prestige" jobs in which they have no skills, and generally setting themselves up for the same kind of failures which have marked their whole lives. Therefore, it becomes vitally important for the staff to give them some meaningful direction and *to supply them with an opportunity for success.* Later in treatment, as more knowledge of self is gained, these goals can change, but initially these patients are always the first to overestimate their talents and the last to admit weakness.

The Patuxent staff does control the treatment. In most penal institutions things like job and shop placement are controlled by "classification officers" and discipline is handled by the custodial force. At Patuxent these are functions of the treatment team. Within reason—internal harmony must always be considered—a man can be placed on a job or taken off a job because it is important to his treatment at the time, not because the job supervisor does or does not want him. Within reason—considering the security of the Institution—discipline can become a learning and therapeutic experience for the man, as he learns that there is a difference between punishment and limit-setting or as he learns that his therapist can impose controls while still holding him in high regard. The staff members are involved in the daily lives of the patients; they are there when the patients need them.

So "support" refers to all aspects of the treatment process: the willingness of the staff to give of themselves, to accept, to empathize, to be available in crises, to help solve problems, to encourage and, when necessary, to direct.

Learning

All of the above enter into the learning process. The four level system may be looked upon as a kind of behavior modification device; there are other opportunities as well for rewards and punishments with regard to job and school performance. But this kind of learning is not enough. Because of their relative inability to generalize, this kind of learning is not likely to follow the men into society. More meaningful is that which the men learn about themselves and their characteristic ways of coping. Because the staff is so intimately involved with them in a variety of situations, there is ample opportunity over the years to instruct them in the methods of self-observation. The end product is more likely to be self-awareness and self-control than basic personality change. Teaching that there are alternative ways to function is meaningless, however, if the men see all around them that the old ways reap the most rewards; that is why the milieu must be different from the traditional prisoner society.

This is not easy to achieve. It depends to a large extent on the involvement of the professional staff with the custodial force. The professional staff has to demonstrate to them, as well as to the patients, that the old ways are not always the best ways, that the expression of even hostile and aggressive feelings is not always a bad thing, and that discipline at its best is a teaching, rather than a punitive, device. On the other hand, custodial personnel do have more sustained contact with the patients and can bring to the therapeutic staff important information about the ways the patients interact with one another. In the therapeutic community, learning takes place at all levels.

I think that some special emphasis must be given to the *imitative* behavior of the patients. Once they learn that their traditional roles are not reinforced, they cast about for new roles to play. This tends to happen at a time when they still have little awareness of real self and when they are in the process of forming a bond with the therapist. Quite often they begin to imitate their therapist and to incorporate some of his values. The imitation can be even more extensive, to the point that it includes an identification with the larger values and principles of the Institution. This in turn can become a loyalty very akin to loyalty toward family. In truth, for many men, the Institution is the most meaningful family they have ever had; they take with them into free society the values the Institution has taught.

CONCLUSION: THE EFFECTIVENESS OF TREATMENT

As I have indicated, Patuxent reports a 7% recidivism rate for a *fully treated* group of patients. Fully treated means that they went through the program in the Institution and then were on parole for three years. For other groups, those who had in-house treatment only or those who were released by the court after only a brief parole, the recidivism rate rises. On the average, a fully treated man spends four years in the Institution and another three on parole/outpatient status.

A program that has much in common with Patuxent's is that at the Center for the Diagnosis and Treatment of Dangerous Persons (29). The Center treats only sex offenders but the patients are committed for an indeterminate period of time; they are subjected to a wide variety of therapeutic techniques, and there is an aftercare program. The recidivism rate for a fully treated group at the Center is reported as 6% and, as at Patuxent, the recidivism rates rise for the partially treated groups, those released by court order against the advice of the institution.

How successful any program is tends to depend upon a variety of factors. Voluntary patients under any circumstances tend to do well if they are really sincere; the very act of volunteering is a good prognostic sign even when the therapy takes place in a prison. Among voluntary patients, those who are more neurotic-like or psychotic-like do better than the most sociopathic, leading in part to the good success rates frequently reported from psychiatric hospitals which treat patients who have been found "not guilty by the reason of insanity." The more clearly sociopathic the patient population, the greater the necessity for some specialized treatment program.

I have cited Patuxent as a model program; but that program is about to change. Perhaps even the Patuxent concept is no longer valid, given the "temper of our times." In the last several years support for the concept of indeterminate sentence has waned. Hersteadvester, which served as a model in Europe, was radically altered a few years ago and the law which governs Patuxent has been changed as of July 1, 1977. Both continue as treating institutions but without the indeterminate sentence for patients/inmates. California now gives fixed sentences and many other states are moving in the direction of the determinate sentence. Society as a whole is disillusioned with prisons as treatment and rehabilitative agencies; our culture is becoming ever more punitive—witness the rush of states to pass death penalty laws—and more reluctant to spend tax money on criminals. Those of us who still believe that criminals can and should be treated are clearly out of step.

The State of Maryland is attempting a solution to the punishment *vs.* rehabilitation conflict which accompanies the new Article 31B (the old Defective Delinquency Law), which went into effect on July 1, 1977. Under the new law, the indeterminate sentence and involuntary commitment are abolished. Patuxent remains as an institution to treat "eligible persons," who are defined as follows:

> "Eligible person" means a person who (1) has been convicted of a crime and is serving a sentence of imprisonment with at least three years remaining on it, (2) who has an intellectual deficiency or emotional unbalance, (3) is likely to respond favorably to the programs and services provided at Patuxent Institution, and (4) can be better rehabilitated through those programs and services than by other incarceration.

The new law also provides that any person who is serving a sentence of at least three years may volunteer for commitment and treatment. He may request a transfer back to the Division of Correction anytime after commitment and his request must be honored. A diagnostic evaluation relating to eligibility for treatment must be made by at least one psychiatrist, one psychologist and one social worker. A treatment plan must be written for each eligible person and it must be reviewed and/or revised every six months. The paroling authority remains the Institutional Board of Review; there is essentially no change in the outpatient programs that existed under the old law. Each eligible person must be seen by the Institutional Board of Review at least once in each calendar year. Parole and/or other conditional release may be granted at any time, without regard to length of sentence, but an eligible person must be released from confinement upon the expiration of his sentence.

After the new law went into effect, about 80 percent of the men already confined at Patuxent elected to remain at Patuxent. The Institution has been swamped with requests for admission from men in penal institutions within the Division of Correction. At this writing we are in the process of evaluating many of these men.

So far there are more problems than solutions. For example, an eligible person is one who is "likely to respond favorably" to programs offered by Patuxent, programs which are not available in other correctional institutions within the State. This basically means psychotherapy. The diagnostic task is to determine who is "treatable," and treatability has never been satisfactorily defined. In addition, many of the volunteers have extremely long sentences, double and triple life, and would ordinarily not be eligible for parole in less than thirty to forty years.

These men have also committed the most heinous crimes; their motivation for treatment is almost certainly related to the more liberal parole situation at Patuxent. Yet we cannot say they are not treatable. And if treatment is successful, would the Institution be subverting the will of society by granting them early conditional release?

Patuxent now has an opportunity to treat dangerous criminals using techniques that have evolved over the years, in a milieu that continues to be therapeutic, but without the indeterminate sentence. Indeterminate sentence may not be needed, given that we can still modify the prisoner society and that we still have control of the parole situation, and given also that the new generation of patients will all be "volunteers." Clearly, therapists must accommodate to what society, through its legislatures, will permit. To keep our values intact and yet be flexible is a challenge we can accept. We know that even though the history of the treatment of sociopathy has been filled with frustration, it has in recent years also had many successes. The sociopath is not untreatable.

REFERENCES

1. CLECKLEY, H. M. *The Mask of Sanity*. (4th ed.). St. Louis: C. V. Mosby Company, 1964.
2. CARNEY, F. L. Treatment of Aggressive Patients. In: D. J. Madden and J. R. Lion (Eds.), *Rage, Hate, Assault and Other Forms of Violence*. New York: Spectrum Publications, Inc., 1976, 223-248.
3. McCORD, W. and McCORD, J. *Psychopathy and Delinquency*. New York: Grune and Stratton, 1956.

4. CLECKLEY, H. M. Psychopathic States. In: S. Arieti (Ed.), *American Handbook of Psychiatry, Vol. 1.* New York: Basic Books,
5. GUNN, J. Forensic Psychiatry and Psychopathic Patients. *Br. J. Psychiat.* spec pub #9:302-307, 1975.
   (Eds.), *Rage, Hate, Assault and Other Forms of Violence.* New York: Spectrum
6. STEADMAN, H. J. Predicting Dangerousness. In: D. J. Madden and J. R. Lion Publications, Inc., 1976, 53-69.
7. ESMIOL, P. Personality Disorders in Private Practice. In: J. R. Lion (Ed.) *Personality Disorders: Diagnosis and Management.* Baltimore: Williams and Wilkins, 1975, 318-333.
8. LION, J. R., AZCARAGE, C., CHRISTOPHER, R., and ARANE, J. D. A Violence Clinic. *Md. State Med.* 23:45-48, 1974.
9. CARNEY, F. L. Outpatient Treatment of the Aggressive Offender. *Am. J. Psychoth.* 31 (2):265-274, 1977.
10. WHITELY, J. S. The Psychopath and His Treatment. *Br. J. Psychiat.* spec pub #9:159-169, 1975.
11. ROTH, L. H. and ERWIN, R. F. Psychiatric Care of Federal Prisoners. *Am. J. Psychiat.* 128:424-430, 1971.
12. BACH-Y-RITA, G. Personality Disorders in Prisons. In: J. R. Lion (Ed.), *Personality Disorders: Diagnosis and Management.* Baltimore: Williams and Wilkins, 1974, 308-317.
13. HALLECK, S. Psychiatry and Correctional Justice. *Bull. of The Menninger Clinic* 35:402-407, 1971.
14. FINK, L. and MARTIN, J. P. Psychiatry and the Crisis of the Prison System. *Am. J. Psychoth.* 27:479-584, 1973.
15. CLARK, R. *Crime in America.* New York: Simon and Schuster, 1970.
16. STURUP, G. K. *Treating the Untreatables.* Baltimore: The Johns Hopkins Press, 1968.
17. CARNEY, F. L. The Indeterminate Sentence at Patuxent. *Crime and Delinquency* 20:135-143, 1974.
18. JEW, C. C., CLANON, T. L., and MATTOCKS, A. L. The Effectiveness of Group Psychotherapy in a Correctional Institution. *Am. J. Psychiat* 129:602-605, 1972.
19. LIEBMAN, M. D. and HEDLUND, D. A. Therapeutic Community and Milieu Therapy of Personality Disorders. In: J. R. Lion (Ed.), *Personality Disorders: Diagnosis and Management.* Baltimore: Williams and Wilkins, 1974, 368-405.
20. SYKES, B. M. *The Society of Captives: A Study of a Maximum Security Prison.* Princeton: Princeton University Press, 1958.
21. GUENTHER, A. L. Compensations in a Total Institution: The Forms and Functions of Contraband. *Crime and Delinquency* 21:243-254, 1975.
22. BRODY, S. A. The Political Prisoner Syndrome. *Crime and Delinquency* 20:97-106, 1974.
23. TOCH, H. *Men in Crisis.* Chicago: Aldine Publishing Co., 1975.
24. BACH-Y-RITA, G. Habitual Violence and Self-mutilation. *Am. J. Psychiat.* 131: 1018-1020, 1974.
25. MAIER, G. J. Therapy in Prisons. In: D. J. Madden and J. R. Lion (Eds.), *Rage, Hate, Assault and Other Forms of Violence.* New York: Spectrum Publications, Inc., 1976, 113-133.
26. LION, J. R. and PASTERNAK, S. E. Countertransference Reactions to Violent Patients. *Am. J. Psychiat.* 130:207-210, 1973.
27. SARGENT, D. A. Confinement and Ego Regression: Some Consequences of Enforced Passivity. *Intern. J. Psychiat. in Medicine* 5:143-151, 1974.
28. VAILLANT, G. E. Sociopathy as a Human Process. *Arch. Gen. Psychiat.* 32:178-183, 1975.
29. KOZOL, H. L., BOUCHER, R. J. and GOROFOLO, R. F. The Diagnosis and Treatment of Dangerousness. *Crime and Delinquency* 18:371-392, 1972.

15

Outpatient Treatment of Psychopaths

JOHN R. LION, M.D.

This chapter serves as a primer for the treatment of the psychopath. Existing literature by other workers deals with intensive psychoanalytic treatment of this type of patient (1, 2) and with therapy within special inpatient and outpatient milieus (3, 4). More recent work has focused on the general clinical problem of manipulation (5). In this section general principles of psychotherapy in an outpatient setting will be presented.

GENERAL PRINCIPLES

Clinicians electing to treat psychopaths must be cognizant of the following principles. First, the therapist must be continually vigilant with regard to manipulation on the part of the patient. Second, he must assume, until proved otherwise, that information given him by the patient contains distortions and fabrications. Third, he must recognize that a working alliance develops, if ever, exceedingly late in any therapeutic relationship with a psychopath.

Developing Trust

The above cautions mitigate against disappointments and frustrations which all too often become converted into therapeutic nihilism by those involved in working with these types of character disorders, for the therapeutic contract is most imperfect. Almost inevitably psychopaths are referred by third parties such as probation officers, courts or lawyers. Even when psychopaths do enter treatment "voluntarily" they usually come under some duress such as that of a spouse who is threatening to leave; hence, covert coercion is present. Coercion and the presence of a

286

third party are not conducive to developing trust. When the clinician is under some obligation to report to an outsider the "progress" of a psychopath, initial mistrust is bound to linger. The only recourse the therapist has is to openly describe the state of progress by sharing with the psychopath all impressions he has about him. I show psychopaths all correspondence generated and received concerning them. Complete frankness and honesty are the only hope for these relationships and often lead to fruitful dialogue in therapy.

There are two sets of magical expectations surrounding the treatment of psychopathy. The first occurs on the part of the third party referring the patient for treatment. If the patient is seen as charming, articulate, and intelligent, he automatically becomes a "good candidate for insight psychotherapy" in the mind of the referring agent. Hence, marvelous things are expected to happen in the treatment process. The second magical expectation comes from the patient himself, who, sensing the alternative of treatment to incarceration or other legal action, sees a chance to manipulate as well as to acquire new skills with which to outwit others. The clinician is immediately endowed with enormous perspicacity and a power of observation which he in fact does not possess. In the initial stages of treatment, psychopaths will "lay themselves bare" and reveal interesting tidbits of information relevant to sexual exploits, grandiose dealings with money, and other matters which are designed to intrigue therapists, particularly those in earlier stages of training. The therapist must constantly be on guard for these distractions; he should be alerted when he finds himself fascinated by the accounts of the psychopath whom he has opted to treat.

Psychopaths are also prone in the early stages of treatment to lavish praise upon the therapist as the person who "genuinely cares" or "understands" him and who will listen to him patiently, in contrast to "those others who always want something." The magnitude of praise and positive statement is proportional to the patient's attempt to seduce the therapist into a position of lowered vigilance, at which point deviant behavior may be forthcoming. At the same time, if he is successful in his seduction, the psychopath reassures himself of the fact that his skills and charms still work, even in the face of a critical professional; the patient thus gains positive reinforcement from his ability to subtly shape the course of therapy.

I have often found it useful to tell psychopaths who are in early treatment phases that their stories are most engrossing but have nothing whatsoever to do with the treatment process. Often such a remark is met with the question: "What do you want me to talk about?" Here one must educate the patient in some respect, since the only language he knows is the language of manipulation. I generally make some statement to the effect that my job is to help him to recognize true and spontaneous emotions, emotions not clouded by the need to win or triumph over others. I also state that I am not interested in issues of money, sexual prowess, or personal glory but merely wish to learn something about his mundane day-to-day life. This kind of statement needs constant repeating, for it forms the basis for therapy and inevitably causes some discouragement in the patient in subsequent treatment.

Irrespective of the etiology of psychopathy, one may take as an operating premise for therapy the concept that the psychopath not only lacks a conscience, but is unaware of the subtleties of affect and fantasy (6) that are adaptive for a normal life-style. Coupled with these deficits is a general narcissistic posture which is prominent in all phases of treatment. Our job is to hold a mirror up to the patient so that he sees his self-centered ways of behaving which, without foresight and reflection, and unencumbered by guilt, are ultimately so destructive for him. Seeing this reflection time and again hopefully converts that which is syntonic into that which is dystonic. Few psychopaths enjoy this process. Introspection and insight are foreign exercises and alien to a life-style of impulsive and hedonistic behavior. The psychopath wants and does; he is loathe to look and think. The narcissism and need to win or "con" are defenses against involvement and means of devaluating other individuals, effectively precluding intimacy.

Thus, in time the psychopath is ultimately put into the position of viewing himself. He will later be confronted with the problem of identity, a crisis he has eluded for too long and dealt with by borrowing the identities of others. In some instances, paranoia develops as the next stage and much anger at the therapist is seen in the transference. Eventually *depression* develops as the narcissism is relinquished and the patient begins to deal with his intrinsically low feelings of self-esteem. Such is a rough, basic synopsis of treatment.

The psychopath enters treatment in the same way he starts any new endeavor. A gusto prevails during early sessions and a honeymoon period ensues. The honeymoon period is concurrent with the time during which the therapist is endowed with special qualities. Yet there exist within the patient underlying feelings of inferiority which mobilize him to take a position of attack. He is apt to launch himself into battles regarding philosophical issues and the treatment process. The patient may begin to read psychiatric texts. Discussions about styles of therapy and schools of psychiatry may dominate the hour, allowing little chance for the therapist to confront the patient with routine issues of affect and behavior. Yet such intratherapeutic contests siphon off adverse behavior. Thus, during the honeymoon phase, the patient becomes quiescent outside of the therapeutic hour and relatives or his spouse are quick to comment that he is making enormous gains in a relatively short time in treatment. These accolades of success, perhaps reported by the patient himself, must basically be ignored.

Sooner or later, the psychopath will "test" the therapist by behaving in some deviant manner at home or work. This "test" of deviance is usually subtle and ambiguous, confronting both patient and therapist with a new transgression in therapy and signalling the end of the honeymoon period. Since there is ambiguity in the transgression, it is difficult to analyze. Often the patient will have been fired from a job for stealing but will claim that he was fired because of union difficulties. Since the therapist cannot easily ascertain the validity of this claim, he is at a disadvantage. The only solution is to begin the painful business of discussing with the patient one's doubts about his credibility, a tactic which ushers in the bilateral mistrust so prominent during the early stages of treatment. The concomitant disillusionment subsequent to this is reflected in anger on the part of the psychopath, accompanied by dismay, rejection, and either feigned or genuine hurt with regard to the therapist's betrayal and mistrust of him. At this point, it is necessary to point out quite firmly to the patient that his primary difficulty is one of mistrust and that it is sad, indeed, that the therapist cannot trust him and that he in turn cannot trust the therapist. Since such general mistrust must exist in outside relationships as well, it must be most unsatisfying and may perhaps be a good focus of therapy.

Additional problems arise when spouses or third parties report deviations in behavior which reflect the return of psychopathic activities. Again, such unsolicited reports evoke the issue of confidentiality and the therapist must share with the patient such breaches, which are an inevitable part of the treatment process. The patient will accuse the therapist of being an agent of the court, etc., while the therapist must stand his ground and state that although his job is to sift the information given him while maintaining as much confidentiality as possible, he may indeed have some allegiance to the court, which places him in a precarious position. Many therapists do not like this and may share this dislike with the patient. Such a shared dislike does not preclude treatment but merely sets out in the open the unpleasantness of third party watchfulness. The following case example summarizes some of the issues involved in the early stages of treatment.

A 20-year-old psychopathic young girl was referred by her father, an attorney, because of pathological lying, shoplifting, and a general life-style of deceit. After the honeymoon period had been entered with magical results at home, the patient was mysteriously fired from her job. The details of this firing were obscure to me but, as often happens in these cases, I learned from a friend of the family that the patient had apparently stolen some money from the cash register and had been dismissed on those grounds. Not knowing what was the truth, and not wishing to act as detective, I confronted the patient with my ignorance of the basis for her firing but stated that I had heard from a third source—and named that source—that there had been some financial indiscretion which alarmed me greatly. I stated that while I was not a lawyer or detective, the patient needed to tell me what was going on. I had no choice except to believe her even though I doubted the veracity of her comments. The patient then launched into a thoroughly believable story about the incident, which led me to comment that her statement made sense but still left me with an uneasy feeling of mistrust, and that I would hope that trust could be reestablished at some time in the future. This made the patient unhappy but clearly stated my position in the treatment process.

In the above case, the informer was a relative of the patient. These situations do indeed happen in treatment of psychopaths, since friends, family, and other third parties feel that the therapist may not "fully know the facts" and are eager to enlighten him with regard to actual behavior on the outside. I personally do not turn off such knowledge, although I do tell whoever calls that I will confront the patient with it and reveal the source. Such confrontations produce enemies, but open communication is the only salvation in the treatment of psychopathy and I cannot disregard outside messages. Again, the only ammunition the therapist has is direct and open honesty, even though the therapy is to some extent being performed in an arena with interested spectators. One can only hope that in time, as behavior returns to normal, the arena will empty and privacy will be restored.

Dealing with Anger and Absences

It is quite obvious that the therapeutic relationship is exceedingly fragile and delicate. The patient, sensing that the therapist has little faith in him or her, is often sullen and rebellious while alternately being grandiose, with a desire to please and manipulate. Anger is often a problem in the early course of coercive therapies, since a patient whose life-style is psychopathic becomes frustrated when he or she cannot cope with situations in the usual manipulative manner. The fragile alliance suffers even more when scheduled appointments are missed because of illness, holidays, or vacations. Psychopaths take any opportunity to break routine and throw the therapist off guard. Absences on the part of the therapist have a demonstrably negative effect upon trust and often weeks of therapy are required to recapture gains previously made. Retaliatory absences are not uncommon even when the clinician goes to great pains to work this through. The following example is illustrative.

A psychopathic patient had been making reasonable progress in therapy, coming to grips with object relations. After treatment of a year, I developed hematuria necessitating frequent visits to a urologist for radiographic studies and cystoscopy. During one absence, I told my secretary that she should telephone the patient and explain to her that I would be absent from a session because of a cystoscopic examination for what was then believed to be kidney stones. I emphasized to the secretary that the detailed explanation was very necessary and the secretary complied. Following this workup, sessions were restored with the patient, at which time the patient entered my office with questions as to how I was feeling and if my "flu" was all better. I replied that I did not have the flu and questioned as to what she had been told on the phone. The patient adamantly stated that she had been told that I had a cold and had missed the session because of this. Subsequently, the patient cancelled a session for no valid reason.

I believe the above example illustrates what I felt to be an inability to tolerate the affect evoked by a detailed revelation of my illness. She used denial and distortion as a defense. The anger having to do with unexpressed alarm over my health was reflected in a retaliatory absence; however, these speculative issues were not amenable to confirmation as we had not reached a level of therapy and trust appropriate to discussion of transference feelings. The point is that the therapy is highly vulnerable, perhaps more vulnerable than one would imagine when first confronted with the apparent coldness of the psychopath. Viewing the patient as a person with a narcissistic personality disorder may make this phenomenon more understandable.

Absences on the part of the patient create problems, since one can never be sure whether the patient is actually sick or is feigning illness to avoid what he or she senses will be a difficult session. The following is an example.

A patient telephoned me to state that his automobile was broken and that he could not attend the session. I told him that I had some time in the afternoon and that he could call me when he knew the state of repair of his car. The patient promised to call, but never did. In the following week's session, he stated that he had been tied up with the towing operations of his car and did not have the time to call me until late in the afternoon when he realized I could no longer see him. I told him that this explanation seemed plausible, but that there was some seed of doubt in my mind regarding the fact that he could not find the time to telephone and at least apprise me of the situation. Again, I reflected to him the issue of mistrust. The patient sat stonily and listened to me without acknowledgment, although I sensed he clearly understood my point.

While one cannot easily ascertain the causes of absences in patients, one can still share with the patient disbelief in a matter-of-fact way without accusation. It is wise to operate on a "gut level" in these instances, since there is little else to go on and therapists should refuse to be put in the position of being a detective. Patients who are psychopathic will often come armed with all kinds of ammunition and alibis, as though they were about to appear before a magistrate. The therapist should state that he is not equipped to handle evidence more appropriate for a court but must rely upon verbalizations rendered by the patient. He can believe or disbelieve these verbalizations according to his intuition, but this is all he has to go on. This makes it very clear to the patient that evidence plays little role in psychotherapy and that affect, not fact, is the issue at stake.

Early countertransference reactions on the part of the therapist fluctuate. During the honeymoon phase, many therapists become enthused with the apparent rapid progress being made by patients who are so verbal and articulate. Rescue fantasies become prominent, particularly with well-to-do psychopaths from influential families; but humility is called for. My own feelings about prognosis suggest that it takes a good working year of therapy in order to determine whether or not a patient is making any reasonable gains with regard to the development of true affective awareness, intimacy and trust.

Acting Out

Problems of acting out become important as the transference develops (7). Generally, the acting out is of an aggressive type having to do with authority figures. Patients who see the therapist as a parental figure may translate feelings into behavior on the outside against their own parents, personnel at school or employers in the job situation. In addition, sexual acting out may become problematic. Every attempt must be made to trace these behaviors to their transference source. This is very difficult for psychopathic patients, who appear to have some ingrained developmental difficulties in translating affective states to conscious and verbal awareness.

Acting out behavior, particularly when deviant, poses problems in the therapy. Often the therapist is being "tested" to see how loyal he is. I have on occasion threatened psychopaths with the termination of therapy if acting out in the form of deviant behavior or absences from therapy does not cease. The injunction needs to be made very clearly; the patient must realize that the therapist will not tolerate certain behaviors and that limit setting will be imposed. The therapist must unambivalently set for himself a threshold for intolerable behavior. I have discharged patients whom I could not control with mutual acknowledgment of the poor therapeutic alliance; some have accepted the discharge while other clamor for return, espousing a new honesty which is certainly suspect.

Payment

Payment is an issue which must be discussed from the outset (6). Generally, I ask for payment prior to each session until such time as a therapeutic relationship is established. For some patients, this is several months; for others it may be longer. There are certain psychopathic patients who have problems with money; from these I accept only cash. Nonetheless, I have been misled on several occasions.

> A charming and handsome middle-aged psychopath with a history of check forging was sent to me for treatment by his wife, an earnest and tearful woman who desired treatment for her "unfortunate" husband. The woman agreed to pay for the husband's treatment and the husband came for three sessions with a check in hand written by his wife. All three checks were returned to me for insufficient funds. While the wife had indeed signed them, she had done so with inadequate bank assets.

The above example illustrates the complexities of exacting payment and demonstrates the need for being firm with regard to money. This may be quite unpleasant for certain therapists who are used to billing monthly or having an agency or professional corporation bill for them. I explain to patients that their general behavior makes me more comfortable with regular weekly payments. Surprisingly, patients understand this, especially when roles are reversed in fantasy and they are asked to imagine how they would feel as the doctor treating a psychopath who is prone to skip payment.

Often patients will omit payment for one session to test the therapist; I allow two such sessions to occur and, if payment is not brought up-to-date, discharge the patient. I ask for cash or a money order from high risk patients and accept checks from those deemed more trustworthy. In no case do I allow third party coverage to reimburse me directly. Signed receipts should be given the patient for money and the money should be scrupulously counted, even though this appears an odious task. On several occasions, I have been underpaid and on one occasion overpaid by a patient who was testing to see whether I would return the extra money. Therapists have a tendency not to look at checks, as though it were a crass and mercenary act, but the amount written on the check should be noted and prompt discussion should ensue if it is incorrect.

Referrals

On occasion, the psychopathic patient may request referral to a lawyer or internist for consultation. In this case, I generally ask the patient to share his request for consultation and its reason with me. The following example illustrates the reasons for careful scrutiny and foresight with regard to a referral. Referrals should not be made casually.

A 30-year-old psychopath asked me for referral to an accountant for help in preparing his income tax form. Since the patient had a history of excessive spending and falsifying expense statements at work, I decided that the best course of action was to refer him to my own accountant, whom I knew to be an exceedingly conservative man. I knew in this instance that the patient would not easily dupe or fool the accountant and I also felt that he would receive reasonable service. I told the patient this, and explained my reasons for the referral. He accepted both and appeared pleased with the result.

On another occasion, the patient asked to be referred to a dentist for both necessary repair of a cavity and some elective restorative work. Again, the general grandiosity of this patient made me apprehensive lest he accumulate a large bill which could not be paid. Accordingly, I chose my own dentist, with the same rationale as above. The patient went to him, settled for a reasonable amount of both elective and necessary dental work, and arranged reasonable terms of payment to which he adhered.

It will be recognized that the above examples illustrate principles quite deviant from the traditional ones in psychotherapy. Upon examination, however, they appear quite logical given the premise of mistrust which is at the heart of all treatment with psychopaths. In another instance, and with a more traditional patient, one might urge the patient to seek his own accountant and dentist in order to foster autonomy and independence.

PROGRESS IN THERAPY: DEPRESSION AND DESPONDENCY

Gains in therapy with these patients are exceedingly slow and arduous. The therapist, rather than accepting the hollow "improvements" mentioned above, should wait for despondency and depression to occur since, as previously mentioned, narcissism and grandiosity are the hallmarks of most psychopaths who seek exploitative ways of manipulating themselves out of unpleasant situations. With persistent confrontation, introspection occurs in time. One eventually reaches a point in therapy at which nihilism appears in the patient and genuine sadness ensues. I have seen such depression develop to the point of requiring antidepressant medication; however, both the patient's capacity and his tolerance for depression must be learned and developed as an adaptive human trait (8).

Psychopathic patients may come to sessions after therapy is well underway and verbalize such sentiments as "there is nothing for me to do." At this point repeated acknowledgments of the despair induced by the absence of manipulative ability are necessary. At this time, even more acting out of the depression—and anger at the therapist for its induction —is a possibility. The patient may quit his job and start a new business venture or enter a grandiose entrepreneurial scheme to avoid this boredom and despondency. Premature attempts at termination and absences from sessions occur. These matters must be monitored closely. The therapist should constantly strive to teach the patient the process of insight and contemplation; the development of an active ability to fantasize and anticipate the consequences of action, as well as an affective awareness, is a prerequisite to efficacious treatment (8).

When the patient can visualize what can happen to him if he should engage in a socially deviant piece of behavior, he has shown progress in treatment; when he can recognize anger, fear, and nuances of affective expression, he has made some improvement. A capacity for intimacy and trust, as revealed both within and outside of the therapy, is indicative of positive change.

Use of Medications

The treatment of aggressive psychopaths differs in several respects from the treatment of non-aggressive psychopaths. With the aggressive psychopath, in contrast to, say, the check forger or the "con artist," problems in the direct handling of hostile urges are issues in therapy (9). With the aggressive psychopath, depression is even more of a risk as the aggression abates and there is a dynamic shift from outwardly directed to inwardly directed anger. Medications may help in the reduction of impulsivity and lability of mood and affect associated with aggressive outbursts, but psychopaths quite often resist taking medication or abuse it.

For those patients who do show responsible willingness to accept drugs to curb aggressiveness and impulsivity, consideration should be made of antianxiety agents such as the benzodiazepines. This class of drugs reduces the tension which often propels patients into impulsive acts and can secondarily diminish the hyper-vigilance often seen as part of the paranoid symptoms shown by some psychopaths (10). The latter patients, in fact, will not usually tolerate antipsychotic agents even though suspiciousness is clinically evident, for these major tranquilizers markedly impair watchfulness and thus may heighten, rather than reduce, paranoia and the tendency to become aggressive. In addition, antipsychotic agents frequently produce subtle side effects intolerable to paranoid and narcissistic individuals.

The anticonvulsants have been shown to reduce aggressiveness in patients who demonstrate epileptoid outbursts of rage (11, 12). Confirmation of underlying brain dysfunction by electroencephalographic examination, neurological evaluation, and psychological testing may provide additional justification for the use of such drugs.

Lithium has also been shown to be of use in certain patients labeled "emotionally unstable." These patients' symptoms probably reflect variants of a bipolar affective disorder manifested not by typical mood swings but by fluctuations in levels of psychomotor agitation, irritability, and aggressiveness (13).

Two classes of experimental drugs bear mention. The central nervous system stimulants used in hyperkinetic children have been anecdotally reported to be of benefit in adults who show clinical pictures of impulsivity, aggressiveness, and antisocial behavior (14). Also, research with progestational agents on sexually deviant and aggressive patients has demonstrated positive effects of these drugs, which act by reducing sexual drive state and thus, secondarily, reducing aggressiveness (15). I have on one occasion administered reserpine to a patient with a severe character disorder with the hope of making him depressed to the point of introspection; such a tactic was experimental, in response to the intriguing question of how to induce depression in patients who deny it and handle it by behavioral means (16). I have felt the value of most psychopharmacologic agents in the treatment of psychopathy—such as the tranquilizers and anticonvulsants—to lie in the propensity of these agents to curb impulsivity and produce a mild state of depression conducive to reflection. (For a more complete discussion of these and other pharmacologic approaches to treatment of the psychopath the reader is referred to Chapter 16 of this volume.)

The "Burning Out" Process

Time is the greatest ally of the therapist. Thus it is observed that the longer an aggressive psychopath is kept locked up, the less likely he is to revert to his old manipulative and aggressive ways of behaving. This "burning out process" probably has to do with physiologic maturation and can be seen in impulsive and aggressive youths who show reduced impulsivity and hostility in their thirties and forties, after having served comparatively long sentences within institution settings. Maturation is an important variable but one which is poorly understood. The "burning out" process most likely represents physiologic changes which have a general dampening effect on psychological parameters of lability and impulsivity. In the "natural experiment" one sees this in the differences between normal adolescents and adults. Maturation or "burning out" also plays a role in outpatient therapy, since the duration of treatment is long. It should be noted, however, that "burning out" may refer more to physically violent criminal activity than to antisocial behavior in general, since there are some data which suggest that psychopaths continue to be socially maladjusted as they age but are less often convicted of criminal activity (17).

Development of Guilt

The development of guilt and a "superego" has been conceptualized as a major task of treatment for all psychopaths. Regrettably, the superego, a derivative of the ego, cannot be so easily shaped. It is felt by most clinicians that milieu treatment with 24-hour custodial and therapeutic care enables feedback to be present at all times so that some rudimentary forms of guilt develop, or, at the very least, the patient learns what is right and wrong. Many tactics in the treatment of psychopaths, including the precipitation of depression mentioned earlier, reflect the desire on the part of clinicians to forcefully confront the patient with issues of good and bad and to induce a state of hopelessness conducive to therapeutic insight.

A psychopathic girl was hospitalized at a private facility. Outpatient treatment had produced little change in her behavior and it was decided on this occasion to keep her on suicide precautions with a one-to-one patient/staff ratio in order to always have a nurse with her. It was thought that this might foster some form of discomfort conducive to reflection and identification. The hospital course proceeded rather smoothly with gains made in introspection. In time she was discharged and later committed suicide.

Another patient prone to violent outbursts was treated on an outpatient basis with anticonvulsants. His violent behavior was markedly reduced but he, too, ultimately killed himself (12).

A third patient was hospitalized. His wealthy family agreed to pay for two staff members who traveled on the hospital grounds wherever he went and always confronted him with any deviant piece of behavior he demonstrated. Few gains were made of any lasting value.

These various examples illustrate complex problems as well as equally complex and imperfect solutions and their hazards.

GROUP THERAPY

Group therapy forms an important treatment modality for psychopaths, since they are apt to be brutally honest with one another while being devious with the primary therapist. There is much peer confrontation in the group setting and it is a useful means of self-confrontation (18). Enhancement of psychotherapy by videotape playback of sessions may also be helpful.

Some groups form on the basis of self-help organizations such as Synanon and Daytop and are, of course, a prime modality of treatment within any hospital milieu. Within the group therapy, it may be useful to pick one particular psychopath as a therapist-leader. This tactic utilizes the dynamic of reaction formation, often most prominently seen in prison settings where there appears to be a thin line between the prisoner and the guard. By elevating a psychopath to the position of responsibility, he may identify with and adopt some values of the therapist, internalizing valuable ideas and norms which become part of his way of behaving. Obviously, this process takes considerable time to develop.

EXPLOITATION IN A HOSPITAL SETTING

Mention should be made of one facet of the inpatient treatment of psychopaths which demonstrates the exploitative power of the patient. The psychopath can create dissension on a hospital ward and actively manipulate events in such a way as to produce staff and patient distrust. Subtle and flagrant violations of ward rules confront everyone with issues of compliance and at the same time produce splits in staff allegiances. The psychopath is particularly skilled at generating conflicts over power and authority, and may become an uncontrollably defiant member of the patient population. Administrative problem solving may center around the psychopath when other issues and other patients are equally important.

Staff impotence must be acknowledged and discussed. Limits must be set and maintained. At the same time, caution must be exercised so that the psychopath does not exploit and exhaust the time that the staff has at its disposal. In time, some manipulation may require benign neglect to be extinguished. I have seen rare instances in which the ward could not tolerate the destructive manipulation of a psychopath and transfer to another facility was warranted. All of these points illustrate the constant need for the therapist to be vigilant and aware of his limitations. Consultation with colleagues is useful for the latter, since psychopaths, inpatient or outpatient, regularly mobilize feelings of helplessness in therapeutic staff.

THERAPEUTIC QUALITIES

The final question remains as to which kinds of therapists are best, or even suitable, for treating psychopaths. There exist in every therapeutic community physicians, psychiatrists and therapists who are particularly willing and able to deal with behavior disorders and psychopaths. Generally, these clinicians are those who have had experience in forensic matters and who are more skilled at detecting manipulation than their more psychoanalytically oriented colleagues, who depend heavily upon the self-reporting and spontaneous introspective processes which are part of the analytic process. In addition, it has been my observation that the therapists most skilled at treating psychopaths have some degree of entrepreneurial spirit which puts them in touch with the narcissism and grandiosity inherent in these patients. Without this "window" into the psychopaths' tendency to exploit in a grandiose style, the clinician cannot understand and internally predict what the psychopath will do. He is thus almost constantly "off guard." Also, the less attuned therapist is apt to be entrapped by his latent exhibitionism *vis à vis* mankind's fascination with psychotropic entrepreneurs, as evidenced by many famous hoaxes and swindles.

The therapist who works with psychopaths carries burdens which require a balance of work with other types of patients—neurotic and psychotic—lest he become hardened in his style. The therapist must constantly suspect his patient's intentions and behavior and work toward the day when an open honesty appears, one which is paradoxically, but quite predictably, accompanied by a depression. This melancholy heralds the beginning of a guilt-like process which can eventually lead to appropriate affects, attachments, and a normal life-style.

REFERENCES

1. EISSLER, K. R. Ego-psychological Implications of the Psychoanalytic Treatment of Delinquents. *Psychoanal. Study Child* 5:97-121, 1950.

2. SCHMIEDELBERG, M. The Analytic Treatment of Major Criminals: Therapeutic Results and Technical Problems. In: K. R. Eissler (Ed.), *Searchlights on Delinquency*. New York: Internat. Univ. Press, 1949.

3. AICHHORN, A. *Wayward Youth*. New York: Viking Press, 1925.

4. JONES, MAXWELL. *The Therapeutic Community*. New York: Basic Books, 1953.

5. BURSTEN, B. *The Manipulator*. New Haven: Yale University Press, 1973.

6. LION, J. R. Diagnosis and Treatment of Personality Disorders. In: J. R. Lion (Ed.), *Personality Disorders*. Baltimore: Williams and Wilkins, 1974.

7. GREENACRE, P. Problems of Patient-therapist Relationship in the Treatment of Psychopaths. In: R. M. Lindner and R. V. Selinger (Eds.), *Handbook of Correctional Psychology*. New York: Philosophical Library, 1947.

8. LION, J. R. The Role of Depression in the Treatment of Aggressive Personality Disorders. *Amer. J. Psychiat.* 129:347-349, 1972.

9. LION, J. R. *Evaluation and Management of the Violent Patient*. Springfield, Ill.: Charles C Thomas, 1972.

10. LION, J. R. Conceptual Issues in the Use of Drugs for the Treatment of Aggression in Man. *J. Nerv. Ment. Dis.* 160:76-82, 1975.

11. MONROE, R. R. The Problem of Impulsivity in Personality Disturbances. In: J. R. Lion (Ed.), *Personality Disorders*. Baltimore: Williams and Wilkins, 1974.

12. MONROE, R. R. Anticonvulsants in the Treatment of Aggression. *J. Nerv. Ment. Dis.* 160:119-126, 1975.

13. LION, J. R., HILL, J., and MADDEN, D. J. Lithium Carbonate and Aggression: A Case Report. *Dis. Nerv. Sys.* 36:97-98, 1975.

14. ALLEN, R. P., SAFER, D., and COVI, L. Effects of Psychostimulants on Aggression. *J. Nerv. Ment. Dis.* 160:138-145, 1975.

15. BLUMER, D. and MIGEON, C. Hormone and Hormonal Agents in the Treatment of Aggression. *J. Nerv. Ment. Dis.* 160:127-137, 1975.

16. LION, J. R., MILLAN, C., and TAYLOR, R. J. Reserpine and the Induction of Depression: A Case Report. *Dis. Nerv. Sys.* 36:321-322, 1975.

17. MADDOCKS, P. D. A Five Year Followup of Untreated Psychopaths. *Brit. J. Psychiat.* 116:511-15, 1970.

18. LION, J. R. and BACH-Y-RITA, G. Group Psychotherapy with Violent Outpatients. *Inter. J. Group. Psychother.* 20:185-191, 1970.

16

Drug Treatment of Personality
Disorders and Delinquents

ROBERT KELLNER, M.D., PH.D.

In this chapter clinical studies of psychotropic drugs in delinquents and patients with personality disorders are surveyed. The survey is not limited to antisocial personalities, because often patients with personality disorders which bear another diagnostic label commit repeatedly antisocial or unlawful acts. A few studies with patients in other diagnostic categories, for example neurotics and epileptics, are summarized because these studies deal with the treatment of symptoms or traits, such as explosiveness, hostility or emotional lability, which are frequently found in personality disorders. The main emphasis is on double-blind, controlled trials; several open label studies have been summarized mainly when the drug was reported to be effective in the treatment of personality disorders and too few controlled studies have been published. Several of the studies discussed in this chapter have been described by the authors themselves in other parts of the present volume.

Throughout the chapter comments are made about the design of each study and the apparent validity of the results. In uncontrolled studies it is usually difficult to assess the contribution of the drug effect to outcome unless at least the reports of independent observers or some other evidence is available, such as outcome without drug treatment. Therefore, when some of the uncontrolled studies are described, merely the author's impressions are summarized and no attempts are made to evaluate the findings. The diagnostic classification used by the authors of the individual studies has been accepted and no changes in the authors' terminology have been made. Unless a syndrome is discussed which was defined by the author of the study, the diagnostic categories of the *Diagnostic and Statistical Manual of Mental Disorders* of the American Psychiatric Association *(DSM II)* have been used. In the comments and conclusions in the present chapter the term antisocial personality disorder of the *DSM II* has been used synonymously with the term sociopathy.

MINOR TRANQUILIZERS AND HOSTILITY

There have been several studies in which the effects of minor tranquilizers on hostility have been examined. These studies are predominantly with normal subjects or neurotic patients and the findings may not be pertinent to patients with personality disorders; therefore, these studies are not summarized—only the main conclusions are listed.

Gardos et al. (1), DiMascio et al. (2), and Salzman et al. (3) carried out studies with normal volunteers in which they compared changes in anxiety and hostility with oxazepam and chlordiazepoxide. They found an increase in hostility on the Buss-Durkee Inventory in anxious subjects who were taking chlordiazepoxide, but not in those who were taking oxazepam. They also found a reduction of anxiety in subjects with high anxiety, whereas, in subjects with low anxiety, there was a "paradoxical anxiety increase."

McDonald (4) carried out a study with female college student volunteers of single doses of 5 mg. or 10 mg. diazepam and of placebo. There was a complex interaction of changes in hostility, dosage and traits. A dose of 5 mg. of diazepam led to a reduction of hostility on the Multiple Affect Adjective Checklist, whereas 10 mg. led to an increase in hostility. "Action-oriented" subjects reported an increase in hostility, whereas "nonaction-oriented" subjects experienced a reduction in hostility. There was no evidence of anxiety reduction.

Gleser et al. (5) compared the effects of a single dose of 20 mg. chlordiazepoxide and placebo in a double-blind study with delinquent boys. There was a significant decrease in rated hostility and anxiety in the boys who received chlordiazepoxide.

Lorr et al. (6) carried out a large, multi-centered, controlled study of meprobamate, chlorpromazine, phenobarbital and placebo with psychotherapy in anxious outpatients attending VA Mental Hygiene Clinics (this study is summarized in the section on major tranquilizers). They found increased hostility ratings at the end of eight weeks with meprobamate, but not at the end of 12 weeks of the trial, when the hostility ratings had decreased to baseline levels.

Feldman (7) compared the effects of benzodiazepines in anxious patients, finding a negligible reduction of hostility with chlordiazepoxide and with diazepam, but a marked reduction with oxazepam.

Podobnikar (8) carried out a double-blind study of chlordiazepoxide and placebo in private practice. He rated four target symptoms, each on a four-point rating scale; "neurotic hyperaggressiveness" decreased with the passage of time. The decrease was significantly greater in the chlordiazepoxide group.

McNair et al. (9) compared the effects of chlordiazepoxide, meprobamate and placebo in 85 new nonpsychotic veteran outpatients. After six weeks of treatment, there was a significantly greater reduction with chlordiazepoxide than with placebo on the anger-hostility scale of the POMS (Psychiatric Outpatient Mood Scales). After eight weeks, the anger and hostility scores remained low, but the placebo group had improved as well and the difference between drug and placebo was no longer significant. In the same study there were no significant differences between meprobamate and placebo.

Rickels and Downing (10) examined changes in hostility during treatment with chlordiazepoxide. They analyzed the data of over 200 anxious outpatients who had participated in drug trials and who were treated with either chlordiazepoxide (40 mg. daily) or with placebo. They found a significant decrease in ratings of the "irritability" and "hostility" items of the Physician Questionnaire and a significantly greater reduction of the anger-hostility factor of the Lipman-Rickels Symptom Checklist with chlordiazepoxide than with placebo. There was no evidence that a greater number of patients treated with chlordiazepoxide had become more irritable and hostile than those receiving placebo; thus, there was no evidence of idiosyncratic hostility side effects. The authors argue that chlordiazepoxide leads to a significant *decrease* in hostility in neurotics and that changes in test scores with normal volunteers should not be equated with increases in clinical hostility. In another study with chlordiazepoxide, in which the Clyde Mood Scale was used, Rickels and Clyde (11) found an increase in scores of the "aggressive" factors but also an increase in the "friendly" factor.

Covi et al. (12) analyzed the hostility ratings and self-ratings in a drug trial of diazepam, imipramine and placebo in a 16-week parallel trial with 212 depressed, nonpsychotic female outpatients. Diazepam increased self-rated hostility as measured by the hostility factor of the POMS; the observer-rated hostility increased on the Lorr Scale in diazepam treated patients participating in group psychotherapy. There was no increase in hostility as measured by the anger-hostility factor of the Hopkins Symptom Checklist. The authors concluded that in depressed female outpatients diazepam induces certain kinds of hostility as reflected by self-rating of mood but not by self-rating of symptoms emphasizing overt aggression or impulses to be overtly aggressive.

There have been rare reports in the literature of paradoxical rage reactions with chlordiazepoxide and with diazepam. These have not been reported with oxazepam (2, 13).

MINOR TRANQUILIZERS IN EPILEPTICS

Monroe and Wise (14) studied the effects of chlordiazepoxide and primidone in an open label study in acutely disturbed psychotic patients who had either seizures or episodic behavioral changes suggestive of altered states of awareness. Chlordiazepoxide was added to the phenothiazine maintenance treatment. Several of these patients appeared to benefit from the addition of chlordiazepoxide in that they became less impulsive. This study is summarized in the section on anticonvulsants.

Monroe et al. (15) studied the effects of various drugs in patients whose EEG's became activated by the administration of alpha chloralose. Fifteen chronic psychotic patients were included in a double-blind crossover study. There were significant differences in activation with various drugs; while taking placebo or no drug there was an activation rate of about 50%. Chlorpromazine and triflupromazine showed an activation rate of about 65%, whereas the rate of activation with chlordiazepoxide was 20%. There was also a marked improvement in impulsive behavior in the patients receiving chlordiazepoxide.

Goddard and Lokare (16) treated with diazepam 16 epileptics who showed hostility and aggressive behavior. It was an open label study which lasted for six months; diazepam was added to the standard anticonvulsant medication. Diazepam was administered in doses between 2 mg. and 10 mg. three times a day orally and was given intramuscularly in doses between 5 mg. and 10 mg. at times of aggressive outburst. Before the study started, paraldehyde or a phenothiazine had been prescribed for the treatment of aggressive outbursts. The patients were evaluated on the Wittenborn Psychiatric Rating Scale. At the end of six months there was a significant decrease in the number of convulsions and significant improvement in the ratings, suggesting a decrease of aggression and hostility.

Sch 12,679 in Aggression

Sch 12,679 is a benzazepine derivative which differs in structure from other psychotropic drugs; it shows similarity to chlordiazepoxide and perphenazine but has different effects on agitated and aggressive behavior in animals. Sch 12,679 differs from the other two drugs in that it inhibits aggression and agitation in Rhesus monkeys without producing sedation or extrapyramidal side effects (17). In rats and mice it antagonizes various kinds of experimentally induced aggression and, unlike other psychotropic drugs, it does so without evidence of concurrent ataxia or neurological impairment (18). This suggests that there may be a final common pathway for the neurophysiology of aggressive behavior and that this might be sensitive to specific drugs. In two uncontrolled studies with schizophrenics (19, 20), Sch. 12,679 appeared to have either weak or no neuroleptic properties. In a pilot study with four severely mentally retarded patients who were uncontrollably aggressive, it appeared to have a substantial calming effect (21). Itil et al. (22) investigated the effects of Sch 12,679 in a four-week open label study in 10 adolescent mentally retarded girls. They used several methods of evaluating changes in aggressive behavior. They concluded that the girls became less aggressive, more attentive and more interested and sociable than during the pre-study placebo period.

Conclusions

The present findings on the effects of minor tranquilizers on hostility can be summed up as follows: There is a complex interaction of minor tranquilizers, anxiety, depression and hostility. Unexpected outbursts of rage have been reported in patients taking chlordiazepoxide and diazepam, but these are rare; no such idiosyncratic side effects have been reported with oxazepam. There is an increase of hostility with chlordiazepoxide and diazepam in normal subjects; different benzodiazepines may have different effects which depend in part on personality factors such as being "action-oriented" or "not action-oriented." Chlordiazepoxide leads to a reduction of hostility and irritability in neurotic outpatients and perhaps increases healthy assertiveness. Diazepam increases hostile mood in depressed female outpatients but does not increase impulses to be overtly aggressive. There is evidence to suggest that oxazepam does not increase hostility and *may* lead to a greater reduction of hostility than other benzodiazepines. The differences among the effects of various benzodiazepines on hostility in neurotic patients will be clarified only after oxazepam and other benzodiazepines have been compared in large scale drug trials. In clinical practice it is rare for a patient who complains of excessive hostility to get a satisfactory result with oxazepam when the older benzodiazepines have failed, but, at the present state of knowledge, oxazepam is a rational choice in anxious and hostile neurotics, particularly if the hostility appears to be a side effect of another drug.

The extent to which the findings in neurotics who are hostile can be replicated in patients with personality disorders is not certain. There is evidence from only one study with juvenile delinquents in which a single dose of chlordiazepoxide reduced hostility. Moreover, most of the studies examined changes in verbal hostility as measured by self-rating scales, not changes in hostile and aggressive behavior. There is no evidence at present that minor tranquilizers are effective in the treatment of hostility and impulsiveness in sociopathic personalities. There is some evidence that benzodiazepines in large doses are effective in patients with the emotional dyscontrol syndrome, particularly if there is evidence that the emotional outbursts are of ictal origin.

Sch 12,679 appears to be a drug with interesting possibilities, but there are no published controlled studies in humans.

At present, because of the larger risk of addiction and greater incidence of toxic effects, there are no indications for prescribing meprobamate in hostile and anxious patients, and there is no evidence that it has any advantages over the safer benzodiazepines (23, 24).

MAJOR TRANQUILIZERS

Neuroleptics have tranquilizing effects in schizophrenic patients. Several controlled studies have shown that both hostility and aggression are reduced in both acute and chronic schizophrenics (25, 26). There are relatively few studies in which neuroleptics have been used in the treatment of patients with personality disorders.

Klein et al. (27) compared the effects of imipramine, chlorpromazine and placebo in over 300 non-chronic voluntary psychiatric patients. A part of this study was single-blind, with placebo as a control substance. The authors' impression was that in emotionally unstable character disorders both imipramine and chlorpromazine were more effective than placebo. However, the symptom of anger occurred more frequently when the patients were treated with imipramine than with either chlorpromazine or placebo. No differences were found between either drug or placebo in patients with hysterical disorders and in patients with passive-aggressive character disorders. This study suggests that patients with hysterical or passive-aggressive character disorders had not been helped by the drugs. The study was not double-blind and therefore subject to observer bias. However, it is the only study which examined the effects of chlorpromazine and imipramine in these personality disorders.

Lorr et al. (6) carried out a double-blind controlled trial of several drugs in a multi-centered VA study with Mental Hygiene Clinic patients. Although the majority of the patients were diagnosed as psychoneurotic, about one-quarter were diagnosed as suffering from personality disorders or psychophysiologic disorders. The medications compared were chlorpromazine 100 mg. daily, meprobamate 1600 mg. daily, and phenobarbital 130 mg. daily. All patients were treated once a week with individual psychotherapy. The patients were evaluated before treatment and at eight and 12 weeks. One hundred eighty patients completed the study. Outcome was assessed on 12 self-rating scales (including a scale of adjectives describing feeling states and scales designed to measure direct and indirect hostility) and 11 therapist's rating scales (which included ratings of anxiety and hostility). There were two control groups.

At eight weeks none of the self-ratings discriminated among the treatments except that the chlorpromazine group and the phenobarbital group reported *more* somatic discomfort than the other groups. Among the therapist's ratings there were no significant differences in anxiety among the groups. Verbalized hostility *increased* significantly for all three drug groups. At the end of 12 weeks there were no significant differences among the various groups, and the increase in hostility which was found at eight weeks had returned to baseline levels.

It is difficult to assess the implications of this study for the drug treatment of personality disorders. The patients participating in this study had various diagnoses and only a small proportion had personality disorders. The dose of chlorpromazine was small. The study suggests that a small dose of chlorpromazine in patients with mixed diagnoses produced no decrease in hostility. On the contrary, a temporary increase in verbal hostility occurred.

Molling et al. (28) examined the effects of perphenazine on the behavior of institutionalized delinquent boys. The boys' ages ranged from 10½ years to 14 years. They were selected for the study for their aggressivity, hostility, overactivity or withdrawn and neurotic behavior; some of the boys had other symptoms as well. Twenty-eight boys living in one cottage were randomly assigned to either perphenazine (up to 16 mg. a day) or placebo; another group in another cottage had no treatment. The outcome was rated by the house parents on a 61-item, four-point behavior rating scale. The medication period lasted for three weeks, followed by a three-week post-treatment observation period.

Both the perphenazine group and the placebo group showed decreases in rating, indicating improved behavior, but there was no significant difference between the two. The boys in the control cottage who had no treatment had deteriorated. On follow-up, the placebo group remained unchanged whereas there was an increase of symptoms in the perphena-zine group. This study showed no difference between the effects of per-phenazine and placebo. However, it is not possible to judge from the results of this study the effects of perphenazine on aggression or on socio-pathic behavior. The study period was too short, the number of boys in each treatment group was small and the symptoms treated were too heterogeneous for a single rating scale to measure treatment effects.

Propericyazine

Propericyazine or pericyazine (PPC) is a piperazine derivative re-sembling trifluoperazine and prochlorperazine (29). It has been claimed to be effective in the treatment of aggression and emotional outbursts in both psychotic patients and in patients with personality disorders (17). It is not available in the United States. There are several reports in the literature of uncontrolled studies of propericyazine in personality disorders.

Nimb (30) carried out uncontrolled studies in a municipal welfare home in Denmark. In one of the studies, 35 patients, mainly males with personality disorders, were treated with PPC. The patients' predominant features were asocial behavior, mood swings, or aggressiveness. According to the author, PPC was more effective than previous neuroleptics in that resentment, restlessness and lability of affect decreased conspicuously. Gayral (31) reported an uncontrolled study with PPC in children and adolescents aged mostly between six and 18 years. He used various psy-chotropic drugs, including neuroleptics, minor tranquilizers and anti-depressants. The children and the adolescents were suffering predomi-nantly from behavior and personality disorders. No results of ratings or self-ratings were described. The author expressed the opinion that PPC is effective in controlling impulsiveness and "acting out."

Bobon et al. (32) reported an uncontrolled study of 269 patients treated with PPC. Patients in this study were adults with sociopathic disorders, senile patients and children. The authors found over 50% "good" and "very good" results and concluded that PPC was effective in reducing aggression, impulsive behavior and "the manifestation of some other abnormal traits." Volmat (33) reported an uncontrolled study of PPC with 25 children and 36 adolescents. The dosages, individually ad-justed, did not exceed 30 mg. daily in most patients. No rating methods are described but the author reported that there was "an improvement of character and instability which was usually accompanied by improve-ment of school and training performance, or activity." The author also expressed the opinion that PPC suppressed anger and aggressive reactions.

Ferguson et al. (34) compared PPC and chlordiazepoxide in 28 patients with antisocial behavior. These medications were added under double-blind conditions to other medications which the patients were already receiving. There were no overall differences in outcome between the two groups, but patients who were receiving PPC were rated as less physically aggressive whereas patients on chlordiazepoxide were rated as less anxious, less depressed and less verbally aggressive. The authors do not describe the statistical methods used. Moreover, the results are difficult to evaluate because most patients were concomitantly taking other psychotropic drugs.

Rajotte and his colleagues (35) compared PPC and chlorpromazine (CPM) in 38 patients with behavior disorders in a double-blind parallel trial. No differences were found between the two drugs in ratings of aggressive behavior. Most of the patients had also been given other psychotropic drugs. Again no conclusions can be drawn from the study about the relative effects of PPC and chlorpromazine in aggressive behavior, mainly because most patients were concomitantly receiving other psychotropic drugs.

Conclusions

The studies on the effects of neuroleptics on behavior disorders are inconclusive. There appear to be differences among individuals in their response to neuroleptics (36) and there may be differences among neuroleptics in their effects on impulsive behavior. Neuroleptics, particularly low potency phenothiazines, which are usually prescribed in large doses (37) tend to lower the convulsive threshold and may precipitate seizures or aggravate behavior disorders (38-40). This perhaps does not apply to thioridazine (41). Thioridazine has also been used in combination with anticonvulsants in the treatment of behavior disorders in studies which are described in the section on anticonvulsants (36, 42).

Most of the studies on the effect of neuroleptics on personality disorders have methodological shortcomings, such as inadequate controls or inadequate statistical evaluations. There are a large number of published uncontrolled studies and many clinicians have used neuroleptics with apparent success in at least some patients with personality disorders; yet there is no conclusive evidence available at present that neuroleptics are useful drugs in the treatment of these patients.

There are a large number of published uncontrolled studies on the effects of diphenylhydantoin (DPH) on aggression, hostility and impulsiveness (40, 43-54). Most of these suggest that the drug has a beneficial effect on behavior disorders, particularly on aggressive and explosive behavior in both adults and children. Several controlled studies with psychiatric patients and with offenders have been published on the effects of DPH on hostility, violence and aggression.

Stephens and Shaffer (55) compared 300 mg. of DPH daily with 15 mg. daily in 30 patients suffering from anxiety neurosis. The smaller dose was used as a control substance instead of placebo. It was a double-blind crossover study lasting for six weeks. The data were analyzed both for a crossover design and for a parallel (between subjects) design. The patients had been carefully selected; an arbitrary score was chosen on the Barron Ego Strength Scale and only patients above this score were included in this study.

Both physician ratings and self-ratings significantly favored 300 mg. DPH over the smaller dose. There was a significantly greater reduction of anxiety symptoms and of symptoms of interpersonal difficulties such as symptoms of irritability, quarrelsomeness, temper outbursts and impatience. This is a well designed study; it shows that in neurotic patients DPH was effective in alleviating hostile symptoms such as irritability and temper outbursts.

Conners et al. (56) compared DPH (200 mg. daily) with methylphenidate (20 mg. daily) and placebo for two weeks in young delinquent boys. There were no differences between the two drugs and neither of the drugs was superior to placebo. This study is summarized more fully in the section on stimulants.

Gottschalk et al. (57) compared DPH 300 mg. daily with DPH 24 mg. (which was regarded as a placebo dose) in 44 inmates of an institution for emotionally disturbed criminal offenders. Only inmates who had breaches of discipline in the previous six months were asked to participate in this study. Outcome was assessed by the Gottschalk-Gleser Content Analysis Method. After six months none of the scales of the Content Analysis Scales discriminated between DPH 300 mg. daily and the smaller dose.

Lefkowitz (58) carried out a controlled study of DPH in delinquent boys with a mean age of about 15 years. All boys in the institution had been committed by the courts for an indefinite period. Fifty boys with the greatest number of episodes of destructive behavior were chosen for the experiment. The design was a parallel matched pair design, double-blind with random assignment to treatments. A dosage of 200 mg. DPH was compared with placebo. Altogether 11 outcome measures were used, including an aggressiveness scale, classroom behavior, inventory rating by psychiatrists, ratings by group activity workers and cottage staff follow-up ratings; these yielded a total of 93 scores. The study lasted for two and a half months. There was a significant decrease in aggressiveness in both groups. None of the measures significantly favored DPH over placebo. Eight subscales either approached or reached a significant level but the placebo group had a significantly *greater* reduction of "distress," "unhappiness," "negativism" and "aggressiveness."

This is a well designed study. Surprisingly, DPH had no beneficial effect on aggression, psychopathology or behavior. The author explained the somewhat greater effects of placebo as "a Hawthorne effect" in that toxicity associated with DPH may have reduced its overall benefit, increasing the relative effectiveness of the benign placebo. This result and the explanation cannot be accepted without replication. Only a few scales out of the total number yielded significant results in favor of placebo; this in itself could have been a chance result. However, the study showed clearly that DPH was not superior to placebo treatment in this population.

Monroe and Wise (14), in a study mentioned in the section on minor tranquilizers, studied the effects of primidone and chlordiazepoxide in acutely disturbed psychotic patients who had either seizures or episodic behavioral changes suggestive of altered states of awareness. It was an uncontrolled study with 55 patients; over one-half of the patients had been diagnosed as schizophrenic. Either chlordiazepoxide or primidone was added to the standard phenothiazine regimen. After having tried various combinations, they found an improvement in some of the patients on the combination of primidone with phenothiazines. Over one-third of the patients in this study were reported to have shown a definite improvement.

Itil and Rizzo (42) described a study of adolescents who had aggressive and explosive traits. They were treated with a combination of diphenylhydantoin up to 300 mg. daily and thioridazine up to 100 mg. daily. Fifteen patients were treated and 10 were in a control group. The authors do not mention whether it was a blind study. They found that a decrease of slow EEG activity, reduction of epileptic-like pattern on the EEG and an increase of alpha index were highly correlated with behavior and a decrease of rated psychopathology. It is somewhat difficult to evaluate the significance of this study. It is not certain whether the combination of these two drugs or one of the drugs alone was responsible for the changes in the EEG and the improvement in the patients' behavior.

Boelhouwer et al. (36) examined the effects of DPH and thioridazine in adolescents and young adults who were admitted because of antisocial behavior or uncontrollable impulsive behavior. They compared the effects in those patients who showed 14 and 6 per second positive spiking on the EEG and those without positive spiking. Seventy-eight patients were included in the study; the treatments were thioridazine 300 or 600 mg. daily, Dilantin 300 mg. daily, either singly or in combination, and placebo. They used a modified Latin-Square design. Each treatment phase lasted for eight weeks. There were significant differences between the responses of the two groups to treatment: The group with positive spiking showed a better response to the combination of thioridazine and diphenylhydantoin than to either drug alone. The group without positive spiking showed the best response to diphenylhydantoin alone.

The results of this study are congruent with those of Itil and Rizzo (42), in that they show a correlation between physiological measures and response to psychotropic drugs, a finding which could have implications for treatment. These studies require replications and extensions. Other studies have not shown consistent relationships between positive spiking and other measures, such as autonomic reactivity or psychological tests.

Carbamazepine differs from other antiepileptic drugs in that it is an iminostilbene derivative; the ring structure is identical to that of opipramol and similar to that of imipramine. A large number of studies have been published on the effects of carbamazepine in epileptics, in epileptic psychoses and in children with behavior disorders. Carbamazepine is an effective antiepileptic drug both in grand mal and partial seizures, including psychomotor seizures. In many of these studies, changes in behavior and in mood have been reported (see Dalby (59) for a recent review). In most uncontrolled studies with epileptics, including epileptic psychoses, the authors report improvement in mood and decreased irritability, impulsiveness and hostility. There have been a large number of reports of substantial improvement in the social adjustment of epileptic patients after treatment with carbamazepine was started. In a few patients an increase in irritability and explosiveness has been reported, particularly when there has been evidence of brain atrophy or dementia. There have been several controlled studies in which the psychotropic effects of carbamazepine in epileptics have been evaluated.

Bird et al. (60) carried out a controlled study with 46 mentally retarded epileptics. The study lasted for 18 months. One group continued with their previous medication, while the other group received carbamazepine instead of their usual anticonvulsants. The study was double-blind. No significant differences were found between the two groups in the number of epileptic attacks nor in behavior or social attitudes as assessed by nurses' observations. No rating scales were used. It is difficult to evaluate this study because of the absence of ratings. Apparently carbamazepine did not lead to conspicuous changes in behavior.

Marjerrison et al. (61) carried out a controlled study with 21 epileptics, most of whom suffered from various psychoses. Two psychiatrists rated the patients using the Inpatient Multidimensional Psychiatric Scale (IMPS). Nurses used the Psychotic Reaction Profile. At the beginning of the study the dosages of the patients' antipsychotic and anticonvulsant drugs were reduced to one-half and either phenobarbital or carbamazepine was substituted. The study was double-blind. During the study there were no significant differences between the number of seizures in the two groups. None of the IMPS factors differentiated significantly between the treatments. Two items of the psychiatrists' ratings and two items of the nurses' ratings favored carbamazepine: The ratings suggested that the patients treated with carbamazepine were more active and less sedated than patients treated with phenobarbital.

Rajotte et al. (62) compared the effects of carbamazepine with DPH in a double-blind controlled study with 24 hospitalized epileptics. It was a crossover design with each treatment block lasting six months. The patients were rated on the Rajotte Rating Scale which is a 16-item, seven-point rating scale that includes symptoms of personality disorders in epileptics such as "violent," "angry" and "quarrelsome." There was no difference between the two groups in the number of grand mal seizures. The scores of the behavior rating scales significantly favored the carbamazepine group. This is a well designed study and the findings suggest that carbamazepine was more effective than DPH in the control of behavior disorders of institutionalized epileptics.

Pryce-Phillips and Jeavons (63) carried out a double-blind parallel drug trial of carbamazepine and placebo in 22 hospitalized epileptics. The study lasted for 16 weeks. The dosage was increased at regular intervals to 600 mg. in the sixth week and then reduced. There was no difference between the two groups in the numbers of convulsions. There was initially a decrease in aggressive behavior and an improvement of ward cooperation with carbamazepine, but this was not maintained. The physical activity of the patients decreased while treated with carbamazepine.

This study did not show significant behavioral changes between the two groups, except that physical activity diminished with carbamazepine.

This was a placebo controlled study whereas in the previous studies the control substances were other anticonvulsant drugs. This may mean that the increased activity and alertness of patients on carbamazepine reported in the previous studies are more likely to be caused by the absence of the sedative effects of the traditional anticonvulsants than by psychotropic effects of carbamazepine.

Rodin et al. (64) compared carbamazepine and placebo in 37 patients who suffered from uncontrolled clinical psychomotor seizures. Their study was preceded by a baseline period of low therapeutic doses of DPH and phenobarbital. The design was a three-week crossover of carbamazepine and placebo. An attempt was made to achieve a therapeutic level of carbamazepine between 5 and 7 μg/ml. (serum). Nurses recorded verbal or physical aggressive outbursts and "behavioral observations" were made by the ward physician. Apparently no ratings were carried out. There was a striking reduction of psychomotor seizures with carbamazepine; there was no change in aggressive outbursts. Although there was a significant reduction of psychomotor seizures on carbamazepine, there were no significant changes in behavior. No ratings were carried out, but this study appears to be in accord with the results of the previous study that in epileptics carbamazepine had no greater effect on aggression than placebo.

Cereghino et al. (65) compared DPH, phenobarbital and carbamazepine (1200 mg. daily) in a double-blind Latin-Square design with each treatment block lasting 21 days. There was a two-week period intervening between the experimental treatments, when patients received their usual anticonvulsant medication. The patients were hospitalized epileptics who suffered predominantly from both grand mal and partial seizures. The authors constructed a rating scale of behavior which consisted of 53 items; 23 were modified from the Ward Behavior Rating Scale (Burdock) and 30 items were added which were devised for this study. Target symptoms which the patient displayed before the study were selected from this scale and subsequently each symptom was rated on a three-point bipolar scale. The changes in behavior were not evaluated statistically; only the percentage of patients who improved, deteriorated or remained the same are listed. There appeared to be greater improvement of behavior with carbamazepine. It is difficult to evaluate the changes in behavior which occurred in this study because the results of the various items or clusters of the scale are not described and no statistical evaluations are reported. Judging by the percentage of improved patients, there was a trend toward greater improvement with carbamazepine.

Rodin et al. (66) compared the effects of a combination of carbamazepine and DPH with those of a combination of primidone and DPH. Forty-five epileptic outpatients, who had either grand mal or psychomotor seizures or both, participated. The patients were initially treated with DPH until an adequate serum level was reached and then either primidone or carbamazepine was added. It was a simple crossover design with each treatment lasting for three months. The study was double-blind for the psychologists who carried out tests and single-blind for the treating neurologist.

There were no significant differences in the incidence of seizures. The authors published only a summary of the psychological test results, which indicated that the patients showed significantly smaller impairment on the repeatable cognitive perceptual motor battery. They became progressively less depressed and scored significantly lower on the psychopathic deviate scale of the MMPI while treated with the carbamazepine-DPH combination. The published summary of the psychological tests suggests that the psychotropic effects of the combination of carbamazepine and DPH were more favorable than those of the combination of primidone and DPH.

Conclusions

Diphenylhydantoin (DPH) was found to be effective in the treatment ment of neurotic patients in that it reduced anxiety and feelings of irritabiilty and hostility. Although there are a large number of favorable reports on DPH in the treatment of aggression and hostility in open label studies, in controlled studies of delinquents and sociopathic personalities DPH was not more effective than placebo. It appears that the irritability and hostility experienced by neurotic patients are amenable to treatment with DPH, but it is largely ineffective in the treatment of similar symptoms in patients with sociopathic personalities.

The disappointing outcome of the controlled studies does not preclude the possibility that there is a small proportion of patients in whom DPH or other anticonvulsants have substantial beneficial effects. For example, in Boelhouwer et al.'s study (36) patients without positive spiking apparently benefited from DPH alone. There is some evidence that combinations of anticonvulsants with other drugs have beneficial effects in the emotional dyscontrol syndrome. The studies by Monroe (67), Monroe and Wise (14), Itil and Rizzo (42) and Boelhouwer et al. (36) suggest that in some patients the combination of an anticonvulsant with another drug may be more effective than the anticonvulsant alone.

In placebo controlled studies, carbamazepine did not improve the behavior of mentally retarded epileptics and the epileptics who were psychotic. Carbamazepine caused less sedation than DPH. In one study with epileptics carbamazepine was associated with a significantly greater improvement in behavior than DPH; a similar trend was found in another study. Epileptic patients were found to be less depressed when treated with a combination of carbamazepine and DPH than when treated with primidone and DPH. The two placebo controlled studies yielded somewhat conflicting results: In one study no changes in behavior were noted while in the other small changes were observed. It seemed that the improvement in mood and behavior with carbamezepine in epileptics was caused, in part, by the decrease in sedation brought about by replacing the previous sedative anticonvulsant drugs.

Carbamazepine appeared to be effective in uncontrolled studies with patients with the emotional dyscontrol syndrome. There have been no controlled studies of carbamazepine in patients with personality disorders who were not epileptic.

STIMULANTS

Beneficial effects of amphetamines and methylphenidate in the treatment of disturbed behavior in children have been found in several controlled studies (68-71). There are two reports of uncontrolled studies with adult psychopaths (72, 73). Three controlled studies have been published in which stimulants were used in delinquent adolescent boys.

Korey (74) carried out one of the early studies of the pharmacological treatment of personality disorders. In 1944, several years before controlled studies became customary in medicine, he compared the effects of amphetamine with placebo in a single-blind controlled study. Twenty boys who were regarded as severely delinquent were selected from inmates of the National Training School for Boys. Their ages ranged from 14 to 19. The boys apparently displayed impulsiveness and were all severely delinquent. In the group treated with amphetamine, about one-half of the boys either reported they were feeling better or their behavior was reported to have improved.

Conners et al. (56) compared the effects of DPH and methylphenidate in delinquent boys. Forty-three delinquent boys (mean age 12 years) in a residential training school were selected as being the most aggressive or disturbing in their cottages. This was a parallel design trial lasting two weeks, with DPH 200 mg. daily, methylphenidate 20 mg. daily and placebo. The cottage parents filled in a 36-item, four-point symptom rating scale. In addition, the staff filled in a daily log of good and bad behavior which two raters examined independently. The school teachers filled in an 11-item behavior rating scale. The Rosenzweig Picture Frustration Test and the Proteus Mazes were administered at the end of the treatment. A structured interview was conducted with each child to evaluate the effect of the drug, including effects on anxiety, sadness, anger and somatic complaints. The boys in the placebo group had more symptoms before treatment. None of the criteria used showed any beneficial effects of either DPH or methylphenidate and subjective reports tended to show negative effects; however, this was a brief study, the number in each group was small, and the groups were heterogeneous, which may have been responsible for the negative outcome.

Eisenberg et al. (75) compared the effects of dextroamphetamine and placebo in delinquent adolescents. Forty-two delinquent Negro boys, living at a boys' village, were selected on the grounds that they were the most troublesome and most difficult to manage. Their ages ranged from 11 to 17, with a median of 14 years. They were divided into three matched groups, one group treated with dextroamphetamine, one with placebo and one group with no treatment. Each boy was rated by his house parents and by his classroom teacher on a four-point, 43-item symptom rating scale. Peer perception and self-perception were evaluated by a sociogram (Bowers and Larson Class Play). The study lasted for four and a half months. There was a significant reduction of rated disturbed behavior with dextroamphetamine, with no significant differences between placebo and the control group. There were no differences among the three groups in self-perception as measured by the sociogram and there was only a nonsignificant trend in the drug group toward improvement in perception by peers. Statistically significant differences were found in favor of amphetamine in that destructive behavior improved, in spite of the fact that it was a small study with only 14 boys in the experimental group.

There are several published reports on drug treatment of adults who have been suspected of having minimal brain dysfunction (MBD). The literature on the relationship of MBD in children to subsequent abnormalities in adult life, including personality disorders, has been reviewed by several authors (76-78). Stimulants have been used in the treatment of these adults in several uncontrolled studies (76, 79, 80) and in one controlled study (78).

Wood et al. (78) carried out a double-blind study with 11 adults who appeared to suffer from MBD and who were judged by history to have been hyperactive in childhood. They used a crossover design with each treatment period lasting for two weeks. The treatments were methylphenidate hydrochloride (up to 60 mg. daily) and placebo. The patients' most prominent symptoms were impulsivity, irritability, inattentiveness, restlessness and emotional lability. Using research diagnostic criteria, the researchers determined that the patients had a variety of nonpsychotic diagnoses, including antisocial disorder, drug or alcohol abuse, and generalized anxiety disorder. The outcome was evaluated on a five-item, seven-point self-rating scale with items such as "calm-nervous" and "concentrating-mind wandering." Four of these five scales significantly favored methylphenidate over placebo; the only exception was the item "happy-sad" which did not discriminate significantly between the two treatments. After the double-blind trial these and an additional four patients were treated, apparently successfully, in an uncontrolled study with either pemoline or a tricyclic antidepressant, both drugs which have been used in children with MBD. None of the patients showed a tendency to abuse methylphenidate; two women who had a tendency to abuse drugs before the trial terminated this behavior when their irritability and anger diminished during the trial.

The findings of this study suggest that methylphenidate, and perhaps other stimulants, are effective in some adults who had symptoms of MBD in childhood and who still manifest some of these symptoms. The findings tend to support the authors' conclusion that some adults who had been diagnosed as having MBD in childhood have a persistent abnormality which is concealed by other diagnostic labels because of the tendency for the symptoms to change in adult life.

Conclusions

Stimulants have been found to be effective in the treatment of juvenile delinquents. One of the studies showed no difference between methylphenidate and placebo, but this study lasted only two weeks and may have been too short to show measurable differences in the effects of the treatments. In the two studies of amphetamines with juvenile delinquents, the findings suggest that at least some boys benefited subjectively and that their behavior improved. There are no long-term studies available and it is not known how long such improvement would be maintained. Moreover, there is a risk that juvenile delinquents would exceed the prescribed dose and abuse stimulants if the treatment was in an outpatient setting.

Methylphenidate was found to be effective in one controlled study with adults who had long-term psychiatric abnormalities, including personality disorders, and who apparently had had symptoms of minimal brain dysfunction in childhood. There are no other controlled studies of stimulants in adults with personality disorders.

LITHIUM

Several studies of the treatment of personality disorders with lithium have been published.

Sheard (81) carried out an open label multiple crossover study with lithium carbonate in 12 young male delinquents. Their common characteristic was that they had shown repeated impulsive and aggressive behavior which frequently got them into trouble with the law. All had personality disorders. The delinquents had a battery of both psychological and behavioral tests before they entered the trial; they were treated for four months inside the institution and had 12 months of follow-up treatment after release. While in the institution the treatment consisted of two periods: four weeks of high lithium level (0.6 to 1.5 meq/L) treatment alternated with four weeks at a low level (less than 0.6 meq/L). During the follow-up an attempt was made to achieve the higher of the two lithium levels, but, as the subjects were unreliable in taking their drugs, the actual serum level varied a great deal. It was found that the number of serious aggressive episodes decreased when the serum lithium was between 0.6 to 1.5 meq/L, as compared to the times when the lithium level was below 0.6 meq/L. It also appeared that serious aggressive incidents decreased more than did the total of all antisocial incidents.

The study was not double-blind; however, some assessments were carried out without the assessor's knowledge of the design (such as tickets by prison authorities and self-ratings). These also favored lithium over placebo. An interesting finding in this study was that, in delinquents whose aggressive behavior appeared to be an integral aspect of their personality, reduction in aggressive affect was associated with a concomitant increase in anxiety and depression. In four individuals whose destructive behavior was a source of anxiety, a reduction of aggressive affect occurred without an increase in depressive affect or anxiety.

Tupin et al. (82) examined the effects of lithium in prisoners who had been selected because they had shown patterns of recurrent violence and reacted rapidly to slight provocations with anger and violent behavior. Commonly encountered features in this population were a history of brain injury and non-specifically abnormal EEG's. The prisoners had various psychiatric diagnoses; the largest group were explosive personalities and the next largest group carried a diagnosis of "schizophrenia" or "possible schizophrenia." The prisoners had been treated previously with phenothiazines, which reduced the psychotic symptomatology in schizophrenic patients but did not control their violent behavior. Outcome of treatment was evaluated from various sources, such as reports from prison guards concerning rule infractions, changes in security classifications, reports from the prisoners and observations by psychiatric staff. There was a significant decrease in the number of disciplinary actions for violent behavior during lithium treatment as compared to the same time period before lithium. The number of non-violent disciplinary actions decreased, but this change did not reach a significant level. Security classifications decreased during the study and the prisoners reported that they experienced a greater capacity to reflect on the consequences of their actions, a greater ability to control angry feelings when provoked and a diminished intensity of angry affect. The psychiatric staff reported a decrease in aggressive behavior. Sixteen of the 21 subjects who were judged to have improved had an abnormal EEG or a history suggestive of brain damage. The dosage of lithium tended to be higher than is necessary for the maintenance treatment of manic-depressive illness. The authors commented that the reduction of aggressiveness seemed to create significant psychic turmoil in many of the prisoners.

This is an uncontrolled study and thus is subject to observer bias. However, the observation that violent and aggressive acts decreased more than non-violent sociopathic behavior is less likely to be biased (an observation which is similar to that made by Sheard) and would suggest that lithium had a specific effect on violent and aggressive behavior.

Rifkin et al. (83) examined the effects of lithium carbonate in patients with emotionally unstable character disorder (EUCD) in a double-blind crossover study with 21 patients. The authors describe the main characteristics of the EUCD as follows: mood swings, chronic maladaptive behavior patterns, poor acceptance of authority, poor work record, manipulativeness, often sexual promiscuity and abuse of drugs. The mood swings are unusually not reactions to environmental or interpersonal events. In this study lithium was found to be decidedly more effective than placebo in reducing the severity of the mood swings.

Patients with EUCD have previously been treated successfully with chlorpromazine in an open label study (27). Although no direct comparison between chlorpromazine and lithium in these disorders has been made, it appears that while chlorpromazine has a calming effect during the episodes of elevated mood, lithium has both a calming and an antidepressant effect. Apart from the important therapeutic implications, this study is of theoretical interest because it suggests a possible relationship between the emotionally unstable character disorders and manic-depressive illness.

Sheard et al. (84) carried out a double-blind study in a correctional institution with young delinquent inmates with severe personality disorders. The main criteria for selection were convictions for serious aggressive crimes such as manslaughter, murder or rape, and a history of either chronic assaultive behavior or chronic impulsive antisocial behavior. The inmates' ages ranged from 16 to 27 with a mean somewhat over 19 years. Eighty inmates started the study and 66 completed it. The drug was preceded by a one-month study period without medication; the trial lasted three months, after which there was a final month of study without medication. It was a parallel (between subjects) design of either sustained release lithium carbonate or placebo. The assignment to treatments was random. The initial evaluation consisted of eight tests and personality inventories, including the Minnesota Multiphasic Personality Inventory, the Rotter Intraversion-Extraversion Scale, the Eysenck Personality Inventory, the Buss-Durkee Hostility Inventory and the Personality Research Form. The same tests were administered after the drug trial was completed, during the final drug-free month. The changes during the study were assessed by the number of infractions of institution rules: major infractions, consisting of seriously threatening behavior or actual assaults, or minor infractions, which were less serious offenses. Another test battery, consisting of four psychological tests, including the Affect Adjective Checklist and the Rosenzweig Picture Frustration Test, was administered and Behavior Rating Scales were completed weekly by the authors. The decrease in the number of infractions was significantly greater in the drug group. There was a striking reduction in the incidence of major infractions in the lithium group, which decreased month by month until at the end of the fourth month it reached zero. The number of infractions increased again in the lithium group after the medication was withdrawn. In a linear discriminate function analysis the infraction scores had the greatest weight and the hostility scale of the MAACL the next greatest weight.

This is a well designed study and the results are impressive. The study has a few flaws—for example, because of a chance result of random assignment there were racial differences between the drug group and the placebo group—but analysis of the data suggests that the demographic differences and differences between prestudy measures of the two gruops did not substantially affect the results of the study. The results confirm the findings of earlier studies that lithium is effective in reducing aggression in personality disorders.

Conclusion

Maintenance treatment with lithium is a promising and hopeful development in the treatment of personality disorders in patients who are explosive, impulsive and emotionally unstable. The effective serum level appears to be similar or perhaps somewhat higher than that which is required to prevent affective episodes in patients with manic-depressive illness. It is possible that the optimum serum level varies among individuals and has to be determined for each patient. Lithium treatment has the disadvantage that its side effects are poorly tolerated by impulsive and emotionally unstable patients and if they experience troublesome side effects they are likely to discontinue the drug. The characteristics of patients who are likely to respond have been described by the various authors; however, the prediction of a good response in any individual cannot be made with accuracy. Patients with personality disorders who show impulsiveness, instability of mood, or unpremeditated aggression should have a trial of treatment with lithium, particularly if the effects of other treatments have been inadequate.

The Effects of Lithium on the Aggressive Behavior of Epileptics

Morrison et al. (85) examined, in an uncontrolled study, the effects of lithium on combative behavior. Several of the patients were epileptics. In the first part of the study 20 inpatients who had been hopsitalized for an average of two years were studied. All of the patients showed hyper-aggressive behavior; 11 had frequent clinical seizures and abnormal EEG's; seven had abnormal EEG's without seizures. Sixteen patients had made repeated physical attacks on ward personnel or other patients or both. Four of the patients with abnormal EEG's appeared to have been impulsive without overt aggression. In the second part of the study seven patients who had been referred because of hyperaggressive behavior were studied; four were schizophrenics and three had personality disorders. Apparently these patients had normal EEG's. The patients were evaluated after three weeks on placebo and after three weeks on lithium by means of the Buss-Durkee Inventory and a nurses' rating scale. In the first part of the study 15 of the 18 patients with abnormal EEG's were found to have improved; there was a reduction in the frequency of hyper-aggressive and assaultive behavior and a decreased tendency to quarrel while treated with lithium. In the second group, the patients who had normal EEG's, behavioral changes were less noticeable.

A few patients who had a history of long-standing aggressive behavior apparently showed conspicuous changes. The part of the study in which the changes were observed was not controlled and it is difficult to evaluate the findings.

Jus et al. (86) examined the effects of lithium in eight female patients with temporal lobe epilepsy. During the study the patients continued with their routine anticonvulsant medication. The number of seizures increased and behavior became more impaired in these patients as compared to a control group which was not receiving lithium.

Erwin et al. (87) reported beneficial effects in the treatment of patients with grand mal epilepsy and psychomotor epilepsy in an open label study with lithium. This study has not been published and cannot be evaluated; the results of this study have been summarized by Lion (88).

Conclusion

The reports on the effects of lithium in epileptics are conflicting. The evidence suggests that both epilepsy and behavior disturbance can be aggravated by the administration of lithium; thus, if lithium is to be tried at all this should be done with caution and only when other treatment modalities have failed. However, the observations in Tupin's study suggest that a history of either brain damage or an abnormal EEG without seizures is not a contraindication to treatment with lithium.

SUMMARY

Compared with schizophrenia, affective disorders and neuroses, there have been only few controlled drug trials in patients with personality disorders. Most controlled studies with personality disorders and delinquents deal with patients who were selected by clinical diagnosis. It is not possible to relate these results to the diagnostical categories derived from factor analytic studies of personality inventories or biographical data or to diagnostic categories derived from psychophysiological experiments.

During the last few years evidence has accumulated that individuals whose behavior is often labeled as sociopathic can benefit from drug treatment if their predominant symptoms are uncontrollable aggression, impulsiveness or lability of mood.

The most promising development in recent years has been the treatment of personality disorders with lithium. Controlled studies suggest that in patients with emotionally unstable character disorders lithium has a beneficial effect. Similarly, in violent offenders lithium reduces the tendency to aggression and violence.

The effects of benzodiazepines on hostility appear to be complex. In normal subjects chlordiazepoxide tends to increase feelings of hostility, whereas in anxious and irritable neurotic outpatients chlordiazepoxide decreases hostility. In depressed, nonpsychotic female outpatients diazepam tends to increase hostile mood but not impulses to be overtly aggressive. In normals diazepam apparently has different effects, depending in part on personality factors such as being "action oriented" or "non-action oriented." Unexpected rage has been reported as an idiosyncratic side effect in the treatment of neurotics with chlordiazepoxide and diazepam but this is a very rare occurrence; no such idiosyncratic side effects have been reported with oxazepam. In controlled studies with normal subjects oxazepam has not been found to increase hostility; in neurotic patients it appears to reduce hostility more than other benzodiazepines. When explosiveness is of ictal origin, benzodiazepines in adequate doses, either alone or in combination with other drugs, may have a beneficial effect; there is inadequate evidence at present that benzodiazepines are effective in the treatment of hostility in personality disorders. Several controlled studies with benzodiazepines will be required to clarify conclusively the effects of benzodiazepines on hostility in neurotic patients and in patients with personality disorders.

Sch 12,679, a benzazepine derivative, is an experimental drug. There is evidence from animal studies to suggest that it has specific antiaggressive effects but there are no controlled studies in humans.

The effects of diphenylhydantoin on hostility tend to vary with the diagnostic category. There is evidence that DPH reduces hostility and anxiety in neurotic patients. The results of drug trials of anticonvulsants with personality disorders are somewhat conflicting. There is no evidence from controlled studies that anticonvulsants are effective in the treatment of antisocial personalities or in delinquents. There is some evidence that anticonvulsants are effective in combination with other drugs in the treatment of impulsive behavior in patients with emotional dyscontrol syndrome. In uncontrolled studies carbamazepine has been reported to be effective in this syndrome. In epileptics carbamazepine was found to be more effective than other anticonvulsants in improving behavior and social effectiveness. There are no published controlled studies of carbamazepine in patients with personality disorders who are not epileptic.

Neuroleptics have been found to reduce hostility and aggression in both acute and chronic schizophrenics but there is no conclusive evidence that they are effective in the control of these symptoms in patients who are not psychotic. In some patients low potency phenothiazines may aggravate the tendency to aggression, apparently because they lower the convulsive threshold. This perhaps does not apply to thioridazine.

Propericyazine, which is not marketed in the United States, has been reported to be more effective than other neuroleptics in the treatment of personality disorders, but there are no adequately controlled studies to support this observation.

Amphetamines have been found effective in the treatment of juvenile delinquents; however, these were short-term studies and it is not known how long the improvement could be maintained. Moreover, in the outpatient treatment of delinquents there is the risk of habituation and drug abuse. There is evidence from one study to suggest that methylphenidate is effective in some adults who were hyperactive in childhood and who perhaps had persisting symptoms of minimal brain dysfunction.

Sociopathic behavior without the tendency to aggression, violence, impulsiveness and mood swings does not appear to be altered by drug treatment. There are no published controlled drug trials with inadequate personalities who have descended into crime, with the "inadequate psychopaths," or the "neurotic psychopaths" of factor analytic studies. While studies in clinical pharmacology have shown that some traits and some target symptoms in personality disorders and delinquents can be effectively treated with psychotropic medications, there is no single drug or class of drugs which is suitable for the treatment of people whose behaviors are labeled deviant or antisocial. Other chapters in the present volume show that diagnosis of sociopathy and its various subgroups is becoming more precise; surveys of drug studies indicate that the design of drug studies has been becoming more rigorous. It is likely that within the next few years more evidence will accumulate for the rational choice of drugs in the treatment of sociopathic behaviors and disorders.

REFERENCES

1. GARDOS, G., DiMASCIO, A., SALZMAN, C. and SHADER, R. I. Differential Actions of Chlordiazepoxide and Oxazepam on Hostility. *Arch. Gen. Psychiatry* 18:757-760, 1968.
2. DiMASCIO, A., SHADER, R. I., and HARMATZ, J. Psychotropic Drugs and Induced Hostility. *Psychosomatics* 10:46-47, 1969.
3. SALZMAN, C., KOCHANSKY, G. E., SHADER, R. I., PORRINO, L. J., HARMATZ, J. S., and SWETT, C. P. Chlordiazepoxide Induced Hostility in a Small Group Setting. *Arch. Gen. Psychiatry* 31:401-405, 1974.
4. McDONALD, R. L. The Effects of Personality Type on Drug Response. *Arch. Gen. Psychiatry* 17:680-686, 1967.
5. GLESER, G. C., GOTTSCHALK, L. A., FOX, R., and LIPPERT, W. Immediate Changes in Affect with Chlordiazepoxide. *Arch. Gen. Psychiatry* 13:291-295, 1965.
6. LORR, M., McNAIR, D. M., WEINSTEIN, G. J., MICHAUX, W. M., and RASKIN, A. Meprobamate and Chlorpromazine in Psychotherapy. *Arch. Gen. Psychiatry* 4:75-83, 1961.
7. FELDMAN, P. E. Current Views on Antianxiety Agents. Pamphlet from a scientific exhibit presented at the Annual Meeting of the American Medical Association, Houston, Texas, November, 1967.
8. PODOBNIKAR, I. Implementation of Psychotherapy by Librium in a Pioneering Rural-Industrial Psychiatric Practice. *Psychosomatics* 12:205-209, 1971.
9. McNAIR, D. M., GOLDSTEIN, A. P., LORR, M., CIBELL, L. A. and ROTH, J. Some Ef-

fects of Chlordiazepoxide and Meprobamate with Psychiatric Outpatients. *Psychopharmacologia* 7:256-265, 1965.

10. RICKELS, K. and DOWNING, R. W. Chlordiazepoxide and Hostility in Anxious Outpatients. *Am. J. Psychiatry* 131:442-444, 1974.

11. RICKELS, K. and CLYDE, D. J. Clyde Mood Scale Changes in Anxious Outpatients Produced by Chlordiazepoxide Therapy. *J. Nerv. Ment. Dis.* 145:154-157, 1967.

12. COVI, L., LIPMAN, R. S., and SMITH, V. K. Diazepam Induced Hostility in Depression. Paper presented at the Annual Meeting of the American Psychiatric Association in Toronto, Canada, May 2-6, 1977.

13. SHADER, R. I. Drugs in the Management of Anxiety. *Curr. Psychiatr. Ther.* 11:81-85, 1971.

14. MONROE, R. R. and WISE, S. P. III: Combined Phenothiazine, Chlordiazepoxide and Primidone Therapy for Uncontrolled Psychotic Patients. *Am. J. Psychiatry* 122:694-698, 1965.

15. MONROE, R. R., KRAMER, M.D., GOULDING, R. and WISE, S. EEG Activation of Patients Receiving Phenothiazines and Chlordiazepoxide. *J. Nerv. Ment. Dis.* 141:100-107, 1965.

16. GODDARD, P. and LOKARE, V. G. Diazepam in the Management of Epilepsy. *Br. J. Psychiatry* 114:213-214, 1970.

17. ITIL, T. M., and WADUD, A. Treatment of Human Aggression with Major Tranquilizers, Antidepressants and Newer Psychotropic Drugs. *J. Nerv. Ment. Dis.* 100:83-99, 1975.

18. BARNETT, A., MALICK, J. B. and TABER, R. I. Chemical and Electrical Treatment of Aggression. *Psychopharm. Bull.* 9:17, 1973.

19. KESKINER, A., ITIL, T. M., HAN, T. H., SALETU, B. and HSU, W. Clinical, Toxicological and Electroencephalographic Study with Sch 12,679 in Chronic Schizophrenics. *Curr. Therap. Res.* 13:714-725, 1971.

20. PARK, S., GERSHON, S., and FLOYD, A. A Clinical Trial of a Benzazepine (Sch 12,679) in Acute Schizophrenic Patients. *Curr. Therap. Res.* 14:298-302, 1972.

21. ALBERT, J. M., LANGLOIS, Y. and GRAVEL, L. Étude Pilote Du SCH-12679 chez des arriérés mentaux profonds présentant des troubles graves du comportement. *L'Union Médicale Du Canada* 104:904-909, 1975.

22. ITIL, T. M., STOCK, M. J., DUFFY, A. D., ESQUENAZI, A., SALETU, B., and HAN, T. H. Therapeutic Trials and EEG Investigations with Sch 12,679 in Behaviorally Disturbed Adolescents. *Curr. Therap. Res.* 14:136-150, 1972.

23. KELLNER, R. Drugs, Diagnoses and Outcome of Drug Trials with Neurotic Patients: A Survey. *J. Nerv. Ment. Dis.* 151:85-96, 1970.

24. KELLNER, R. Unwanted Effects of Minor Tranquilizers and Hypnotics. *Psychiatric Annals* 5:457-463, 1975.

25. KLEIN, D. F. Importance of Psychiatric Diagnosis in Prediction of Clinical Drug Effect. *Arch. Gen. Psychiatry* 16:118-126, 1967.

26. KLEIN, D. F. Psychiatric Diagnosis and a Typology of Clinical Drug Effects. *Psychopharmacologia* 13:359-386, 1968.

27. KLEIN, D. F., HONIGFELD, G., and FELDMAN, S. Prediction of Drug Effect in Personality Disorders. *J. Nerv. Ment. Dis.* 152:183-198, 1973.

28. MOLLING, P. A., LOCKNER, A. W., SAULS, R. J., et al. Committed Delinquent Boys. *Arch. Gen. Psychiatry* 7:96-102, 1962.

29. NINEHAM, A. W. An Outline of the Chemical and Pharmacological Properties of Pericyazine. In: F. A. Jenner, et al. (Eds.), *Proceedings of the Leeds Symposium on Behavioural Disorders.* London: May and Baker LTD, 1965.

30. NIMB, M. Experience with Pericyazine in a Welfare Home. In: F. A. Jenner, et al. (Eds.), *Proceedings of the Leeds Symposium on Behavioural Disorders.* London: May and Baker Ltd., 1965.

31. GAYRAL, L. A Clinical Report on Treatment of Behavior and Personality Dis-

orders in Children and Adolescents. In: F. A. Jenner, *et al* (Eds.), *Proceedings of the Leeds Symposium on Behavioural Disorders*. London: May and Baker LTD, 1965.

32. BOBON, J., GERNAY, J. M., COLLARD, J., GOFFIOUL, F., and BREULET, M. Bad Character and Neuleptil; on a Belgian Luxemburger Clinical Experience (1963-1964). *Acta Neurol. Psychiatr. Belg.* 68:154-162, 1968.

33. VOLMAT, R. Three Years Experience with Pericyazine in the Treatment of 650 Patients with Disorders of Character and Behaviour. In: F. A. Jenner, *et al.* (Eds.), *Proceedings of the Leeds Symposium on Behavioural Disorders*. London: May and Baker LTD, 1965.

34. FERGUSON, K., BAN, T. A., LEHMANN, H. E., and LEE, M. A. Etude comparative de la propericiazine dans le controle du comportement antisocial. *L'Union Med. du Canada* 96:448-449, 1967.

35. RAJOTTE, P., GIARD, N., and TETREAULT, L. A Controlled Trial of Propericyazine and Chlorpromazine in Behavior Disorders. *Curr. Therap. Res.* 8:166-174, 1968.

36. BOELHOUWER, C., HENRY, C. E., and GLUECK, B. C. Positive Spiking. A Double-Blind Control Study on Its Significance in Behavior Disorders, Both Diagnostically and Therapeutically. *Am. J. Psychiatry* 125:65-73, 1968.

37. ITIL, T. M. and MYERS, J. P. Epileptic and Anti-epileptic Properties of Psychotropic Drugs. *International Encyclopedia of Pharmacology and Therapeutics*, Vol. 2, Section 19, Mercier, J. (Ed.). Oxford and New York: Pergamon Press, 1973.

38. FABISH, W. The Effect of Chlorpromazine on the EEG of Epileptics. *J. Neurol. Neurosurg. Psychiat.* 20:185, 1957.

39. HANKOFF, L. D., KAYE, H. E., ENGELHARDT, D. M., and FREEDMAN, N. Convulsions Complicating Ataractic Therapy, Their Incidence and Theoretical Implications. *N.Y. State J. Med.* 57:2967-2974, 1957.

40. JONAS, A. D. *Ictal and Subictal Neurosis, Diagnosis and Treatment.* Springfield, Ill.: Charles C Thomas, 1965.

41. KAMM, I. and MANDEL, A. Thioridazine in the Treatment of Behavior Disorders in Epileptics. *Dis. Nerv. Syst.* 28:46-48, 1967.

42. ITIL, T. M. and RIZZO, A. E. Behavior and Quantitative EEG Correlations During Treatment of Behavior-Disturbed Adolescents. *Electroencephalogr. Clin. Neurophysiol.* 23:81, 1967.

43. BALDWIN, R. and KENNEY, T. J. In: J. Hellmuth (Ed.), *Learning Disabilities II Seattle.* Special Child Publications of the Seattle Sequin School, Inc., 1966.

44. BRILL, N. Q. and WALKER, E. F. Psychopathic Behavior with Latent Epilepsy. *J. Nerv. Ment. Dis.* 101:545-549, 1945.

45. FREYHAN, F. A. Effectiveness of Diphenylhydantoin in Management of Nonepileptic Psychomotor Excitement States. *Arch. Neurol. Psychiat.* 53:370-374, 1945.

46. KALINOWSKY, L. B. and PUTNAM, T. J. Attempts of Treatment of Schizophrenia and Other Nonepileptic Psychoses with Dilantin. *Arch. Neurol. Psychiat.* 49:414-420, 1943.

47. KLEIN, D. F. and GREENBERG, I. M. Behavioral Effects of Diphenylhydantoin in Severe Psychiatric Disorders. *Am. J. Psychiatry* 124:847-849, 1967.

48. PASAMANICK, B. Anticonvulsant Drug Therapy of Behavior Problem Children with Abnormal Electroencephalograms. *Arch. Neurol. Psychiat.* 65:752-766, 1951.

49. PUTNAM, T. J. and HOOD, O. E. Project Illinois: A Study of Therapy in Juvenile Behavior Problems. *Western Med.* 5:231-233, 1964.

50. RESNICK, O. The Psychoactive Properties of Diphenylhydantoin: Experiences with Prisoners and Juvenile Delinquents. *Int. J. Neuropsychiat.* 1:30-48, 1967.

51. SILVERMAN, D. The Electroencephalograph and Therapy of Criminal Psychopaths. *J. Crimin. Psychopathol.* 5:439, 1934.

328

52. TURNER, W. J. The Usefulness of Diphenylhydantoin in Treatment of Nonepileptic Disorders. *Int. J. Neuropsychiat.* 3:8-20, 1967.
53. WALKER, C. F. and KIRKPATRICK, B. B. Dilantin Treatment for Behavior Problem Children with Normal Electroencephalograms. *Am. J. Psychiatry* 103:484-492, 1947.
54. ZIMMERMAN, F. T. Explosive Behavior Anomalies Children on an Epileptic Basis. *N.Y.J. Med.* 56:2537-2543, 1956.
55. STEPHENS, J. H. and SHAFFER, J. W. A Controlled Study of the Effects of Diphenylhydantoin on Anxiety, Irritability, and Anger in Neurotic Outpatients. *Psychopharmacologia* 17:169-181, 1970.
56. CONNERS, C. K., KRAMER, R., ROTHSCHILD, G. H., SCHWARTZ, L., and STONE, A. Treatment of Young Delinquent Boys with Diphenylhydantoin Sodium and Methylphenidate. *Arch. Gen. Psychiatry* 24:156-160, 1971.
57. GOTTSCHALK, L. A., COVI, L., ULIANA, R., and BATES, D. Effects of Diphenylhydantoin on Anxiety and Hostility in Institutionalized Prisoners. *Compr. Psychiatry* 14:503-511, 1973.
58. LEFKOWITZ, M. M. Effects of Diphenylhydantoin in Disruptive Behavior: Study of Male Delinquents. *Arch. Gen. Psychiatry* 20:643-651, 1969.
59. DALBY, M. A. Chapter 18 in *Advances in Neurology,* Vol. II (Eds. J. K. Penry, D. D. Daly) New York: Raven Press, 1975.
60. BIRD, C. A. K., GRIFFIN, B. P., MIKLASCEWSKA, J. M., and GALBRAITH, A. W. Tegretol (Carbamazepine): A Controlled Trial of a New Anticonvulsant. *Br. J. Psychiatry* 112:737-742, 1966.
61. MARJERRISON, G., JEDLICKI, S. M., KEOGH, R P., HRYCHUK, W., and POULAKAKES, G. M. Carbamazepine: Behavioral, Anticonvulsant and EEG-effects in Chronically Hospitalized Epileptics. *Dis. Nerv. Syst.* 29:133-136, 1968.
62. RAJOTTE, P., JILEK, W., JILEK L., PERALES, A., GIARD, N., BORDELEAU, J.-M., and TÉFREAULT, L. Propertes Antiepileptiques et Psychotropes de la Carbamazepine. *Union Med. Can.* 96:1200-1206, 1967.
63. PRYCE-PHILLIPS, W. E. M. and JEAVONS, P. M. Effect of Carbamazepine on the Electroencephalographic and Ward Behaviour of Patients with Chronic Epilepsy. *Epilepsia* 11:263-273, 1970.
64. RODIN, E. A., RIM, C. S., and RENNICK, P. M. The Effects of Carbamazepine on Patients with Psychomotor Epilepsy. Results of a Double-Blind Study. *Epilepsia* 15:547-561, 1974.
65. CEREGHINO, J. J., BROCK, J. T., VAN METER, J. C., PENRY, J. K., SMITH, L. D., and WHITE, B. G. Carbamazepine for Epilepsy. *Neurology* 24:401-410, 1974.
66. RODIN, E. A., RIM, C. S., KITANO, H. A Comparison of the Effectiveness of Primidone Versus Carbamazepine in Epileptic Outpatients. *J. Nerv. Ment. Dis.* 163:41-46, 1976.
67. MONROE, R. R. *Episodic Behavioral Disorders.* Cambridge, Mass.: Harvard University Press, 1970.
68. CONNERS, C. K. and EISENBERG, L. The Effects of Methylphenidate on Symptomatology and Learning in Disturbed Children. *Am. J. Psychiatry* 120:458-464, 1963.
69. CONNERS, C. K., ROTHSCHILD, G., EISENBERG, L., SCHWARTZ, L. S. and ROBINSON, E. Dextroamphetamine Sulfate in Children with Learning Disorders. *Arch. Gen. Psychiatry* 21:182-190, 1969.
70. EISENBERG, L., CONNERS, C. K., and SHARPE, L. A Controlled Study of the Differential Application of Outpatient Psychiatric Treatment for Children. *Jap. J. Psychiatry* 6:125-132, 1965.
71. EPSTEIN, L. C., LASAGNA, L., CONNERS, C. K., and RODRIGUEZ, A. Correlation of Dextroamphetamine Excretion and Drug Response in Hyperkinetic Children. *J. Nerv. Ment. Dis.* 146:136-146, 1968.

72. HILL, D. Amphetamine in Psychopathic States. *Br. J. Addiction* 44:50, 1947.
73. SHOVRON, J. J. Benzedrine in Psychopathy and Behavior Disorders. *Br. J. Addiction* 44:58, 1947.
74. KOREY, S. R. The Effects of Benzedrine Sulfate on the Behavior of Psychopathic and Neurotic Juvenile Delinquents. *Psychiatr. Quart.* 18:127-137, 1944.
75. EISENBERG, L., LACHMAN, R., MOLLING, P. A., LOCKNER, A., MIZELLE, J. D. and CONNORS, C. K. A Psychopharmacologic Experiment in a Training School for Delinquent Boys: Methods, Problems, Findings. *Am. J. Orthopsychiat.* 33:431-447, 1963.
76. MANN, H. B. and GREENSPAN, S. I. The Identification and Treatment of Adult Brain Dysfunction. *Am. J. Psychiatry* 133:1013-1017, 1976.
77. SCHUKIT, M. A. and PETRICH, J. Hyperactivity: Diagnostic Confusion. (Awaiting Publication).
78. WOOD, G. R., REIMHERR, F. W., WENDER, P. H., and JOHNSON, G. E. Diagnosis and Treatment of Minimal Brain Dysfunction in Adults. *Arch. Gen. Psychiatry* 33:1453-1460, 1976.
79. ARNOLD, L. E., STROBEL, D., and WEISENBERG, A. Hyperactive Adult: Study of the "Paradoxical" Amphetamine Response. *JAMA* 222:693-694, 1972.
80. GROSS, M. D. and WILSON, W. C. *Minimal Brain Dysfunction.* New York: Brunner/Mazel, 1974.
81. SHEARD, M. H. Effect of Lithium in Human Aggression. *Nature* 230:113-114, 1971.
82. TUPIN, J. P., SMITH, D. B., CLANON, T. L., KIM, L. I., NUGENT, A., and GROUPE, A. The Long-Term Use of Lithium in Aggressive Prisoners. *Compr. Psychiatry* 14:311-317, 1973.
83. RIFKIN, A., QUITKIN, F., CARRILLO, C., BLUMBERG, A. G., and KLEIN, D. F. Lithium Carbonate in Emotionally Unstable Character Disorder. *Arch. Gen. Psychiatry* 27:519-523, 1972.
84. SHEARD, M. H., MARINI, J. L., BRIDGES, C. I., and WAGNER, E. The Effect of Lithium on Impulsive Aggressive Behavior in Man. *Am. J. Psychiatry* 133:1409-1413, 1976.
85. MORRISON, S. D., ERWIN, C. W., GIANTURCO, D. T., and GERBER, C. J. Effect of Lithium on Combative Behavior in Humans. *Dis. Nerv. Syst.* 34:186-189, 1973.
86. JUS. A., VILLENEUVE, A., GAUTIER, J., PIRES, A., CÔTÉ, J. M., JUS, K., VILLENEUVE, R., and PERRON, D. Some Remarks on the Influence of Lithium Carbonate on Patients with Temporal Epilepsy. *Int. J. Clin. Pharmacol.* 7:67-74, 1973.
87. ERWIN, C. W., GERBER, C. J., MORRISON, S. D., *et al.*, The Effect of Lithium on Convulsive Disorders. Paper read at World Congress of Psychiatry, Mexico City, 1971.
88. LION, J. R. Conceptual Issues in the Use of Drugs for the Treatment of Aggression in Man. *J. Nerv. Ment. Dis.* 160:76-82, 1975.

Subject Index

331

Name Index